Ancient Greek Lists

Ancient Greek Lists brings together catalogic texts from a variety of genres, arguing that the list form was a preeminent ancient Greek mode of expressing value through text. Ranging from Homer's Catalogue of Ships through Attic comedy and Hellenistic poetry to temple inventories, the book draws connections among texts seldom juxtaposed, examining the ways in which lists can stand in for objects, create value, act as methods of control, and even approximate the infinite. Athena Kirk analyzes how lists come to stand as a genre in their own right, shedding light on both under-studied and well-known sources to engage scholars and students of Classical literature, ancient history, and ancient languages.

ATHENA KIRK is Assistant Professor of Classics at Cornell University.

T0370901

Ancient Greek Lists

Catalogue and Inventory across Genres

ATHENA KIRK

Cornell University, New York

CAMBRIDGE
UNIVERSITY PRESS

CAMBRIDGE
UNIVERSITY PRESS

Shaftesbury Road, Cambridge CB2 8EA, United Kingdom

One Liberty Plaza, 20th Floor, New York, NY 10006, USA

477 Williamstown Road, Port Melbourne, VIC 3207, Australia

314–321, 3rd Floor, Plot 3, Splendor Forum, Jasola District Centre, New Delhi – 110025, India

103 Penang Road, #05–06/07, Visioncrest Commercial, Singapore 238467

Cambridge University Press is part of Cambridge University Press & Assessment, a department of the University of Cambridge.

We share the University's mission to contribute to society through the pursuit of education, learning and research at the highest international levels of excellence.

www.cambridge.org
Information on this title: www.cambridge.org/9781108744959

DOI: 10.1017/9781108887397

First published 2021
First paperback edition 2023

A catalogue record for this publication is available from the British Library

ISBN   978-1-108-84113-9   Hardback
ISBN   978-1-108-74495-9   Paperback

To Elsa, who counts the letters

Contents

Figures

Acknowledgements

This book began as a doctoral dissertation and extended footnote to the study of Greek literacy (a near-anagram of seriality). In the intervening years its letters have been replaced and rearranged into this final form thanks to countless institutions, colleagues, and friends, too many to name. First thanks are due to my advisors at Berkeley, and especially Leslie Kurke, who has shaped and encouraged this work from the start. A semester at the Center for Hellenic Studies afforded me crucial time to write, and an exceptional community of Hellenists; the CHS's generous sponsorship of our "Logic of Lists" workshop further enhanced this study. I benefited from an Affinito-Stewart grant of the President's Council for Cornell Women and from collaborative initiatives at Cornell, including a CIVIC Media Studies Fellowship and a Brett de Bary Interdisciplinary Mellon Writing Group at the Society for the Humanities. Thanks are due too to the institutions whose audiences welcomed and engaged with presentations based on these studies, expanding my thinking at so many turns.

The longest list in this book comprises everyone who has eschewed the infinite to bring about its completion. I owe an endless great debt of gratitude to my colleagues and students at Cornell, all of whom have greatly enriched my scholarly life. The graduate students in my 2016 Catalogues seminar taught me so much about the Greek texts here, as did many others I impelled to opine on them. None of this would have occurred were it not for the leadership and support of department chairs Charles Brittain, Sturt Manning, Verity Platt, and Éric Rebillard, or the eternal wisdom of my department mentors, Hayden Pelliccia and Courtney Roby. Alan Nussbaum, Piero Pucci, and Jeff Rusten shared their profound expertise with me on several occasions.

The book entered production as the COVID-19 pandemic descended on the US and UK; it has materialized due to the efforts of Bethany Johnson and Michael Sharp at CUP. Chris Jackson detected many infelicities in the copy, and Mary Danisi and Rebecca Marratta gave invaluable assistance indexing and proofreading. Two anonymous readers for CUP improved the manuscript at multiple stages. Polly Low, Kirk Ormand, and Jonathan

Ready generously workshopped individual chapters, as did members of the Classics+ and DeBary groups at Cornell. So many others have given of their time and minds to me during this project, and they have my deepest thanks, φιλότητος ἀπόδεξις ἥδε· Annetta Alexandridis, Ben Anderson, Merike Andre-Barrett, Yelena Baraz, Caitlín Barrett, Abigail Burleson, Julia Chang, David Crane, Joshua Daniel, Chiara Formichi, Meg Foster, Jill Frank, Eli Friedman, Nicole Giannella, David Goldstein, Jenny Goldstein, Jessica Gordon-Roth, Denise Green, Kim Haines-Eitzen, Johanna Hanink, Ella Haselswerdt, Drew Hicks, Katherine Lu Hsu, Isabel Köster, Virginia Lewis, Min Lieskovsky, Alex Livingston, Doug MacMartin, Eli Marshall, Aaron, Jen, and Nate Maclaughlin, Chloe, Doug, and Edith McLaren, Klas Molde, Jennifer Nelson, Astrid van Oyen, Nandini Pandey, Thomas Pepper, Felipe Rojas, Joel Rygorsky, Jeffrey Saletnik, Stephen Sansom, Lauren Shea, Rebecca Slayton, Jennifer Stager, Fernanda Veiverberg, Andrew Witkin, and Nancy Worman.

The love and support of my family has meant everything, as they know. I am so grateful to all the Moiseys, GUT, UP, TM, and ΘN; and especially to my parents, Artemis and John, and my brother, Kimon. Andrew, and Elsa, you make all things possible.

Abbreviations

I have used standard abbreviations for texts and authors. The following additional abbreviations appear.

ID   J. Coupry, ed. *Inscriptions de Délos: Période de l'amphictyonie attico-délienne: Actes administratifs (nos. 89–104–33).* Paris 1972.

IG   *Inscriptiones Graecae.* Berlin 1873–.

K-A   R. Kassel and C. Austin, eds. *Poetae Comici Graeci.* Berlin 1983–.

LSAG²   L. H. Jeffery, *The Local Scripts of Archaic Greece*, 1961; revised edition with a supplement by A. W. Johnston. Oxford 1990.

LSJ   H. G. Liddell, R. Scott, H. Stuart Jones, R. McKenzie, P. G. W. Glare, *Greek–English Lexicon*, with a revised supplement, 9th ed. Oxford 1996.

Milet   P. Herrmann (†), W. Günther, N.Ehrhardt, *Inschriften von Milet. Teil 3, Inschriften n. 1020–1580.* Berlin and New York 2006.

SEG   *Supplementum Epigraphicum Graecum.* Leiden 1923–.

The list is the origin of culture.

Umberto Eco, interview in *Der Spiegel*, 2009

In the treatise *On Hunting*, during a discussion of how to raise and train dogs, Xenophon offers some additional advice on what to call them (*Cyn.* 7.5):

> τὰ δ' ὀνόματα αὐταῖς τίθεσθαι βραχέα, ἵνα εὐανάκλητα ᾖ. εἶναι δὲ χρὴ τοιάδε· Ψυχή, Θυμός, Πόρπαξ, Στύραξ, Λογχή, Λόχος, Φρουρά, Φύλαξ, Τάξις, Ξίφων, Φόναξ, Φλέγων, Ἀλκή, Τεύχων, Ὑλεύς, Μήδας, Πόρθων, Σπέρχων, Ὀργή, Βρέμων, Ὕβρις, Θάλλων, Ῥώμη, Ἀνθεύς, Ἥβα, Γηθεύς, Χαρά, Λεύσων, Αὐγώ, Πολεύς, Βία, Στίχων, Σπουδή, Βρύας, Οἰνάς, Στέρρος, Κραύγη, Καίνων, Τύρβας, Σθένων, Αἰθήρ, Ἀκτίς, Αἰχμή, Νόης, Γνώμη, Στίβων, Ὁρμή.

> Give them names that are short, so that they are easy to call out. They should be like these: Soul, Spirit, Handle, Spike, Spear, Snare, Lookout, Guard, Lineup, Sworder, Cutthroat, Blazer, Courage, Crafty, Ringwood, Wily, Lusty, Charger, Passion, Roarer, Outrage, Burster, Might, Bloomer, Youngblood, Cheerful, Joy, Eagle-eye, Sunbeam, Turner, Force, Lineman, Gusto, Eagle-owl, Rock-dove, Rugged, Screech, Killer, Whirlwind, Toughguy, Air, Beam, Pique, Mind, Brain, Tracker, Rush.

Almost fifty examples later, one has presumably gotten the idea. Why include this litany, so charmingly excessive? Perhaps the aristocratic sportsman needed so many suggestions, or perhaps they were culled from the population of dogs known to the author. But more likely, the passage underscores a very basic aesthetic premise, and one from which this book begins: the ancient Greeks liked lists, catalogues, inventories, enumerations. Long ones. They liked composing them, performing them, hearing them, reading them, writing them down, and cutting them into marble. They did not think they were dull or uninspired, and they probably did not skip over them when they cropped up in the midst of a perfectly good narrative sequence.

Lists, though, were not merely entertaining flourishes or chances for an author to demonstrate erudition and virtuosity. As this book will argue, Greek lists functioned from the earliest literature on as the consistent and continuous means of expressing cultural value in text. Ultimately, they came not only to record value, but to create it. This system can often be circular: items of intrinsic value are included in lists, but inclusion in a list endows an item with extrinsic value, thus making it worth re-listing. Robin Coste Lewis's 2015 narrative poem *Voyage of the Sable Venus* deploys this feature of lists to expose the historical violence done to Black bodies. The work consists, in the author's words, "solely and entirely of the titles, catalog entries, or exhibit descriptions of Western art objects in which a black female figure is present, dating from 38,000 BCE to the present."[1] Through the relentless selection and positioning of source texts, Lewis arranges and redisplays these dismembered objects in all their diachronic horrors of design and description. Thus a passage from the section "Catalog I: ANCIENT GREECE & ANCIENT ROME" lists:[2]

[Two Nubian Prisoners Bound
to a Post] Protome [Probably

The Handle of a Whip
or Other Implement] Oil Flask Back

View Head of an African Prisoner
Statue of Prisoner Kneeling Arms

Bound at the Elbows
Left Arm Missing

Bust of a Nubian Prisoner
with Fragmentary Arms

As Lewis re-curates Western art through each set of entries, she also exposes the catalogue form itself as a powerful tool for propagating, but also revising, ingrained cultural systems of worth. *Voyage of the Sable Venus* shows moreover that catalogues can manipulate objects in time and space, preserving what is long lost, and spotlighting what is otherwise invisible.

In the ancient Greek world, the list in its many manifestations became the recognizable mode of expressing quantifiable and lasting value in contexts sometimes lacking standards. The sheer quantity of lists in Greek literature hints at the importance of the form. From the *Iliad*'s monumental Catalogue of Ships to Aeschylus' account of war dead in the *Persians* or Callimachus' list of

[1] R. C. Lewis 2016: 35.   [2] R. C. Lewis 2016: 47.

Sicilian cities, the literary record boasts an enduring tradition of interrupting long narrative sequences with enumerations. Similarly robust, if less well-preserved, is the tradition of longer, stand-alone poetic catalogues, such as the Hesiodic *Catalogue of Women* – indeed, the list form may underlie some of the oldest Greek poetry.[3] At the same time, lists pervaded an apparently entirely separate tradition: the vast corpus of documentary inscriptions. Amidst scores of decrees, laws, and dedications, one can peruse as many casualty lists, ship manifests, inventories, building accounts, and tribute records. While scholars have long analyzed and mined these primary materials for evidence about their historical contents, only rarely have they entered discussions focused on literary list and catalogue. The mandate of Armayor, who decades ago noticed numeric correspondences between Homeric and Herodotean catalogue, still holds: "What we have to contend with here is not coincidence but Catalogues, Greek Catalogues with themes and rules of their own which we have not yet begun to understand."[4] Although many of our texts share cultural heritages, audiences, and perhaps even authors, we tend to treat literary lists and epigraphic lists as entirely different beasts. This book aims to align these two discourses, working toward a poetics of Greek lists across genres, and inquiring into common traditions, mechanics, and underlying objectives. In lists of the archaic and Classical periods, the Greeks exhibit a previously unexplored preoccupation with amassing, displaying, and counting prestige objects, real or imagined. These enumerations do not simply exhibit items: rather, as they mirror physical collections they create permanent virtual facsimiles of personal and public wealth. As a result, list-texts take on a worth so culturally weighty that they supplant and supersede physical objects themselves.

An additional contention of this book is that listmaking represents a distinct and autonomous tradition in the Greek world, often transcending the bounds of poetry and prose, literature and document.[5] Greek lists do not function discretely *within* genres and registers: they more properly form a genre unto themselves. Apparently disparate examples overlap in their uses and abuses of the list format, presenting intertextualities throughout the Classical period that ultimately anticipate the fused archival and literary cataloguing practices of the Hellenistic period. Thus studying lists brings together not only literature and epigraphy, but disparate theories of genre and medium. The Greek list was a transmedial phenomenon,[6] a text-form with a cohesive set of functions and

---

[3] See, e.g., Kühlmann 1973: 11–13.   [4] Armayor 1978: 7.

[5] For lists in the Roman tradition, cf. now Riggsby 2019, chapter 1. Galjanić 2007 treats the Indo-European tradition of enumeration.

[6] As separate from "intermedial," though some lists also are this. For distinctions between these terms, see Rajewsky 2005. Martin 2008 outlines useful approaches to Greek object–text relations; see e.g. 337–339 on representation.

behaviors in a variety of manifestations – from oral performance to written text to inscribed surface. While this book focuses on texts from the archaic period on, much of this material discussed here shows affinities with the palace records of goods so well-preserved for Mycenean culture. While the Linear B evidence is beyond the scope of this book,[7] it is clear that the written text in Bronze Age Greece had become an established means of documenting wealth, and making a list of important items appears to have been a regular administrative practice well before the Homeric poems became solidified. The Linear B evidence is beyond the scope of this book but would make for productive future study.

"What's in a List?" Revisited

This book engages particular lists on their own terms, but it also revisits broader thematic concerns about lists.[8] Lists have often been related to questions about ancient literacy and orality, due in no small part to Jack Goody's chapter-length treatment of them nearly half a century ago in *The Domestication of the Savage Mind.*[9] For Goody, who discussed lists primarily in early writing systems of the Near East but also gestured to Greek evidence, lists led to knowledge:

> [I]t was the keeping of such chronicles and the re-ordering of materials by means of the visual inspection of the written word, that permitted wider developments in the growth of human knowledge, more particularly in knowledge of the past, but also in knowledge about the natural world.[10]

While Goody's broader claims about literacy and the Greek alphabet have met with ample and appropriate criticism in the intervening decades, more specified applications like this have received less attention and critical engagement and run the risk of persisting in the received scholarly understanding of the topic.[11] Lists, like writing itself, should be understood as

---

[7] For more general ideas about the function of the written tablets, see, e.g., Schwink 1999 and Palaima 2003.

[8] Examples of longer specialized studies include: Trüb 1952, Kühlmann 1973 on (mostly) epic catalogue, Ormand 2014 on Hesiod, Minchin 1996, Gaertner 2001, and Sammons 2010 on Homer, Asquith 2005 and 2006 on Hesiod and Hellenistic poetry, R. Hamilton 2000 on the Delian inventories, Gordon 1999 on magical lists, Harris 1995 on inventories of the Athenian Acropolis, Aleshire 1989 on the inventories of Asclepius, Spyropoulos 1974 on Aristophanes.

[9] Goody 1977: 74–111.   [10] Goody 1977: 90.

[11] But for a more a nuanced account of "List Literacy" and Greek documentary culture, see Thomas 2009: 30–42; cf. also Thomas 1989: 287–288 and mentions of lists throughout Thomas 1989, and Davies 2003 and 1994.

a product, and not a prerequisite, of human knowledge. Moreover, it is not easy to separate ancient lists by their presumed level of sophistication. A division between epic lists and other apparently more mundane lists also informed, separately, Kühlmann's monograph on the topic,[12] and the roots of this kind of approach inhere in the overall tendency to treat archival "documentary" lists as separate from "literary" ones, and oral ones apart from written ones. As this book aims to show, however, the cultural functions of Greek lists did not wholly depend on their status as oral or written, or as "document" or "literature." In fact, features of Greek oral poetic lists persisted in written texts; meanwhile, in other contexts, such as performed drama or historical inquiry, one can scarcely categorize lists as one medium or another. And, as we shall see, it is not always clear whether the list was transmitted to its audience via "visual inspection" or aural reception; moreover, these media do not always correspond precisely to different goals and purposes. Thus this book also interrogates Umberto Eco's claim, quoted in the epigraph, that the "list is the origin of culture," by considering how the diverse range of lists from across Greek culture operate.[13] In the case of the Greeks, there is much to be learned from how they organize and present their valuable information.

Several previous studies, Kühlmann's included, have shed light on the relationship of lists to various Greek textual genres. For Kühlmann, lists in epic are modes of presenting truth and fact, and of eliding the authorial voice. Gordon's study of magical lists, itself a short anthropology of ancient listmaking, responds to both Goody and Kühlmann. Taking his title from Goody's chapter heading, Gordon softens Goody's claims, putting forth that "with the advent of writing, listing of many different kinds became institutionalized in Greek and Roman culture." In dialogue with Kühlmann, he highlights the uncertainty of the list:[14]

> [I]s it best understood as an active, purposive fragmentation of the world, an act of magisterial disarticulation, or as a passive collection of things that are lying about, that need to be brought together? Does the list break down the unity of experience in order to assert the power of the list-maker over, and with, the matter in question; or does it rather tend towards holism, assembling *disjecta membra* into an implied totality? ... part of the rhetorical achievement of a list may be precisely this uncertainty about the grain or flavour of its reading.

While no theoretical framework can account for every example, and indeed no one study can encompass the vast range of Greek lists without itself

---

[12] Kühlmann 1973: 18.   [13] Eco 2009.   [14] Gordon 1999: 246–247.

being reduced to a catalogue, this book inclines toward the theory that lists do "tend towards holism" and approach "an implied totality," with the caveat that such a totality is, almost by definition, incomplete. In this I follow in part the more specific theory of Umberto Eco that the list is a kind of representation that "suggests infinity almost physically, because it in fact does not end, nor does it conclude in form."[15] I would revise the formulation slightly to suggest that the form may appear to end, but its recursive potential to contain the infinite persists.

Beyond their importance to literacy and orality, Greek lists crucially impinge on several other areas of intellectual inquiry. One that has recently received more scholarly attention is the topic of ancient numeracy, that is, in Cuomo's recent definition, "the ability to count, calculate, and measure."[16] Often evidence about Greek counting and measurement is couched within lists, and, as I shall discuss below, lists themselves can enable the act of counting itself. In this regard, the term "tally" bears special significance to this project. Originally denoting a stick with notches to mark debts and repayments (from Lat. *tālea*, cutting, rod, stick), it came to mean a record or account of such values, in the form of a list. Thus it encapsulates one of the central themes of the book, that catalogues and inventories always retain an intimate connection to physical objects of value, and themselves become the objects of value over time. The study of lists also relates closely to the study of collecting. Not only does listing often follow upon collecting: the list too is its own form of collection.[17] More broadly, lists crucially inform our understanding of knowledge production in antiquity, of generic boundaries and intersections, and of performance cultures. The story of ancient historiography, for instance, is not complete without consideration of such projects as genealogies and chronicles, or catalogic documentary sources.[18] Meanwhile, debates about the composition of Homeric epic inevitably turn to the origins of catalogic sections, as either older relics or newer additions; moreover, the genre of the catalogue poem seems closely related to the origin of epic.

What Is a List? (What Is It Not?)

The studies in this book treat a range of ancient evidence, from Homeric epic to Hellenistic inscriptions and much in between. Many of the texts here have

---

[15] Eco 2009: 17.   [16] Cuomo 2012: 1; see also Netz 2002.

[17] On collecting, see, e.g., Elsner and Cardinal 1994, Pearce 1994 and 1995, Bounia 2004, and Tanselle 1998.

[18] On these questions see, e.g., S. West 1985 and 1991, Moyer 2002, Kosmetatou 2013.

been categorized by other scholars with various labels such as "catalogue," "inventory," "account," "enumeration," and "chronicle." While each of these schemata has its own set of potentially useful nuances, in general I treat all as sub-groups of the blanket term "list." In this, I depart from previous scholarship that insists on a definition of a list as a bald, laconic series of short, unconnected, and concise entries, to be contrasted with, for instance, a "catalogue," which is usually taken to be a longer, further elaborated, and perhaps more expressive textual form. In addition, I concentrate on lists that could be classified as "inventories," in that much of the discussion focuses on lists that describe cohesive collections of objects, often physical ones. This term is usually applied in the context of documentary records, such as those of the sacred dedications discussed in Chapter 4; yet it could equally apply to many of the Homeric lists in Chapter 1, though these are generally called "catalogues." While I am in favor of collapsing these putative distinctions, for the sake of clarity I have continued to employ conventional terms applied to key texts, such as the Iliadic Catalogue of Ships, the Attic inventories, or the Lindian Chronicle.

Goody distinguished three kinds of lists, based partly on the temporal relationship between the list and its contents: the "record of outside events"-type, which archives past events, the "shopping list"-type, which serves as a "guide for future action," and the "lexical list."[19] Yet these groupings are limiting and uneven: they fail to account for examples such as a temple inventory, which both records the past and guides future behavior. As such they become logically dubious, for the list-type does not always correspond to the "correct" location of the list in time relative to events: rather, the direction-of-fit can change. This problem of intentionality in a shopping list, for instance, was brilliantly dramatized by Elizabeth Anscombe two decades before Goody:[20]

> Let us consider a man going round a town with a shopping list in his hand. Now it is clear that the relation of this list to the things he actually buys is one and the same whether his wife gave him the list or it is his own list; and that there is a different relation where a list is made by a detective following him about. If he made the list itself, it was an expression of intention; if his wife gave it him, it has the role of an order. What then is the identical relation to what happens, in the order and the intention, which is not shared by the record? It is precisely this: if the list and the things that the man actually buys do not agree, and if this and this alone constitutes

---

[19] Goody 1977: 81–82; at 84ff he further categorizes lists: "administrative lists, event lists," etc.
[20] Anscombe 1957: 56.

a mistake, then the mistake is not in the list but in the man's performance (if his wife were to say: "Look, it says butter and you have bought margarine," he would hardly reply: "What a mistake! we must put that right" and alter the word on the list to "margarine"); whereas if the detective's record and what the man actually buys do not agree, then the mistake is in the record.

In the case of many Greek texts, where we often have no information about the intentions of the listmaker or the list-user, any one of Anscombe's hypotheticals could be the reality. Thus I resist most formal distinctions about lists not as a reductive move, but because they tend to limit the analytical possibilities for serial texts, which can shift categories at will. Instead, I pursue a formal but liberal definition of a list influenced by Eco: a kind of text that is either presented as or is recognizably serial, and that is recursive, potentially extendable *ad infinitum*.[21] Discussions of lists also often posit a minimum number of elements (typically three) that a series should have to be determined a "list"; yet I contend that a very small or even null set can be a list if it is introduced as one.

This open-ended definition of lists draws also from educational psychology, in which listmaking constitutes an "epistemic game" of implicit questions, where, "if the answer to these questions must be discovered, rather than recalled or looked up, then the listmaking process is an inquiry process and the resulting list constitutes new knowledge."[22] Thus just "eggs, milk, tomatoes, bread" suggests "What do we need from the grocery store?," "eight hundred stallions, sixteen hundred mares, and a huge amount of dogs" answers "Why should we believe you about the Babylonians?" This all amounts to a kind of speech act that functions much as would a magical list, which, most agree, is essential to a charm's efficacy.[23] In authored literary texts, too, lists serve a specific and identifiable function beyond the decorative or the expository. Instead of effecting a charm or curse, though, the nonmagical list, as a means of presenting a facsimile of a physical reality to an audience as evidence, has a curatorial aim.

---

[21] Eco 2009 does not precisely define lists, but his essay focuses on their visuality, their qualities of infinite possibility, and potentially infinite form.

[22] Collins and Ferguson 1993: 27.

[23] The exact principles by which the list works in ancient magic remain contested. In summarizing several views, Collins 2008: 83–86 surmises that neither (1) a sense of completeness nor (2) parallels to administrative text style provide adequate explanation for the list's ubiquitous presence. Collins partially espouses rhetorical explanations such as those of Weiner 1983 and Gordon 1999, but stresses the importance of cross-cultural influences on the Greek and Roman world too. For a recent summary of the complications of that topic as regards the Near East, see Noegel 2010: 22–23. Collins is right, I think, to introduce the connection of body-part enumerations with healing *ex votos* that depict body parts. An approach to a related topic that examines compositional, rhetorical, and cross-cultural elements of healing together is that of Watkins 1995: 537–539 on Indo-European medical doctrine.

What Lists Do

While this book suggests that listmaking works in distinct ways for ancient Greek culture, some of their analytical possibilities can be illuminated at the outset by recourse to modern texts, as we have already seen in the case of *Voyage of the Sable Venus*. A second example is Camus' *The Stranger*, in which the enigmatic murderer Meursault, imprisoned in solitary confinement, whiles away his time by composing mental lists of the objects in his old room. This game soon becomes a generative and creative enterprise, as he progressively lengthens his inventory with each performance (98).

> Sometimes I would exercise my memory on my bedroom and, starting from a corner, make the round, noting every object I saw on the way. At first it was over in a minute or two. But each time I repeated the experience, it took a little longer. I made a point of visualizing every piece of furniture, and each article upon or in it, and then every detail of each article, and finally the details of the details, so to speak: a tiny dent or incrustation, or a chipped edge, and the exact grain and color of the woodwork. At the same time I forced myself to keep my inventory in mind from start to finish, in the right order and omitting no item. With the result that, after a few weeks, I could spend hours merely in listing the objects in my bedroom. I found that the more I thought, the more details, half-forgotten or mal-observed, floated up from my memory. There seemed no end to them.

This passage encapsulates several of what this study defines as the central functions of inventories. Some of these are perhaps self-evident, but it is worth setting them out together. Lists can:

1 COLLECT a series of important items into one place
2 COUNT, whether implicitly or explicitly, the sum of the items
3 COLLATE the items into an order or into sub-groupings
4 CONJURE items without their physical presence
5 CREATE a new, composite item (i.e., the list) that rivals the value of the items listed.

Meursault's inventory collects and counts its contents, if not numerically, still for the sake of completeness; it also collates them, attending to their spatial order. We can also read this list as a conjuring act. On one hand, it is an exercise that seems neatly emblematic of Meursault's person: obsessive and detached, pathological and indifferent. Yet behind all this perhaps lurks a *horror vacui*, an anxious attempt to materialize what cannot be present, to fill an empty prison cell and a troubled mind with the trappings of a free life, and to forge object-bonds to a civilization of which he was never fully part. Or so we perhaps merely hope: it could be that, for this man who does not grieve his mother's death, who shot a man five times because the weather was hot, and who will never leave prison alive, an inventory of his possessions stands only as the ultimate act of nihilistic perversity.

Whatever the case, Meursault's last comments point to a final quality of lists this book will pursue: its recursive possibilities. "So I learned," he airily concludes, "that even after a single day's experience of the outside world a man could easily live a hundred years in prison." Given just a brief glimpse of a collection, one can produce an infinite, ever-extendable inventory. This passage thus presents the inventory as, potentially, a powerful remedy for isolation and loss, a means of coping with disconnection and emptiness, and a tool for amplifying the briefest of material interactions.

Medium and Material

But lists can also create, or be generative of, material. Presented as a series of nouns with no surrounding narrative, lists assert the agency of objects, or, as Latour would call them, "a population of actants that mix with things as well as with societies."[24] This kind of agency is exemplified by a very different modern work: Tim O'Brien's *The Things They Carried*, a collection of stories about a platoon of American soldiers in Vietnam. The eponymous first story specifies (2):

> The things they carried were largely determined by necessity. Among the necessities or near-necessities were P-38 can openers, pocket knives, heat tabs, wrist watches, dog tags, mosquito repellent, chewing gum, candy, cigarettes, salt tablets, packets of Kool-Aid, lighters, matches, sewing kits, Military payment Certificates, C rations, and two or three canteens of water. Together, these items weighed between fifteen and twenty pounds, depending upon a man's habits or rate of metabolism. Henry Dobbins, who was a big man, carried extra rations; he was especially fond of canned peaches in heavy syrup over pound cake. Dave Jensen, who practiced field hygiene, carried a toothbrush, dental floss, and several hotel-size bars of soap he'd stolen on R&R in Sydney, Australia. Ted Lavender, who was

---

[24] Latour 1993: 90.

scared, carried tranquilizers until he was shot in the head outside the village of Than Khe in mid April.[25]

Here, objects in the list work together to evoke the material realities of an experience unimaginable to those outside it. The list distills the soldier's tour of duty into so many pieces of metal, plastic, and organic matter, each "necessity" a trivial-seeming object, but each contributing to a weighty collective burden, physical and emotional, and entwined in a human narrative from start to tragic finish. The list of objects allows a reader, separated in space and time, an entrée into the soldier's physical and emotional world. The crucial transformative power of this part of the story rests not just in the material, but in the material *recreated as text*. And yet lists do not merely replicate objects, but also return them to us. Perhaps more than other types of text, they mediate the relationship between human actors and the physical world, illustrating Latour's contention that "interest in texts does not distance us from reality, for things too have to be elevated to the dignity of narrative ... why deny [texts] the grandeur of forming the social bond that holds us together?"[26] It is by translating the material, and then transporting it, that lists can carry objects across vast expanses of time and space. The lists in *The Stranger* and *The Things They Carried* also share one more specific salient feature. Both describe objects far removed from the lister and the audience, unavailable to them, and perhaps lost. As such, they both hint at the power of lists to stand in for objects, to act as the interfaces by which we access them. As a result, these lists become our experience of the things in them; more than just mediators or translations, they *are*, in some sense, the things themselves.

In the Greek world, even more than the modern one, lists exemplify the cultural necessity of codifying objects and of translating their abundance and matter into the verbal realm. Ancient Greek literature inhabits a world far removed from that of Meursault's Algiers or Ted Lavender's Than Khe. And in contrast to the *The Stranger* and *The Things They Carried*, which portray the most extreme forms of social isolation and removal from civilization, in Greece lists and listmakers flourish in all of the commonest human contexts. Obsessive lists and visions of their powers are not the province of people driven to the borders of sanity, but of Homeric heroes, state officials, famous intellectuals, erudite poets, and comic caricatures of "everyman."

Moreover, ancient Greek sources display little of the information-angst expressed in postmodern attitudes about lists. Their worldview contrasts

[25] O'Brien 1990: 2.   [26] Latour 1993: 90.

sharply with that described by, for instance, John Durham Peters, who argues that:[27]

> We live ... in a time of promiscuous knowledge, and the list is one strategy to cope with and make use of our temptations amid information abundance. The comically preposterous juxtapositions of lists repeatedly point to how the world escapes our concepts. There can also be a certain desperation in a list, an exasperation that the universe is so wide and our time is so short.

Nor do ancient Greek sources seem to share the disaffected critiques of tradition and catalogue illustrated in modern popular culture, such as by the song lyric:[28]

> But nobody wants to hear this tale
> The plot is clichéd, the jokes are stale
> And baby we've all heard it all before
> Oh, I could get specific but
> Nobody needs a catalog
> With details of love I can't sell anymore

Greek texts project instead a celebratory quality, and a belief in the form's generative and recuperative power, even in the face of cultural loss. The ubiquity and normalization of extended lists is apparent not only in Xenophon's dog names, but in any number of contexts. In Aristophanes' *Acharnians*, the protagonist, Dicaeopolis, an average Athenian citizen, lampoons his city's willingness to escalate conflict with Sparta on any pretext, giving an absurd example. "Come on," he scoffs, "what if one of the Lacedaemonians had sailed out on a canoe, taken a Seriphian puppy, and put it up for sale? Would you all have sat still in your houses?" His answer launches into a vivid description of the likely consequences (543–551):

ἦ πολλοῦ γε δεῖ·
καὶ κάρτα μέντἂν εὐθέως καθείλκετε
τριακοσίας ναῦς, ἦν δ' ἂν ἡ πόλις πλέα   545
θορύβου στρατιωτῶν, περὶ τριηράρχους βοῆς,
μισθοῦ διδομένου, παλλαδίων χρυσουμένων,
στοᾶς στεναχούσης, σιτίων μετρουμένων,
ἀσκῶν, τροπωτήρων, κάδους ὠνουμένων,
σκορόδων, ἐλαῶν, κρομμύων ἐν δικτύοις,   550
στεφάνων, τριχίδων, αὐλητρίδων, ὑπωπίων·

[27] Peters 2015: 9.   [28] "Invisible Ink," Clayton Scoble and Aimee Mann (*Lost in Space*, 2002).

Far from it.

All the more, you immediately would have hauled out
three hundred ships, and the city would be full   545
of soldiers' clamor, of shouting round the admirals,
of wages being paid, of Pallas-statues being gilt,
of the stoa groaning, of foodstuffs being measured out,
of wineskins, of leather oar thongs, of people buying jugs,
of garlic, of olives, of onions in mesh bags,   550
of garlands, anchovies, flute girls, black eyes.

This imagined scene of the city comprises an asymmetrical collection in which sights mix with sounds, events, and activities; people and produce jostle one another for space in the verse-lines. The list enables these disparate elements to combine as one entity, here forming a synesthetic portrait of the city that ultimately becomes a cipher for war and its multi-sensory chaos. The presentation of this description as a list of nouns and participles, rather than a narrative with clauses, varied structures, relational words, or descriptors, speaks to the cultural import of the form. It is the list, not another kind of poetic composition, that creates and materializes this hypothetical version of the city for the play's audience, evoking its fullness and placing the theatergoers within it. The list brings the world of the work alive.

Inventory, Collecting, and Archive

While theories of the list often remain tethered to the written text, catalogues and inventories are imbricated with more material concepts, such as the "collection" and the "archive," two terms that have garnered scholarly attention since the 1990s. Useful theories of collecting and archivism for this study highlight the symbiotic relationship between collections or archives and the past. Thus Susan Stewart writes:[29]

> The collection does not displace attention to the past; rather, the past is at the service of the collection, for whereas the souvenir lends authenticity to the past, the past lends authenticity to the collection. The collection seeks a form of self-enclosure which is possible because of its ahistoricism. The collection replaces history with classification, with order beyond the realm of temporality.

[29] Stewart 1993: 151. See also Muensterberger (1994) on the psychology of collecting.

For Stewart, a "collection" creates a self-contained, hermetic world with its own completeness and authority. This book argues that the Greek inventory, too, by creating its own definitive version of the objects in its store, takes their place "beyond the realm" of both time and space.

Meanwhile, theories of the archive have burgeoned[30] in the wake of Derrida's *Archive Fever* and paid particular attention to the ways in which archives both display and mask data.[31] The approach here has benefited from ideas such as those expressed by Achille Mbembe, that the archive is a method of controlling the past and its memory.[32] Finally, studying the interaction of the list and its contents as outside, physical things also impinges on scholarship related to materiality and text. As Haas presciently wrote, "the word material is not meant to invoke conventional binary distinctions like material/immaterial, physical/mental, body/mind. Rather, texts written or read are at once material and immaterial, and writers and readers engage one another in realms that are both physical and mental."[33] This too occurs in the writing and reception of catalogues and inventories, which evoke, and ultimately create, the material world of another time.

Outline of the Book

The chapters of this book comprise six interlocking case studies of catalogues and inventories in multiple Greek authors and genres, from archaic epic to its reception by the Alexandrian poets. Throughout the book, a key Greek term will be the verb καταλέγω, "recount," the verb from which "catalogue" derives. Beginning with Homer, use of this verb is one rough metric by which we can gauge subsequent authors' interest in and use of lists. While quantitative data do not stand in for an author's program or style, some trends nonetheless prove provocative. Homer, Herodotus, and Aristophanes, for instance, all employ this verb disproportionately often compared with other authors, and they also display especial interest in catalogic sequences in their works. Homeric καταλέγω also reappears in the allusive world of early Hellenistic poetry, in which poets engage in complex games of emulation and variation, often involving listed information.

Chapter 1 argues that the list in Homer serves as a mode of counting and establishing authoritative standards of numeration. In the pre-coinage context of the Homeric poems, authors and speakers use lists to project

---

[30] Derrida 1996; cf. Kittler 1996.   [31] E.g. Greetham 1999.
[32] Mbembe 2002; cf. Greetham 1999.   [33] Haas 1996: 4.

authority and accountability to an audience; the poet himself, moreover, emerges as the ultimate meta-counter. More than a literary device, catalogues of objects in Homer allow for the comparison, valuation, and trade of items in the absence of other standards of measurement. Finally, drawing on Eco's conception of the list as "potentially infinite," I suggest further that these sets of texts engage in a paradoxical and deliberately obfuscating practice of presenting their contents as uncountably large.

Chapter 2 explores the poetics of epic catalogue in the best evidence we have for the archaic catalogue poem, the Hesiodic *Catalogue of Women*. While Greek lists in some instances impart official value to a collection of objects, this chapter explores the idea of the catalogue as a mode of gendered control and a marker of loss. Alongside the Odyssean catalogue of women in the *Nekuia* and Semonides' catalogue of women, we can read the genre of woman-catalogue more generally as an attempt to typologize and collapse the individuality of women, all the while treating them as objects similar to any saleable prestige item. Chapter 3 continues the exploration of listing valuable objects by shifting to the world of Classical prose. It treats Herodotus' use of the catalogue and the general problem of quantifying goods on a large cultural scale, as well as the specific use of the list as a cipher for imparting value. In the *Histories*, I argue, the genre of historiography and the nascent administrative inventory tradition coalesce. We find multiple examples of lists used to prove points and express value, and the characters and audience of the *Histories*, deeply invested in quantifying and displaying their wealth and possessions, use the list format to enact and prove their own worth. Meanwhile, Herodotus' use of the term *apodeixis* for his work – also the technical word for an inscribed inventory – reveals that he conceives of his project as a grand multimedia catalogue of everything of importance to the Greek world. He has transferred the discrete uses of lists available to him to his own new type of text, thus incorporating old forms while distinguishing the *Histories* from previous genealogical works. At the center of this study, Chapter 4 treats the genre of the epigraphic inventory within the context of earlier Greek literature. It argues through detailed re-examination of these enigmatic texts that they are calculated in their layout and design to "display" and "replace" the dedications in their store for the viewers of the text. Moreover, whether or not they serve as ongoing useful records for the officials involved, they allow both the polis administration and the public to grapple with multiple forms of deterioration and loss.

Chapter 5 returns us to the literary world of Classical Athens and Greek comedy. Here, the administrative uses of listing have become increasingly entwined in civic domestic life and the elite literary arts. Whereas the previous chapters have drawn parallels among literary and epigraphic texts without postulating direct allusion, this chapter advances the argument that the comedies of Aristophanes consciously draw on the poetics of both literary and administrative catalogues. The plays contain lists that parody the archaic poetic catalogue tradition; meanwhile, in various scenarios, Aristophanic characters display a preoccupation with the listing-behaviors we have already begun to outline: counting, valuation, quantifying, and establishing authority. The comedies thus represent a deep integration of the literary and administrative spheres through their use of the inventory. Chapter 6 examines aspects of the reception of catalogue in early Hellenistic poetry, focusing on Callimachus and Hermesianax. These poets, I argue, exploit catalogue as a non-mimetic form, using it to defy traditional ways of counting, and traditional orderings and boundaries of space and time. In their hands, the catalogue poem becomes a locus of disorder and fantasy.

The Conclusion gestures toward the listed dynamics of counting and materialization in later texts through the brief examples of the Parian Marble and Lindian Chronicle. These monumental inscribed text-objects can be understood as literal transformations of cultural value into list form, extreme inventories untethered from their contents.

1 | A Number of Things

Homeric Catalogue, Numerical Authority, and the Uncountable

As foundational texts for both the Greeks and for modern Classical scholarship, the epics of Homer furnish a natural starting point for considering the diachronic poetics of Greek lists. In the last two decades, two monographs have renewed focus on this textual form, highlighting its centrality to epic narrative, rhetoric, and genre. Sammons has skillfully illuminated many catalogic passages and highlighted the ways in which catalogue enriches the epics with elements and narratives external to the main story. Perceau, meanwhile, has sought to elevate the generic importance of catalogue, focusing our attention on the "inventory poetics" of Homer, and its key terms and dynamics.[1] The present chapter, along with this book, has a different aim: it situates Homeric catalogic texts within the greater context of Greek literature and culture, focusing specifically on the poetics of value and counting. Beginning with Homer, the catalogue will become a cultural technique for expressing value in something, and creating value from nothing.

Focusing mainly on catalogues of objects in Homer, I argue that these texts enact the expression and control of value through counting.[2] In a context without fixed numerical standards, but great gains and losses at stake, the list serves as a mode of counting and of displaying numerate authority; ultimately it gains its own intrinsic, fiduciary value as a tool of exchange.[3] Speakers in the poems use lists to project their prestige through the ability to count, and lists in turn lend legitimacy to the counters, including the poetic voice. Moreover, as it provides an interface between counting and power, the list format also allows for the expression of

---

[1] Sammons 2010 and Perceau 2002. Other studies of the form include: Minton 1962, Beye 1964, M. W. Edwards 1980, Minchin 1996, Gaertner 2001, Tsagalis 2010, Perceau 2015; Trüb 1952, Austin 1965, Kühlmann 1973. For summary of earlier scholarship, see Sammons 2010: 4–8.

[2] As in the rest of the book, I take an inclusive definition of catalogue/list here, not discriminating on the basis of previously determined catalogue status (cf. Sammons 2010: 9), nor insisting on a distinction between catalogue and list (cf. Minchin 1996: 75).

[3] See Peacock 2013: 68–104 for discussion of the evolution of units of "money" in Homer.

infinite, or potentially infinite, sets of information. Eco proposed that verbal and visual lists inspire "a subjective feeling of something greater than us ... an emotional condition, a potential infinity." For Eco, the list, like the epic catalogue, "suggest[s] infinity almost physically because in fact it does not end, nor does it conclude in form."[4] But I aim to show that the *Iliad* and *Odyssey* "suggest infinity" in more explicit ways too. The programmatic language that surrounds lists of things contains certain commonly repeated elements: a statement of boundlessness or infinity and a verb of naming. Far from invalidating the list, claims that its contents cannot be counted in fact emphasize their abundance as approaching infinity and form part of the poetics of catalogue. Listing in Homer thus enacts the counting of what is functionally (if not actually) infinite. In this context, we can return to and revise the observation of Beye, who said that Homeric catalogues "all share in the essential quality of a list, namely, isolated pieces of information that gain a modest coherence or unity by the simple fact of juxtaposition."[5] Rather, these isolated pieces of information gain *value* by the simple fact of juxtaposition. Moreover, this chapter argues that lists project specific characters' ability to display control of numerical data. In the *Iliad* the projection occurs between Agamemnon and his men, as well as among the muses, the poet, and the audience. In both epic poems, Odysseus stands out as a character of extraordinary numeric and catalogic ability, a skill that becomes his mode of re-asserting authority and identity. Meanwhile, the complex interplay of counting and listing emerges in the contrastive terms *onomainō*, "name off" and *katalegō*, "recount."

Counts and Kings

At the start of *Iliad* 2, Agamemnon expresses shame at the prospect of quitting Troy and wasting the Achaean resources deployed there. He describes how dramatically the Greek forces outnumber the Trojans in an elaborate metaphor (2.123–128):[6]

> εἴ περ γάρ κ᾽ ἐθέλοιμεν Ἀχαιοί τε Τρῶές τε
> ὅρκια πιστὰ ταμόντες ἀριθμηθήμεναι ἄμφω,
> Τρῶας μὲν λέξασθαι ἐφέστιοι ὅσσοι ἔασιν,   125

---

[4] Eco 2009: 62.

[5] Beye 1964: 345. His further interpretation of this quality as "something alien to narrative, no matter how paratactic the style in which the narrative is cast" is a conclusion that I will not readily espouse here.

[6] Translations are mine unless otherwise noted. Texts of Homer are from van Thiel 2010 and 1991.

ἡμεῖς δ᾽ ἐς δεκάδας διακοσμηθεῖμεν Ἀχαιοί,
Τρώων δ᾽ ἄνδρα ἕκαστον ἑλοίμεθα οἰνοχοεύειν,
πολλαί κεν δεκάδες δευοίατο οἰνοχόοιο.

For if we wished, Achaeans and Trojans as well,
to cut oaths of fidelity and count our sum,
collect as many Trojans as are in their homes, 125
and split up us Achaeans into groups of ten –
and we then chose one Trojan each to bear our wine,
many a group of ten would be winebearerless.

While Agamemnon himself seems to comprehend the absolute values of the troops, he guides his audience to non-arithmetic understanding of quantities. Dividing the Greeks into groups of ten forms them into subsets easily represented on the fingers, or perhaps even with tactile counters, which, as Netz has argued, ultimately became "the medium of numerical manipulation par excellence" in the Greek world.[7] Even if the act of counting is presented as a joint endeavor here (Ἀχαιοί τε Τρῶές τε), the total sum is known only to Agamemnon. What is important, rather, is his audience's ability to comprehend the comparison between both sides – this kind of presentation also calls to mind counters on abaci, whose display highlights relative rather than absolute values.[8] The moment soon passes, and indeed Agamemnon goes on to note that Trojans are in fact much greater with the strength of their allies added, but the visualization of the troops and their incorporation conjures up a mental inventory in the minds of the assembly. He has them imagine physically collecting (λέξασθαι) the troops who are physically at home (ἐφέστιοι) in the here-and-now, and then assembling them into parties with a winebearer – an image that may also suggest to them a comforting power differential.

While Agamemnon presents a description of what counting everyone (ἀριθμηθήμεναι) would entail, he in fact never arrives at a number or sum, but only at an imagistic quantity. The scene focuses rather on his skills in numeration and arithmetic proportions. If, however, he can invent and present this visual thought-experiment, he has himself presumably understood the relevant figures in their more abstract numerical terms. The ability both to digest and to reformulate numerical data for the masses thus sets Agamemnon apart from the group, reinforcing his general authority over

---

[7] Netz 2002: 329; it is not clear how archaic such devices may have been, but digital counting works similarly. Cf. van Berkel 2017 on orality and numeracy.

[8] That is, counters themselves placed in different value-columns can in theory represent whatever units one assigns to them.

them and also his effectiveness: the soldiers, having listened to him, initially take his suggestion to leave Troy.[9] While his reference to the numbers may appear at first to be an act of transparency, it in fact constitutes a carefully conceived display of numerical calculation that in its turn reinforces his own decision-making power and control of information.

This passage is not a catalogue, and yet it has a great deal to do with catalogues. Scholars have seen Agamemnon's numerical interests here as a precursor to the "real" Catalogue of Ships that will soon follow, and indeed as part of a unique interest in counting in Book 2.[10] Rather than having some generally unifying effect on just this book, however, I contend that a focus on numeracy persists throughout Homer, expressed in catalogues and lists. Moreover, it highlights a more specific triangular tension, among the nodes of: absolute countability (as reckonable, e.g. by Agamemnon or other authority figures), relative countability (as reckonable, e.g. for the audience), and the uncountable or infinite (as reckonable only to the most gifted narrators, such as the muses or the poet). Catalogues in both epics, I argue, consistently navigate among these three vertices. We can see shades of this tension in the series of similes for the army that appear later in Book 2 (455–483). Whereas the earlier passage focused us on Agamemnon's numerical prowess, these similes highlight the army's uncountable mass in a series of comparisons to difficult-to-count natural entities: fire, birds, numberless leaves and flowers, swarming flies.[11] At turns, the poem struggles to characterize how to value the things it presents as most dear.[12]

Counting in the Catalogue of Ships

Here enters the list. Unlike metaphors for the army, the Catalogue of Ships will speak of explicit sums, and yet it too turns on the three-pronged contrast of absolute, relative, and non-countability.[13] At the beginning of the Catalogue,

---

[9] G. S. Kirk 1985: 131 notes a stylistic shift in these lines: "until now the speech has been undramatic and routinely cumulative in expression, with conventional verse-structure and moderate enjambment. The present graphic and hypothetical calculation, set out in a single long and progressively enjambed sentence and brought to an epigrammatic climax in 128, noticeably elevates the style."

[10] Sale 1994: 54–55 and Rabel 1997: 64; see also Sammons 2010: 153 n.62.

[11] G. S. Kirk 1985: 163ff.

[12] Cf. Allen 1921: 34: "Dignity is given to the list by the repeated similes emphasizing the size of the multitude, and by the invocation to the muses to help the poet in his hard task."

[13] It is not impossible that the Agamemnon passage was composed as a deliberate gesture toward the Catalogue of Ships. For the relative chronology of the Catalogue and the rest of the poem, see Kullmann 2012, who argues that the Catalogue is an independent, earlier text; cf. Visser

the poet famously pleads numeric ignorance, claiming an inability to speak or name the multitude (2.485–493)[14]:

> ἔσπετε νῦν μοι Μοῦσαι Ὀλύμπια δώματ᾽ ἔχουσαι·
> ὑμεῖς γὰρ θεαί ἐστε πάρεστέ τε ἴστέ τε πάντα,
> ἡμεῖς δὲ κλέος οἶον ἀκούομεν οὐδέ τι ἴδμεν·
> οἵ τινες ἡγεμόνες Δαναῶν καὶ κοίρανοι ἦσαν·
> πληθὺν δ᾽ οὐκ ἂν ἐγὼ μυθήσομαι οὐδ᾽ ὀνομήνω,
> οὐδ᾽ εἴ μοι δέκα μὲν γλῶσσαι, δέκα δὲ στόματ᾽ εἶεν
> φωνὴ δ᾽ ἄρρηκτος, χάλκεον δέ μοι ἦτορ ἐνείη,   490
> εἰ μὴ Ὀλυμπιάδες Μοῦσαι Διὸς αἰγιόχοιο
> θυγατέρες μνησαίαθ᾽ ὅσοι ὑπὸ Ἴλιον ἦλθον·
> ἀρχοὺς αὖ νηῶν ἐρέω νῆάς τε προπάσας.

> Tell me, Muses who hold homes on Olympus,
> for you are goddesses and you are present and know all,
> while we hear only the story and know nothing.
> And I could not speak nor name off the multitude,
> not even if I should have ten tongues and ten mouths,
> and an unbroken voice, and in me a bronze heart,   490
> should the Olympian muses, aegis-bearing Zeus's
> daughters, not remind how many went to Troy;
> I now will speak the ships' leaders and all the ships.

For the poet to say he could not name the multitude, even with super-human physical traits, unless the muses remind him – but then apparently to do so anyway – introduces, as Sammons put it, "serious logical problems."[15] But

---

  1997, Danek 2004 and Nünlist 2013, who stress its oral features and composition, along with the rest of the poem. Previous studies include: Page 1959 and Lazenby and Hope Simpson 1970, who pressed for the Mycenean origins of the Catalogue; and Niese 1873 and Giovannini 1969, who understood it as describing Greece in the eighth/seventh century BCE. Jachmann 1958 argued for a post-Homeric date. G. S. Kirk 1985 remained agnostic on the relative date of composition. See also: Allen 1910 and 1921, Leaf 1922, Burr 1944, Crossett 1969, M. W. Edwards 1980.

[14] On the Catalogue recently, see Danek 2004, Kullmann 2009, Sammons 2010: 135–196, Strauss Clay 2011: 117–118, Kullmann 2012, Marks 2012, Fayer 2013, Faraone 2013, and with additional bibliography given by Sammons 2010: 5–7. For an interactive map of the place-names in the text, see Strauss Clay's "Mapping the Catalogue of Ships," http://ships .lib.virginia.edu/home>

[15] For his list, see Sammons 2010: 153. Cf. G. S. Kirk 1985: 167–168:

> the poet has declared that he can deal with the leaders, provided the Muses help him; the troops would be beyond his powers even if he had ten tongues, and so on – unless the Muses reminded him of how many came to Troy. In other words, it is not after all the sheer size of the task (requiring ten tongues), it is lack of knowledge that is the impediment.

what sort of information does the poet promise to give and in fact provide, and how do the muses assist in this venture (or not)? G. S. Kirk, following propositions by Krischer to interpret ὅσοι as indirect interrogative, addressed this issue numerically, by suggesting that "the [Muses'] 'reminding' (μνησαίαθ') can be reconciled with the poet's professed physical inability to deal with such large numbers: he is not about to tell *who* were the troops as he had with the leaders … but rather *how many* they were, (ὅσοι)."[16] And yet, in the catalogue itself, the poet, like Agamemnon, does not provide any direct or cohesive sum of troops or leaders, but rather controls the nature of the data and its computation.[17] More apt perhaps then is the view that this passage is a *recusatio*, in Ford's words a "refusal to give a presentation of complex things," which for Ford relates to an expression of the numerical sublime.[18] But the poet does not exactly refuse, but rather plays with types of numeracy, first setting us up for non-countability (πληθὺν δ' οὐκ ἂν ἐγὼ μυθήσομαι οὐδ' ὀνομήνω), next gesturing toward an absolute value via the muses (ὅσοι), and finally in the catalogue giving subtotals that are useful as relative values.

Like Agamemnon's presentation of the troops, intended to emphasize relative rather than absolute values in digestible decads, the Catalogue of Ships gives specific numbers that are impossible to tally in their complete sum.[19] Instead of base ten, however, it operates on larger groupings, most commonly of forty, thirty, occasionally sixty, and once ninety; these are presented in regular structures with formulaic wording that corresponds to the numbers.[20] One-off, non-rounded figures are given as well, perhaps for the sake of verisimilitude and variation. The two most common and regular formulae are for contingents with forty and thirty ships:

> Forty ships: τοῖς δ' ἅμα τεσσαράκοντα μέλαιναι νῆες ἕποντο
> (nine times, plus three with fifty and eighty)
> "and along with them forty black ships followed"

> Thirty ships: τοῖς δὲ τριήκοντα γλαφυραὶ νέες ἐστιχόωντο (four times, with slight variations)
> "and with them thirty hollow ships lined up"

---

[16] G. S. Kirk 1985: 167, Krischer 1965. For problems and further references, see Sammons 2010: 154.

[17] For a "democratic" reading of the catalogue, see Heiden 2008.

[18] On the *recusatio*: Martin 1989: 223–224, Ford 1992: 73, de Jong 2001: 281–283, Sammons 2010: 150–155, and González 2013: 7.2.

[19] See Huxley 1966 for an argument to take the numbers of the Catalogue seriously.

[20] For types, see G. S. Kirk 1985: 171–173.

Thus when the numbers shift, the corresponding modifiers and verbs also change. An audience listening to the catalogue therefore has more markers of quantity than just numerical terms. The modes of description reinforce the quantities, and, in theory, if listeners tuned out and missed the number at the beginning of the hexameter, they might fairly reliably fill it in upon hearing the rest of the line. The catalogue, then, is structured to facilitate and reinforce a sense of group-by-group reckoning, and a comparison between and among the contingents – not a total sum. It may even also allow for simple, one-time calculations, such as in the two exceptional cases in which the poet states the number of men per ship, for the Boiotians (494–510) and the contingent led by Philoktetes (716–720):

> The Boiotians' contingent:
> τῶν μὲν πεντήκοντα νέες κίον, ἐν δὲ ἑκάστῃ
> κοῦροι Βοιωτῶν ἑκατὸν καὶ εἴκοσι βαῖνον.
>
> Of these there were 50 ships, and on each
> 120 sons of the Boiotians embarked.
>
> Philoktetes' contingent:
> τῶν δὲ Φιλοκτήτης ἦρχεν τόξων ἐΰ εἰδὼς
> ἑπτὰ νεῶν· ἐρέται δ' ἐν ἑκάστῃ πεντήκοντα
> ἐμβέβασαν τόξων ἐΰ εἰδότες ἶφι μάχεσθαι.
>
> Of them, Philoktetes, well-versed in the bow, was leader
> over seven ships. And on each fifty rowers,
> men well-versed in the bow to fight by force embarked.

Perhaps an attentive listener might be able to multiply these sets, especially if some belong to later strata of composition. The use of fifty as the factor in each passage may have facilitated such a calculation for any later listener in possession of a counting-board in the hand or the mind's eye.[21] The format of the catalogue entries does not, however, enable any running tally of total ships or total forces. In an echo of the power structure between Agamemnon and his men, and between the muse and the poet,

---

[21] See Netz 2002: 326, who explains how Western abaci employed positional counting to facilitate calculation, with columns based on fives and tens; thus Philoktetes' total numbers, for instance, could be represented by seven counters in the "fifty" column of an abacus, which could then be resolved by representing sets of two fifties as one counter in the "hundred" column, to arrive at 3 (100) plus 1 (50) = 350 rowers. The calculation required for the Boiotians is more extensive. The abacus was in use from at least the fifth century BCE; the earliest extant example is the Salamis abacus from ca. 300 BCE, which has a fifty column.

the audience is not given the tools or the complete information necessary to come up with a total sum.[22]

Instead, the catalogue encourages either the processing of singular, entry-specific information, or the overall impression of a huge mass of forces, where there are many more Greeks than Trojans. This last effect is amplified by the stark contrast in the bulk and length of the Achaean catalogue, which has an average of about nine lines per entry (29 entries over 266 lines, 494–760), and of the Trojan catalogue, with an average of just under four lines per entry (16 entries over 62 lines, 816–877).[23] Thus each contingent of the Achaean forces actually "feels" bigger, in addition to there being more contingents in total. Again the audience is placed into the position of Agamemnon's men, who can sense, but not themselves count, the quantitative difference between the two sides. In presenting the catalogue the poet can be seen as both telling and not telling the *plēthus* – a term whose scope is itself contested.[24] He avoids a sum total, but he points the audience to tools to form a comparative opinion of how large it could be.[25] In the end, they cannot speak or name the multitude either, but they know something of its greatness.

We return then to the muses. Sammons reads the line of the invocation, ἀρχοὺς αὖ νηῶν ἐρέω νῆάς τε προπάσας, "I now will speak the ships' leaders and all the ships," as the poet's own, ambiguous solution, and one that does not quite clarify the extent of the muses' assistance. Maslov, however, has recently suggested the invocation of the muses is a diagetic device for the genre of catalogue poetry more generally, with which the muses were connected from the earliest times.[26] If Maslov is right, we can read the muses here as a generic prerequisite; such a reading would accord well with the idea that they represent programmatic reckoners of the uncountable. As such, they function to help us imagine the ways in which one could quantify, since they are beings knowledgeable of how to grasp infinity.[27]

---

[22] Cf. here Sammons' discussion of the "palpable tension between the poet's cataloguing and the king's," in reference to Priam's ransom in *Iliad* 24 (2010: 213). In extended lists, my suspicion is that the speaker and narrative voice become indistinguishable; this may be similar to the view of genealogy as para-narrative; see Alden 2000: 153–178.

[23] Total number of entries taken from G. S. Kirk 1985: 250.

[24] Usually taken to mean the multitude of the army and not just its leaders; see Ford 1992: 72–73, Heiden 2008, Sammons 2010: 156–158.

[25] Compare here Thucydides' understanding that numbers of ships imply numbers of men.

[26] Sammons 2010: 154, Maslov 2016: 423–425.

[27] A related question that Sammons poses is how to grasp zero – "it remains unclear what quality of glory accrues to the hero who kills a succession of nonentities" (Sammons 2010: 156).

I Could Not Name the Sum

As the list to end all lists, the Catalogue of Ships, one might imagine, behaved in ways distinct from other lists in Homer with its own singular poetics. And yet its programmatic rhetoric of an unreckonable total, and its alleged inability to be spoken, accompany other far less grand catalogic contexts with more easily digestible numbers. Versions of the so-called *recusatio* formula, πληθὺν δ' οὐκ ἂν ἐγὼ μυθήσομαι οὐδ' ὀνομήνω (And I could not speak nor name off the multitude), appear three more times in the *Odyssey*.[28] In that poem, a speaker, as opposed to stating that she or he cannot name the πληθύν, stands back from stating "all" the examples in the catalogue, using a form of πᾶς in the first position, and a quantitative correlative introducing the matter at hand. For Sammons, the idea of refusal relates ultimately to the tension between the all-encompassing knowledge of the muses on the one hand, and poetic innovation on the other; and between the imaginary "ideal" catalogue and the one that actually occurs.[29] My view is of a less literal poet, and one who is interested instead in highlighting the potential of catalogue to communicate, and in fact approximate, the infinite. While the formula does not always introduce a catalogue, it always invokes one, and it would seem to be part of an underlying poetics of catalogue poetry.

In Book 11, the formula appears twice, first to conclude Odysseus' catalogue of women in the underworld – a passage to which I will return in Chapter 2. Odysseus states (328–329):

πάσας δ' οὐκ ἂν ἐγὼ μυθήσομαι οὐδ' ὀνομήνω,
ὅσσας ἡρώων ἀλόχους ἴδον ἠδὲ θύγατρας·

I could not speak or name all the women,
However many wives and daughters of heroes I saw.

Here, as de Jong and Sammons note, in contrast to their appearance in *Iliad* 2, these words are used as a "breaking-off" formula, to end the list.[30] Later,

---

[28] *Od.* 4.240, 11.328, 11.517. See Sammons 2010: 150–158. Cf. also *Hom. Hymn Dem.* 149, ταῦτα δέ τοι σαφέως ὑποθήσομαι ἠδ' ὀνομήνω, a positive version of the formula.

[29] Poetic innovation, ideal versus actual catalogue: Sammons 2010: 164–165. Sammons' view of the Catalogue also seeks to contextualize it within the narrative context of the poem as we have it.

[30] De Jong 2001: 281–283. The variation in use here may be due to the relative chronology of the *Nekuia*. Sammons 2010: 150–151 aptly compares *Il.* 17.260–261, where a catalogue is also interrupted; but the formulaics of the "*recusatio*" phrase are somewhat different there.

in *Odyssey* 11, they appear in Odysseus' response to Achilles' inquiry about his son Neoptolemos (11.517–518):

> πάντας δ' οὐκ ἂν ἐγὼ μυθήσομαι οὐδ' ὀνομήνω,
> ὅσσον λαὸν ἔπεφνεν ἀμύνων Ἀργείοισιν

> I could not speak or name them all,
> All the people he killed, blameless, for the Argives

After Odysseus emphasizes the impossibility of naming all of Neoptolemos' victims, he mentions just one; thus the formula can signal that either very many, one, or no more may follow.[31] But no matter which, he invokes the catalogue form for the audience, and specially signals its essential features of recursion, flexibility, and, in Eco's formulation, *potential* infinity. The programmatic statement here stands less as a refusal or a break than a way to characterize what-could-be-stated-as-a-catalogue (and maybe what was one, in certain performances). In this poetic world, catalogues are uncountable in total, ever-extendable. οὐκ ἂν ἐγὼ μυθήσομαι οὐδ' ὀνομήνω gives an oral poet leave to make the ensuing catalogue however long he sees fit; perhaps, these words even prime an audience to prepare for a long passage.[32]

How we define what follows this formula, however, is not always obvious. A third appearance in the *Odyssey* occurs as Helen tells Telemachus of his father (*Od.* 4.240–241):

> πάντα μὲν οὐκ ἂν ἐγὼ μυθήσομαι οὐδ' ὀνομήνω,   240
> ὅσσοι Ὀδυσσῆος ταλασίφρονός εἰσιν ἄεθλοι·

> And I could not describe nor name off all of them,   240
> how many are determined Odysseus' struggles.

Here, at first glance, a proper list does not accompany Helen's lines – the opening seems to be an earnest *recusatio*, in which the speaker warns that there is too much to tell but, as de Jong describes, gives instead a paradigmatic example in the form of an embedded narrative.[33] Yet on an extra-narrative level, this passage in Book 4 in fact does signal a grand

---

[31] On this beginning in the context of priamel, see Race 1982: 33–35; cf. Ford 1992: 73–74, who argues for the poet's emphasis on selectivity in these passages.

[32] Eco 2009. For the separate Aristotelian idea of "potential" versus "actual" infinity, see *Physics* 208a 7–8.

[33] On the relationship of these moments to Kant's numerical sublime, see Ford 1992: 76. Cf. Allen's own account of the ancient scholarship related to the Catalogue of Ships: "Endless works were written either upon it or upon its subject, the nations and families that went to Troy" (1921: 31).

catalogue to come in the remainder of the poem following the Telemacheia: Odysseus' own account of his struggles. Beginning in Book 5, the *Odyssey* amounts to a narrative of precisely what Helen says she cannot tell. And, while perhaps any one version of the epic may not name them *all*, each version gives a large enough set to fulfill the requirements of abundance and, like the Catalogue of Ships, approximate completeness and grapple with the infinite.[34] The Odyssean examples, moreover, occur in contexts of embedded narration that closely parallel the meta-poetic statement of *Iliad* 2. One suspects that the characters of Odysseus and Helen engage in a similar ironical poetics here as did the Iliadic poet. While others have seen this practice as signaling the selectivity of the poet and the dynamism of the text, numerically speaking, these formulaics prime an audience to expect that the so-called infinite will be illustrated with a finite set. Stated otherwise, the actual arithmetic difference between the quantity listed and infinity is not significant within this rhetorical framework. Rather, abundance is conceptualized in a way that a modern reader might find irrational: as closer to infinity than to a countable number.[35] In this, the poem also illustrates the idea that "in some collections the estimate is probably more accurate than a full inventory."[36]

Naming and Counting

The speakers in these passages claim to be unable to describe their subject in two ways: neither μυθέομαι, "tell" nor ὀνομήνω, "name." But in each example, the object of the verbs is a numerical entity: a form of πᾶς later referenced by a form of ὅσος, or, in *Iliad* 2, the πληθύς.[37] The confusion of counting and naming, of names and numbers, is worth considering in its relation to the catalogue and to the act of counting – what set of implications do these two terms collectively and contrastively evoke? The content

---

[34] Consider also a more focused, localized example of the same phenomenon. At the start of Book 5, Athena sits among the assembly of the gods and is said to remind them of the hero's plights (5.5–6: τοῖσι δ' Ἀθηναίη λέγε κήδεα πόλλ' Ὀδυσῆος | μνησαμένη) – a statement reminiscent of Helen's. Her list that follows (5.7–20) accomplishes what Helen says she could not, though Athena could not be said to really do justice to the κήδεα πόλλα in the limited examples she gives.

[35] If this is so, the Homeric Greeks would not be unique in their (to our sensibilities) distorted perception. It has been observed that cultures that do not deal with large-number arithmetic treat smaller, single-digit integers as if they were spaced further apart than large, far-off ones. The system functions much as does visual perspective, in which distant objects appear to be closer together than immediate ones. See, e.g., Bellos 2010: 13–41.

[36] Peters 2015: 349.   [37] Most take this to refer to the masses of the army, not just the leaders.

of *mutheomai* (*muthos*), an authoritative performative speech act, Martin showed, can be clearly distinguished from *epos*, a more basic message-utterance.[38] But it also contrasts with *onoma*. In these list-passages, the phrase's formulaic use shows that ὀνομαίνω signals an act of enumeration, as opposed to the storytelling inherent in μυθέομαι.[39] Moreover, ὀνομαίνω denotes the original, first-hand act of naming a complete sum in list form, rather than repeating one – an action described by the more obviously catalogic καταλέγω, as we will see. The semantic move from "calling (of one person) by name" to "listing" is illustrated in an exchange between Hera and personified Sleep, in which she promises to give him one of the Graces in return for sedating Zeus (*Il.* 14.277–279):

> Ὣς ἔφατ᾽, οὐδ᾽ ἀπίθησε θεὰ λευκώλενος Ἥρη,
> ὄμνυε δ᾽ ὡς ἐκέλευε, θεοὺς δ᾽ ὀνόμηνεν ἅπαντας
> τοὺς ὑποταρταρίους οἳ Τιτῆνες καλέονται.

> Thus he spoke, and the goddess white-armed Hera
> did not disregard him,
> but swore as he asked, and she named all the gods
> below Tartarus, who are called Titans.

Here the act of naming takes on a transactional significance, amplified by its quantitative and completist poetics. ὀνομαίνω is no mere list of names, but the surety for an oath; perhaps line 278 even plays at an etymological connection with ὄμνυε. Though this list itself does not appear in our version of the *Iliad*, it acts as a guarantee in a context of neither written record nor universal standards of value. This transactional nature of the named list is nowhere more apparent than in Agamemnon's catalogue of reparations for Achilles (9.122–156, repeated at 265–298). Agamemnon introduces the gifts to the assembled commanders (9.120–121), saying ἂψ ἐθέλω ἀρέσαι δόμεναί τ᾽ ἀπερείσι᾽ ἄποινα | ὑμῖν δ᾽ ἐν πάντεσσι περικλυτὰ δῶρ᾽ <u>ὀνομήνω</u>, "I would like to appease him and give boundless return / and among you all I shall name splendid gifts." Yet the ensuing enumeration, like the Catalogue of Ships, constitutes not so much a naming but a count, for the quantity of the gifts is arguably of greater importance in many cases than their individual identities. Furthermore, like the Catalogue of Ships, the list includes several items not named individually, but counted up in subtotals, as at the very start (9.122–124, repeated at 9.264–266):

---

[38] Martin 1989.

[39] Here we might contrast Apollonius of Rhodes' version, discussed below, Chapter 6.

ἕπτ' ἀπύρους τρίποδας, δέκα δὲ χρυσοῖο τάλαντα,
αἴθωνας δὲ λέβητας ἐείκοσι, δώδεκα δ' ἵππους
πηγοὺς ἀθλοφόρους, οἳ ἀέθλια ποσσὶν ἄροντο.

Unburnished tripods seven, and ten gold talents,
and twenty glittering cauldrons, and twelve horses
strong, prizebearing, who raise up prizes with their feet.

But unlike the men and ships in *Iliad* 2, which have comparable units, these goods, as so many epic treasures, are disparate items lacking a standard. As has often been noted, in the Homeric economy there is no coinage and thus no single unit of prestige goods, or of payment or wealth.[40] While certain parameters apply (in Schaps' memorable terms, "no number of cucumbers could ransom a hero"), the category of prestige goods comprises a disparate array of objects whose total value is impossible to sum up.[41] Because of this disparity, the list form becomes a guarantee of value where neither standard nor physical document is available: the "named" list takes on a contractual capacity and also serves as receipt. As a result, the list not only expresses or guarantees a certain value, it also operates as a constitutive form, creating and enhancing the worth of both its contents. In this scenario, the utterer of the list occupies the role of numerical controller. And just as the list imbues objects with value, the person who performs the act of ὀνομαίνω – Agamemnon, Hera, Helen, Odysseus, or the poet – becomes vested with a count-driven power. Here too, the listener receives no translation into a reckonable total. The theoretically countable items on offer (seven tripods, ten talents, twenty cauldrons, ten horses, seven women, twenty Trojan women, one daughter, seven cities) are sufficiently interpolated with description that one loses track of them; moreover, each represents a different unit. It is the promissory force of ὀνομαίνω and the list form, rather than its particular content, that lends credibility to the transaction.[42]

Thus the verb of "naming" encodes the act of listing for a contractual or probative purpose, by the original person who controls the numbers. The

---

[40] See, e.g., Schaps 2004: 65–67.   [41] Schaps 2004: 66.

[42] On the exchange politics of Agamemnon's offer, see Donlan 1993, supported by, e.g., Muellner 1996: 141–142, Lateiner 2004: 25–26; see also Donlan 1989: 5–6, Redfield 1995 [1975]: 103–106 and, on exchanges more generally, Donlan 1982. Sammons 2010: 121–122 has argued against Donlan on the grounds that a) his theory at its most extreme does not allow for a variety of power relationships possible in the heroic world, and b) the other characters treat the offer too favorably for it to be so evidently hostile to an audience. Sammons instead maintains that "[g]ifts characterize the donor as much as the recipient, and the portraiture is entirely flattering." See also Wilson 2002 and Scodel 2008, with further discussion below.

interplay of naming, listing, and counting is complicated by the reprise of Agamemnon's catalogue, which Odysseus recounts for Achilles in his hut later in Book 9 (265–298). While the contents of the list are repeated verbatim (with first person changed to third), Agamemnon's original offering statement is further altered. Odysseus says (262–263):[43]

> εἰ δὲ σὺ μέν μευ ἄκουσον, ἐγὼ δέ κέ τοι <u>καταλέξω</u>
> ὅσσά τοι ἐν κλισίῃσιν ὑπέσχετο δῶρ᾽ Ἀγαμέμνων·

> Come then, if you will, listen to me, and I will enumerate
> for you how many gifts in his hut Agamemnon has promised:

καταλέξω replaces Agamemnon's original ὀνομήνω, while ὅσσα δῶρα stand in for Agamemnon's ἀπερείσια ἄποινα.[44] Here at last we find the expected *terminus technicus* for the catalogue – καταλέγω, a verb whose relationship to the "inventory poetics" of Homer has been richly explored.[45] Indeed, this verb may align with a cross-linguistic pattern of words that mean both "tell" and "count" (e.g. German *zählen*, Spanish *contar*, and the Germanic ancestors of English "tell").[46] But its peculiarly reiterative nature, signaling the repetition of a previously stated catalogue, has not been sufficiently emphasized.

Here, whereas Agamemnon was creating the list for the first time, Odysseus is about to give an authoritative recitation – an "authorized recording," in modern legal parlance.[47] Hainsworth insists that "Odysseus' verbatim report is not so much a careful statement of the terms of a contract as the normal epic convention when orders, messages, etc. are delivered."[48] However, this *is* indeed a special situation. Successful or not, this offer is no

---

[43] For the minor differences between the passages at 264–299 and 122–157 and an interpretation, see, e.g., Hainsworth 1993: 98. He does not, however, comment on these preceding lines.

[44] καταλέγω is an apt verb for listing, but even when it does not denote what its English cognate does it seems to have some relationship to counting, e.g. when Laertes asks Odysseus (in disguise) to recount for him how many years it is since he (allegedly) saw his son (*Od.* 24.287–289): ἀλλ᾽ ἄγε μοι τόδε εἰπὲ καὶ ἀτρεκέως κατάλεξον· | πόστον δὴ ἔτος ἐστίν, ὅτε ξείνισσας ἐκεῖνον, | σὸν ξεῖνον δύστηνον, ἐμὸν παῖδ᾽, εἴ ποτ᾽ ἔην γε;

[45] Perceau 2002, Krischer 1971: 131–157, Kyriakidis 2007: 68–70; Couloubaritsis 2006: 252–257; see Sammons 2010: 7–8, with additional bibliography there. Also see: Bakker 1997: 55–60, Finkelberg 1998: 121–129.

[46] For a media-theory perspective on the phenomenon, see Ernst 2003: 147–157; while I take issue with Ernst's statements about the history of the Greek alphabet and the Catalogue of Ships, the broader discussion of the two verbs provides useful background and discussion of the history of the idea.

[47] Here and in the case of ὀνομήνω the future directly preceding the list seems performative rather than temporal; on this, see Christensen 2010, who interprets first-person futures in Homer in performative utterances as precursors to the similar phenomenon found in epinician poetry.

[48] Quotation from Hainsworth 1993: 98, citing Bowra 1952: 254–258.

ordinary message, and καταλέγω marks it as such. Moreover, Odysseus is not just any messenger, nor are the length of the message and its contents anything short of extraordinary. The capacity for list-repetition, as opposed to list-composition, may inform the poet's own use of ὀνομαίνω in the *recusatio* in *Iliad* 2. The poet cannot "ὀνομαίνω" the Catalogue of Ships in the sense of not being able to generate it, but in theory he could repeat it. Thus while Agamemnon and the muses know and can generate the data of their respective catalogues, Odysseus and the poet, respectively, are endowed with the ability to recite them. The act of doing so also, however, establishes the authority and credibility of Odysseus himself as the re-lister, issues that will be at the core of his identity in the *Odyssey*.

Odysseus the καταλόγιος

Understanding Odysseus' specialized powers of catalogic recitation in *Iliad* 9 illuminates instances of listing in the *Odyssey*. The verb καταλέγω characterizes key moments of the narrative: this is the term Alcinous will use when he asks Odysseus to tell his own story in *Odyssey* 8, and that Odysseus will use as he challenges Demodocus to tell the tale of the Trojan horse.[49] But as the poem proceeds, the ability to correctly inventory and recite lists of objects becomes crucial to Odysseus' recovery of power, wealth, identity, and family. His catalogic abilities bookend the Ithacan section of the *Odyssey*, beginning with his counting of gifts from the Phaeacians in Book 13 and ending with the catalogue of Laertes' trees in Book 24. We can observe the empowerment associated with listing and inventorying from the moment Odysseus at long last arrives in Ithaca. As he surveys the shore, he has a brief internal struggle and performs an act of accounting (13.203–218):

> ὤ μοι ἐγώ, τέων αὖτε βροτῶν ἐς γαῖαν ἱκάνω;
> ἦ ῥ' οἵ γ' ὑβρισταί τε καὶ ἄγριοι οὐδὲ δίκαιοι,
> ἦε φιλόξεινοι καί σφιν νόος ἐστὶ θεουδής;   205
> πῇ δὴ χρήματα πολλὰ φέρω τάδε; πῇ δὲ καὶ αὐτὸς
> πλάγξομαι; αἴθ' ὄφελον μεῖναι παρὰ Φαιήκεσσιν
> αὐτοῦ· ἐγὼ δέ κεν ἄλλον ὑπερμενέων βασιλήων
> ἐξικόμην, ὅς κέν μ' ἐφίλει καὶ ἔπεμπε νέεσθαι.
> νῦν δ' οὔτ' ἄρ πῃ θέσθαι ἐπίσταμαι, οὐδὲ μὲν αὐτοῦ   210

---

[49] On Odysseus' authority in *Odyssey* 8, see recently Olsen 2017, who illuminates the roles of dance and movement in performing authority.

καλλείψω, μή πώς μοι ἕλωρ ἄλλοισι γένηται.
ὢ πόποι, οὐκ ἄρα πάντα νοήμονες οὐδὲ δίκαιοι
ἦσαν Φαιήκων ἡγήτορες ἠδὲ μέδοντες,
οἵ μ᾽ εἰς ἄλλην γαῖαν ἀπήγαγον· ἦ τέ μ᾽ ἔφαντο
ἄξειν εἰς Ἰθάκην εὐδείελον, οὐδ᾽ ἐτέλεσσαν.   215
Ζεύς σφεας τείσαιτο ἱκετήσιος, ὅς τε καὶ ἄλλους
ἀνθρώπους ἐφορᾷ καὶ τείνυται, ὅς τις ἁμάρτῃ.
ἀλλ᾽ ἄγε δὴ τὰ χρήματ᾽ ἀριθμήσω καὶ ἴδωμαι,
μή τί μοι οἴχωνται κοίλης ἐπὶ νηὸς ἄγοντες.
ὣς εἰπὼν τρίποδας περικαλλέας ἠδὲ λέβητας   220
ἠρίθμει καὶ χρυσὸν ὑφαντά τε εἵματα καλά.
τῶν μὲν ἄρ᾽ οὔ τι πόθει·

Ah me, what people's land have I come to this time?
Men arrogant and savage and not civilized,
or ones hospitable and of god-fearing minds?   205
Where should I bring all these goods? And I, where shall I
take myself to? I should have stayed right where I was
in Phaeacia, and then I would have come to meet
another mighty king who would have welcomed me
and sent me home. But as it is, I do not know   210
where I should store them, nor will I just leave them here,
in case to my chagrin they become others' loot.
Gah! Not wholly in their right minds nor civilized
were they, the Phaeacian leaders and counselors,
who led me to some other land, when they told me   215
they'd take me to fair Ithaca, but let me down.
May Zeus punish them, Zeus who cares for suppliants,
who surveils men and punishes whoever sins.
But come, I shall count up the goods, and let me see –
lest they left and took some on the hollow ship.   220
And saying thus he counted the gorgeous tripods
and cauldrons; the gold and the lovely woven clothes.
From these nothing was missing.

As Odysseus ponders how to proceed, his focus alternates between concern for his own welfare and that of the goods, to which he obsessively returns with the resumptive statements *νῦν δ᾽* (210) and *ἀλλ᾽ ἄγε* (218). The passage juxtaposes his person and his possessions in parallel as if to equate them, as visible in the anaphoric questions πῇ δὴ χρήματα πολλὰ φέρω τάδε; πῇ δὲ καὶ αὐτὸς | πλάγξομαι; Meanwhile, his solutions to the problems of where to go or how to cope with not being in Ithaca (or so he believes) involve the counting and care of his treasure. Thus his final proposition and subsequently described action of counting (ἀριημήσω, 218 and ἠρίθμει, 221) seem to satisfy him. Yet practically this accounting and inventory-taking solves little: if anything, it merely reiterates the problem of storage.[50] But in the act of taking an inventory of the goods, Odysseus performs an authoritative accounting role that establishes him as king, much like Agamemnon in the *Iliad*, though he has no dominance over anyone at the moment.[51] Once again in the region in which he rules (if unwittingly so), he once again behaves like a ruler.

While the final books of the *Odyssey* restore Odysseus to power and status in multiple ways, perhaps his ultimate reclamation of self, lineage, and innate identity occurs when he reveals himself to Laertes in Book 24. At the start of the scene between the two men, Odysseus (disguised as the stranger) foreshadows the catalogue of trees he will later recite as proof of his identity, commenting to his father (24.244–247):

> ὦ γέρον, οὐκ ἀδαημονίη σ' ἔχει ἀμφιπολεύειν
> ὄρχατον, ἀλλ' εὖ τοι κομιδὴ ἔχει, οὐδέ τι πάμπαν,   245
> οὐ φυτόν, οὐ συκῆ, οὐκ ἄμπελος, οὐ μὲν ἐλαίη,
> οὐκ ὄγχνη, οὐ πρασιή τοι ἄνευ κομιδῆς κατὰ κῆπον.

> Old man, you show no ignorance of orchard-tend-
> ing; no, your care is good, and not in any way,   245
> not plant, nor fig, nor vine nor even olive branch,
> nor pear nor plot goes uncared for in your garden.

While this casual list of items sounds like a rhetorical device of emphatic praise, it also hints at Odysseus' hidden catalogic knowledge of the garden's features. But even before his revelation, the stranger again shows his ability to inventory, presenting a list of gifts he supposedly gave Odysseus as a guest-friend (24.273–279):

> καί οἱ δῶρα πόρον ξεινήϊα, οἷα ἐῴκει.
> χρυσοῦ μέν οἱ δῶκ' εὐεργέος ἑπτὰ τάλαντα,
> δῶκα δέ οἱ κρητῆρα πανάργυρον ἀνθεμόεντα,   275
> δώδεκα δ' ἁπλοΐδας χλαίνας, τόσσους δὲ τάπητας,
> τόσσα δὲ φάρεα καλά, τόσους δ' ἐπὶ τοῖσι χιτῶνας,
> χωρὶς δ' αὖτε γυναῖκας ἀμύμονα ἔργα ἰδυίας
> τέσσαρας εἰδαλίμας, ἃς ἤθελεν αὐτὸς ἑλέσθαι.

---

[50] M. L. West 2014: 233: "He checks to see that his possessions are all there. They are, but he is still miserable."

[51] I use the term "king" loosely; for discussion of what monarchy meant in Homeric Greece, see, e.g., Luraghi 2013: 132–135.

... and I furnished him guest-friend gifts, such as befit.
I gave him seven talents' worth of well-wrought gold,
and gave to him a silver flowered mixing bowl,   275
also twelve simple cloaks, and just as many rugs,
as many lovely shrouds, also as many vests.
Apart from these, four women, knowing blameless works
attractive ones, whom he himself was glad to choose.

Here again, the stranger presents a catalogue as both proof of the story he tells about the meeting, and as a testament to his upright character. Thus well before revealing his identity to Laertes he has established himself as both an appreciator of the orchard and trees, and a friend to Odysseus with intimate knowledge of his possessions.[52] Taken together, these two mini-catalogues prefigure the one Odysseus presents as ultimate proof – which his father accepts – that he is himself the son of Laertes. Odysseus recites the list that Laertes originally counted off for him, a historical act signaled by the past tenses of ὀνομάζω and ὀνομαίνω. While Odysseus does not state a verb for his own list, he acts here again, as in *Iliad* 9, ὁ καταλέγων, the reciter of the list once created by his father (24.338–344):[53]

διὰ δ᾽ αὐτῶν
ἱκνεύμεσθα, σὺ δ᾽ ὠνόμασας καὶ ἔειπες ἕκαστα.
ὄγχνας μοι δῶκας τρεισκαίδεκα καὶ δέκα μηλέας,   340
συκέας τεσσαράκοντ᾽· ὄρχους δέ μοι ὧδ᾽ ὀνόμηνας
δώσειν πεντήκοντα, διατρύγιος δὲ ἕκαστος
ἤην· ἔνθα δ᾽ ἀνὰ σταφυλαὶ παντοῖαι ἔασιν,
ὁππότε δὴ Διὸς ὧραι ἐπιβρίσειαν ὕπερθεν.

We walked
through them, and you named off and spoke each one.
You gave me thirteen pear trees and ten apple trees,   340
and forty figs. Thus you spelled out that you would give
me fifty vine-rows, each one to be gathered in
succession. And they have all kinds of clumps of grapes
whenever Zeus's seasons rain down over them.

Here we see a combination of all the nuances that ὀνομαίνω bore when Agamemnon employed it in *Iliad* 9, if with a different result. When Laertes

---

[52] See Pucci 1996: 12, Henderson 1997.

[53] Pucci 1996: 6 stresses the role of lineage and the transfer of the inheritance, as well as the act of repetition on the part of the heir: "By learning the names of trees, the infant enters into the world of language in the wake of the father, into an orderly cataloguing of things, alien to all inventive rhetoric." On the role of farming knowledge as a sign of authority, see Murnaghan 2006.

named off his catalogue, the verb denoted a contractual offer, a binding promise of the gift; moreover, like Agamemnon, Laertes was the creator of the catalogue and the owner of the goods within it, with the power to bestow them on another. Here too the verb denotes a formal offer of gifts or compensation in the form of a catalogue, not just a promise. This analysis can perhaps resolve lexical issues associated with the collocation here of ὀνόμηνας plus the future infinitive δώσειν in line 341. LSJ and Autenrieth render ὀνόμηνας here as "promise to do," based on a meaning such as "speak."[54] Such may be the implication of Laertes' words, but the interpretation of ὀνόμηνας should attend instead to the presence of the cognate ὀνομάζω in line 339 and the special resonance of the denominative of ὄνομα with transactional listmaking to a transactional end.[55] Here, as we have seen it used before, ὀνομαίνω is deployed specifically in recounting, naming off again for inventory purposes, a series of commodities for exchange in an inventory. Thus we may consider ὀνόμηνας δώσειν as closer to "you listed with the intent to give," somewhat akin to the future infinitive with μέλλω.

The catalogic importance of ὀνομαίνω, and its distinction from καταλέγω and ὀνομαίνω emerges in full in one final example, a passage in which the shepherd Eumaeus tells Odysseus (in disguise) of his master's former wealth (14.96–104):

> ἦ γάρ οἱ ζωή γ᾽ ἦν ἄσπετος· οὔ τινι τόσση
> ἀνδρῶν ἡρώων, οὔτ᾽ ἠπείροιο μελαίνης
> οὔτ᾽ αὐτῆς Ἰθάκης· οὐδὲ ξυνεείκοσι φωτῶν
> ἔστ᾽ ἄφενος τοσσοῦτον· ἐγὼ δέ κέ τοι <u>καταλέξω.</u>
> δώδεκ᾽ ἐν ἠπείρῳ ἀγέλαι· τόσα πώεα οἰῶν,   100
> τόσσα συῶν συβόσια, τόσ᾽ αἰπόλια πλατέ᾽ αἰγῶν
> βόσκουσι ξεῖνοί τε καὶ αὐτοῦ βώτορες ἄνδρες·
> ἐνθάδε τ᾽ αἰπόλια πλατέ᾽ αἰγῶν ἕνδεκα πάντα
> ἐσχατιῇ βόσκοντ᾽, ἐπὶ δ᾽ ἀνέρες ἐσθλοὶ ὄρονται.

Indeed was his wealth boundless. Not so great was that
of any lordly man, not on the dark mainland,
nor in Ithaca itself. And not to twenty men
was there such plenteousness. I'll recount it for you:

---

[54] Heubeck et al. 1992: 399 liken ὀνομαίνω + future infinitive to ὑπισχνέομαι but admit that the usage "lacks close parallels in epic" (the further interpretation of *Il.* 18.449 and 9.515 as having an implied future infinitive seems somewhat dubious as well).

[55] ὀνομάζω seems to overlap somewhat in semantic range, appearing at *Il.* 18.449 and 9.515 in reference to Agamemnon's "promise" of gifts. We might adduce here Thetis' language as she explains to Hephaestus and Charis the quarrel between Achilles and Agamemnon, recounting key events, including the embassy and Agamemnon's offer, *Il.* 18.448–449: τὸν δὲ λίσσοντο γέροντες | Ἀργείων, καὶ πολλὰ περικλυτὰ δῶρ᾽ ὀνόμαζον.

On the mainland twelve herds of cows, so many sheep,   100
so many droves of pigs, so many packs of goats
as pasture goatherds, foreign or of his own kind.
And also here feed packs of goats, elevenfold,
on the outskirts, and skilled men keep watch over them.

Here, though this exact catalogue has not appeared within the narrative before, Eumaeus nonetheless recounts it as an inventory he has heard, of an already established collection that no longer exists (or so he thinks): ἢ γάρ οἱ ζωή γ᾽ ἦν ἄσπετος. Eumaeus, consistent with the other scenes we have observed, uses καταλέγω for his act of recollection and restating, not originating, the inventory. Here the nuance of this word emerges most clearly: the one who employs ὀνομαίνω is the inventor of the list and the controller of its content; he who performs καταλέγω feels in charge of the list's preservation and reperformance. At the same time, this passage emphasizes the restorative force of the reperformance, allowing both lister or listener to repossess, in some sense, what is theirs. Eumaeus is perhaps doubly poised to do this through his closeness to Odysseus, but also through his affinity to the poet.[56]

Counting the Countless

Eumaeus' list of Odysseus' holdings also introduces our final term of inquiry. At the start of his speech he proclaims that his master's wealth (ζωή) was "boundless," or more literally "unspeakable," ἄσπετος. Thereupon, however, he immediately provides a spoken account of the precise bounds of the wealth.[57] This apparent rhetorical subversion occurs in many other key passages too. Earlier in *Odyssey* 13, when Odysseus leaves Scheria asleep on the ship, the poet first mentions the gifts from Alcinous, saying (13.134–138):

οἱ δ᾽ εὕδοντ᾽ ἐν νηῒ θοῇ ἐπὶ πόντον ἄγοντες
κάτθεσαν εἰν Ἰθάκῃ, ἔδοσαν δέ οἱ ἄσπετα[58] δῶρα,   135
χαλκόν τε χρυσόν τε ἅλις ἐσθῆτά θ᾽ ὑφαντήν,

---

[56] For a reading of these kinds of connection as various forms of slavery, see Schmidt 2006.

[57] ἄσπετος, as ἐννέπω, < PIE *sekʷ*.

[58] van Thiel: ἀγλαά. The reading ἄσπετα δῶρα is defensible on analogy to 20.342, where Telemachus offers same to the suitor who would marry Penelope. The choice of ἀγλαά is based on comparison with 16.230 and on the frequency of this adjective, which appears fairly commonly with δῶρα and ἄποινα in this position, while ἄσπετος accompanies δῶρα only one other time (supra) and in a different part of the line.

πόλλ’, ὅσ’ ἂν οὐδέ ποτε Τροίης ἐξήρατ’ Ὀδυσσεύς,
εἴ περ ἀπήμων ἦλθε, λαχὼν ἀπὸ ληΐδος αἶσαν.

They led him asleep on the swift ship over seas
and sent him to Ithaca, gave him countless gifts:　　135
bronze and gold and woven clothes, in heaps, many,
so as Odysseus would never have won at Troy,
had he come back with ease, taking his lot of spoil.

These ἄσπετα δῶρα are the same ones that Odysseus will count once he awakes in Ithaca some eighty lines later, yet here they have been outlined as uncountable and unspeakable. On the one hand, the apparent inconsistency of being able to count the explicitly countless here seems remediable – perhaps we should read the adjective as hyperbolic, or perhaps we should not expect such close continuity between books of the poem. Regardless, a stock epithet need not be congruous with the immediate context in which it appears.[59] Finally, some editors reject ἄσπετα in favor of ἀγλαά (the phrase ἀγλαά δῶρα appears at 16.230). I would like to suggest instead that more is at work in designations of quantified amounts as infinite than simply a bleached epithet or a simple exaggeration. Here, both the adjective ἄσπετος and the quantifying statement in line 137 (πόλλ’, ὅσ’ ἂν οὐδέ ποτε Τροίης ἐξήρατ’ Ὀδυσσεύς) emphasize the vastness of the treasure, and the latter perhaps momentarily calls into question Odysseus’ desert of it. But the doubt does not linger long, for his counting the goods upon reaching Ithaca confirms his rightful ownership of them. Though their exact sum might elude a less-skilled character, Odysseus, like Agamemnon and Zeus, is set apart by his ability to count what most people cannot. The short list of items at lines 217–218, ὣς εἰπὼν τρίποδας περικαλλέας ἠδὲ λέβητας | ἠρίθμει καὶ χρυσὸν ὑφαντά τε εἵματα καλά, echoes but does not repeat the description of them at 137 (χαλκόν τε χρυσόν τε ἅλις ἐσθῆτά θ’ ὑφαντήν), but gives more detail of what the objects were as Odysseus is described counting them, and thereby both enacts his inventory and affirms his rightful ownership of them.

---

[59] Parry 1987: 14 and 21–23 insisted that the "ornamental epithet" functions exclusively as a compositional building block, having "no relation to the ideas expressed by the words of either the sentence or the whole passage in which it occurs" (quotation 21). Sale 1993: 139–140 has discussed instances in which a normal formula is replaced with a less common one to avoid such potential absurdities as "Of the Cretans, Idomeneus, leader of the Cretans, was the leader." Janko 1992 calls these substitutes "equivalent formulae." M. W. Edwards 1997: 272–277 summarizes further scholarship on the topic, to which we may add later references given by Latacz et al. 2000: 52–57 and Hackstein 2010: 417–418.

Odysseus' and Eumaeus' acts of counting the countless are not unique. A similar but more common phrase, ἀπερείσια ἄποινα, "boundless ransom," is invoked multiple times throughout the *Iliad* and *Odyssey*, and often followed by an enumeration.[60] Following Wilson's study of heroic ransom and ἄποινα and ποινή, it has been surmised that ransoms are always described as "boundless" from the point of view of the ransom-giver; as Scodel puts it, "the person offering the ransom sees it as boundless not because of its economic value, but by transference from the good he seeks to recover, whose value to him is limitless."[61] I contend instead that, paradoxically, limited lists of so-called "boundless" ransoms and treasures *reinforce* their size through the kind of obfuscating quantification we have already seen, and through the infinity-rhetoric surrounding catalogue more generally. While it might initially appear that a catalogue "lays bare the rhetoric of limitlessness,"[62] in fact the listing of the so-called infinite serves as an expression of its abundance and *potential* infinity, in Eco's sense. The best-known example of the boundless-ransom formula occurs in a list we have already encountered – Agamemnon's offering of *Iliad* 9 (119–156):

ἀλλ' ἐπεὶ ἀασάμην φρεσὶ λευγαλέῃσι πιθήσας,
ἂψ ἐθέλω ἀρέσαι δόμεναί τ' <u>ἀπερείσι' ἄποινα</u>.   120
ὑμῖν δ' ἐν πάντεσσι περικλυτὰ δῶρ' ὀνομήνω
<u>ἕπτ'</u> ἀπύρους τρίποδας, <u>δέκα</u> δὲ χρυσοῖο τάλαντα,
αἴθωνας δὲ λέβητας <u>ἐείκοσι</u>, <u>δώδεκα</u> δ' ἵππους
πηγοὺς ἀθλοφόρους, οἳ ἀέθλια ποσσὶν ἄροντο.
<u>οὔ κεν ἀλήϊος εἴη ἀνὴρ ᾧ τόσσα γένοιτο</u>,   125
<u>οὐδέ κεν ἀκτήμων ἐριτίμοιο χρυσοῖο</u>,
<u>ὅσσά μοι ἠνείκαντο ἀέθλια μώνυχες ἵπποι</u>.
δώσω δ' <u>ἑπτὰ</u> γυναῖκας ἀμύμονα ἔργα ἰδυίας
Λεσβίδας, ἃς ὅτε Λέσβον ἐϋκτιμένην ἕλεν αὐτὸς
ἐξελόμην, αἳ κάλλει ἐνίκων φῦλα γυναικῶν.   130
τὰς μέν οἱ δώσω, μετὰ δ' ἔσσεται ἥν τότ' ἀπηύρων
κούρη Βρισῆος· ἐπὶ δὲ μέγαν ὅρκον ὀμοῦμαι
μή ποτε τῆς εὐνῆς ἐπιβήμεναι ἠδὲ μιγῆναι,
ἣ θέμις ἀνθρώπων πέλει ἀνδρῶν ἠδὲ γυναικῶν.
ταῦτα μὲν αὐτίκα <u>πάντα</u> παρέσσεται· εἰ δέ κεν αὖτε   135
ἄστυ μέγα Πριάμοιο θεοὶ δώωσ' ἀλαπάξαι,
νῆα ἅλις χρυσοῦ καὶ χαλκοῦ νηησάσθω

---

[60] The phrase appears eleven times. See Scodel 2008: 76–80.
[61] Wilson 2002: especially 39, 78–79. Scodel 2008: 80; cf. Sammons 2010: 111.
[62] Sammons 2010: 111.

εἰσελθών, ὅτε κεν δατεώμεθα ληΐδ' Ἀχαιοί,
Τρωϊάδας δὲ γυναῖκας ἐείκοσιν αὐτὸς ἑλέσθω,   140
αἵ κε μετ' Ἀργείην Ἑλένην κάλλισται ἔωσιν.
εἰ δέ κεν Ἄργος ἱκοίμεθ' Ἀχαιϊκὸν οὖθαρ ἀρούρης
γαμβρός κέν μοι ἔοι· τίσω δέ μιν ἶσον Ὀρέστῃ,
ὅς μοι τηλύγετος τρέφεται θαλίῃ ἔνι πολλῇ.
τρεῖς δέ μοί εἰσι θύγατρες ἐνὶ μεγάρῳ εὐπήκτῳ   145
Χρυσόθεμις καὶ Λαοδίκη καὶ Ἰφιάνασσα,
τάων ἥν κ' ἐθέλῃσι φίλην ἀνάεδνον ἀγέσθω
πρὸς οἶκον Πηλῆος· ἐγὼ δ' ἐπὶ μείλια δώσω
πολλὰ μάλ', ὅσσ' οὔ πώ τις ἑῇ ἐπέδωκε θυγατρί·
ἑπτὰ δέ οἱ δώσω εὖ ναιόμενα πτολίεθρα   150
Καρδαμύλην Ἐνόπην τε καὶ Ἱρὴν ποιήεσσαν
Φηράς τε ζαθέας ἠδ' Ἄνθειαν βαθύλειμον
καλήν τ' Αἴπειαν καὶ Πήδασον ἀμπελόεσσαν.
πᾶσαι δ' ἐγγὺς ἁλός, νέαται Πύλου ἠμαθόεντος·
ἐν δ' ἄνδρες ναίουσι πολύρρηνες πολυβοῦται,   155
οἵ κέ ἑ δωτίνῃσι θεὸν ὣς τιμήσουσι
καὶ οἱ ὑπὸ σκήπτρῳ λιπαρὰς τελέουσι θέμιστας.

But since I was a fool to trust my sorry heart,
now I want to appease and give boundless ransom.   120
Before you all I shall name off illustrious gifts:
Seven unfired tripods, ten talents of gold,
and twenty gleaming cauldrons, ten prize-bearing strong
horses, who raise up victory prizes with their feet.
Not mean would be the man who got so many things,   125
nor would he be in want of highly precious gold,
who attained all the prizes my swift horses won.
And I will give him seven women, Lesbian,
who know of blameless works, whom I myself picked out
when I sacked well-built Lesbos, who surpassed races   130
of women in their beauty. These I'll give to him,
and with them will be Briseus' daughter, whom I took
from him. And I will swear a solemn oath that I
at no point mounted her bed or mingled with her
as is the norm for humans, for women and men.
All these things will be his right now; and if later   135
the gods grant us to ravage Priam's great city,
let him go in and load his ship with gold and bronze
in heaps. When we Achaeans divvy up the spoil,
let him choose twenty Trojan women for himself
who are (after Argive Helen) the loveliest.   140

And should we reach Achaean Argos, lushest land,
he'd be my son-in-law, of equal honor to
my favored son Orestes, raised in great plenty.
I have three daughters in my well-constructed halls –
Chrysothemis, Laodike, Iphianassa –   145
let him lead off the one he likes with no bride-price
to Peleus' house. I'll give dowry-gifts besides,
so much as none has given for his daughter yet.
And I will give him seven well-settled cities,
Kardamyle, Enope and grassy Hire,   150
and divine Pherae and rich-meadowed Antheia
and lovely Aipeia and viny Pedasus.
And they're all by the sea, near to sandy Pylos.
In them live men rich-flocked in cattle and in sheep
who will bestow him god-like honor with their gifts   155
and under the scepter complete his splendid will.

The first section contains a rapid succession of theoretically processable numbers and items.[63] In addition to increasing in uniqueness and value, the items in the list increasingly defy quantification, and Agamemnon's presentation of them contributes to the effect. His qualification of the horses at lines 125–127 creates a quantitatively unclear compendious comparison early on. While the value statement "οὔ κεν ἀλήϊος εἴη ἀνὴρ ᾧ τόσσα γένοιτο | οὐδέ κεν ἀκτήμων ἐριτίμοιο χρυσοῖο" ("Not mean would be the man who got so many things | nor would he be in want of highly precious gold," 125–126) might at first seem to refer to the preceding gifts, it becomes in line 127 part of a more convoluted numerical comparison to the horses' winnings that feels almost like an afterthought (" . . . [so many things] . . . as the prizes my swift-footed horses have won"). What initially appeared to be the cap to a short list turns out to be an elaboration of just one entry, and the audience is invited to count even objects not within the catalogue at hand. As the gifts become more lavish in kind, not only do interruptions continue, but a reversal of expectations occurs: more easily valuated objects such as precious metals and dowry-gifts do not receive specific counts, whereas the people and cities do. Thus Agamemnon promises seven Lesbian women, twenty Trojan ones, and seven cities, but in vague terms "gold and bronze in heaps" (ἅλις χρυσοῦ καὶ χαλκοῦ, 137),

---

[63] Cf. Sammons, who frames the passage in terms of specificity: "this begins as an unusually generous but quite conventional list of objects: seven tripods, ten talents of gold, twelve horses, seven Lesbian women, and Briseis. The latter items are again made less generic by means of short elaborative description"(2010: 117).

and "very many dowry-gifts, so many as no man has given for his daughter" (μείλια ... πολλὰ μάλ', | ὅσσ' οὔ πώ τις ἑῇ ἐπέδωκε θυγατρί 147–148).[64] As in the Catalogue of Ships, the audience gets such an onslaught of items that, even if they could count each constituent part, they could not easily keep track of a running total. The point seems to be that they lose count entirely. The great illusion of the lavish gift-giver, as of the lover in Catullus' "give me 1,000 kisses" scheme, is to confuse his audience into not knowing the total sum, so that it is uncountable and *appears* to be infinite. This kind of list-design, with a statement of infinity followed by a combination of specificity, variation, and distraction, creates what we might call an *apeiron*-effect.[65] Moreover, the nature of oral epic poetry is such that catalogues of boundless goods are ever-extendable, and in a performance any one of them could be elaborated, in theory, forever. The catalogue thus rhetorically presents these ransoms as potentially infinite, and in fact they really are so. Whereas Wilson has argued that the phrase "unlimited *apoina*" here invokes an "*apoina* theme" following the Greeks' losses in Book 8, on a formal level the phrase more generally sets up the audience to hear an enumeration.[66]

The correspondence between list and the boundless emerges again in *Iliad* 24, where the poet inventories Priam's goods in real time as the king collects them together (24.228–237):

ἦ, καὶ φωριαμῶν ἐπιθήματα κάλ' ἀνέῳγεν·
ἔνθεν δώδεκα μὲν περικαλλέας ἔξελε πέπλους,
δώδεκα δ' ἁπλοΐδας χλαίνας, τόσσους δὲ τάπητας,   230

---

[64] Macleod's analysis of Achilles' refusal of Agamemnon through the lens of Book 24 is worth bearing in mind here. When Hector says his father will give "gold in heaps" in exchange for sparing his life, Achilles responds that even ten and twenty times the ransom (δεκάκις τε καὶ εἰκοσινήριτ' ἄποινα) will not change his mind and keep him from throwing Hector's body to the dogs (22.349–352).

> The theme of the wrath of Achilles is extended from the quarrel with Agamemnon to the vengeance for Patroclus; and as the first wrath came to an end, so must the second. Nor would Hector's death be able to extinguish it. If it is to come to an end, then it must first be represented as unyielding and horrifying; otherwise the story would lack shape or point or grandeur. Hence the description of how Achilles insulted, in words and in deed, his dead enemy goes well beyond what we read elsewhere in the poem; and it begins where he refuses to think of accepting a ransom. (1982: 21)

[65] The Homeric adjective ἀπερείσιος etymologically accords with the later philosophical term for the infinite, τὸ ἄπειρον. While ἄπειρος and ἀπερείσιος follow different derivational paths, they are ultimately tied to the same root; Chantraine suggests further that ἀπερείσιος could have undergone influence from ἀπείρων (s.v. πεῖραρ, of ἀπειρέσιος and ἀπείριτος: "ces mots ont pu subir l'influence de ἀπείρων, etc.").

[66] Wilson 2002: 78.

τόσσα δὲ φάρεα λευκά, τόσους δ᾽ ἐπὶ τοῖσι χιτῶνας.
χρυσοῦ δὲ στήσας ἔφερεν δέκα πάντα τάλαντα,
ἐκ δὲ δύ᾽ αἴθωνας τρίποδας, πίσυρας δὲ λέβητας,
ἐκ δὲ δέπας περικαλλές, ὅ οἱ Θρῇκες πόρον ἄνδρες
ἐξεσίην ἐλθόντι, μέγα κτέρας· οὐδέ νυ τοῦ περ   235
φείσατ᾽ ἐνὶ μεγάροις ὁ γέρων, περὶ δ᾽ ἤθελε θυμῷ
λύσασθαι φίλον υἱόν.

He spoke and opened up the lovely coffer-lids.
From these he took out very lovely broadcloths, twelve,
also twelve simple cloaks, and just as many rugs,   230
and as many white shrouds, also as many vests.
He weighed and brought out gold – all told ten talents' worth,
and brought out two glittering tripods, four cauldrons,
and then a very lovely cup the men of Thrace
once gave him on an embassy – a great treasure.   235
Not even this did the old man save in his home,
so did he wish in his heart to ransom his son.

Immediately the listener conceives of the offering as a lavish but finite collection, drawn generously from Priam's rich stores and tailored to please its recipient. Yet in the remainder of Book 24 we hear the ransom spoken of as ἀπερείσια, boundless, not once but at three key moments in which its size should be clear: first as Priam's sons load it onto his chariot (276), then by Priam himself as he tells Achilles what he has brought with him (502), and finally again as Achilles accepts the gifts and his men unpack them (576).[67] Rather than undermine the initial presentation of the items, the epithet and preceding catalogue operate jointly to highlight the opulence of the offer. The stark enumeration with its repeated quantifying words (δώδεκα, τόσσα, etc.), as Macleod noted, emphasize the quantities involved, while the paratactic structure and unvaried connections with δέ emphasize each item.[68] As a whole, the effect on an audience is – ironically – one of abundance rather than limits, for listeners receive an onslaught of numbered items rather than any sum total of them. Moreover, the list prepares them to think of the ransom as exceedingly large later, when it is described as such. Finally, the list form presents the sum of the ransom's parts as overflowingly abundant and *potentially* infinite, with the possibility of another addition at any point to the constituent parts. Though the list reaches a climactic finale with the singular heirloom cup, the previous

---

[67] As Scodel 2008: 76 observes, "[i]ts limits are completely palpable."
[68] Macleod 1982: 108, with reference to a similar use of repeated quantifiers elsewhere in Homer.

items (just as many ... just as many ...) could continue recursively. Once the poet focuses in on this last item, the audience is distracted from the exact count of how many came before. Eumaeus' account of Odysseus' wealth, too, includes the same kind of quantifying words used of Priam's ransom. It does not prepare a listener for the later-stated boundlessness of the listed items, but rather confirms it, proving through an actual tally just how abundant the wealth in question was. In a variety of combinations then, the two components – a statement of boundlessness plus a list – together result in signifying unreckonably large magnitudes, both within internal narrative and to the external audience.

Positing an established formulaics of "boundless" plus list accounts for truncated versions of this combination, such as when Adrastus begs Menelaus to spare him in exchange for a ransom at *Il.* 6.45–50:

> Ἄδρηστος δ᾽ ἄρ᾽ ἔπειτα λαβὼν ἐλίσσετο γούνων·   45
> ζώγρει Ἀτρέος υἱέ, σὺ δ᾽ ἄξια δέξαι ἄποινα·
> πολλὰ δ᾽ ἐν ἀφνειοῦ πατρὸς κειμήλια κεῖται
> χαλκός τε χρυσός τε πολύκμητός τε σίδηρος,
> τῶν κέν τοι χαρίσαιτο πατὴρ ἀπερείσι᾽ ἄποινα
> εἴ κεν ἐμὲ ζωὸν πεπύθοιτ᾽ ἐπὶ νηυσὶν Ἀχαιῶν.   50
>
> Then Adrastus clasped him by the knees and begged: 45
> Take me living, son of Atreus, and yourself
> receive a worthy ransom: because many lie
> the treasures in my wealthy father's residence.
> Bronze and gold and iron, wrought laboriously,
> from which my father would give you boundless ransom
> should he learn I'm alive by the Achaean ships.   50

First the speaker describes and defines the contents of the list (ἄξια ἄποινα, κειμήλια), and then he elaborates with a very brief (in this case) list (χαλκός, χρυσός, πολύκμητος σίδηρος). Following the contents, the speaker restates (perhaps in synonymous terms) the heading: ἀπερείσια ἄποινα. That this kind of framing occurs even with so brief an enumeration suggests this to be a formulaic feature and not a practical one – surely an audience would not lose track in one or two lines of what was being described.[69] But the presence of even the shortest of catalogues signals the amplitude of the offer.

---

[69] A similar kind of framing occurs in dedication scenes, such as Hector's injunction to Hecuba to bring an offering to Athena (*Il.* 6.269–279), which begins and ends with the words ἀλλὰ σὺ μὲν πρὸς νηὸν Ἀθηναίης ἀγελείης ἔρχεο (ἔρχεο).

Inventing the Inventory

Expressions of abundance highlight the ways in which epic presents numeracy – the ability to deal accurately in numerical sums and values – as the province of elite characters with claims to power. The connection emerges both through kings' and generals' performance of counting (often in list form) and through their offering up an enumeration to validate or prove their status. This act of counting is intimately linked to and realized through listmaking. Finally, the programmatic language that surrounds lists of things thus contains some commonly repeated elements: a statement of boundlessness or infinity and a verb of naming. Far from invalidating the list, claims that its contents cannot be counted in fact emphasize their abundance as to approach infinity and, as this chapter has argued, are part of a greater poetics of object-cataloguing. Listing in Homer thus functions as a counting of the rhetorically and potentially infinite. It furthermore emerges that counting is difficult to separate from naming, and thus verbs based on *onoma* come to denote listmaking. The verb *onomainō* in particular signals that the person in possession of the objects will present a list of them. It is the enumeration and its utterance – by either character or narrator – that constitutes part of a contractual offer.

The subsequent chapters of this book trace these features, in various guises, through catalogues and inventories of other genres and periods. Archaic and poetic ways of showing quantities and wealth persist into the historical world of documents. As a final example, we might examine a use of extended description as a practical feature of inventories of goods. While perhaps the elaborations here relate to the general magnificence of this catalogue, they also take part in an extended history of describing items for identification purposes. As subsequent chapters will show, more mundane lists, such as Herodotus' enumeration of Croesus' dedications to Delphi or Athenian sacred inventories, all employ stock modifiers to describe items, adding or omitting them at will. The inventory entry is an expandable and collapsible form that employs mainly a limited vocabulary of stock phrases, thus behaving somewhat like formulaic poetry, with occasional specialized descriptions of standout items.

We can see the practice at work in such moments as the descriptions in dressing scenes and offerings. The following passage, for example, describes the gifts Antinous and others bring for Penelope, *Od.* 18.290–303:

> ὣς ἔφατ' Ἀντίνοος, τοῖσιν δ' ἐπιήνδανε μῦθος.   290
> δῶρα δ' ἄρ' οἰσέμεναι πρόεσαν κήρυκα ἕκαστος.

Ἀντινόῳ μὲν ἔνεικε μέγαν περικαλλέα πέπλον,
ποικίλον· ἐν δ' ἄρ' ἔσαν περόναι δυοκαίδεκα πᾶσαι
χρύσειαι, κληῖσιν ἐϋγνάμπτοισ' ἀραρυῖαι·
ὅρμον δ' Εὐρυμάχῳ πολυδαίδαλον αὐτίκ' ἔνεικε,   295
χρύσεον, ἠλέκτροισιν ἐερμένον, ἠέλιον ὥς·
ἕρματα δ' Εὐρυδάμαντι δύω θεράποντες ἔνεικαν
τρίγληνα μορόεντα, χάρις δ' ἀπελάμπετο πολλή·
ἐκ δ' ἄρα Πεισάνδροιο Πολυκτορίδαο ἄνακτος
ἴσθμιον ἤνεικεν θεράπων, περικαλλὲς ἄγαλμα·   300
ἄλλο δ' ἄρ' ἄλλος δῶρον Ἀχαιῶν καλὸν ἔνεικεν.
ἡ μὲν ἔπειτ' ἀνέβαιν' ὑπερώϊα δῖα γυναικῶν,
τῇ δ' ἄρ' ἅμ' ἀμφίπολοι ἔφερον περικαλλέα δῶρα·

Thus spoke Antinous, and what he said pleased them,   290
and each man sent a herald forth to bear his gifts.
Antinous' brought a great and very lovely cloak,
multi-colored. And on it were twelve brooches all
in gold, and fitted on with bending fasteners.
Eurymachus' then brought a cleverly wrought chain,   295
golden, adorned with amber, gleaming like the sun.
And servants brought to Eurydamas two earrings,
triple-clustered, and shining from them much grace.
A servant from lord Peisander, Polyctor's son
brought out a necklace, a very lovely trinket.   300
And different servants brought out different lovely gifts.
But she, noblest of women, went up to her loft,
and there her handmaids brought the very lovely gifts.

In the passage, we find a collection of items intended for a woman, described in reasonable but not terribly original detail: remarkably, we see περικαλλής three times in the identical line position. Though some of the collocations of the gifts are unique in Homer (e.g. περικαλλέα πέπλον), the most arguably elaborate entry is that of the earrings, which are the same as those Hera dons at *Il.* 14.183 (identical to line 298 here). The use of stock adjectives (such as περικαλλής) comes as no surprise in the context of oral-formulaic verse: the poet has a few descriptors and some longer phrases, as for the earrings, and arranges them together to make a catalogue, condensing and embellishing at will. We associate this shuffling of stock words and phrases with oral composition in particular, in which a poet relies on known building blocks to form original arrangements. But a similar mode of composition may have created a new type of later, purely written document: the inscribed inventory. An especially apt comparandum may be found in the treasure records of Artemis Brauronia, which list primarily articles of clothing dedicated to the goddess in the fourth century. The entries tend to be repetitive and formulaic, employing a handful of uncommon yet limited adjectives and garment-types: bordered, dark blue, sea-green, short tunic, shawl, and so forth. The repetition also emphasizes the use of stock phrases in making the list and an expandability principle, whereby any one item can receive a fuller treatment or have further attributes added to it. That the list is expanded here instead of just summarized as περικαλλέα δῶρα without elaboration suggests that it is important to inventory items for this kind of scene and describe them in some detail. At the same time, it is an example to keep in mind in subsequent chapters, where we will examine the formulaics at work in inventory texts of the fifth and fourth centuries.

In Homer, the catalogue behaves as a key mode of accessing and presenting numeric value in the absence of physical goods, or in the context of an "infinite" or potentially infinite sum. A brief but telling pivot point from the Homeric world to that of Classical Greece occurs just after Odysseus anxiously counts his treasure following his arrival in Ithaca. At Athena's encouragement, Odysseus safeguards the goods in a cave (*Od.* 13.366–371):

ὣς εἰποῦσα θεὰ δῦνε σπέος ἠεροειδές,
μαιομένη κευθμῶνας ἀνὰ σπέος· αὐτὰρ Ὀδυσσεὺς
ἆσσον πάντ᾽ ἐφόρει, χρυσὸν καὶ ἀτειρέα χαλκὸν
εἵματά τ᾽ εὐποίητα, τά οἱ Φαίηκες ἔδωκαν.
καὶ τὰ μὲν εὖ κατέθηκε, λίθον δ᾽ ἐπέθηκε θύρῃσι   370
Παλλὰς Ἀθηναίη, κούρη Διὸς αἰγιόχοιο.

Thus spoke the goddess and went into the dim cave,
contriving hiding places there. And Odysseus
carried everything near, gold and unyielding bronze
and well-made clothes, which the Phaeacians had given him.
These he safeguarded well, and Pallas Athena   370
daughter of aegis-bearing Zeus walled up the door.

This passage prefigures the later Greek world of dedication, storage, and treasury. Just as in the historical period, the contents of Odysseus' treasure are collated, separated, and listed according to material (gold, bronze, clothing), and put away for safe-keeping. The verb κατέθηκε merits particular attention, for in the Classical world, in keeping with the material-verbal analogues we encounter in Herodotus, κατατίθημι will come to denote the registering and recording of payments, goods, and memories.[70] Again, though we have seen a small list of the items already, a brief catalogue renames them following (and thus defining) πάντα: χρυσὸν καὶ ἀτειρέα χαλκὸν | εἵματά τ' εὐποίητα ... With the re-cataloguing and the act of storing the goods behind a closed door, Odysseus enacts both the essential functions of a treasurer, with the goddess at hand to witness careful curatorship of precious items just as would occur in a sacred storage space. The list – as it will continue to do throughout Greek literary and administrative tradition – unfailingly accompanies the storage and safeguarding of those objects most precious to be remembered and, through text, preserved. Thus hoarding and safeguarding give way to accounting and record-keeping. In both the epics, Odysseus stands out as a character of particular numeric and catalogic ability. But the ability to correctly inventory and recite lists of objects becomes central to Odysseus' recovery of his sense of place, space, and personhood. Through the lens of the *Iliad*, we can see that Odysseus is one of a select few characters who exhibit the ability to count accurately and master numbers through listing. Moreover, the connection of Homeric catalogues to the infinite, uncountable, and unspeakable lends further gravity to what Odysseus is seeking to regain. His reestablishment of self will be no small feat, and what he regains no small kingdom. Rather, it is, like the Phaeacians' gifts, like his former wealth, and like Agamemnon's ransom, a "boundless recompense."

---

[70] Register of payment: Xen. *Oik.* 9.8; to record, register in a book or account: Dem. 61.2.

2 | "Or Such a Woman as..."

Exchange Value in the Hesiodic *Catalogue of Women*

In the Homeric world, the last chapter has argued, catalogues enact the control of quantities and the assessment of value. In this context, lists serve as an authoritative reckoning tool for characters and poet alike. They can even bring about a brand of magical counting: less can seem like more, and values can shift and deceive without warning. Yet the physical reality of objects, however remote or imagined, remains an implicit constant in the background of these texts, and most of them impart value to putative collections of objects in a single place or time. Through Homeric catalogue, possessors document and assert ownership over what they hold dear; just as well, however, can they employ lists to grapple with the anxiety of lack, the *horror vacui* that accompanies absence, destruction, and disintegration. Thus, for instance, while we have understood Odysseus' inventories as performative reclamations and positive reassertions of self and worth, they also stand as uneasy attempts to grasp at what little he has and all he hopes to regain.

As much as it is a tool for controlling quantities, the list thus serves as the ideal vehicle for navigating and encompassing slippery commodities, things that threaten to shift, escape, or change owners. This chapter examines the list's function as marker of this loss, or potential loss, in the case of one of the most slippery commodities in the Greek literary imagination: women.[1] We have already seen women appear as line-items in Homeric catalogue, inserted among so many gold tripods or bronze cauldrons; seven women of Lesbos, Briseis, twenty Trojan women, and one daughter of Agamemnon are included in his list of reparations to Achilles in *Iliad* 9. The point here is not so much that women are so starkly commodified or objectified – which is unsurprising – but that archaic Greek poetic lists present a mode of both valuing and possessing women

---

[1] On the possession and commodification of women in the historical democratic context, see Gilhuly 2014: 188, who discusses the establishment of Athenian public prostitution as a way for "young men [to] still have what does not belong to them, without impinging on the integrity of another man's household."

even when one cannot "have" them. The presence of women in listed content also allows for some reflection on the gendered nature of catalogic performance. Archaic Greek catalogue can be understood as a fundamentally masculine form of expression, as opposed to genres like lament or lyric that seem more available to female voices. The sentiment famously expressed in the priamel of Sappho 16 suggests this distinction, juxtaposing an anaphoric list of military objects of male admiration with a singular, female one: "Some say that cavalry, some that infantry, some that an army of ships is the most beautiful thing on the dark earth. But I say it is whatever you love." If indeed the poem alludes here to epic topics and even the Catalogue of Ships itself, it comments on list form's potential as a vehicle for (in DuBois' words) "men trading women, men moving past women."[2] There are certain exceptions: Helen, for instance, both resists being lost in the list and can herself perform catalogue, as the previous chapter suggested. But in the main, Greek catalogues are a tool for men. The notion of trading women raises further questions about their use value and exchange value – economic concepts that often conflict, but which catalogues of women attempt to reckon with.

In *Iliad* 9, Ajax himself provides an analysis of Agamemnon's reparations catalogue that illuminates the problems of use and exchange value in the case of women specifically. He attempts to persuade Achilles to accept the offer by weighing out the worth of both women and men (*Il.* 9.636–642):

> … σοὶ δ' ἄλληκτόν τε κακόν τε
> θυμὸν ἐνὶ στήθεσσι θεοὶ θέσαν εἵνεκα κούρης
> οἴης· νῦν δέ τοι ἑπτὰ παρίσχομεν ἔξοχ' ἀρίστας,
> ἄλλά τε πόλλ' ἐπὶ τῇσι· σὺ δ' ἵλαον ἔνθεο θυμόν,
> αἴδεσσαι δὲ μέλαθρον· ὑπωρόφιοι δέ τοί εἰμεν   640
> πληθύος ἐκ Δαναῶν, μέμαμεν δέ τοι ἔξοχον ἄλλων
> κήδιστοί τ' ἔμεναι καὶ φίλτατοι ὅσσοι Ἀχαιοί.

> … but the gods put an implacable, bad
> spirit in your breast, for the sake of a single girl.
> But now we supply you with seven, far and away the best,
> and many other things as well. So have a gracious spirit.
> Have a care for your house; we are under its roof too, you know,   640
> out of the multitude of the Danaans, and we wish to be your
> main concern and your most beloved, however many Achaeans there are.

[2] DuBois 1978: 96.

Ajax's argument rests on two complementary numerical statements that both recall previous catalogues in the poem. The first, at 637–638, recalling Agamemnon's catalogue, operates on the contrast of οἵης (one/single) with ἑπτά (seven) and ἄλλά τε πόλλ' (many others), where he asserts that women ought to have a fixed exchange value just like any other chattel – in what universe can one be worth as much as seven? This conclusion owes not so much to Ajax's "bluff mind" or lack of empathy, as commentators have suggested, as to the underlying tension between women's exchangeability and (at least to some) individual appeal.[3] For Ajax, Achilles' inability to accept Agamemnon's listed offer amounts to a failure to understand the economics of listed women. In his second value statement, however, he employs precisely the opposite argument about men: that Achilles should consider the worth of the few men of the embassy above the less valuable πληθύς (multitude). In this, his speech pivots to recall not Agamemnon's catalogue of goods, but the Catalogue of Ships and Achaean leaders and troops, which had systematically outlined the πληθύς and its worth. Lines 640–642 emphasize the embassy's higher per capita value relative to the Achaean masses: πληθύος ἐκ Δαναῶν . . . ἔξοχον ἄλλων . . . and ὅσσοι Ἀχαιοί (from the multitude of the Danaans . . . beyond the others . . . as many as are Achaeans).[4] While this passage is often thought to reflect on the principles of Homeric honor,[5] it speaks equally to the gendered dynamics of exchange, and a list's ability to count men and women differently. These distinctions result in part from contrastive socioeconomics (Ajax and Achilles' aristocratic friendship versus the commercialization of Briseis et al.), and yet they persist for high-status women too.

The catalogues of women presented in this chapter operate within this kind of framework and introduce still more nuanced systems of valuation and control. The Hesiodic *Catalogue of Women*, Semonides Fragment 7, and the catalogue of women in the Odyssean *Nekuia* provide complex modes of commercializing and measuring the worth of high-status women and share a vested interest in serving as remedies for their loss. Each poetic context offers unique circumstances for this loss. In the case of the *Odyssey*, the overt context is the women's death and physical removal from the

---

[3] "Bluff mind": Griffin 1995 ad loc. Hainsworth 1993 ad loc. similarly discredits Ajax's character ("[his] failure to understand the θυμαλγής λώβη suffered by Akhilleus verges on the comic") instead of the economic systems he attempts to uphold.

[4] Here again I question whether Ajax's message is, in Griffin's paraphrase, "We are your friends, and we represent the whole army"; the idea is more that "we are better than the rest of the army."

[5] See, e.g., Hainsworth 1993 ad loc. 637–639: "Whether Agamemnon seized one woman or the seven he now promised was all the same. In matters of honour it is the nature of the offence that counts; profit and loss do not come into it."

earth. In the Hesiodic *Catalogue*, loss accompanies the end of human–divine unions and, as Ormand has argued, a bygone social structure.[6] Semonides' catalogue, meanwhile, showcases more subtle types of loss associated with mortal married wives – their apathy, their failure to meet expectations, and their unruly behaviors.[7] While other studies have highlighted the contrastive elements of woman-catalogues,[8] I attempt to illustrate shared generic poetics and goals surrounding the counting, recuperation, and even rematerialization of women-as-goods. In all these examples, we find an attempt to exert minute control over a particular social category, yet an ultimate failure to quantify it fully. This reading also provides a framework for interpreting later documentary texts dealing with transient commodities, from perishable objects to perishable people. The cataloguer's (or catalogue's) desire to impart order over the collection manifests itself as an attempt to grasp at its elusive contents. The list becomes more than just a tool for imposing orders, but a mode of constituting them.[9]

From Ships to Women: Infinite to Countable

We have seen previously that the Iliadic Catalogue of Ships serves as a definitional and metapoetic catalogue, outlining a clear set of contents, but also engaging in an elusive poetics of infinity through which the poetic voice ultimately confounds the audience's faculties of reckoning. This kind of infinity-poetics, which presupposes male subjects counted by male cataloguers for male audiences, contrasts directly with catalogues of women, which instead present women as eminently countable, even in their illustriousness. The catalogue in the *Nekuia* at *Od.* 11.225–327, in which Odysseus lists all the illustrious women he encountered on his visit

---

[6] Ormand 2014; on the heroic age, González 2010. See also recent and different global interpretations of the poem in Tsagalis 2017. Koning 2017 sees the poem as a marker of the end of the Heroic Age. See Sammons 2017 for a useful discussion of the *Catalogue of Women* in relation to the types of catalogue found within epic.

[7] On modern models of "unruly women," see, e.g., Rowe 1995 and Peterson 2017.

[8] See, e.g., Sammons 2010: 74–102 for a useful reading of the *Nekuia* as a threat to the surrounding narrative, with pertinent bibliography. For him, the Homeric catalogue of women "has no single theme that can be pinned down to serve a paradigmatic function." On the Hesiodic *Catalogue* as contrasted with Semonides, see Osborne 2005.

[9] The same poetics is at work not only in other poetry, such as Aeschylus' catalogue of Persian dead, but also in epigraphic documentary catalogues, such as lists of casualties and decommissioned or repurposed dedications. While individual entries in these texts may inspire specific remembrances, it is in the list-text as a whole that the deepest expression of loss resides.

to the underworld, presents a kind of foil to the Catalogue of Ships. The opening lines of the catalogue at first seem to echo the Iliadic catalogue, recalling its quantifying and aggrandizing language with markers like ὅσσαι and ἄριστος (as many [women] as … best …) (11.225–227).

> αἱ δὲ γυναῖκες
> ἤλυθον, ὤτρυνεν γὰρ ἀγαυὴ Περσεφόνεια,
> ὅσσαι <u>ἀριστήων</u> ἄλοχοι ἔσαν ἠδὲ θύγατρες.

> The women
> came, for noble Persephone urged them,
> as many as were wives and daughters of chiefs.

Yet unlike the Catalogue of Ships, the *Nekuia* passage despite its generous heading (ὅσσαι ἀριστήων ἄλοχοι ἔσαν ἠδὲ θύγατρες) will not name an uncountable multitude; the ensuing catalogue names only thirteen women in all (six of these in two groups of three) with more focus on their divine liaisons than their relationships with the ἀριστῆες ("best men" / "chiefs"): the heading, in a sense, sets up a false and unrealized expectation; the audience is primed to anticipate a longer account but in fact receives a manageable one. The interplay between preface and content may depend in part on the history of the Odyssean catalogue, its possible origin as a longer text, and its relationship to the greater genre of woman-catalogue. Yet in presenting a concise and manageable list of women, it seems to correspond to a policy of keeping womens' numbers quantifiable and digestible.

It is in this context that we can also understand the Hesiodic *Catalogue*, which despite its length does not aim to overwhelm the listener with an uncountable mass, invoking an ungraspable infinitude; rather, it attempts to separate its women into manageable subsets, likely grouping them according to genealogical lines, themselves presented geographically.[10] Cingano has argued accordingly that the *Catalogue* "originates from the need to create a broad, systematic and panhellenic arrangement by families which might accommodate the main genealogies of the entire Greek world, and complement the cosmogonic plan of the *Theogony*."[11] Yet the cataloguing of women has different effects from divine genealogizing, even if it follows upon it. Members of families are not all of equal worth, and their systematic arrangement privileges certain players and moments in the

---

[10] Ormand 2014: 47, following Merkelbach-West's editorial principles, explicated by M. L. West 1985: 31–124.
[11] Cingano 2005: 123.

generative process. Cataloguing women does not accomplish the same goals as cataloguing men. If inclusion in the Iliadic Catalogue of Ships perhaps ultimately distinguished the Achaean leaders, singling them out from the rest of men, the Hesiodic *Catalogue* works rather to file women under finite typologies and determine a value for each one. Even if the poem's original overall structure was otherwise, its few extant programmatic fragments reveal an interest in categorizing women according to which god they went to bed with. The opening invocation to the muses sets the parameters (fr. 1.1–5 M-W):[12]

> Νῦν δὲ γυναικῶν ⌊φῦλον ἀείσατε, ἡδυέπειαι
> Μοῦσαι Ὀλυμπιάδε⌊ς, κοῦραι Διὸς αἰγιόχοιο,
> αἳ τότ' ἄρισται ἔσαν⌊
> μίτρας τ' ἀλλύσαντο .⌊
> μισγόμεναι θεοῖσ⌊ιν

> Now sing of the race of women, sweet-versed
> Olympian Muses, daughters of aegis-holding Zeus,
> who at that time were the best ...
> and loosened their girdles ...
> mixing with the gods

The poem here both defines the women it will describe as the "best" ones (ἄρισται) but also defines the capacity in which their excellence lies: namely, their openness to intercourse with the gods (ἀλλύσαντο and μισγόμεναι).[13] It then goes on to point out that such women are no longer of this world – as West observed, the "poet had a clearly defined and individual view of the heroic period as a kind of Golden Age in which the human race lived in different conditions from the present and which Zeus terminated as a matter of policy."[14] We can perhaps place the easy differentiation and evaluation of types of women among these terminated conditions. As the fragment goes on, the poet asks the muses to tell not merely *who* the women were who comingled with the gods in this magical age, but *how many* each divinity slept with (fr. 1.6–22 M-W):

> ξυναὶ γὰρ τότε δα⌊ῖτες ἔσαν, ξυνοὶ δὲ θόωκοι
> ἀθανάτοις τε θε⌊οῖσι καταθνητοῖς τ' ἀνθρώποις.
> οὐδ' ἄρα ἰσαίωνες ομ⌊

---

[12] Texts of Hesiod are taken from Solmsen, Merkelbach, and West 1990, with exceptions as noted. Translations are my own except as noted.

[13] Cf. Kyriakou 2017, who argues for the women of the *Catalogue* as independent empowered characters with a kind of *aristeia*.

[14] M. L. West 1985: 3.

ἀνέρες ἠδὲ γυναῖκες ε[
ὀϛϛόμεν[ο]ι φρ[εσὶ] γῆρ[ας   10
οἳ μὲν δηρὸν ε.[..]κ.[
ἠΐ[θ]εοι, τοὺς δ᾽ εἶθ[αρ] ε.[
ἀ[θ]ἀνατοι [νε]ότητ[
τάων ἔσπετε Μ[οῦσαι
ὀϛϛ[αι]ϛ δὴ παρελ[έξατ᾽ Ὀλύμπιος εὐρύοπα Ζεὺς   15
σ]περμαίϳνων τὰ ⸤πρῶτα γένος κυρδῶν βασιλήων,
.]ϛ τε Π[̣ο]ϛειδάω[ν
. . . . . .]ν τ᾽ Ἄρης [
. . . . . .].ηι̣.ιντ[
. . . .].ϛτοοπ[20
. . . . Ἑ]ρμῆς .[
. . . .] βίη Ἡ[ρακλῆος

For at that time feasts were in common and councils were in common
among immortal gods and mortal humans.
And not of equal life-span
men and women
seeing old age in their hearts   10
some for a long time
young, but others right away
immortals youth…
Of these tell me, Muses …
with how many lay wide-seeing Olympian Zeus   15
begetting …
… Poseidon
[with how many] Ares …
[with how many] Hephaistos …
[with whom] Hermes …   20
[with how many] the might of Herakles

It is likely that the quantitative ὅσσαις appeared before each god's mention;[15] if so, the poem repeatedly proclaims its focus on numbers rather than stories. This repetition signals the sum of the gods' collective conquests, counting the notches on each one's bedpost, as it were.[16]

The proem of the Hesiodic *Catalogue* thus succeeds in establishing three connected points. First, the "best" women gave themselves to the gods for

---

[15] This restoration appears in the text of Most 2007, following the suggestion of Stiewe.

[16] Sammons 2010: 66–69 discusses a related passage: Zeus's lists of erotic conquests in *Iliad* 14, which he situates in the narrative context of *apate* – for Sammons, the catalogue shows that Zeus is both conquerer and conquered (by *eros*). No such context is available here, but the passage here does not seem to engender the same kind of interpretive ambivalence.

procreation; second, the times in which such women lived are gone; third, the poem should tell their number, which is in fact each god's number of conquests. The catalogue becomes therefore an inventory of divine possessions, and within it a concatenated appraisal of just how much they are worth. Analyzed this way, the poem presents itself as a document of what was and no longer can be: namely, a world in which women give themselves freely to men of higher status.[17] I will maintain that the act of cataloguing these liaisons serves as a remedy for their absence from the social structure of the poem's own time, whether or not an audience can find other ways to approximate them too.

Typology and Formulaics

This emphasis on quantity in the proem and the use of ὅσσαις as a structuring device contrasts with the formula the rest of the poem famously employs at the start of its entries: : ἦ οἵη, "or such a woman as . . .," a phrase that focuses on quality and indefiniteness. This formula has often been treated as a generic feature already devoid of synchronic meaning by the time of the *Catalogue*'s composition. West believed it originated in a separate poetic tradition that simply listed women, rather than placing them within a more complex Hesiodic genealogical schema.[18] Rutherford, agreeing that the formula is "at odds with the overall structure" of the *Catalogue* also interprets it as an adaptation from earlier *ehoie*-poetry combined with the genealogical tradition, in an example of generic "crossing" or "automatization."[19] More recently, however, Irwin has convincingly argued that the formula "remained present in the text" and situates it within the tradition of the symposium.[20] I wish to propose an additional interpretation: that the formula serves in this context to remind an audience of the underlying exchangeability and relative *sameness* of women. By introducing each woman as οἵη, the poem subtly suggests that its entries are endlessly interchangeable, and the catalogue itself recursive. Although the women of the

[17] In an innovative reading of the poem's sexual vocabulary, Irwin 2005 has argued that the bygone context of such hierarchical sexual liaisons can be replicated in the symposium, between citizens and *hetairai*.

[18] M. L. West 1985: 167.

[19] Rutherford 2000: 91–93; see 265 nn.40 and 41 for further explanations of the terms "crossing" and "automatization" (the latter borrowed from Russian formalism). See also Nasta 2006, who analyzes the formula as a signal of embedded narration.

[20] Irwin 2005: 51–52. D'Alessio 2005 considers the influence of genealogical poetry on Pindar and Bacchylides.

catalogue enjoy special status, the initial pronoun undermines their uniqueness. True, the women of the *Catalogue* may fetch differing values. However,
the echoing ἢ οἵη introduces an exemplar but also presents her as transfer-
able, in the sense that a number of others might do in her stead. As such, the
poem sets itself up as a typology into which all heroic women may be fitted,
and a detailed expansion of the *Theogony*'s "tribes of women," to use
Loraux's classic formulation.[21] As a genre, then, woman-catalogue uses
typologizing formats to manage and grasp at its elusive subject.[22]

While most instances of the ἢ οἵη formula come at the start of an extant
fragment, the fragment that precedes the start of the *Shield of Heracles*
provides some possible surrounding context to support this reading (fr.
195 M-W, with *Scutum* 1–3):

> ⋯⋯ ⋯⋯]θεν ἀνηγ.[   ]ο̣[
> ⋯⋯ ⋯⋯ ⋯] καὶ νη[ΐδος] ἠϋκόμ[οιο
> ⋯⋯ ⋯⋯ ⋯]. καλ[λίσφυ]ρον Ἠερόπ[ειαν
> ⋯⋯ ⋯⋯ .πρὸ]ς δῶμα [φίλη]ν κεκλῆ[σθαι ἄκοιτιν·
> ἢ τέκε ⋯.]βιον καὶ ἀρηΐφι[λον] Μενέ[λαον   5
> ἠδ' Ἀγαμέμ]νονα δῖον, ὃς ['Άργεος ε]ὐρυχό[ροιο
> ⋯⋯ ⋯].ϊ πατρὶ ἄναξ κ[αὶ κοίρ]ανος ἦεν.
>
> ἢ' οἵη προλιποῦσα δόμους καὶ πατρίδα γαῖαν
> ἤλυθεν ἐς Θήβας μετ' ἀρήιον Ἀμφιτρύωνα
> Ἀλκμήνη, θυγάτηρ λαοσσόου Ἠλεκτρύωνος·

> … and of the lovely-haired Naiad
> … and beautiful-ankled Aeropea
> … to his home to be called his dear wife
> who bore …-bion and war-loving Menelaus   5
> and god-like Agamemnon, who of Argos with wide spaces
> … to his father was lord and ruler.

> Or such as she, who leaving her home and native land
> came to Thebes following warlike Amphitryon,
> Alcmene, daughter of Electryon who stirs the people.

The disjunctive ἢ(ἐ) immediately relates the next entry to the last, but it
also introduces Alcmene as an alternative to Aeropea: in the greater
context, the formula suggests that the poet has thus asked the muse to
sing of any one of a set of genealogically related women, not all of them: her,

[21] Loraux 1993: 72–110.
[22] For a creative meditation on visual typologies of women and modes of resistance to them, see
    B. Schmidt 2016.

or her. The resulting narrative suggestion is that we never in fact arrive at the definitive total of ἄρισται – just a representative sample. οἵη, meanwhile, points forward to the next exemplar but also introduces her as similar to other possibilities: indeed, an audience might think on many mythological women who, as in Alcmene's case, forsook their own country for a man. I do not mean to press meaning into every repetition of the formula, but its force seems to be, at least in part, that the broad plotline of each woman's life is not utterly unique to her; it may be, however, unique within the context of the catalogue, which provides the audience with an overview of kinds of women based on their behaviors and personalities, and good or bad value. Thus the famous figures of the catalogue become more significant as archetypes or exemplars than as individuals, despite their luminous reputations. The formula signals that their stories may be substituted for each other. In turn, it becomes a repeated reminder that while women of the audience's era cannot compare to those of the past, nor can the unions they form and offspring they produce, one can still grasp at them via the *Catalogue*.

By establishing behavioral types of women and likening them to one another, the Hesiodic *Catalogue* aligns with Semonides' list of types of women in Fr. 7, a poem with which it has been contrasted.[23] Semonides' poem, I suggest, engages in the same mode of typologizing as the Hesiodic *Catalogue* and the Odyssean *Nekuia*, but to a more extreme and nuanced degree, in a distortion of the woman-catalogue genre. The unceremonious start of the poem almost instantly sets up a formula that all others will follow (Sem. fr. 7.1–4):

χωρὶς γυναικὸς θεὸς ἐποίησεν νόον
τὰ πρῶτα. <u>τὴν μὲν</u> ἐξ ὑὸς τανύτριχος,
τῇ πάντ' ἀν' οἶκον βορβόρῳ πεφυρμένα
ἄκοσμα κεῖται καὶ κυλίνδεται χαμαί·

From the start, god made the mind of woman
other.[24] (He made) one from a long-bristled swine.
Everything in her house lies fouled in mud,
Unkempt, and rolls on the ground.

The simple discourse device τὴν μέν, which will predictably be followed by successive repetitions of τὴν δέ for the remainder of the poem, signals immediately that this will be a series, functioning as

---

[23] See, e.g., Ormand 2014: 217–222; Loraux 1993: 90 presents Semonides' poem as a "polemical reading" of the concept of the race of women in the *Theogony* and *Works and Days*.

[24] Or: "diverse." For the problems of the interpretation of χωρίς, see, e.g., Lloyd-Jones 1975: 63–64 and Loraux 1993: 90–91.

a structuring device akin to the ἦ οἵη formula. Even this shorter iambic catalogue emerges as a tool of division and conquest. Meanwhile, the initial description "everything in her house lies fouled with mud" reveals that the poet will give generalizations with illustrative details, rather than portraits of specific women. Semonides' association of each type of woman with a particular animal (or in a few cases, natural element) reinforces this idea, emphasizing categorical difference rather than individual uniqueness. While Loraux insisted that "we must also stop looking for something like a systemic classification in which the different types of women might refer to an order in the animal world," an important intervention in the face of previous scholarship seeking one-to-one scientific correlations,[25] I argue that we cannot dispense entirely with the poem's typologizing aim and particularly its connection to its generic catalogic predecessors.

In this, the poem also emphasizes the species of women as different from that of men, for, as Payne has insightfully observed, "its premise is that marriage is not a union between two human beings, but between a husband who is fully human and a wife who, despite her human appearance, is in fact something nonhuman in human form."[26] In this scheme, all women belong to one of ten types: sow, vixen, dog, ass, weasel, mare, monkey, bee, or the inanimate earth and sea. The poem thus likens women to things that do not generally receive individuated differentiation; this is perhaps clearest in the case of the sea or earth, but it informs the ancient understanding of non-human animals as well.[27] With the exception of the land- and sea-types, each entry begins identically: "another (type) is from [animal x]" (τὴν δὲ ἐκ ...). The structural organization of the list itself thus reflects the categories it imposes; at the same time, it reflects an anxious (if perhaps satirical) attempt to control unruly types.[28]

This overt catalogic – and even woman-catalogic – structuring suggests a mode of compensation, of apprehending groups characterized by their intractable natures. The animal-female behaviors of the poem are connected by a notion that they are unmanageable, unreasonable, and unresponsive to changes in circumstance. Thus the dog-woman barks incessantly, and her husband is powerless to stop her (lines 16–20):

---

[25] Loraux 1993: 98.   [26] Payne 2010: 112.

[27] There are of course notable exceptional cases, e.g. Odysseus' dog Argos, the Calydonian boar, or Lucius the Ass, but these are hardly the norm. For discussion of ancient speciesism, see Newmyer 2006: 103, who presents Plutarch as an ancient anti-speciesism activist.

[28] On the seriousness of the invective, see Payne 2010: 112.

οὐδ' εἰ χολωθεὶς ἐξαράξειεν λίθωι
ὀδόντας, οὐδ' ἂν μειλίχως μυθ<εό>μενος,
οὐδ' εἰ παρὰ ξείνοισιν ἡμένη τύχηι,
ἀλλ' ἐμπέδως ἄπρηκτον αὐονὴν ἔχει.

Not if he rages and knocks out her teeth
with a stone, nor if he speaks to her softly,
nor even if she happens to be at another's home,
but she is incessant in her uncontrollable whining.

The natural remedies of either violence or pacification are thus unavailable to these husbands, whose general plight is summed up in the idea of ἄπρηκτον, used of things that are useless and unprofitable, as well as which "cannot be remedied," as a disease. The sea-woman presents similar challenges, with the added difficulty of being unreliable. She too is characterized by a series of alpha-privatives that suggest her husband's *aporia* (32–36):

τὴν δ' <u>οὐκ ἀνεκτὸς</u> οὐδ' ἐν ὀφθαλμοῖς ἰδεῖν
οὔτ' ἄσσον ἐλθεῖν, ἀλλὰ μαίνεται τότε
<u>ἄπλητον</u> ὥσπερ ἀμφὶ τέκνοισιν κύων,
<u>ἀμείλιχος</u> δὲ πᾶσι κἀποθυμίη   35
ἐχθροῖσιν ἴσα καὶ φίλοισι γίνεται·

This one is not tolerable to look upon with the eyes
nor to come close to, but she rages then,
unapproachable, like a dog with her puppies,
and she is implacable and hateful   35
to her enemies and friends alike.

This woman frustrates the efforts of those who would look at her, approach her, or attempt to mollify her; moreover, her description recapitulates that of the dog-woman in its embedded simile, echoing earlier ἄπρηκτον with ἄπλητον and emphasizing that her attitude is indifferent to friend or foe (cf. also ἀρρήκτον in line 116). Thus the poem presents women as displaying moods and behaviors potentially impervious to male modes of control.[29] Some respite, however, comes in the form of the categorization and organization of knowledge. If a man is familiar with the various types of women, the poem seems to suggest, he can analyze potential mates,

---

[29] For some other types of wife, violence and kindness may be effective modes of influencing women's behavior. Yet even in these instances further problems arise, including, most notably, the drainage of resources. Thus the ass-woman, who "when subject to force and violence grudgingly obliges" (σύν τ' ἀνάγκη σύν τ' ἐνιπῆσιν μόγις ἔστερξεν, 44–45) nonetheless is reckless and indiscriminate in her eating and pursuit of paramours.

and at least come to the recognition that there is nothing to be done. In return, he is absolved of responsibility for women's bad behavior.[30]

In conjunction with describing women as variously unsupportable, the catalogue is framed with the idea of Zeus-driven destiny, a notion that further emphasizes the irremediable plight of men. By the end of the poem, Semonides has recapitulated and repackaged the idea of women as a god-given plague for men, ultimately framing it as a source of commonality and even an opportunity for male bonding. Even if women besides the bee-type are impossibly maddening, one is in good company in knowing that "all these other kinds" of women are the norm as created by Zeus for men (τὰ δ' ἄλλα φῦλα ταῦτα μηχανῆι Διὸς / ἔστιν τε πάντα καὶ παρ' ἀνδράσιν μενεῖ, 95–96). At the close of the poem, the poet notes that, while each man praises his own wife and blames another's, "we are unaware that we have the same fate" (ἴσην δ' ἔχοντες μοῖραν οὐ γινώσκομεν, 114). At this point the narrative voice has shifted abruptly to the inclusive first-person plural, turning to face the audience in an act of gendered solidarity – "we are all Menelaus." The moment contrasts starkly with the rest of the poem, which describes only indeterminate third-person subjects who interact with women, usually "a/the man who … " (ἀνήρ, lines 16, 54, 62, 76) or a definite article with a participle.[31] Concluded in this way, the catalogue, despite all its pessimism, offers itself up a remedy of sorts, a method for the allied front to divide and conquer, and assert some semblance of order.

Finally, the poem's conclusion invokes the therapeutic and unifying function of catalogue through its apparent allusion to Helen. The idea that woman has been an evil "ever since Hades received those men fighting for the sake of a woman" (ἐξ οὗ τοὺς μὲν Ἅιδης ἐδέξατο / γυναικὸς εἵνεκ' ἀμφιδηριωμένους, 117–118), considered in the context of woman-catalogue, recalls the catalogic sequences of the *Nekuia* and gestures toward a similar imagined catalogue of dead men. The addressees of the poem share not only a synchronic common plight with one another but a diachronic one linked to the first generation of fettered men: the heroes of the Trojan War.

---

[30] Here again I break with Loraux's argument (1993: 100) that "it must be clear that each woman is always an incomplete combination of several broader types of female behavior." On the contrary, I read the catalogue as interested only in broad strokes rather than nuance, compartmentalization as conquest.

[31] The indefinite pronoun τις is twice employed to emphasize the rare cases in which "someone" might be satisfied with his wife: first, regarding the mare-woman, who "is an evil to the man who has her, unless he is some tyrant or scepter-holder, the kind of person who is pleased with such behaviors in his heart" (ἢν μή τις ἢ τύραννος ἢ σκηπτοῦχος ἦι, ὅστις τοιούτοις θυμὸν ἀγλαΐζεται, 69–70); then, about the singularly lucky husband of the bee-woman (τήν τις εὐτυχεῖ λαβών·, 83).

Through the same poetic structures that can be employed to typologize and divide women, the addressees of Semonides' poem, considered as a collective, can now be included within the most prestigious of Greek genealogies.[32] Via the catalogue, the shared "bane" of woman is recast as a source of male nobility and pride.

Rates of Exchange

Semonides' poem raises specific anxieties about women inherent in the Hesiodic *Catalogue* too, including the central concern that a wife will prove to be bad value. The conclusion of the poem reiterates these two points in its general summation of the perils of cohabitation, first addressing the problem of food supply and women who drain too many resources (100–102):

> ὅστις σὺν γυναικὶ †πέλεται
> οὐδ᾽ αἶψα Λιμὸν οἰκίης ἀπώσεται,
> ἐχθρὸν συνοικητῆρα, δυσμενέα θεῶν.

> For whoever ?stays with a woman
> will not soon push hunger out of his home,
> hateful housemate, hostile to the gods.

This caveat is followed closely by concerns about honesty and faithfulness (108–111):

> ἥτις δέ τοι μάλιστα σωφρονεῖν δοκεῖ,
> αὕτη μέγιστα τυγχάνει λωβωμένη·
> κεχηνότος γὰρ ἀνδρός, οἱ δὲ γείτονες
> χαίρουσ᾽ ὁρῶντες καὶ τόν, ὡς ἁμαρτάνει.

> And whatever woman seems the most prudent,
> she ends up doing the greatest damage.
> For while her husband gapes, the neighbors
> enjoy seeing how he too is duped.

While narrative context is not so readily available in the Hesiodic poem, we find there too efforts to quantify the net worth of women through various systems of exchange. The most organic way of expressing the women's value is via the quantity and quality of their offspring; hence the catalogue

---

[32] Compare here the inhuman genealogy of women, who are strange diachronic hybrids born from (ἐκ) their various animals.

often includes passages such as the following one about Thyia, daughter of
Deukalion (fr. 7 M-W):

> ἣ δ' ὑποκυσαμένη Διὶ γείνατο τερπικεραύνωι
> υἶε δύω, Μάγνητα Μακηδόνα θ' ἱππιοχάρμην,
> οἳ περὶ Πιερίην καὶ Ὄλυμπον δώματ' ἔναιον

> And she, becoming pregnant, bore to thunderbolt-delighting Zeus
> two sons, Magnes and chariot-happy Macedon,
> who lived in palaces around Pieria and Olympus

The vivid description of Thyia's pregnant state as ὑποκυσαμένη points
physically to the procreative process, almost as if to provide visual proof of
the lineage's pedigree: the verb means "to swell," though in post-Homeric
texts the simplex κύω can also be used in the active of the male role in
conception. The image reminds us of Poseidon's truism that "the beds of
the immortals are not barren" (οὐκ ἀποφώ[λιοι εὐναὶ ἀθανάτων, fr.
31 M-W). Yet the account quickly transitions into a less bodily mode.
The gender-neutral verb γείνατο (either "beget" or "bear" a child) shifts the
poem's focus from the process of gestation or childbirth to the genealogical
impact of Thyia's role. In between ὑποκυσαμένη and γείνατο the poet elides
the pregnancy, the act of the labor, and the process of the birth itself,
necessary though it may be to the production of heroes.[33] In the following
lines, moreover, we find no notion of the offspring's infancy but learn
instead of their adult attributes: their names, the epithet "rejoicing in
chariots" (ἱππιοχάρμην), and their places of residence.

In fact, six times in the fragments of the *Catalogue*, there is a similar
collocation describing a woman as she bears a new generation of offspring.
The phrase consists of the article/pronoun ἣ followed by a particle δὲ and the
participle ὑποκυσαμένη, "pregnant."[34] Elsewhere the same phrase appears with
τίκτω, as at, for example, the genealogy of the Myrmidons (fr. 205 M-W line 1):

> ἥδ' ὑποκυσαμένη τέκεν Αἰακὸν ἱππιοχάρμην . . .

> And she, becoming pregnant, gave birth to Aiakos who delights in horse-
> chariot.

---

[33] Again here I depart from Kyriakou 2017, who interprets statements of τέκεν and γείνατο as
indicators of female power in the genealogical process. Because so much of the process is elided,
I read these formulaics as, on balance, effacing the crucial importance of women. Sammons
2017, along related lines, proposes that the *Catalogue of Women* results in a catalogue of men.

[34] Tsagalis 2009: 164 lists this formula among others he identifies in the text; see also his more
general discussion of formulaics at 162–178.

In both these examples the main verb appears fairly close to the participle, but other placements of γείνομαι or τίκτω are possible. The participle, however, appears only in one context, following ἣ δ' at the start of the line. And though the simplex verb κύω is rather more common, the compound ὑποκύω is rare, used only in the middle and only in this context;[35] scholia and lexicographers gloss it repeatedly, perhaps because of its opacity to later audiences. For these reasons, it is worth considering where this formal feature appears and what its significance in the *Catalogue* might be.

The attestations in the *Catalogue* leave us little context; in most of them the phrase comes at the beginning of the fragment.[36] Its three attestations in Homeric epic allow for deeper exploration.[37] Significantly, in both the *Iliad* and the *Odyssey*, it always appears as part of a genealogical or catalogic section of the poem, with twin or multiple births.[38] At the start of *Iliad* 6, it describes the nymph Abarbarea, mother of Pedasos, whose lineage is given as Euryalos kills him. Pedasos was the child of the nymph and the shepherd Boukolion, who lay with Abarbarea as he was tending his flock (*Il.* 6.25–26):

> ποιμαίνων δ' ἐπ' ὄεσσι μίγη φιλότητι καὶ εὐνῇ,
> ἣ δ' ὑποκυσαμένη διδυμάονε γείνατο παῖδε.

> And shepherding on the mountains he mixed with her in love and bed, and she becoming pregnant birthed twin boys.

Abarbarea is described as ὑποκυσαμένη following a brief description of the sexual encounter (25). In line 26, ἣ δ' coupled with the participle serves to connect the offspring and their birth to the moment of conception. This may seem to be an over-obvious point, but genealogical passages do not always trace out all the steps of succession, often skipping blithely from one generation to the next with little mention of the birds and bees. Thus it is at the will of the poet to choose which milestones to include. The presence of ἣ δ' ὑποκυσαμένη does not merely state the obvious but emphasizes the lasting importance of the sexual encounter, and links it chronologically and biologically to the ultimate important content of the passage – the number and names of the twin offspring. The verbal and structural connection of the sex act to the remarkable offspring in this way legitimizes

---

[35] Simplex κυομένη appears at *Theogony* 125 and 405, and in the *Catalogue* at fr. 17a M-W line 15, but in variable position and without the pronoun and conjunction.

[36] The phrase appears at fr. 7.1 M-W, 26.27 M-W, 145.15 M-W, 205.1 M-W, 10a.42a M-W, 10a 47.

[37] For discussion of the dating of the *Catalogue*, see, e.g., Ormand 2014: 3 n.5.

[38] I treat as exceptional its appearance in the Homeric *Hymn to Selene* 13, a poem generally considered post-archaic, though cf. A. E. W. Hall 2013.

both the act and the woman whose body links the generations of men. For this reason, the specific choice of ὑποκύω, a word that implies the physical, visual manifestation of conception and pregnancy, becomes all the more pointed: the woman in question demonstrates the efficacy and significance of what initially may sound like just a gratuitous mention of a tryst. Meanwhile, in its resumptive force, ἣ δ' snaps us abruptly out of the bedroom and back into the archival world of the verbal genealogy, from voyeur to diagrammer. The image of the woman swollen and pregnant provides a brief memento of the union, but little significant narrative, before the poem returns to the business of listing names.

The story of Abarbarea and Boukolion in its abbreviated form does not include an elaborated sex scene from which to divert our attention; but an example from the *Odyssey* does. There ἣ δ' ὑποκυσαμένη appears again at the start of the *Nekuia* catalogue, describing Tyro, who gives birth to twins. Particularly important for the study of the Hesiodic *Catalogue* is that the phrase here is doubly embedded in catalogue and genealogy, first within the catalogue of women, and then Tyro's genealogy therein. It describes her following a detailed account of her rape by Poseidon, a vividly described and striking scene (*Od.* 11.238–246):

ἣ ποταμοῦ ἠράσσατ' Ἐνιπῆος θείοιο,
ὃς πολὺ κάλλιστος ποταμῶν ἐπὶ γαῖαν ἵησι,
καί ῥ' ἐπ' Ἐνιπῆος πωλέσκετο καλὰ ῥέεθρα.   240
τῷ δ' ἄρα εἰσάμενος γαιήοχος ἐννοσίγαιος
ἐν προχοῇς ποταμοῦ παρελέξατο δινήεντος·
πορφύρεον δ' ἄρα κῦμα περιστάθη οὔρεϊ ἶσον,
κυρτωθέν, κρύψεν δὲ θεὸν θνητήν τε γυναῖκα.
λῦσε δὲ παρθενίην ζώνην, κατὰ δ' ὕπνον ἔχευεν.   245
αὐτὰρ ἐπεί ῥ' ἐτέλεσσε θεὸς φιλοτήσια ἔργα,
ἔν τ' ἄρα οἱ φῦ χειρὶ ἔπος τ' ἔφατ' ἔκ τ' ὀνόμαζε·
'χαῖρε, γύναι, φιλότητι· περιπλομένου δ' ἐνιαυτοῦ
τέξεαι ἀγλαὰ τέκνα, ἐπεὶ οὐκ ἀποφώλιοι εὐναὶ
ἀθανάτων· σὺ δὲ τοὺς κομέειν ἀτιταλλέμεναί τε.   250
νῦν δ' ἔρχευ πρὸς δῶμα καὶ ἴσχεο μηδ' ὀνομήνῃς·
αὐτὰρ ἐγώ τοί εἰμι Ποσειδάων ἐνοσίχθων.
ὣς εἰπὼν ὑπὸ πόντον ἐδύσετο κυμαίνοντα.
ἣ δ' ὑποκυσαμένη Πελίην τέκε καὶ Νηλῆα,
τὼ κρατερὼ θεράποντε Διὸς μεγάλοιο γενέσθην ἀμφοτέρω·   255

She loved Enipeus a river-god,
who rushed over the earth, by far beautifullest of rivers,
and she used to frequent his beautiful streams.   240

Likening himself to Enipeus, the earth-holder and shaker
lay beside her in the eddying mouth of the river,
and a deep blue wave stood up around them like a mountain,
swollen, and hid the god and mortal woman.
And he loosened her virgin girdle, and he poured sleep down on her. 245
When the god was done with his amorous deeds,
he took her hand in his and he spoke a word and called on her:
Rejoice, woman, in lovemaking, and when a year has gone around,
you will bear shining children, since the gods' beds
are not barren. Tend to them and rear them. 250
Now: go home and hold silent, and do not name names.
But I tell you, I am Poseidon the earth-shaker.
He spoke and sank under the swelling sea.
And she, becoming pregnant, bore Peleus and Neleus,
who both became strong attendants of Zeus. 255

We see here an extended and elaborated sexual encounter in the midst of the genealogy. But the passage itself also prefigures the formula in etymological play with the notion of swelling and the k root κυ- (< IE *kuh_1-): first in the form of the wave (κῦμα) that swells, like a mountain, to cover the pair, then in the swell of the sea (κυμαίνοντα) as Poseidon dives back in. κυρτωθέν, "swollen" may also be felt to be part of this group, though its derivation is unknown.[39] This same swell is then transferred to Tyro herself, who ends up ὑποκυσαμένη. As before, I would argue that here, too, the phrase ἡ δ᾽ ὑποκυσαμένη returns us to the succession, linking (this time etymologically) the moment of conception with the subsequent double offspring through the figure of the pregnant woman. As such, it rivals some of the functions that scholars have identified for the phrase ἢ οἵη in the Hesiodic *Catalogue*. While Ormand has lamented that "nothing like the ehoie formula surfaces" in the Odyssean catalogue of women, I would contend that ἡ δ᾽ ὑποκυσαμένη may be just such an element.[40] Indeed, it is perhaps this very passage that represents the point of reference for the formula in the Hesiodic *Catalogue*. Certainly it is ripe with Hesiodic intertext, as has often been discussed (though not resolved).[41] If we accept the hypothesis of Rutherford that the *Catalogue* "is the culmination of a tradition of catalog poems, sharing key formal and thematic features . . .

---

[39] For theories, see Beekes 2010 s.v. κυρτός.   [40] Ormand 2014: 43.

[41] In the *Catalogue* we find scattered several of its narrative elements of this episode: the loosening of the girdle (as the rubric for the entire poem, fr. 1 M-W line 4), Tyro herself among its elements, her love for Enipeus and union with Poseidon, and specifically lines 249–250 (= fr. 31 M-W lines 2–3); the text possibly told of Poseidon's dive back into the water. For discussion of the relationship of the two texts, see, e.g., Rutherford 2000: 93–97, Ormand 2014: 43–44.

such as the *ehoie*-formula,"[42] it would seem that this formula, too, belongs to a tradition of genealogy.[43] Rutherford has further suggested that the *ehoie*-formula once functioned to signal an abrupt transition from one branch of a family to another, becoming a formal device.[44] In a similar way, ἣ δ᾽ ὑποκυσαμένη may have once highlighted twin births, and the resumption of the genealogy after a digression however long or brief to a particularly elaborate or extraordinary union scene. This might be Poseidon disguised as a river sleeping with a woman under a wave; or, equally extraordinary, a group of mares impregnated by the North Wind disguised as a stallion. Such is the story that appears in the Trojan genealogy, about the mares of Erichthonius who give birth to twelve foals (*Il.* 20.219–225):[45]

> Δάρδανος αὖ τέκεθ᾽ υἱὸν Ἐριχθόνιον βασιλῆα,
> ὃς δὴ ἀφνειότατος γένετο θνητῶν ἀνθρώπων·   220
> τοῦ τρισχίλιαι ἵπποι ἕλος κάτα βουκολέοντο
> θήλειαι, πώλοισιν ἀγαλλόμεναι ἀταλῇσι.
> τάων καὶ Βορέης ἠράσσατο βοσκομενάων,
> ἵππῳ δ᾽ εἰσάμενος παρελέξατο κυανοχαίτῃ·
> αἳ δ᾽ ὑποκυσάμεναι ἔτεκον δυοκαίδεκα πώλους.   225

> Dardanus in turn had a son, King Erichthonius,
> who became the wealthiest of mortal men.   220
> His three thousand horses were pastured in a marsh,
> mares, adorned with delicate colts.
> Boreas fell in love with these as they were pasturing,
> and likening himself to a dark-haired stallion he lay beside them.
> And they, becoming pregnant, bore twelve foals.   225

Again the text highlights an unusual tale of divine disguise. Like Poseidon, Boreas shifts shapes between natural phenomenon and animate character, but in reverse. Following this episode the participle of the pregnant woman

---

[42] Rutherford 2000: 89.

[43] Rutherford's idea of the evolution of the genre is complex; he posits separate traditions of (1) *ehoie*-poetry and (2) genealogical poetry that fuse together into a new genre of (3) *ehoie*-catalogues of women (2000: 92).

[44] Rutherford 2000: 84. See also Tsagalis 2009: 160–161 and Hirschberger 2004: 30: "The *e hoie* formula is an elliptical expression employed to introduce a story or a genealogy. It seems that it is a relic of an older epic phase, in which it functioned as an 'oral lemma' within a series or chain of women stories."

[45] It is not clear how many mothers are imagined among the mares, nor is M. W. Edwards' suggestion that "presumably Boreas fell in love with and serviced only twelve of the mares" certain (1991: 318).

breaks and transitions us to the topical focus: the offspring, about whose wondrous powers we hear in the subsequent lines.

Regrettably, the Hesiodic *Catalogue* as it stands is too tattered to know what immediately preceded the attestations of ἡ δ᾽ ὑποκυσαμένη there, and to test fully the hypothesis I have laid out. Most of the time, the phrase appears at the beginning of a fragment, so whatever preceded it is lost. But if the rest of the Hesiodic tradition is any indication, it may have accompanied the introduction of certain extraordinary unions and offspring there too. The phrase also appears twice in one last genealogical place, the *Theogony*. It first modifies Echidna, who unites with Typhon to produce a series of new monsters (306–308):

> τῇ δὲ Τυφάονά φασι μιγήμεναι ἐν φιλότητι
> δεινόν θ᾽ ὑβριστήν τ᾽ ἄνομόν θ᾽ ἑλικώπιδι κούρῃ·
> ἡ δ᾽ ὑποκυσαμένη τέκετο κρατερόφρονα τέκνα.

> And they say Typhon mixed with her in love,
> he fearsome and outrageous and lawless, her the maiden with
>   flashing eyes.
> And she becoming pregnant bore dauntless children.

While this episode is not singular, embedded as it is in a long line of monstrous generations, the union here is highlighted as particularly bizarre and incredible, as perhaps marked by the narrative distancing of φασι, "they say." And if the phrase's function is to resume the genealogical progression and move us from conception to children, it certainly does that: we are introduced to Orthos, Kerberos, and the Hydra, important for their connection to Herakles, but also because Echidna bears the next generation too, with Orthos as father. Finally, in the *Theogony* the formula also introduces the birth of Hekate, to Asteria (409–412):

> γείνατο δ᾽ Ἀστερίην εὐώνυμον, ἥν ποτε Πέρσης
> ἠγάγετ᾽ ἐς μέγα δῶμα φίλην κεκλῆσθαι ἄκοιτιν.
> ἡ δ᾽ ὑποκυσαμένη Ἑκάτην τέκε, τὴν περὶ πάντων
> Ζεὺς Κρονίδης τίμησε

> And she bore good-named Asteria, whom Perses once
> led to his great house to be called his dear wife.
> And she becoming pregnant bore Hekate whom above all
> Zeus the son of Kronos honored.

In this instance, we hear less about the encounter that produced the pregnancy than about the offspring that resulted from it. And yet the phrase draws narrative attention to the start of the lengthy and mysterious so-called "Hymn to Hekate," which intrudes into the text and for which Hesiod "appears to drop everything."[46] The purpose of the interlude on Hekate remains a matter of debate, but ἣ δ' ὑποκυσαμένη at the very least functions here as a strong indication to pay attention to the offspring that follow.[47] Perhaps in the *Theogony* the phrase functions to flag either a particular union or an especially significant offspring. As for the *Catalogue*, we could postulate something similar. Yet as Nagy has explained: "the continuity of narration in the transition from *Theogony* to *Catalogue* is an aspect of the same oral traditions that resulted in the texts that we know as the *Theogony* and *Catalogue*. Seen in this light, the composition of Hesiodic poetry is an ongoing process";[48] thus the *Catalogue* may have used the formula in the kinds of immediate context we have seen here, or in some new, performance-specific ways.

On a semantic level, the ἣ δ' ὑποκυσαμένη phrase prevents women from becoming the focus of the narrative, compressing their role in the entire generative process into one participle. Placed directly after the sexual encounter, this reference to a woman's pregnancy may indeed interrupt the reverie of the erotic scene, but it cannot rival the significance of the genealogical project, for ἣ δ' ὑποκυσαμένη is not the part of the story that counts. Osborne may indeed be right in his assessment that the *Catalogue* runs on male desire, and that its women "all fit into essentially the same order of things, an order where women are sexually attractive to men, made into sexual partners on a more or less permanent basis, and bring forth offspring."[49] By the sixth century BCE, during which the *Catalogue* as we have it was perhaps composed, ὑποκυσαμένη was not likely a household term. Instead, it belonged to poetry of the past, and, as I have argued, to specific contexts within that tradition. Like the *ehoie* formula, ἣ δ' ὑποκυσαμένη signals doubly that "we are in a catalogue of women," and that "we are in a genealogy." If the women serve as nodes, links from one generation of men to the next, they just as well serve as transports from one generation of poets to another. In the "pregnant" participle, we can recognize a conduit not only between father and son, but within the poetic genealogy of which it forms part. For the catalogue, the events in the process of childbearing turn out to be the moment of male desire, the visible manifestation of its

[46] Clay 1984: 27; she posits that Hekate's prominence is due here to her status as an intermediary between the old and new order, gods and men.

[47] Osborne 2005: 16 emphasizes the contrast between the characterization of women in the *Theogony* and *Catalogue*, the latter being far more focused on the physically attractive traits of the women.

[48] Nagy 2009: 295.   [49] Osborne 2005: 17.

fruition and gender-neutral fact of the birth, and the renown of the offspring. Perhaps more robustly than its predecessors, the *Catalogue* emphasizes a two-pronged value of women, initially as visible carriers of divine seed but ultimately as, almost literally, worth their weight in children.

Other Modes of Valuation

Yet offspring are not the only metric by which the *Catalogue* measures and imparts women's value. The traffic in women is alive and well here: the number of a woman's suitors and the amount of gifts (δῶρα) or bride-price (ἕδνα) she could fetch form critical components of her entry in the catalogue.[50] Consider, for example, the exceptional case of Demodike (fr. 22 M-W):

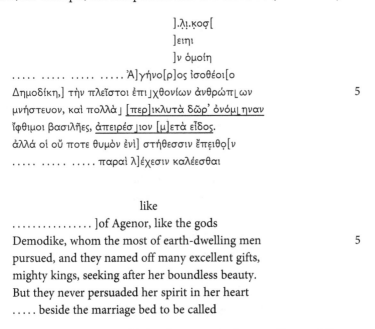

```
                    ].λι.κοσ[
                    ]ειηι
                    ]ν ὁμοίη
..... ..... ..... .....Ἀ]γήνο[ρ]ος ἰσοθέοι[ο
Δημοδίκη,] τὴν πλεῖστοι ἐπι[χθονίων ἀνθρώπ[ων        5
μνήστευον, καὶ πολλὰ] [περ]ικλυτὰ δῶρ' ὀνόμ[ηναν
ἴφθιμοι βασιλῆες, ἀπειρέσ[ιον [μ]ετὰ εἶδος.
ἀλλά οἱ οὔ ποτε θυμὸν ἐνὶ] στήθεσσιν ἔπειθο[ν
..... ..... .....παραὶ λ]έχεσιν καλέεσθαι
```

                      like
.............]of Agenor, like the gods
Demodike, whom the most of earth-dwelling men   5
pursued, and they named off many excellent gifts,
mighty kings, seeking after her boundless beauty.
But they never persuaded her spirit in her heart
..... beside the marriage bed to be called

Here the poet expresses Demodike's value in multiple ways. First and foremost she has the most suitors (πλεῖστοι); more importantly, they (or a kingly subset of them, ἴφθιμοι βασιλῆες) name off many, very renowned gifts. Moreover they do not merely offer the gifts but name them. The phrase περικλυτὰ δῶρ'

---

[50] Ormand 2014: 64–72 argues that ἕδνα and δῶρα are two distinct terms in the *Catalogue*, the former more specific to "competitive bidding," the latter applicable to more generalized gift-giving. Here I am less concerned with the difference between the two terms than with the fact that both can rather precisely quantify a woman. On the presence of bride-price as opposed to dowry in the *Catalogue*, see Ormand 2014: 52–64 and Osborne 2005: 17–18.

ὀνόμηναν reflects the vocabulary and practice of Homeric commodity exchange, echoing the formalized offer of gifts from Agamemnon to Achilles for his return (cf. περικλυτὰ δῶρ' ὀνομήνω, *Il.* 9.121), as well as Odysseus' catalogue of Laertes' trees (ὄρχους δέ μοι ὧδ' ὀνόμηνας | δώσειν πεντήκοντα, "and you named off fifty vines to give me," *Od.* 24.341–342).[51] Yet more than either of these passages, the *Catalogue* states clearly the terms of the exchange: the gifts are presented as the worth of Demodike's infinite beauty (ἀπειρέσιον εἶδος). We have seen that the idea of "boundlessness" also figures in the Homeric formula "boundless recompense" (ἀπερείσια ἄποινα), which is offered up by, e.g., Priam for Hector's body and Agamemnon for Achilles' return to battle. Yet the *Catalogue* reverses the terms, applying the epithet not to the offer (the δῶρα) but to the *desideratum* – Demodike's boundless beauty. It is perhaps for this reason that the offer, uncharacteristically, is unsuccessful: the commodity itself cannot be bought at any price. At the same time, the poet immortalizes it, as if to remind an audience that the work preserves not only unions that produced heroic genealogies, but all the noble former women of Greece. As Kurke elucidates in her study of Pindar, these kinds of exchange are aristocratic and heroic, rather than strictly commercial.[52] This kind of reading also informs Ormand's discussion of ἕδνα and δῶρα: those commodities can be exchanged for boundless beauty, since in aristocratic exchange the point is not strict valuation but rather the establishment of a social bond.

Perhaps the most striking examples of women's value come in the fragments surrounding Helen and Mestra, both of whom are quantified in the poem through discussion of their market exchange price. Mestra's shape-shifting ability makes her into both a valuable and replenishable source of income.[53] Her father, Erysichthon, sells her to a suitor for a hefty bride-price, and she in turn changes to an animal form to escape the new husband; they then repeat the scam on further unsuspecting men of means. When the duped suitor Sisyphus brings Erysichthon to trial, he receives a ruling that defends the sale of women as χρήματα and invokes rules of exchange (fr. 43a.41–43 M-W):

ε]ὖτέ τις ἀντ' ὤνοιο χατίζηι χ[ρῆ]μ' ἀνελ[έσθαι,
ἀ]μφὶ μάλα χρῆν ὤν[ον . . . .]. τῖμον [
οὐ γ]ὰρ δὴ μεταμειπ[τόν, ἐπὴν τὰ] πρῶτ' [ἀποδώηι.

If someone desires to carry off a good for a price,
it is crucial [that] the price … value …
for it is not exchangeable, once he has sold it.

---

[51] See discussion above, 28–31 and 34–36.   [52] Kurke 1991.

[53] For the idea of shape-shifting as "keyed to gender," see Ormand 2014: 86–87. On brides as "dangerous gifts" see Lyons 2003.

The lacunose apodosis could contain any one of several ideas: that a price should be fixed in relation to the value of the goods; that it must be agreed upon; or that it cannot be changed once determined.[54] Whatever its precise meaning, it highlights that Erysichthon has gone against basic rules of commerce in his scheme. A double-entendre in the final line cleverly reiterates Mestra's specific brand of trickery, for μεταμειπτόν implies that the item cannot be exchanged or re-sold, but also that it cannot be *metamorphosed*; Mestra has done both.[55]

Mestra's literal elusiveness and ability to escape the marriage contract by supernatural means also serve as a literal manifestation of the general slipperiness of women. She is the ultimate unstable commodity, but also the ultimate bad wife, unreliable and a poor value disguised as quality. The legal dispute and apparent legislation here thus represents another attempt to grasp onto elusive women and protect against their loss. The ruling gives insurance for both the value and the sustained possession of what an owner has purchased.

In the scheme, Mestra has value mainly for her father, most of which consists in her shape-shifting abilities and dishonesty, though she potentially would be useful as a child-bearer to Glaukos. In contrast to her, Helen fetches prices by virtue of her beauty, so much so that her value is even marked by another mini-catalogue of her suitors (fr. 196–200 and 204 M-W). Whereas other women fetch large bride-prices (perhaps with brief lists of objects) for their worth, and although some other women of the *Catalogue* do provoke wooing contests, Helen's value is by far the largest.[56] The catalogue of suitors is not a mere contest, but a reckoning of her worth as figured in the unit of suitors.[57] In this way the suitors-catalogue to some degree echoes the function of the *Catalogue* as a whole. Moreover, the suitors themselves, though they are situated close to the narrative time-frame of the rest of the poem, woo at a distance from Helen.[58] The poet speaks explicitly of this distance in emphasizing that suitors had no contact with Helen (fr. 199.1–9 M-W):

---

[54] The interpretation of these lines has received much discussion. For a history of the problems, see Ormand 2014: 95 with n.20, and his new interpretation at 242–244; see also Irwin 2005: 69–70, Ormand 2004, and Steinrück 1994: 294–298, who includes a summary of previous readings.

[55] The verb μεταμείβω can apply to each of these scenarios. For the notion of exchange, cf. Pi. O.12.12, of exchanging good for bad; for metamorphosis of precisely this kind, cf. Mosch.2.52, of Zeus changing Europa from a cow back into a woman. Note that it is unclear whether Mestra is sold as an animal or a woman; see Ormand 2014: 88–89.

[56] On other contests for marriage, see Cingano 2005: 125.

[57] M. L. West 1985: 117 argues for an original total number of twenty-five to thirty suitors.

[58] Cingano 2005: 122 observes that the catalogue of suitors "marks the transition to quite a different subject, time, and tone from the *Catalogue of Women*."

Κάστορί θ᾽ ἱπποδάμωι καὶ ἀεθλοφόρωι Πολυδεύκει,
ἱμείρων Ἑλένης πόσις ἔμμεναι ἠυκόμοιο,
εἶδος οὔ τι ἰδών, ἀλλ᾽ ἄλλων μῦθον ἀκούων.
ἐκ Φυλάκης δ᾽ ἐμνῶντο δύ᾽ ἀνέρες ἔξοχ᾽ ἄριστοι,
υἱός τ᾽ Ἰφίκλοιο Ποδάρκης Φυλακίδαο   5
ἠύς τ᾽ Ἀκτορίδης ὑπερήνωρ Πρωτεσίλαος·
ἄμφω δ᾽ ἀγγελίην Λακεδαίμονάδε προΐαλλον
Τυνδαρέου π[οτ]ὶ δῶμα δαΐφρονος Οἰβαλίδαο,
πολλὰ δ᾽ ἔεδν[α δίδον,] μέγα γὰρ κλέος [ἔσκε γυ]ναικός

… to Castor tamer of horses and prizebearing Polydeuces,
desiring to be the husband of beautiful-haired Helen,
though not knowing her or having ever seen her, but hearing stories
     from others.
And from Phylake wooed two exceedingly excellent men,   5
Podarkes, son of Iphiclos, himself son of Phylacos,
and good Protesilaos, overbearing son of Aktor.
And both repeatedly sent messages to Lakedaimon,
to the home of wise Tyndareos, son of Oebalus
and they gave many gifts, for the woman's fame was great.

Unlike the other women of the *Catalogue*, whom suitors generally have
seen or met in person, the appeal of Helen rests on second- or even third-
hand reports of her beauty. In this sense, she already functions as an absent
commodity even in her own time, unavailable to most men save Menelaus,
and, as the audience knows, even to be lost to him.[59] Both Hesiod and
Semonides, I have argued, use the catalogue form to evaluate women and
cope with their slippery elusiveness. The absence of women emerges
metapoetically within this very context of control: the Hesiodic
Catalogue, even as it proclaims its focus on women, is more concerned
with their husbands, divine suitors, and offspring than the women themselves. The genealogical tradition, while it necessarily includes the female
members in the family line, nonetheless also exists to legitimate the succession of male heroes. If we can gingerly speak of the poem as a whole, we
might say that it employs the pretext of "women" to create what is in fact
more properly a catalogue of conduits for patronage. While Osborne has
argued that "what drives the *Catalogue* along is men's inability to resist an
attractive woman," one might equally contend that the poem is instead
fueled by an underlying apprehension that this "natural" order of desire
may not be sufficient anymore.[60] As Ormand has shown, the *Catalogue*

---

[59] Idomeneus also woos her in person: 204.56–64.   [60] Osborne 2005.

expresses lament for "the inevitable decline in bloodlines, the 'mixing' of birth between *kalos* and *kakos*."[61] As such, the work also attempts to resuscitate those bloodlines, or at least preserve them, through a systematically quantified account of what was.[62]

Postscript: Listing Loss, Materializing the Dead in the Athenian *katalogos andron*

This chapter has aimed to show that in the archaic poetic record, catalogues of women afford peculiar structures, poetics, and functions distinct from those of catalogues of men, as represented by the example of the Catalogue of Ships. As a nostalgic text, the *Catalogue of Women* looks back beyond the current generation; yet in the democratic world of the Athenian polis, an analogous desire to list and remember the war dead develops, in the form of the casualty list. This kind of listing takes a hybrid form: on the one hand, the heroes of the state are listed by affiliation with Cleisthenic tribes, but at the same time they are commemorated using archaic, pre-democratic forms of *kleos*, expressed in Homeric language. In this context, women become not the only humans treated as commodities by Greek catalogue. As Gayle Rubin pointed out long ago, "men are of course also trafficked – but as slaves, hustlers, athletic stars, serfs, or as some other catastrophic social status, rather than as men. Women are transacted as slaves, serfs, and prostitutes, but also simply as women."[63] The Athenian citizen – though not exactly a "catastrophic social status" – had trade value as a sheer numerical presence on juries, in the council and assembly, and, especially, in the military. On the one hand these offices carry more specific labels than just "man," but the requirements for holding them were often no more than being a free-born male. As such, men too were subject to loss and the concomitant remedy of it. Perhaps nowhere does the struggle with the loss of men emerge more clearly than in the war context. Though Thucydides' Pericles tells the parents of the dead how fortunate it is to have sons die nobly in battle, even he acknowledges the difficulty of loss.[64]

Funerary speeches and public graves were one mode of coping with this loss, but the inscribed casualty lists that accompanied them provide a tangible

[61] Ormand 2014: 216.
[62] Cf. again here Ormand's discussion of ἕδνα, 2014: 76–77, which, he argues, seem to imply a competition among woman but really exist "to establish a hierarchy among the competing men."
[63] Rubin 1975 [1973]: 175–176.   [64] See Thuc. 2.44.2.

textual analogue to lost men.[65] Beginning in the early fifth century, the Athenians created annual tallies of names of the war dead on marble *stelai* to be displayed alongside public gravesites.[66] These monumental texts were set up in the Athenian public burial ground (*demosion sema*) in groups of ten, for each of the Athenian demes. Arrington has recently re-examined the lists as physical objects, compellingly arguing that they "created a monumental, visual rhetoric of collective resilience and strength that capitalized on Athenian notions of manhood."[67] As such, his study has innovatively linked the lists with concepts of defeat rather than of victory.[68] Here, I highlight some of the ways in which they interact with the Greek catalogue in the *longue durée*, concentrating on the recovery of loss.

The tradition of making annual casualty lists began in Athens sometime before the earliest dated example of 464 BCE, earlier in the epigraphic record than other regular inscribed accounts, such as the Athenian Tribute Lists or inventories from the Parthenon and other treasuries.[69] Thus it would seem they do not follow upon other genres of catalogic inscriptions but instead perhaps have roots in the literary tradition.[70] Ebbott has argued that these monuments influenced the catalogue of war dead in Aeschylus' *Persians* (472 BCE); they also themselves reflect the archaic poetic tradition before them.[71]

The casualty lists consist of columns of names arranged according to the ten Attic tribes, often preceded by a heading and at times accompanied by a label as to the men's position. Importantly for this study, many of the lists include epigrams at their tops or bottoms, or on their bases. The epigrams coupled with the lists themselves reveal the inscriptions' concentration on coping with loss. While several of the lists' headings note merely that "the following men died" (οἵδε ἀπέθανον),[72] the epigrams repeatedly employ the rhetoric of loss. Several contain variants of the verb *apollumi* in reference to

---

[65] For extended discussion of public military burial and commemoration, see recently Arrington 2015, especially 55–90, with Low 2010.

[66] *IG* i³ 1144–1193, plus new fragments *SEG* 46.29.

[67] Arrington 2011: 179; see also Arrington 2015: 93–108.   [68] Arrington 2015: 93–95.

[69] Bradeen 1969, followed by others, argued for a date in the late sixth or early fifth century. Perhaps the earliest example, *IG* i³ 1477 (= *LSAG²* 307 (no. 59)), from Hephaistia in Lemnos, is variously dated to the first few decades of the fifth century.

[70] Bakewell 2007: 90 and 99 suggests that military lists of four kinds (for eligible, summoned, serving, and deceased soldiers) existed as early as the 460s, generated and maintained by individual generals; of these types in the earlier fifth century we have epigraphic evidence only for public production and dissemination of casualty records.

[71] Ebbott 2000 argues that the casualty lists would have been an epigraphic genre familiar to an Athenian audience at the play's first performance in 472. While this chronology is possible, it does not preclude the underlying influence of earlier literature on the creation of the lists.

[72] For a detailed description of the lists' format, see Arrington 2011: 83.

the men's lives. The epigram for *IG* i³ 1163 (a list of disputed date and context)[73] begins with a heroic address to the dead in epic style (34–35):

τλέμονες ℎοῖον ἀγῶνα μάχες τελέσαντες ἀέλπ[το]
φσυχὰς δαιμονίος ὀλέσατ᾽ ἐμ πολέμοι·

O bold men, you accomplished such a struggle in unexpected battle
and lost your marvelous souls in war.

The simplex verb with object ψυχάς echoes Homeric phrasing;[74] meanwhile, it focuses the monument's audience on what is missing, and what the monument hopes to replace. Other casualty-list epigrams prominently highlight the men's loss of their youth (ἥβη) (*IG* i³ 1181):

⌊χαίρετε ἀριστ̄ες πολέμο μέγα⌋ κῦδο⌊ς⌋ ἔχοντες⌋
⌊κο̑ροι Ἀθεναίον, ἔχσοχοι ℎιππ⌋οσύνα⌊ι⌋·
⌊ℎοί ποτε καλλιχόρο περὶ πατ⌋ρίδος ὀ⌊λέσαθ᾽ ℎέβεν⌋,
⌊πλείστοις ℎελλάνον ἀντία μ⌋αρνάμε⌊νοι⌋.

Hail you, best ones, who hold great honor in war,
Athenian sons, outstanding horsemen.
You who once lost your youth for your homeland of fine dancing-
    grounds,
fighting against the greatest part of the Hellenes.

The monument for casualties from Chersonesos, Byzantion, and other wars (447 BCE) invokes youth almost as an exchange for glory (*IG* i³ 1162.45–48):

ℎοίδε παρ᾽ ℎελλέσποντον ἀπόλεσαν ἀγλαὸν ℎέβεν
βαρνάμενοι, σφετέραν δ᾽ εὐκλέϊσαμ πατρίδα,
ℎόστ᾽ ἐχθρὸς στενάχεμ πολέμο θέρος ἐκκομίσαντας,
αὐτοῖς δ᾽ ἀθάνατον μν̄εμ᾽ ἀρετ̄ες ἔθεσαν.

These men lost their shining youth by the Hellespont
fighting, and they brought glory to their country,
so that the enemy groaned reaping the fruits of war,
and they set up for themselves an undying memorial of manliness.[75]

---

[73] The monument has often been dated to 447/6; Arrington 2012 revisits the issue and argues convincingly for a date of 424/3 in commemoration of the battle at Delion.

[74] Cf., e.g., *Il*. 13.763 (of strong Trojans sought by Hector): χερσὶν ὑπ᾽ Ἀργείων κέατο ψυχὰς ὀλέσαντες, "they lay, having lost their souls at the hands of the Argives."

[75] Translation of line 48 assumes epic reflexive αὐτοῖς, following Arrington 2015: 99; but also plausible is "and they (the Athenians) set up an undying memorial of manliness for them (the fallen)." This latter option perhaps gives better sense.

The opening line of the epigram casts the men's loss of their young selves in tangible, physical terms: while ἀπόλεσαν ἀγλαὸν ἥβην ("they lost their shining youth") may sound like a euphemism for "they died," it pointedly recalls the men's physical aspect, now absent, by emphasizing visual qualities. ἀγλαός highlights the visual appearance of their bodies, as it would a beautiful object. In this the poem echoes the Homeric use of ἀγλαός, which commonly describes gifts and ransoms, water and groves. Yet at the same time in Homer ἀγλαός also most frequently modifies sons (υἱοί). In the epigram then, the men's lost *hebe* is presented as both beautiful object and living being – a treasure to be recovered. ἥβε itself too denotes not only the abstract quality of youth, but also the young physical body, or a group of them. This sense appears, perhaps not coincidentally, in the context of Aeschylus' *Persians*, in which the messenger reports (511–512): "thus the city of the Persians groans, longing for the beloved youth of the land" (ὡς στένειν πόλιν Περσῶν, ποθοῦσαν φιλτάτην ἥβην χθονός). There too, ἥβη is something that can be lost forever, and the verb ποθέω denotes yearning for something specifically *absent*.[76] A similar configuration appears in the epigram for the Potideia casualty list, which notes (*IG* i³ 1179.10): ἄνδρας μὲμ πόλις hέδε ποθεῖ καὶ δὲ͂[μος Ἐρεχθο͂ς] ("This city and people long for the men of Erechtheis"). In the Chersonesos epigram, the detail "by the Hellespont" further highlights the geographical distance of the loss, which occurred far from Athens: the *hebe* is absent, not close at hand. The middle lines of the epigram go on to glorify the men, momentarily setting aside their absence in favor of a description of their heroism, but the final pentameter returns us to the issue and offers a compensation: the list is presented as a remedy for the perishing of the men's *hebe*, whose loss has also become the city's loss. As an ἀθάνατον μνε͂μ' ἀρετε͂ς, the monument stands in for them, providing *arete* where they can no longer.

As in the case of epic catalogue, the crucial mechanism of remedy and replacement lies in the verbal bulk of list itself. The majority of the *stele* is taken up not by the epigram (which appears almost as an afterthought, small and compressed), nor by the heading, but by the names of the casualties arranged by *phylai*. This arrangement and the intervening spaces serve as a way to recover the lost dead spatially, while the prominence of each tribe's name verbally repatriates them to their native localities. A viewer whose gaze moves up and down the columns of names both laments the casualty and finds an almost physical comfort in its presence on the stone. As Arrington argues, not only do casualty lists commemorate

---

[76] "Like a lover," muses Arrington 2011: 193.

both victories and defeats, but "the more massive the defeat, the larger the stone."[77] This observation supports the conclusion that the list, as in archaic poetry, recovers those commodities held dear but now destroyed. Much like marriageable women, male youth and vigor – ἀρετή, in short – represented a valuable asset to the polis and an important mechanism for its continued health and security. By exploiting archaic poetics on the one hand and the newer medium of the monumental inscribed *stele* on the other, the city found a way to compensate symbolically for the depleted male population.

[77] Arrington 2015: 105.

3 | Displaying the Past

Inquiry as Inventory in Herodotus

The previous chapters have argued that Homeric and Hesiodic *Catalogue* effect modes of cultural valuation and counting, and that this is an early step in the materialization or objectification of lists that denote physical things. The genre of woman-catalogue, meanwhile, illustrated the ways in which lists enable the commodification of women, creating verbal systems of control. Finally, moving out of the world of the Heroic Age, a brief comparison to Athenian casualty lists suggested the potential of lists as a historical mode of processing absence and loss, not just an epic trope. The connections among recording-keeping, death, and historiography may seem at first distant, yet, as Achille Mbembe notes in his conception of archives:[1]

> Examining archives is to be interested in that which life has left behind, to be interested in debt. However, it is also to be preoccupied with debris. In this sense, both the historian and the archivist inhabit a sepulchre. They maintain an intimate relationship with a world alive only by virtue of an initial event that is represented by the act of dying.

This chapter considers lists and archival practice in the work of Herodotus. Considering the historian in similar terms to an archivist of past forms may help account for Herodotus' use of the list as a central stylistic form in the *Histories*, and the choice to adapt a traditionally poetic form to his work. One way of framing this discussion is to appeal to the idea of Herodotus as "both a *logopoios* and an historian, who molded the two fields into a unity."[2] As historian, on the one hand, he presents the content of lists as a record of physical evidence, perhaps even autopsy, and a pledge of authenticity. As

---

[1] Mbembe 2002: 25.

[2] Pritchett 1993: 5. Vannicelli 2001 studies Herodotus' often autophobic glorification of the Egyptian λόγιοι as foundational historiographers, pointing out, nevertheless, that for all this Herodotus still has a "unitary historical vision" in which he inserts Greek tradition (234). Luraghi 2006 has usefully discussed what *historie* is and is not and, further, reorients the question in such a way as to bridge the divide between the so-called "liar school of Herodotus" and those who named it, pointing out, typically, that there are more than two sides to that particular coin.

logopoios, on the other, he employs the form of the list in accordance with an old and authoritative tradition of catalogue in his literary predecessors, as well as in the written documents of the non-Greeks he presents. In this view, the historian deals in data, the *logopoios* in its arrangement. Herodotus, though, is explicitly *not* a *logopoios*; he uses the term disparagingly, first of the fabulist Aesop and then soon thereafter of Hecataeus of Miletus, placing that historian's work in negative distinction to his own.[3] *Logopoioi*, as he casts them, contrive pleasant fictions; Herodotus deals in something rather more serious. As such, certain features of Herodotus' lists function to impart value to a collection that may no longer exist, or that his audience for other reasons would be unable to see. In his textual presentation of them too, they can be contained as a unified collection: as I will discuss in further detail below, Herodotus frames his lists with introductory and conclusive statements, treating them as contained units. This structure lends them a kind of prominence approaching that of a physical container, such as an actual treasury full of dedications or other important objects might. Ultimately, I will argue, Herodotus' lists function in much the same way as physical storehouses, but through verbal means.

Herodotus faces the general problem of quantification on a large cultural scale and makes specific use of the list as a cipher for imparting value. In the *Histories*, the genres of historiography, the epic catalogue, and the nascent administrative inventory tradition coalesce.[4] We find multiple examples of lists used to prove points and express value, and the characters and audience of the *Histories*, deeply invested in quantifying and displaying their wealth and possessions, use the list format to perform and prove their own worth. Both short- and long-form lists serve as constative narrative forms for the *Histories*. Lists in Herodotus perform expressions of control over people, places, and objects, through processes of counting, naming, and containing them. This is perhaps why, among his myriad censures of Herodotus, Plutarch twice condemns him as a collector, first, "of men's calamities" (θνητῶν ἐκλέγων τὰς συμφοράς, *Mal. Hdt.* 2 [*Mor.* 855d]), and later, of the base and irrelevant in favor of the true and good (866 c–d):

ὁ δὲ τὴν Ἀμάσιδος ἀποψόφησιν καὶ τὴν τῶν ὄνων τοῦ κλέπτου προσέλασιν καὶ τὴν τῶν ἀσκῶν ἐπίδοσιν καὶ πόλλ᾽ ἄλλα τοιαῦτα συναγαγὼν καὶ διαμνημονεύων, οὐκ ἀμελείᾳ δόξειεν ἂν καὶ ὑπεροψίᾳ προΐεσθαι καλὰ μὲν ἔργα καλὰς δὲ φωνάς, ἀλλ᾽ οὐκ εὐμενὴς ὢν πρός ἐνίους οὐδὲ δίκαιος.

---

[3] Beecroft 2010: 133–139 explores this facet of Herodotus' rhetoric; see also Luraghi 2009 and Kurke 2010, chapter 10.

[4] See Kosmetatou 2013, who argues that Herodotus accessed temple inventories in his composition of the *Histories*.

> But the man who compiles and records Amasis's gas-passing, the driving of the thief's asses, the giving of wineskins and many other such things does not seem to me to have omitted noble deeds and beautiful speeches out of negligence and unawareness, but rather because he is neither well nor justly disposed toward certain individuals.

While Plutarch focuses throughout on Herodotus' bias in representing cities and characters, it is worth dwelling momentarily on the criticism implicit in ἐκλέγων and συναγαγών, for Herodotus indeed on many occasions stockpiles all manner of information. He enumerates most famously and at length the Persian satrapies and tributes (3.89–96) and armed forces (7.61–98), but also Croesus and Amasis' offerings at Delphi (1.50–52, 2.176, 182), the gifts Cambyses sends for the Ethiopians (3.20), the rivers in Scythia (4.48–49), the animals in Libya (4.192), and the cities of the Hellespont (6.33). While the longest catalogic sections are often thought of as "digressive," they are hardly expendable, serving instead as central components of Herodotus' history-making and narrative authority. And while questions about Herodotus' use of source material resist scholarly consensus, it seems that he draws on a variety of recognizable list predecessors.[5] Kosmetatou has presented a compelling portrait of Herodotus' use of documentary sources, positing that his composition and style in several passages argue for his use of inscribed inventory lists from Delos and Delphi.[6] At the same time, it has been argued that Herodotus modeled his catalogues of the Persians not on native sources but on archaic Greek precedents, including the Homeric Catalogue of Ships.[7] Finally, as Ceccarelli has pointed out, catalogues are an important medium for representing geographical space in the *Histories*.[8]

Yet Herodotus' text also contains forms of catalogic rhetoric that transcend the documentary, poetic, or historiographic traditions alone, belying an ardent and innovative interest in the collection and repetition of accounts of all kinds – stories, numbers, measurements, and other "factoids," and an abiding belief in the authority of lists. This chapter first establishes some stylistic properties of Herodotus' lists, arguing that his modes of list-framing, -naming, and containment, while perhaps rooted in other genres, imbue the *Histories* with a data-driven catalogic authority.

---

[5] For a sampling of views on sources, see, e.g., Fehling 1989, S. West 1991, Murray 2007a and 2007b, Luraghi 2013.

[6] Kosmetatou 2013.

[7] Armayor 1978. For a summary of scholarly views on the sources of the Persian catalogues, see, e.g., Asheri 2007: 479–481.

[8] Ceccarelli 2016.

The chapter then examines two key terms of the *Histories*' narrative program, both fundamentally related to the act of listing. First, *katalego* becomes for Herodotus a historiographical stylistic cue, retaining the Homeric qualities of narrative recapitulation, but also referring to his presentation of original sourced research, often in the form of data catalogues. As well as expanding *katalego*, Herodotus also introduces a new term to the idea of catalogic display: the verb *apodeiknumi*, "show," which he uses to denote verbal-visual enumerations. This verb and its derivatives take on a crucial and novel significance in both specific passages and in the *Histories* as a whole, which Herodotus famously presents as an *apodexis* of history.

Frame, Name, Contain: Catalogic Control

Herodotus alerts the reader when he includes lists, employing a framing device that contains a heading and concluding tail. This framing both sets off the content of the catalogue as specialized knowledge and signals the importance of the section to an audience. References to the beginning and end of a series usually take the form of a demonstrative pronoun or other deictic element. It is not enough simply to allow an enumeration to speak for itself: it should be both introduced and acknowledged afterward. This is true for the long Persian catalogues: the satrapy list begins (3.89):[9] ἀρχὰς δὲ καὶ φόρων πρόσοδον τὴν ἐπέτειον κατὰ <u>τάδε</u> διεῖλε, "the provinces and the annual revenue of tributes were divided in the following ways." Following the account of twenty ἀρχαί, Herodotus sums up (3.97): αὗται μὲν ἀρχαί τε ἦσαν καὶ φόρων ἐπιτάξιες, "those were the provinces and assessments of tribute." The catalogue of Persian forces, usually considered as a unit from 7.61 to 7.98, in fact comprises several smaller internal catalogues – of the land armies, their generals, the cavalry, their captains, the ships, their admirals, other famous captains. The land contingents begin with ὅδε (7.61): οἱ δὲ στρατευόμενοι <u>οἵδε</u> ἦσαν, Πέρσαι μὲν ὧδε ἐσκευασμένοι, "the following were the ones marshalled; the Persians were outfitted in the following way," and end with ταῦτα (7.81): ταῦτα ἦν τὰ κατ' ἤπειρον στρατευόμενά τε ἔθνεα καὶ τεταγμένα ἐς τὸν πεζόν, "those were the groups marching on land and arranged for the infantry." Similar framing occurs in the internal elements, and the final summation seems to come after the naval captains, following the focus on the exemplary Artemisia (7.99): ἐς μὲν

---

[9] Texts of Herodotus are taken from Wilson 2015. Translations are my own except as noted.

τοσόνδε ὁ ναυτικὸς στρατὸς εἴρηται ("up to this much the naval contingent has been accounted). While elements of these catalogues, such as their Hellenocentric geographies and their ring composition, may impart a Homeric flavor and even show direct influence, they differ in effect. Most pointedly, while Homeric catalogue deals in the potentially infinite, scrupulously avoiding sum totals, Herodotean framings clearly delineate the ends of the lists both rhetorically and numerically. In the list of the Persian forces, the ending ἐς μὲν τοσόνδε suggests a finite quantity, and indeed several subtotals have been given: 80,000 horsemen (7.87), 3,000 total ships (7.97), and, most famously, 1,700,000 in the infantry, counted in spatial groups of 10,000 (7.60).[10] And in what might be a direct contrast to Homeric descriptions of heroic leaders like Agamemnon and Odysseus, who know and control the counts of their men, Herodotus at the close of his catalogue glosses over Xerxes' numerical agency, pointedly employing the passive voice (7.100): Ξέρξης δέ, ἐπεὶ ἠριθμήθη τε καὶ διετάχθη ὁ στρατός, ἐπεθύμησε αὐτός σφεας διεξελάσας θεήσασθαι ("Xerxes, when his army was counted and arranged, desired to ride through them and look upon them"). Xerxes' subsequent conversation with Demaratus (102–103) likewise suggests he is more interested in the general hugeness of his forces than their exact number. Herodotus by contrast presents himself as the controller of exact quantities.

One could argue that narrative bracketing is only logical and useful in long, "digressive" catalogic sections, especially those disseminated through oral performance, where an audience might lose track without cues. Yet Herodotus employs similar framing even when it seems unnecessary. The formulaic pattern of "these are the X" – [list of X] – "those are the X" is no mere practicality but rather a signal for Herodotus' specialized, data-oriented knowledge, even when very brief. An almost comically extreme example occurs in a mini-catalogue of Medean tribes (1.101, taking the MS reading τοσάδε instead of Wilson's τάδε in the first line.):

> ἔστι δὲ Μήδων τοσάδε γένεα· Βοῦσαι, Παρητακηνοί, Στρούχατες, Ἀριζαντοί, Βούδιοι, Μάγοι. γένεα μὲν δὴ Μήδων ἐστὶ τοσάδε.

> And there are this many tribes of the Medes: the Bousai, Paretakenoi, Strouchates, Arizantoi, Boudioi, Magoi. So many are the tribes of the Medes.

The list is so short that clearly no one would need reminding of its content, yet still he includes the repeated head and tail, complete with the backward-

---

[10] On counting in Herodotus, see Purves 2006 and Sergueenkova 2016.

looking μέν familiar from longer catalogic sections.[11] The framing signals a potentially forgettable sequence of names as important and alerts an audience to the presentation of new, insider information. We can observe a similar effect in his presentation of Scythian rivers, which are introduced with an appeal to nameability, a concept that, as we have seen, is closely allied to countability (4.47).

> ὅσοι δὲ ὀνομαστοί τέ εἰσι αὐτῶν καὶ προσπλωτοὶ ἀπὸ θαλάσσης, τούτους ὀνομανέω, Ἴστρος μὲν πεντάστομος, μετὰ δὲ Τύρης τε καὶ Ὕπανις καὶ Βορυσθένης καὶ Παντικάπης καὶ Ὑπάκυρις καὶ Γέρρος καὶ Τάναϊς.

> And however many of (the Scythian rivers) are nameable and accessible by sea, these I will name: first the five-mouthed Ister, then the Tyre and the Hypanis and the Borysthenes and Pantikapes and Hypakyris and Gerros and Tanais.

Here again, Herodotus signals that specialized enumerative information will follow, of the sort that might not be available elsewhere – a listener or reader should attend to the narrator's content.

In addition to showing numerical expertise, catalogic framing also creates a verbal enclosure for the items in catalogues, materializing them into spatially containable collections – a useful tool both for encapsulating physical goods and for the metaphoric "containment" of foreign powers. This kind of framing occurs in collections of precious objects, such as the accounts of Croesus' offerings to Delphi (1.50–52, resumed at 1.92), which I discuss further below, and the lists of dedications Amasis sent to Greece, bracketed as if they might be stand-alone pieces (2.182):

> <u>ἀνέθηκε δὲ καὶ ἀναθήματα ὁ Ἄμασις</u> ἐς τὴν Ἑλλάδα, τοῦτο μὲν ἐς Κυρήνην ἄγαλμα ἐπίχρυσον Ἀθηναίης καὶ εἰκόνα ἑωυτοῦ γραφῇ εἰκασμένην, τοῦτο δὲ τῇ ἐν Λίνδῳ Ἀθηναίῃ δύο τε ἀγάλματα λίθινα καὶ θώρηκα λίνεον ἀξιοθέητον, τοῦτο δ' ἐς Σάμον τῇ Ἥρῃ εἰκόνας ἑωυτοῦ διφασίας ξυλίνας, αἳ ἐν τῷ νηῷ τῷ μεγάλῳ ἱδρύατο ἔτι καὶ τὸ μέχρις ἐμεῦ, ὄπισθε τῶν θυρέων. ἐς μέν νυν Σάμον ἀνέθηκε κατὰ ξεινίην τὴν ἑωυτοῦ τε καὶ Πολυκράτεος τοῦ Αἰάκεος, ἐς δὲ Λίνδον ξεινίης μὲν οὐδεμιῆς εἵνεκεν, ὅτι δὲ τὸ ἱρὸν τὸ ἐν Λίνδῳ τὸ τῆς Ἀθηναίης λέγεται τὰς <τοῦ> Δαναοῦ θυγατέρας ἱδρύσασθαι προσσχούσας, ὅτε ἀπεδίδρησκον τοὺς Αἰγύπτου παῖδας. <u>ταῦτα μὲν ἀνέθηκε ὁ Ἄμασις.</u>

---

[11] Probably most easily analyzed as having a resumptive force to begin the next section, thus "so much for the tribes of the Medes, now (δέ) on to. . . ." But we should not disregard its reflection of the opening list bracket as well.

> Amasis dedicated offerings in Hellas; first a gilded statue of Athena and an
> image of his own likeness in painting, then to the temple of Athena at Lindos
> two stone statues and a linen corslet worthy of being seen; then at Samos to
> Hera a pair of images of himself made out of wood, which were standing in
> the great temple even up to my own time, behind the doors. Now, at Samos
> he made dedications because of the guest-friendship between himself and
> Polycrates the son of Aeaces, but at Lindos on account of friendship with no
> one, but because the daughters of Danaus are said to have founded the
> temple of Athena at Lindos when they arrived on land there in their flight
> from the sons of Aegyptus. These things Amasis dedicated.

The concluding sentence of the section recapitulates both the introductory
clause and, with ταῦτα, the series of demonstratives τοῦτο μέν . . . τοῦτο
δέ . . . τοῦτο δέ. This deictic language, along with such details as ὄπισθε τῶν
θυρέων, has the effect of a virtual display, approximating an autopsy of
these items for the audience in words. In fact, this kind of spatial situating
also occurs fairly frequently in epigraphic inventories, which commonly
include such locative phrases as ἐμ πλαισίῳ "in the box," or περὶ τῷ ἕδει,
"by/on the statue." Specific interpretations of how these terms reflect
placement and storage practices in sanctuaries vary; minute practicalities
aside, however, spatial cues serve both in Herodotus' text and in inscriptions to align the lists' contents as closely as possible with the collections
they describe. Moreover, that tendency only grows stronger as the verbal
medium supersedes the physical collection, and written records and archives become both increasingly authoritative and ever more abstracted from
the objects they represent. Herodotus, though he presents a collection of
goods that perhaps never stood together physically, can nonetheless perform a kind of verbal curatorship to amass them in text. It seems imperative
that the text realize this material quality formally; thus the last sentence of
the Amasis passage forms a precise parallel to the close of the list of
Croesus' dedications (1.52), which I discuss below. In leading up to these
endings, however, Herodotus characteristically interpolates into the list
tangential anecdotes about the various dedications, to the point that
some translators even omit ταῦτα μέν ἀνέθηκε ὁ Ἄμασις, presumably since
it seems to create a *non sequitur*. It attests to the established formulaics of
the list that the Greek text includes an almost superfluous bracketing
sentence.

The list format often reinforces spatial and material realities even to the
point that logic is compromised. In his account of Scythian burial practice,
Herodotus describes the space of the tomb beyond the deceased's body in
a sentence that transforms midway into a verbal collection (4.71):

ἐν δὲ τῇ λοιπῇ εὐρυχωρίῃ τῆς θήκης τῶν παλλακέων τε μίαν ἀποπνίξαντες θάπτουσι καὶ τὸν οἰνοχόον καὶ μάγειρον καὶ ἱπποκόμον καὶ διήκονον καὶ ἀγγελιηφόρον καὶ ἵππους καὶ τῶν ἄλλων ἁπάντων ἀπαρχὰς καὶ φιάλας χρυσέας· ἀργύρῳ δὲ οὐδὲν οὐδὲ χαλκῷ χρέωνται·

> And in the rest of the available space of the tomb they bury, suffocating them, one of the king's mistresses, his cupbearer, his cook, his horse-trainer, his attendant, his message-bearer, his horses, a first-offering of all his other things, and cups of gold; they do not employ silver and bronze at all.

The participle ἀποπνίξαντες, "suffocating" or "strangling," properly governs only the people and possibly the horses buried in the tomb, not the inanimate objects; yet no break in the syntax signals this shift.[12] Rather, the momentum of the list takes over the passage, and everything within the closed space of the tomb is effectively "suffocated." Herodotus' parataxis increases this effect, as well as lending vividness and authenticity to the account, accurate or not.[13] Thus lists in Herodotus present specific numerical, ethnologic, and spatial data in an authoritative way, from the most elaborate to the most attenuated examples. Listing is not just an inherited stylistic device or a digressive tic, but a mode of framing, naming, and containing the unique sets of information he possesses.

Herodotus the καταλόγιος

The authoritative powers of Herodotus' listing depend not just on framing stylistics but on semantic innovations to the traditional vocabulary of Greek catalogue. In the Homeric epics, we have seen exemplified particularly through the figure of Odysseus that the term *katalego* takes on a set of interwoven significations. For a Homeric speaker, *katalego* signals that this is not the first collection or utterance of the given information, but rather an accurate reprisal of a catalogue of objects or facts. Moreover, this act of repetition, far from undermining the speaker's credibility, vests him with numerical and narrative authority; in the case of Odysseus, it even serves to reaffirm his identity. Given this compound's narrative flexibility and Homeric antiquity, it is perhaps no wonder that a later prose text should

---

[12] For details on this element of the practice, see Asheri et al. 2007: 633, who states this cause of death was "aimed at avoiding bloodshed," and that archaeological evidence for how buried horses died is mixed, some having suffered blows and others not.

[13] On parataxis in Herodotus, see Immerwahr 1966; on the inaccuracy of the final sentence, see Asheri et al. (Corcella) 2007: 633.

contain dozens of examples of *katalego*.[14] But other historians do not use the word nearly so frequently.[15] I argue that, just as for Homeric epic, *katalego* is a narrative *mot-clé* for Herodotus, one that he often deploys to refer both to the act of listing proper and to his own self-citation within the composition of the *Histories*. Study of this term on the one hand aligns with scholarship that brings Herodotus together with the figure of Odysseus.[16] On the other, however, analysis of *katalego* attests to Herodotus' interest in the act of cataloguing as an important historiographic and ethnographic practice – an idea that does not emerge in Homer. We can analyze at least two different spheres in which *katalego* operates within Herodotus, with some overlap between them. First, it is used of listed genealogies, also an inherently repeated rather than inventive utterance. Second, in keeping with its use in Homer as a verb signaling reprisal, it serves to mark important repeated information offered as an authoritative account. Herodotus deploys this nuance to lend accountability to his own research, using *katalego* to characterize cited lists of anthropological or geographical information.

Genealogy to Ethnography

Herodotus employs *katalego* perhaps most narrowly to describe serial genealogical recitation. As in Homer, the speaker of *katalego* gives authoritative information, the definitive account of a particular succession. This set of nuances echoes that which we observed earlier in *Odyssey* 24, where the act of re-cataloguing Laertes' trees becomes coterminous with Odysseus' reestablishment of his own genealogy. In Herodotus we see a more explicit connection of genealogy with recitation: *katalego* used of such figures as the Egyptian priests, for instance, who recount the lineage of kings for Herodotus from a papyrus roll (κατέλεγον, 2.100). It also marks moments of individual genealogical importance, such as the one we find in the story of Demaratus, king of Sparta, whose birth from Ariston had been

[14] Powell s.v. cites thirty-six attestations in Herodotus, excluding the five instances of κατεῖπον, "disclose a fact," considered as a separate lemma.

[15] Thucydides uses the compound only three times, always in the specialized sense of military selection or assembly (3.75, 7.31, 8.31). Xenophon uses καταλέγω 13 times across a corpus of 315,469 words, versus 36 attestations over a corpus of 185,554 words in Herodotus (total word counts from TLG). As frequencies per 10,000 words, these can be expressed as .417 (Xen.) versus 1.94 (Hdt.); thus by this metric Herodotus uses καταλέγω over four times (and nearly five times) more frequently than Xenophon.

[16] Exemplified by Marincola 2007; on the idea of Odysseus as ethnographer, see Dougherty 2001.

questioned (6.68). His mother later tells him the strange and authoritative account of her union with a phantom version of Ariston, markedly promising him "the entire (genealogical) truth will be recounted to you" (πᾶν ἔς σε κατειρήσεται τὠληθές, 6.69). "Genealogical" *katalego* appears several times, but one example in particular illustrates how the simple genealogical project – something Herodotus generally distances himself from, save in exceptional cases – develops from a personal, individual birth story into the broader lineage of entire groups or peoples.[17] One such moment occurs in Herodotus' story about the typical Lycian man, who, when asked who he is, "will genealogize himself from his mother" (1.173, καταλέξει ἑωυτὸν μητρόθεν).[18] Here the act of genealogy becomes generalized to an alleged cultural practice, akin to other peculiar behaviors Herodotus ascribes to non-Greeks. Moreover, if, as Asheri suggests, Herodotus here is "reporting a malicious rumor current among the neighboring peoples," we see other cultures' practices reflected in this story as well.

Herodotus' discussion of the Dorian kings illustrates a still more apparent slippage of *katalego* between individual and ethnic lineage (6.53):

> ταῦτα μὲν Λακεδαιμόνιοι λέγουσι μοῦνοι Ἑλλήνων, τάδε δὲ κατὰ τὰ λεγόμενα ὑπ' Ἑλλήνων ἐγὼ γράφω <...> τούτους τοὺς Δωριέων βασιλέας μέχρι μὲν Περσέος τοῦ Δανάης, τοῦ θεοῦ ἀπεόντος, καταλεγομένους ὀρθῶς ὑπ' Ἑλλήνων καὶ ἀποδεικνυμένους ὡς εἰσὶ Ἕλληνες· ἤδη γὰρ τηνικαῦτα ἐς Ἕλληνας οὗτοι ἐτέλεον. ἔλεξα δὲ μέχρι Περσέος τοῦδε εἵνεκα, ἀλλ' οὐκ ἀνέκαθεν ἔτι ἔλαβον, ὅτι οὐκ ἔπεστι ἐπωνυμίη Περσέϊ οὐδεμία πατρὸς θνητοῦ, ὥσπερ Ἡρακλέϊ Ἀμφιτρύων· ἤδη ὧν ὀρθῷ λόγῳ χρεωμένῳ μέχρι Περσέος {ὀρθῶς} εἴρηταί μοι· ἀπὸ δὲ Δανάης τῆς Ἀκρισίου καταλέγοντι τοὺς ἄνω αἰεὶ πατέρας αὐτῶν φαινοίατο ἂν ἐόντες οἱ τῶν Δωριέων ἡγεμόνες Αἰγύπτιοι ἰθαγενέες.

> These things the Spartans alone among the Greeks say. But I relate these things according to what is said by the Greeks in general – that these Dorian kings going back to Perseus son of Danae, not including the god (Zeus), are correctly genealogized by the Greeks, and they are shown by enumeration to be Greeks. For already so early on they were reckoned among the Greeks. But this is why I said "going back to Perseus" but did not take it back any farther: because Perseus has no name derived from a mortal father, as Heracles has Amphytrion, for instance. Thus I was right

---

[17] See below for discussion of his contradistinction from Hecataeus in this regard, who "genealogizes" (γενεαλογέω) when Herodotus does not. On "inquiring kings" see Christ 1994.

[18] Cf. 2.115, of Paris giving his lineage to Proteus, ὁ δὲ καὶ τὸ γένος κατέλεξε καὶ τῆς πάτρης εἶπε τὸ οὔνομα καὶ δὴ καὶ τὸν πλόον ἀπηγήσατο ὁκόθεν πλέοι, "and he listed his ancestry and stated the name of his country and also related the details of his voyage."

to say "going back to Perseus." But if one genealogizes the ancestors all the way back from Danae, daughter of Acrisius, the leaders of the Dorians would turn out to be natural Egyptians.

Here, the ancestral identity of peoples depends on individual genealogies – that is, the ethnic identity of all the Dorian kings is wrapped up in how far one chooses to recount the ancestry of Perseus. This passage also links genealogic catalogue (καταλέγω) to the act of enumerative display encompassed in the term ἀποδείκνυμι (καταλεγομένους ὀρθῶς ὑπ' Ἑλλήνων καὶ ἀποδεικνυμένους), a connection that will be discussed fully below.

Historical Ethnographic Catalogue

Seriality, repetition, and genealogy are thus fundamental and inherited nuances of καταλέγω that persist in Herodotus. But, as these genealogical passages that extend to entire peoples suggest, the verb takes on a new ethnographic and geographical significance. Combining the archaic rhetoric of repetition with his subject, Herodotus deploys καταλέγω as an index of learned citation and self-reference of lists of ethnographic and geographic content.[19] This tendency is most observable in the repeated phrase τὰ καταλεχθέντα, usually understood as "the aforementioned things," but almost always referring more specifically to a previous list of data. Versions of this phrase occur throughout the *Histories*, pointing the audience not only to general information already cited, but specifically to previously given or implied lists of learned ethnographic and geographical information. Thus "the things καταλεχθέντα" are really "the specialized knowledge just listed" – usually land regions, rivers, or ethnic groups. A collection of notable examples appears in discussions of the Scythians, about whom Herodotus is particularly keen to demonstrate his knowledge and research.[20] Three times during his account of Scythian geography he employs the phrase in reference to an earlier listed description of a geographical formation: ἡ καταλεχθεῖσα ... γῆ and ἡ καταλεχθεῖσα

---

[19] On ethnographic writing generally in Herodotus, see Dorati 2011.

[20] Examples of "ethnographic citation" outside of Book 4 include: 3.101, τῶν Ἰνδῶν τῶν κατέλεξα, "of the Indians I (just) listed" (of the preceding list of tribes at 98–100, to be contrasted with the subsequent northern group); 5.52, where Herodotus lists the four rivers of Armenia and then specifies the difference between the two called "Zabatos" (the Upper and Lower Zab): ὁ μὲν γὰρ πρότερος αὐτῶν καταλεχθεὶς ἐξ Ἀρμενίων ῥέει, ὁ δ' ὕστερος ἐκ Ματιηνῶν ("the first listed of these flows out of Armenia, the last out of Matiene"); 6.33, a reference to the five "aforelisted" regions of the European side of the Hellespont. On this and Herodotus' use of Aristeas, see Asheri et al. 2007: 549.

πᾶσα χώρη (4.23 and 4.28), both of the regions of Scythian land he earlier listed, and τουτῶν τῶν καταλεχθέντων (4.83), of the rivers he just listed. Later in Book 4, τῶν καταλεχθέντων ἐθνέων (4.118, "the aforementioned peoples") describes the neighboring ethnic groups he catalogued earlier (4.102–109), whose assembled chiefs the Scythians will warn about the Persians' advance. The phrase τὰ καταλεχθέντα thus reminds the audience both of the previous list and of the detailed ethnographic information Herodotus has provided, signaling his research prowess and the unique content of his work.[21] As he states toward the end of his subsequent account of Libya (4.185): μέχρι μὲν δὴ τῶν Ἀτλάντων τούτων ἔχω τὰ οὐνόματα τῶν ἐν τῇ ὀφρύῃ κατοικημένων <u>καταλέξαι</u>, τὸ δ' ἀπὸ τούτων οὐκέτι, "Up to the Atlantes I am able to authoritatively list the names of the inhabitants of the embankment, but thenceforth no longer."[22]

Herodotus thus echoes the Homeric poetics of recapitulation and cata-logic authority, but embeds them in a new historiographic agenda. In the narrowest sense, *katalego* describes the act of genealogizing, of listing ancestors, and, in the broadest, the *ars technica* of the ethnographer. Accordingly, Herodotus himself is most often the agent of *katalego* in Book 4. Yet the few examples with other characters as subjects also prove telling, subtly aligning key momentary-anthropologists from within the narrative with Herodotus' own self-presentation.[23] The Amazons, for example, when explaining to Scythian men why they (the Amazons) could not live in harmony with the Scythian women, provide a list of their cultural differences: Amazons shoot bows, throw spears, and ride horses, whereas, they point out, "your women do none of these things we listed" (αἱ δὲ ὑμέτεραι γυναῖκες τούτων μὲν οὐδὲν τῶν ἡμεῖς κατελέξαμεν ποιεῦσι, 4.114). The verb here underscores the ethnographic validity of the Amazons' argument not to move to Scythia, as based on researched cultural evidence. These listed activities are echoed in Herodotus' subse-quent description of the women of the Saurometae (116). Earlier on in Book 4, Darius' brother Artabanus, often thought of as a "wise advisor" figure,[24] counsels Darius not to invade Scythia by "citing the difficulty of reaching the Scythians" (καταλέγων τῶν Σκυθέων τὴν ἀπορίην, 4.83). Here

---

[21] It is hard to say whether it also signals firsthand versus learned knowledge, a distinction not always discernable, but it may well do so. On this issue generally, see Asheri et al. 2007: 549.

[22] For the opposite case (things Herodotus could list but chooses not to), cf. 5.72, on Timesitheus of Delphi, τοῦ ἔργα χειρῶν τε καὶ λήματος ἔχοιμ' ἂν μέγιστα καταλέξαι ("whose feats of action and spirit I could list as very great").

[23] On Herodotus as anthropologist, see, e.g., Redfield 1985, Dench 2007, Skinner 2012.

[24] Lattimore 1939.

again, as the agent of *katalego*, Artabanus gives authoritative ethnographic detail to support intelligent advice.[25]

And yet *katalego* is not the way Herodotus describes the overall project of his work – this is not a *katalogos histories*. This may be because the work does more than give sets of data, or because *katalego* sometimes carries an undertone of deception. In two pivotal strategic moments for the Persians and Greeks, we find the verb used of characters who markedly repeat crucial military advice. First, the chresmologue Onomacritus, a figure whose work depends on the selective repetition of information, gives a carefully curated set of oracles to Xerxes at Susa to persuade him to embark on his expedition against Hellas (7.6):

> τότε δὲ συναναβὰς ὅκως ἀπίκοιτο ἐς ὄψιν τὴν βασιλέος, λεγόντων τῶν Πεισιστρατιδέων περὶ αὐτοῦ σεμνοὺς λόγους, κατέλεγε τῶν χρησμῶν.

> And then once he arrived whenever he came into the company of the king, with the Peisistratidae saying grand things about him, he recited from his oracles.

While Onomacritus is notable (including earlier in this passage) for his forgeries and interpolations, Herodotus describes his oracular recitation as an act perceived as authoritative – even if at best semi-honest and not credible in the eyes of Herodotus himself.[26] As in Homer, *katalego* thus marks repeated, serial, and authoritative utterances, but occasionally in an untrustworthy character. In Book 8, *katalego* again clearly marks repeated authoritative speech in the context of Themistocles' decision to engage with the Persians at Salamis, upon advice from the elder Athenian Mnesiphilos,[27] which he repeats to Eurybiades without crediting him (8.58):

> ἀπικόμενος δὲ ἔφη ἐθέλειν οἱ κοινόν τι πρῆγμα συμμῖξαι. ὁ δ' αὐτὸν ἐς τὴν νέα ἐκέλευε ἐσβάντα λέγειν, εἴ τι θέλοι. ἐνθαῦτα ὁ Θεμιστοκλέης παριζόμενός οἱ καταλέγει ἐκεῖνά τε πάντα τὰ ἤκουσε Μνησιφίλου, ἑωυτοῦ ποιεύμενος, καὶ ἄλλα πολλὰ προστιθείς, ἐς ὃ ἀνέγνωσε <μιν> χρηίζων ἔκ τε τῆς νεὸς ἐκβῆναι συλλέξαι τε τοὺς στρατηγοὺς ἐς τὸ συνέδριον.

---

[25] Herodotus endorses Artabanus' admonishment; whether Darius was right to ignore it, and to what extent his campaign might be judged successful, are a matter of debate. Tuplin 2010 gives a survey of evidence and previous scholarship. For a novel reading of the campaign's difficulties and the "uncountability" of the Scythians, see Purves 2006.

[26] See Martínez 2011 on Onomacritus' forgery. Dillery 2005 discusses the nature of Onomacritus' authority. For a reading of his passage in the context of the political shaping (i.e. by Xerxes of literary texts), see Haubold 2007: 52–55.

[27] On the relationship between Themistocles and Mnesiphilos, see Frost 1971.

And when he arrived he said that he wanted to speak on an issue common to them both, and Eurybiades asked him to come aboard his ship and speak, if he wanted. Then Themistocles, sitting by him, retold him all those things he had heard from Mnesiphilos, making them out to be his own ideas, and adding many other things, until he induced him with his petitions to disembark from the ship and collect the generals for a war council.

While we are perhaps meant to understand that this was Themistocles' idea all along,[28] he runs the risk of sounding deceitful, and even derivative. Thus while *katalego* describes acts of enumerating specific facts and figures, and of authoritative repetition, it also is a term too complicated, perhaps too ambivalent, for Herodotus to adopt for the work as a whole.

Apodexis: **Enumerative Display**

To examine how Herodotus frames his project instead, we must turn to a different and less overt set of list-words: the verb *apodeiknumi*, and the noun *apodexis*, which can mean "show," "display," or "inventory." The passage quoted above, on the genealogy of the Dorian kings, illustrates some of the distinctions between these roots and *katalego*. There, Herodotus said, the true origins of the kings were shown by the non-Spartan Greeks in two contrastive but overlapping ways: καταλεγομένους ὀρθῶς ὑπ' Ἑλλήνων καὶ ἀποδεικνυμένους ὡς εἰσὶ Ἕλληνες, "they were genealogized correctly by the Greeks and shown through this list to be Greeks." Mapping the semantic range of the stem of *apodeiknumi* in the *Histories* reveals that it often denotes a specialized kind of display, one that blends physical indexing or proof with verbal enumeration. Understanding these nuances, in turn, allows us to reanalyze both specific passages and Herodotus' greater historiographic program. The elaborate description of Croesus' offerings to Delphi provides a useful example from which to begin (1.51–52):

> ἐπιτελέσας δὲ ὁ Κροῖσος ταῦτα ἀπέπεμπε ἐς Δελφοὺς καὶ τάδε ἄλλα ἅμα τοῖσι· κρητῆρας δύο μεγάθεϊ μεγάλους, χρύσεον καὶ ἀργύρεον, τῶν ὁ μὲν χρύσεος ἔκειτο ἐπὶ δεξιὰ ἐσιόντι ἐς τὸν νηόν, ὁ δὲ ἀργύρεος ἐπ' ἀριστερά. μετεκινήθησαν δὲ καὶ οὗτοι ὑπὸ τὸν νηὸν κατακαέντα, καὶ ὁ μὲν χρύσεος κεῖται ἐν τῷ Κλαζομενίων θησαυρῷ, ἕλκων σταθμὸν εἴνατον ἡμιτάλαντον καὶ ἔτι δυώδεκα μνέας, ὁ δὲ ἀργύρεος ἐπὶ τοῦ προνηΐου τῆς γωνίης, χωρέων

ἀμφορέας ἑξακοσίους· [. . .] καὶ πίθους τε ἀργυρέους τέσσερας ἀπέπεμψε, οἳ
ἐν τῷ Κορινθίων θησαυρῷ ἑστᾶσι, καὶ περιρραντήρια δύο ἀνέθηκε, χρύσεόν
τε καὶ ἀργύρεον [. . .] . ἄλλα τε ἀναθήματα οὐκ ἐπίσημα πολλὰ ἀπέπεμψε
ἅμα τούτοισι ὁ Κροῖσος καὶ χεύματα ἀργύρεα κυκλοτερέα, καὶ δὴ καὶ
γυναικὸς εἴδωλον χρύσεον τρίπηχυ, τὸ Δελφοὶ τῆς ἀρτοκόπου τῆς
Κροίσου εἰκόνα λέγουσι εἶναι. πρὸς δὲ καὶ τῆς ἑωυτοῦ γυναικὸς τὰ ἀπὸ τῆς
δειρῆς ἀνέθηκε ὁ Κροῖσος καὶ τὰς ζώνας. ταῦτα μὲν ἐς Δελφοὺς ἀπέπεμψε.

And Croesus, having finished all these things, sent them to Delphi, and along
with them the following other things: two great big mixing bowls, one gold
and the other silver, of which the golden one used to stand on the right-hand
side as you enter the temple, and the silver on the left, but these also were
changed around after the temple burned down, and the golden bowl now lies
in the treasury of the people of Clazomenae, having a weight of eight and a half
talents and twelve pounds more, while the silver one lies in the corner of the
foyer and holds six hundred amphoras [. . .] And he also sent four silver wine
jars, which stand in the treasury of the Corinthians, and two vessels for lustral
water, one gold and the other silver [. . .] and along with these he sent many
other unspecified dedicatory offerings, including round silver cast bowls, as
well as a golden likeness of a woman three cubits high, which the Delphians
say is a statue of Croesus' baker. Moreover Croesus dedicated the ornaments
from his own wife's neck and her girdles. So those things he sent to Delphi.

Herodotus provides here a formal inventory of everything at Delphi put
there by Croesus. He sometimes includes more detail about some items,
and the locations and conditions of others, but it is in its basic structure an
account – a document that attests both to Croesus' considerable efforts to
propitiate the oracle and to the realities of what was on display at the
sanctuary at a particular moment. Herodotus perhaps composed it himself
based on autopsy, or possibly he embellished a Delphic record he encountered, whether oral or written.[29] Regardless, certainly the idea of taking
stock of treasure in an organized list was not a completely new one, nor is it
one that has gone completely unnoticed. Almost a century ago, Casson
suggested that Herodotus, as well as Thucydides, refers to official military
inventories in scattered examples, and that both authors describe them
with the verb *apodeiknumi* and the noun *apodexis/apodeixis*.[30] He argued
that the term was part of the legalese surrounding the army's practice of
taking inventories as a kind of safeguard or collateral; in his view,

---

[29] S. West 1985: 280 suggests possible access to a written source for this scene; others caution
against assuming that Herodotus made use of many written archival documents (Thomas 1989:
3–4, Murray 2007a: 22–23). For the purposes of this study, the story behind the inventory's
composition is of less interest than its function in the *Histories*.
[30] Casson 1914 and 1921.

Herodotus believed that Xerxes' army went to Delphi to inventory the treasure there, while the idea that they also intended to plunder it came later, from the Delphians (8.35):

> ἐπορεύοντο δὲ ταύτῃ ἀποσχισθέντες τῆς ἄλλης στρατιῆς τῶνδε εἵνεκα, ὅκως
> συλήσαντες τὸ ἱρὸν τὸ ἐν Δελφοῖσι βασιλέϊ Ξέρξῃ <u>ἀποδέξαιεν</u> τὰ χρήματα.
> πάντα δ᾽ ἠπίστατο τὰ ἐν τῷ ἱρῷ ὅσα λόγου ἦν ἄξια Ξέρξης, ὡς ἐγὼ
> πυνθάνομαι, ἄμεινον ἢ τὰ ἐν τοῖσι οἰκίοισι ἔλιπε, πολλῶν αἰεὶ λεγόντων,
> καὶ μάλιστα τὰ Κροίσου τοῦ Ἀλυάττεω ἀναθήματα.

> And they proceeded separated from the rest of the army at that time for the following reasons: in order that they might sack the temple at Delphi and inventory the items there for King Xerxes. Xerxes knew of all the things in the temple worth mentioning, as I learned, better than the ones he had left in his palace at home (from the many people telling him about them), especially of the dedications of Croesus, son of Alyattes.

Although Herodotus offers both motivations, Casson surmised that the sacking of the temple (expressed in the participle συλήσαντες) was subordinate to Xerxes' principal mission, namely, to inventory the treasures there.[31] The word *apodexis*, he correctly pointed out, does appear in later epigraphic texts to denote an official inventory made by a governing body and published, perhaps as an inscription.[32]

But associating those types of document with this passage raises an entirely new question that has not been addressed: under what linguistic, literary, and social circumstances did *apodexis*, literally a "display" or "show," come to denote an inventory or a list in the first place? In answer, I will propose here that before the term enters the bureaucratic lexicon, Herodotus provides a glimpse into how its extension from a physical show of important items to their figurative exposition in words occurred. Through a study of Herodotus' diction and contextual usage, we can observe the development of the meaning of *apodexis* from denoting a physical display of goods or power to describing a symbolic display that occurs via either a representative monument or ultimately simply a text.[33] My study is not the first to address Herodotus'

---

[31] Casson 1914: 146.

[32] "This process of inventory-taking was, I suggested, a recognized military method of ensuring the neutrality of the party taking the inventory. If that party infringed its neutrality, everything set down on the list was seized by those who held the inventory" (Casson 1921: 144, in reference to Casson 1914). While I concur with his semantic analysis, I seriously doubt Casson's overarching assertion (1914) that the Persian expedition to Delphi at 8.35 was for the purpose of inventorying and not for plunder; part of Herodotus' point is that Xerxes already knew the contents of the treasury at Delphi, at least by word of mouth.

[33] In canonical historical linguistic terms, this change would perhaps fall under the category of semantic "metaphoric extension" or "broadening"; Fortson 2003: 650, however, points out the

use of *apodexis* and related compounds; the word has been the subject of considerable attention, mainly because of its appearance in the prologue to the *Histories*, to which I will return. With a view to explicating the famous opening words of the text, Bakker 2002: 20–28 has also undertaken to examine the use of the word elsewhere in Herodotus. My focus here, however, is on the mechanisms and breeding grounds for the word's novel uses apparent in Herodotus, and specifically for its new application to inventories.[34] Following this discussion, I offer reflection on how this semantic mapping affects the meaning of the prologue and work as a whole. Behind this approach lies the idea that a written list can function as a virtual collection, either a facsimile of the physical or a usurpation of it. An inventory thus implies or even conjures up a physical manifestation.[35] Herodotus, I contend, exhibits novel techniques for making these verbal shows of goods and power in the literary tradition. Moreover, I argue, his use of the verb *apodeiknumi* and its derivative *apodexis* signal this intermingling of material and verbal collection and display. In Herodotus' enumerations of objects and concomitant diction, we can observe *apodexis* denoting acts that move from physical displays to verbal ones, in the form of lists.

Let us first take a brief semantic survey of *apodeiknumi* and its relationship to visual and verbal displays. In the *Histories*, Powell has analyzed the verb as having the following distinctions in meaning.[36] In the active: (1a)

---

relative inutility of such typologies, for "they leave entirely untouched the reanalyses (innovations) that are the true changes and that are of primary interest." My goal here thus is to probe Herodotus' own reanalysis of these words and its significance to his work as a whole.

[34] Traugott and Dasher 2002: 16–19 distinguish three kinds of word meaning: (i) conventional, established usage; (ii) community-specific meanings, called "crystallized invited references" (16), which may be later cancelled in subsequent utterances; and (iii) "invited references that have not been crystallized into commonly used implicatures" (17). My argument here would situate Herodotus' use of ἀποδείκνυμι in (iii), such that the enumerative-display meaning arises in a context where the audience "not only reads passively but also actively makes inferences and may begin to exploit these inferences in a way similar to those of the writer," as well as seeking "the relevance of what has been said to the situation, including the task at hand, and perhaps some larger task such as improvement of knowledge structure" (17–18).

[35] For an introduction to the discourse on the topic outside of the ancient world, see, e.g., Swann 2001 and the introduction to Belknap 2004. Eco 2009 brings together a catalogue of the artworks and artifacts that exemplify what he terms "visual lists," that is, works exhibiting "the intention to attain the effect of abundance, of the ineffability of variety suggested" (44). Most scholarship related to the issue in antiquity treats magical texts; in summarizing several views while discussing body-part lists on curse tablets, D. Collins 2008: 83–86 surmises that neither (1) a sense of completeness nor (2) parallel administrative text style provides an adequate explanation for the list's ubiquitous presence. He partially espouses rhetorical explanations such as those of Weiner 1983 and Gordon 1999, but stresses the importance of cross-cultural influences on the Greek and Roman world. Collins is right to introduce the connection of body-part enumerations with healing *ex votos* that depict body parts.

[36] Powell 1938: 38. He gives 137 attestations in total (75 active, 62 middle).

show, point out; (2a) prove, demonstrate; (3a) appoint (as a leader); (4a) produce (offspring, etc.). In the middle: (1m) declare, (2m) perform, (a deed), (3m) display (a quality), (4m) execute (public works, etc.). Regrouping each of these definitions into one of two categories, according to whether they refer to demonstrations in words or in physical actions, yields the following:[37]

Physical	Verbal
$1a_1$ show	$1a_2$ declare (3)
3a appoint	2a prove (13)
4a produce	1m declare (24)
2m perform	
3m display	
4m execute	

Of the 137 total occurrences of ἀποδείκνυμι, only those in the right-hand column (a total of 40) denote a verbal showing; of these, the 24 that mean "declare" (1 m) all govern the noun γνώμη as object, as a periphrastic idiom – "show one's opinion." Thus the word does not denote "declare" unmarked, without the aid of γνώμη in this context; we might call 1 m a subset of 3 m, "display." Likewise, two of the three examples of ἀποδείκνυμι meaning "declare" in the active ($1a_2$) appear with a form of *logos*, which, like *gnome*, specifies the verbal component of the action: ἀπεδείκνυσαν τὸν λόγον ("they put forth their speech," 7.119), and ἐγὼ ἀποδείκνυμι τῷ λόγῳ ("I show in my account," 2.18). The third instance denotes a law of Amasis mandating that each Egyptian ἀποδεικνύναι . . . ὅθεν βιοῦται ("show how he makes his living," 2.177) – something he might well do by action, and which by no means necessarily implies a verbal declaration.

It remains to examine the thirteen examples labeled 2a, "prove," a meaning common in later prose. As in the case of $1a_2$, several of these examples also specify that the actor is using words, because they appear with a form of λόγος, λέγω, or other similar marking.[38] One passage also

---

[37] Some terminology: for the sake of clarity and diplomacy I intend "verbal" to refer to the use of words, be it by pen or by tongue. I will use "written" and "oral" (or "spoken") when impelled to refer to the ever-weakening poles of the literacy debate. On the notion of verbal accounts of the physical, and ἀπόδεξις, cf. Immerwahr 1960 and Nagy 1987 and 1990: 217–255.

[38] ἀποδεικνύοιμεν ἂν τούτῳ τῷ λόγῳ χρεώμενοι (2.15); ἐν τοῖσι ὄπισθε λόγοισι ἀποδέξω (5.22); ἀποδεικνύντες τε λόγῳ (5.94); τοσαῦτα εἴπας Ἀρτάβανος, ἐλπίζων Ξέρξην ἀποδέξειν λέγοντα οὐδέν (7.17).

specifies that the proof came about ἔργῳ, through deed, thus also obviating the need to give ἀποδείκνυμι a verbal meaning (4.8). The seven remaining instances of ἀποδείκνυμι – those that have been interpreted as "prove" but do not have an accompanying speech-marking – will form the subject of my analysis below.[39]

In light of this data, I would venture that Herodotus does not, and cannot, use ἀποδείκνυμι absolutely to refer to a statement without explicitly specifying that words were involved: the verb has not yet acquired an implicit connotation of speech. In later texts, by contrast, ἀποδείκνυμι commonly denotes a verbal showing, or a proof, without any qualification, and eventually the inclusion of λόγος or γνώμη would be redundant. Thus Plato's Socrates, for example, has no problem applying ἀποδείκνυμι to his defense speech (*Ap.* 20d): ταυτί μοι δοκεῖ δίκαια λέγειν ὁ λέγων, κἀγὼ ὑμῖν πειράσομαι ἀποδεῖξαι τί ποτ' ἐστὶν τοῦτο ὃ ἐμοὶ πεποίηκεν τό τε ὄνομα καὶ τὴν διαβολήν. ἀκούετε δή, "The man who says this seems right to me, and I will try to show you what it is that has created this name and slander against me. So listen." In the *Histories*, however, it does not appear without an accompanying mention of the verbal component. It therefore seems plausible that the application of ἀποδείκνυμι to verbal utterances is a relatively new one in Herodotus' time, and one still undergoing change.

Indeed, pre-Herodotean uses of ἀποδείκνυμι show no evidence of its denoting speech. In archaic poetry, ἀποδείκνυμι in its relatively few attestations given below describes exclusively physical displays, often of status or strength. So in *Prometheus Bound*, the winds array their forces as one of a series of apocalyptic events (1080–1088): καὶ μὴν ἔργωι κοὐκέτι μύθωι | χθὼν σεσάλευται, | … σκιρτᾶι δ' ἀνέμων | πνεύματα πάντων εἰς ἄλληλα | στάσιν ἀντίπνουν ἀποδεικνύμενα, "Truly in deed, no longer in word the earth shakes … and gusts of all the winds flit about displaying blows of strife against each other." In the second stasimon of the *Agamemnon*, the chorus describes the lion cub born gentle but who in time "showed its inborn nature from its parents" (ἀπέδειξεν ἦθος τὸ πρὸς τοκέων, 727), while in the *Eumenides*, Athena uses the verb as she leads the procession to accompany the Erinyes below the earth (1003–1005 *bis*):

χαίρετε χὐμεῖς, προτέραν δ' ἐμὲ χρὴ
στείχειν θαλάμους
ἀποδείξουσαν πρὸς φῶς ἱερὸν   1005
τῶνδε προπομπῶν.

---

[39] 2.16, 2.133, 2.142, 2.143 (*bis*), 2.144, 6.53, 7.118.

> Farewell to you too, but first I must
> go to show you your chambers
> by the sacred light of　　　　　　　　　　　　1005
> these attendants.

The sense is explicitly quite visual, and the showing involves light and perhaps gesture, but hardly words.

Pindar provides perhaps a more complex example in his praise of the victor Alcidamas in *Nemean* 6, who, he has said at the start of the ode, "bears witness for all to see that his lineage is like the fruit-bearing land." He later praises the victor's ancestral home of Aigina (45–49):

> πλατεῖαι πάντοθεν λογίοισιν ἐντὶ πρόσοδοι　　　　　45
> νᾶσον εὐκλέα τάνδε κοσμεῖν· ἐπεί σφιν Αἰακίδαι
> ἔπορον ἔξοχον αἶσαν ἀρετὰς <u>ἀποδεικνύμενοι</u> μεγάλας,
> πέταται δ᾽ ἐπί τε χθόνα καὶ διὰ θαλάσσας τηλόθεν
> ὄνυμ᾽ αὐτῶν·

> Wide all around are the avenues for those skilled with words　　45
> to adorn this renowned island, since the Aeacidae
> furnished an outstanding lot, displaying their great excellent deeds,
> and their name flies over the earth and far across the sea.

This passage foreshadows some of the liberal use of metaphor we encounter in Herodotus.[40] In making display of their excellence, possibly not only in deed but also via victory and monument (be that a statue or a poem), the Aeacidae have equipped those who are λόγιοι (e.g. Pindar) to extol them. If we take the poet at his word, the final clause suggests that the vehicle facilitating this visual manifestation of excellence (ἀρετάς) is none other than their flying name (ὄνυμα). For Herodotus, I suggest, *apodeiknumi* will refer not only to physical displays of wealth and worth as put on by the rich and famous, but also to verbal accounts of them. These verbal accounts, when signaled by the verb *apodeiknumi* used absolutely, consist in catalogues of items. Herodotus uses *apodeiknumi* and *apodexis* to refer to displays of the physical variety and to newer, more metaphoric ones. As I have suggested above, the data fall into three fairly well-delineated

---

[40] An example from Sophocles, also referring to non-verbal action, may perhaps precede Herodotus. At the end of the *OT* Oedipus twice denounces marriage, for among other evils κἀπεδείξατε | πατέρας ἀδελφούς, παῖδας αἷμ᾽ ἐμφύλιον, | νύμφας γυναῖκας μητέρας τε, χὠπόσα | αἴσχιστ᾽ ἐν ἀνθρώποισιν ἔργα γίγνεται, "you revealed fathers as brothers, children as kindred blood, brides as wives and mothers, and all the most wicked deeds as transpire among men" (1405–1408). As neither the *OT* nor the publication of the *Histories* is securely dated, I adduce it here merely for interest, with no claims of chronological certainty.

sub-groups: first, pure physical display; second, verbal display or proof with accompanying speech-word; and third, a small group of examples that may denote verbal displays but are not explicitly marked as such. The visual and arguably earlier sense "make a physical display" is most common. Thus Herodotus describes Mitridates' presentation to Harpagus of the dead child supposed to be Cyrus (1.113): φύλακον αὐτοῦ καταλιπών, ἐλθὼν δὲ ἐς τοῦ Ἁρπάγου ἀποδεικνύναι ἔφη ἕτοιμος εἶναι τοῦ παιδίου τὸν νέκυν, "leaving his post and coming to the palace of Harpagus, he said that he was ready to make a showing of the boy's corpse." In a similar way, ἀποδείκνυμι can also refer to actions that demonstrate or provide evidence for a certain human trait or tendency (not so unlike Pindar's characterization of the Aeacidae). In this general vein, too, Herodotus describes the Phoenicians' ingenuity and efficiency in digging the trench at Sane as compared with other peoples, who attempted the same task with inferior results and more work (7.23): οἱ δὲ Φοίνικες σοφίην ἔν τε τοῖσι ἄλλοισι ἔργοισι ἀποδεικνύνται καὶ δὴ καὶ ἐν ἐκείνῳ, "And the Phoenicians make show of their skill, among their other deeds, especially in that one." As to the other side of the spectrum, we have seen examples above of ἀποδείκνυμι with accompanying speech-word, such as the statement at 2.18: μαρτυρέει δέ μοι τῇ γνώμῃ, ὅτι τοσαύτη ἐστὶ Αἴγυπτος ὅσην τινὰ ἐγὼ ἀποδείκνυμι τῷ λόγῳ, "And the oracle coming from Ammon also bears witness to my statement that Egypt is just as great as I show it to be in my account."

Consequently, for an extension of meaning such as this from physical to verbal, we might seek contexts in which the new meaning could arise. The smallest and final sub-group of examples provides evidence of just these kinds of liminal space, where ἀποδείκνυμι denotes neither a strictly physical nor yet a strictly verbal display. These intermediate moments occur in discussions of various influential public figures' displays of their wealth, and most (as accords with the technical meaning of ἀπόδεξις as "inventory") constitute enumerated lists of some sort. But in the following instances, ἀποδείκνυμι and ἀπόδεξις imply enumeration in a less specialized sense. Moreover, reanalyzing these examples both affords fresh insight into some well-known passages of the text and ultimately proves revealing about Herodotus' historiographic program.

When Herodotus discusses the Ionians' traditions about the Egyptians, after giving details about the Egyptian landmass, he states a correction, saying Ἕλληνάς τε καὶ αὐτοὺς Ἴωνας ἀποδείκνυμι οὐκ ἐπισταμένους λογίζεσθαι, οἵ φασι τρία μόρια εἶναι γῆν πᾶσαν, "I show that the Greeks and Ionians themselves do not reckon it right, when they say that the whole earth consists of three parts" (2.16). The proof is in the counting, for, as he goes on to state, the Egyptian Delta forms a fourth part. Here we see that Herodotus' method of "proof" – that is, the action behind ἀποδείκνυμι – consists not so much in words as in enumerating correctly the parts of Egypt in a short list of four. A similar pattern emerges elsewhere: the crafty King Mycerinus, faced with a prophecy that he will live only six years more, stays awake day and night in an effort to re-reckon years, attempting to "prove the oracle false" by enumeration (τὸ μαντήιον ψευδόμενον ἀποδέξαι, 2.133). Likewise, the Thasian Antipater receives Xerxes' army and as evidence gives the sum total enumeration of his expenditure: ἀπέδεξε ἐς τὸ δεῖπνον τετρακόσια τάλαντα ἀργυρίου τετελεσμένα, "He invoiced 400 silver talents spent for the dinner" (7.118). Finally, as we have seen, Herodotus uses the word in reference to the catalogue of the Greek generations (6.53):

> τούτους γὰρ δὴ τοὺς Δωριέων βασιλέας μέχρι μὲν δὴ Περσέος τοῦ Δανάης, τοῦ θεοῦ ἀπεόντος, καταλεγομένους ὀρθῶς ὑπ' Ἑλλήνων καὶ ἀποδεικνυμένους ὡς εἰσὶ Ἕλληνες.

> [The Greeks say] that these Dorian kings going back to Perseus son of Danae, not including the god (Zeus), are correctly genealogized by the Greeks, and they are shown by enumeration to be Greeks.

Again, ἀποδείκνυμι is an act closely linked to enumeration. Even if it involves words and the verbal performance of the enumeration to an audience, it is not so much a plain utterance as a speech act.

An extended series of examples of ἀποδείκνυμι appears later in Book 2 – perhaps unsurprisingly, for these are the sections in which Herodotus refers to the Egyptian dynasties. He uses ἀποδείκνυμι three times to denote the Egyptians' own records of people and accomplishments as related to him by the priests. First, he applies it to the genealogy they give him after he has completed his own account of the succession of kings ending with Sethos, priest of Hephaestus (2.142):

> ἐς μὲν τοσόνδε τοῦ λόγου Αἰγύπτιοί τε καὶ οἱ ἱρέες ἔλεγον, ἀποδεικνύντες ἀπὸ τοῦ πρώτου βασιλέος ἐς τοῦ Ἡφαίστου τὸν ἱρέα τοῦτον τὸν τελευταῖον βασιλεύσαντα μίαν τε καὶ τεσσεράκοντα καὶ τριηκοσίας ἀνθρώπων γενεὰς γενομένας καὶ ἐν ταύτῃσι ἀρχιερέας καὶ βασιλέας ἑκατέρους τοσούτους γενομένους.

> To this point of the account the Egyptians and the priests, enumerating, from the first king to this last one (the priest of Hephaestus), told me of 341 generations of men having come and gone, and in this time just as many of both high priests and kings having come and gone.

Commentators and translators generally interpret ἀποδεικνύντες here as a verb of speaking, introducing an indirect statement with γενομένας and γενομένους, and referring to a claim the priests made about the kings and priests: "declaring *that* there were 341 generations."[41] But if, as shown above, ἀποδείκνυμι used alone cannot denote a plain verbal declaration, a more nuanced meaning ought to hold here. And indeed, the rest of the passage reveals that the priests are doing something beyond just speaking plainly; they are making a formal display of the generations of the past, one by one, in list form, with γενομένας and γενομένους as attributive. The verb ἀποδείκνυμι refers then to words, but of a ritualized and performative nature.[42] Moreover, and perhaps even more significantly, the priests also engage in a simultaneous physical display of the genealogy. We later see that each of the items in the list, in addition to verbally representing a human being, has a material correlate on display in the temple in the form of a wooden likeness (2.143–144):

πρότερον δὲ Ἑκαταίῳ τῷ λογοποιῷ ἐν Θήβῃσι γενεηλογήσαντι ἑωυτὸν ἀναδήσαντί τε τὴν πατριὴν ἐς ἑκκαιδέκατον θεὸν ἐποίησαν οἱ ἱρέες τοῦ Διὸς οἷόν τι καὶ ἐμοὶ οὐ γενεηλογήσαντι ἐμεωυτόν. ἐσαγαγόντες ἐς τὸ μέγαρον ἔσω ἐὸν μέγα ἐξηρίθμεον δεικνύντες κολοσσοὺς ξυλίνους τοσούτους ὅσους περ εἶπον· ἀρχιερεὺς γὰρ ἕκαστος αὐτόθι ἱστᾷ ἐπὶ τῆς ἑωυτοῦ ζόης εἰκόνα ἑωυτοῦ· ἀριθμέοντες ὦν καὶ δεικνύντες οἱ ἱρέες ἐμοὶ ἀπεδείκνυσαν παῖδα †πατρὸς ἑωυτῶν ἕκαστον† ἐόντα, ἐκ τοῦ ἄγχιστα ἀποθανόντος τῆς εἰκόνος διεξιόντες διὰ πασέων, ἐς οὗ ἀπέδεξαν ἁπάσας αὐτάς. Ἑκαταίῳ δὲ γενεηλογήσαντι ἑωυτὸν καὶ ἀναδήσαντι ἐς ἑκκαιδέκατον θεὸν ἀντεγενεηλόγησαν ἐπὶ τῇ ἀριθμήσι, οὐ δεκόμενοι παρ' αὐτοῦ ἀπὸ θεοῦ γενέσθαι ἄνθρωπον· ἀντεγενεηλόγησαν δὲ ὧδε, φάμενοι ἕκαστον τῶν κολοσσῶν πίρωμιν ἐκ πιρώμιος γεγονέναι, ἐς ὃ τοὺς πέντε καὶ τεσσεράκοντα καὶ τριηκοσίους ἀπέδεξαν κολοσσοὺς {πίρωμιν ἐκ πιρώμιος γενόμενον}, καὶ οὔτε ἐς θεὸν οὔτε ἐς ἥρωα ἀνέδησαν αὐτούς.

And before, when the chronicler Hecataeus gave his own genealogy in Thebes and traced back his lineage to a god sixteen generations back, the priests of Zeus did the same thing for him as they did for me, though I did

---

[41] Herodotus 1996: 138: "They declare that three hundred and forty-one generations separate the first king of Egypt from the last I have mentioned"; Herodotus 1987: 193 seems closer to the mark with "they counted ... three hundred and forty-one generations of men, and in these generations there had been, in each, a king and a high priest."

[42] Again, a speech act of sorts. I hesitate to press this comparison in part because the list does not readily fall into one of the categories of illocutionary acts outlined by Austin 1975. While it does fulfill the actions of "labeling" and perhaps "repeating" of "primitive speech acts" (Dore 1975), this apodeictic genealogy as well as Herodotus' other lists "do" something more: almost like magical texts, they conjure the physical presence of what they describe.

not give my own genealogy. Bringing each of us into the great temple, they showed us wooden statues and counted them up, as many as the number I said, for each high priest erects right there a likeness of himself during his life. Thus counting them and showing them, the priests enumerated for me each one of them, being the child of the father [who came before him?], going through all of them from the likeness of the one who died most recently up until they had listed absolutely all of them. And when Hecataeus had traced his descent and connected his family with a god in the sixteenth generation, they traced a descent in opposition to this, besides their numbering, not accepting it from him that a man had been born from a god; and they traced their counter-descent thus, saying that each one of the statues had been *piromis* son of *piromis*, until they had enumerated all 345 statues [each one being a *piromis* son of a *piromis*]; and neither with a god nor a hero did they connect their descent.

These statues, then, stand as the physical manifestation of the genealogy, making up a collection to which the list serves as verbal analogue. And here, as before, several factors speak in favor of interpreting ἀποδείκνυμι as meaning something more specific than the usual rendering (i.e., that the priests "assured" Herodotus or "demonstrated" to him that each priest was the son of the one before him). First, the sequence ἀριθμέοντες ὦν καὶ δεικνύντες οἱ ἱρέες ἐμοὶ ἀπεδείκνυσαν, all with continuous aspect, implies that the two participles together form part of the action of the main verb. This is to say, ἀπεδείκνυσαν describes an ongoing act that comprises both counting and showing. To interpret the meaning as a perfective "they proved" or "they demonstrated" begs an explanation for the imperfect. Continuous aspect makes good sense, however, if the priests are in fact reciting a catalogue.[43] The subsequent iteration of the verb in the aorist after the listing is complete – ἐς ὃ ἀπέδεξαν ἁπάσας αὐτάς – then sums up, simply, the fact that the priests have just given the complete genealogy, from the first to the last (English idiom favors a pluperfect with past uses of "until" for good aspectual reason). By contrast, analyzing ἀπεδείκνυσαν παῖδα πατρὸς ἑωυτῶν ἕκαστον ἐόντα as a head verb and participial indirect statement (as opposed to an attributive participle) renders the later aorist ἀπέδεξαν violent in its change of usage, or even nonsensical – this may in fact explain some editions' choice to translate only one of the two

---

[43] *Contra* Powell 1938 and Filbey, who cites this passage in an account of ἀποδείκνυμι plus supplementary participle but remains vague as to how his general rule would apply here: "Hdt. uses ἀποδείκνυμι with a s[upplementary] p[article] to indicate the proving of what should rather be regarded as a hypothesis than a fact" (Filbey 1917: 12). As to his question of why the passage "lapses into the infinitive" (1917: 13), surely we might simply classify these last sentences as indirect statements dependent on an implicit verb that is not ἀποδείκνυμι.

ἀποδείκνυμι phrases.[44] Finally, the discussion of the honorific *piromis* that follows reconfirms that ἀποδείκνυμι describes a demonstrative sequence, a list. Since the priests have just stated that each statue represents the son of the previous *piromis* (φάμενοι ἕκαστον τῶν κολοσσῶν πίρωμιν ἐκ πιρώμιος γεγονέναι), it does not follow that the next clause should mean that they "asserted" or "proved" this, but that they listed each example in succession, until they had named them all, ἐς ὃ τοὺς πέντε καὶ τεσσεράκοντα καὶ τριηκοσίους ἀπέδεξαν κολοσσοὺς πίρωμιν ἐκ πιρώμιος γενόμενον. As above, Herodotus reverts to the aorist in the abbreviated account of how the listing progressed, from first to last.

The syntax then supports reevaluating ἀποδείκνυμι, but even more so do the curious contents of this collection itself. Imagine for a moment its composition: a group of countable and visually quantifiable objects, statues representing people, arranged in the central space of the temple. Herodotus himself understands, as he distances himself from Hecataeus, that these statues constitute a visual genealogy, commensurate with the succession list he hears, and a standard accompaniment to the verbal tally of names.[45] At a certain point, too, the distinction between historical figure and statue seems to disintegrate. The final lines of the passage fuse human and statue completely: "until they had enumerated all 345 statues, each one being a *piromis* son of a *piromis*." At the same time, just as the statues themselves become one with the men they represent, so too does the act of pointing them out merge with the act of listing their names. The verb ἀπεδείκνυσαν, then, has double valence, referring quite literally to the priests' physical demonstration to Herodotus, but to their verbal genealogy as well. The statues themselves stand as an example of a visual list, a surrogate for the actual humans that make up the genealogy, which may not have a written form but at the very least exists inasmuch as the priest verbalizes it. What the priests provide Herodotus, as he describes it, is a kind of proto-inventory, a verbal account that must take place in real time alongside its physical contents. The verb ἀποδείκνυμι refers to these two qualities – the listing (verbal) and the showing (physical). At its roots, then, the inventory begins as an accompaniment to a collection, not an autonomous entity. In the absence of the collection, though, the inventory not only persists, but also

[44] For example, de Sélincourt 1996: 139.
[45] Moyer has usefully re-examined this episode from a perspective that shuns previous Hellenocentric and orientalizing analytical models: "[t]he confrontation, therefore, of the Ionian historians with the statues of the Theban priests signifies an important intersection of Greek and Egyptian notions of the past, and a reorientation of Greek historical awareness" (Moyer 2002: 87).

threatens to displace the collection itself. While the physical artifacts begin as the authentic entities, the verbal record eventually supersedes them.

For Herodotus, this display, together with its verbalization in a series, constitutes a fundamental method of making history. It is, however, one he aims to improve upon, and this is one crucial difference between his methodology and that which he ascribes to Hecataeus. As Herodotus presents it, Hecataeus essentially regurgitates his own genealogy when presented with the Egyptians' multimedia verbal and visual list, and in doing so rather misses the point.[46] Herodotus, by contrast, engages with the physical Egyptian collection as both a group of objects and a list of names, and accordingly describes it in Greek terms, with ἀποδείκνυμι. The episode with the priests thus encapsulates both authors' entire works: Hecataeus' as mere γενεαλογίαι, Herodotus' as ἀπόδεξις.[47]

This is not the only moment in which Herodotus applies ἀποδείκνυμι and ἀπόδεξις to the Egyptians' account of their history. In his description of the deeds of the kings he includes two examples (2.101):

> τῶν δὲ ἄλλων βασιλέων, οὐ γὰρ ἔλεγον οὐδεμίαν ἔργων ἀπόδεξιν, †κατ' οὐδὲν εἶναι λαμπρότητος,† πλὴν ἑνὸς τοῦ ἐσχάτου αὐτῶν Μοίριος. τοῦτον δὲ ἀποδέξασθαι μνημόσυνα τοῦ Ἡφαίστου τὰ πρὸς βορέην ἄνεμον τετραμμένα προπύλαια, λίμνην τε ὀρύξαι, τῆς ἡ περίοδος ὅσων ἐστὶ σταδίων ὕστερον δηλώσω, πυραμίδας τε ἐν αὐτῇ οἰκοδομῆσαι, τῶν τοῦ μεγάθεος πέρι ὁμοῦ αὐτῇ τῇ λίμνῃ ἐπιμνήσομαι. τοῦτον μὲν τοσαῦτα ἀποδέξασθαι, τῶν δὲ ἄλλων οὐδένα οὐδέν.

> But as to the other kings, because they did not state any enumeration of their deeds, none is particularly outstanding besides one toward the end, Moeris. This one, as the record shows, built the gates of the Hephaestus temple facing north, and the harbor, the measurements of whose perimeter I shall mention later, and built the pyramids on it, whose size I shall recount to be about the same as that harbor. This one made a display of so many deeds, but none of the others made any.

---

[46] On this passage see Dewald 2002. See Murray 2007a: 22–23 on the general lack of a tradition of genealogy in Greece; Bertelli 2001 for the view that the Greek historiographic tradition was distinct from Egyptian and Near Eastern ones, innovating on both. For a different opinion, see S. West 1991: 159, who concludes that Herodotus is not "so much concerned about a snub to Hecataeus' pride in his lineage as with the devaluation of his genealogical researches, impressive as they might seem by Greek standards, when their results are compared with the Egyptian historical traditions."

[47] For the notion that Hecataean genealogy is the background to Greek written historiography, see Bertelli 2001: 72. In discussing this scene, Bertelli (91) notes but does not offer a reason why Herodotus does not quote Hecataeus; this is perhaps in part because Herodotus prefers the Theban audiovisual style of genealogy to the Ionian one.

When Herodotus says that Moeris "made a display of so many deeds," I would suggest that he is speaking not so much of his public works as of an account or catalogue of them, as must be the meaning of ἀπόδεξις at the start of the passage, too. It may denote something very formal, such as a boasting inscription of the type common among Egyptian and Near Eastern kings, or perhaps just an oral catalogue with a visual component, a tour-guide's account of each building, or even a list of the monuments, such as the brief one he himself gives here. Again, however, from an initial physical showing, ἀποδείκνυμι takes on a specialized meaning, still with the sense of a visual display, but involving words.[48] This semantic range seems particularly fitting in the case of a monumental inscription, which makes an iconic as well as a verbal impact on a viewer or reader. At the same time, the change entails a metaphoric leap on the part of the user: whereas one can quite literally make an ἀπόδεξις of a physical collection of goods, there must be a general faith in the authority of inscriptions or words for them to serve as displays of wealth, and for ἀπόδεξις to refer to them.[49] For someone in the possession of a collection of impressive works, then, displaying them corresponds with presenting a verbal catalogue of them, and cataloguing them, in turn, becomes an acceptable manner of display. Once the semantic range of ἀποδείκνυμι allows for this less strictly physical sense, "display a collection in words," it can then apply to any verbal demonstration or proof of a point.

It is of course not without great significance that Herodotus uses ἀποδείκνυμι in the sense of "list" to describe a sequence of events leading from the past to the present, and to discuss the production of monuments and cultural memory. Both the genealogy and the description of Moeris' deeds bear consequence for Herodotus' self-definition as author and producer of history. In the first place, these moments of ἀπόδεξις sharply distinguish Herodotus' brand of historiography from Hecataeus'. At the same time, they do not wholly align him with foreign traditions either; while he admires the Egyptians' educational show-and-tell, he also clearly views his own project as something beyond its scope, and – crucially – not requiring visual aid.[50] And so, when we return to the prologue of the

---

[48] This is not strictly one of the seven intermediate examples, but the semantics are clear in it, too. Powell interprets it as "display a concrete object."

[49] This is one manifestation of "material engagement" of a symbolic sort, as outlined, e.g. by Renfrew 2004.

[50] Vannicelli 2001: 234 points out that, for all his glorification of the Egyptian λόγιοι as foundational historiographers, Herodotus still maintains a "unitary historical vision" into which he inserts the Greek tradition.

Histories, Herodotus' famous titling emerges all the more innovative (1.1)[51]:

Ἡροδότου Ἁλικαρνησσέος ἱστορίης ἀπόδεξις ἥδε, ὡς μήτε τὰ γενόμενα ἐξ ἀνθρώπων τῷ χρόνῳ ἐξίτηλα γένηται, μήτε ἔργα μεγάλα τε καὶ θωμαστά, τὰ μὲν Ἕλλησι, τὰ δὲ βαρβάροισι ἀποδεχθέντα, ἀκλέα γένηται, τά τε ἄλλα καὶ <δὴ καὶ> δι' ἣν αἰτίην ἐπολέμησαν ἀλλήλοισι.

This is the display of inquiry of Herodotus of Halicarnassus, so that neither the events of men become effaced in time, nor great and wondrous deeds, some done by Greeks and others by non-Greeks, become unspoken of, nor above all does the cause for which they fought against one another.

Much has of course been made already of this passage, and especially of the presence of the word ἀπόδεξις in it.[52] I will not attempt to engage all of these studies here, but rather suggest that the semantics I have outlined in the rest of Herodotus reveal an alternative and perhaps clearer interpretive possibility to this opening. Previous interpretations tend to define the word in accordance with their overall view of the *Histories'* generic affinities or mode of composition. So it may mean "written publication," "(oral) performance," or, for those interested in aligning Herodotus with other intellectual genres, "work-in-progress."[53] In an insightful explication, Bakker has come to the conclusion, based partly on formulaics and etymology, that ἀπόδεξις means "the enactment of an accomplishment."[54] While his definition fits numerous examples of passages with ἀποδείκνυμι or ἀπόδεξις, and while I follow him in rejecting such simple renderings as "proof" or "performance" for this context, I nonetheless believe that we can be somewhat more precise. Herodotus gives the name ἀπόδεξις to a work that is neither a simple statement nor of course something purely physical, but rather a text that delivers, via the medium of words, all the marvels of

---

[51] As Bakker has stated, albeit with a different interpretation of ἀπόδεξις: "*historiēs apodexis*, far from being a mere title or a characterization of the 'medial' aspects of the work, is a bold, even provocative, expression stating nothing less than the communicative purpose and ambition of Herodotus' work" (Bakker 2002: 12).

[52] Asheri 2007: 72 provides a fairly exhaustive bibliography, to which ought to be added especially Bakker, who also provides a summary (2002: 8 n.11).

[53] Asheri 2007: 72–73 also suggests understanding either publication or performance, but limits his commentary to general remarks: "The main idea of the sentence is clear: Herodotus wants to save from oblivion or all-devouring time what deserves to be remembered." Among the main recent proponents of differing views, including those that Bakker 2002 takes up, are Nagy 1990 ("performance"), Thomas 1992: 125–126 and 2000: 262–264 ("oral presentation, prepublication, as scientific ἐπίδειξις, whence work-in-progress"), and Lateiner 1989: 7, 9–10 ("demonstration of research").

[54] Bakker 2002: 29.

autopsy. It achieves on its own what the Egyptians require a timed audio-visual presentation to convey; it is a special verbal facsimile of all he has seen and discovered, and it singularly carries the double valence of "display" and "enumeration." The question of what ἀπόδεξις means is perhaps not so much one of oral versus written exposition, or of performance versus publication, but rather of figurative versus physical, metaphoric versus material.

I do not intend to discount the binary apparent in the rest of the sentence, of happenings effaced and deeds going unspoken of, in which we may well read a juxtaposition of the written and oral traditions, especially as ἐξίτηλα seems a term often earmarked for describing inscriptions as well as, as Pelliccia has argued, genealogical extinction.[55] I would suggest that ἀπόδεξις in the sense of "multimedia inventory," rather than aligning Herodotus' work with an oral or written genre, also satisfies the requirements of both media, for, as we have seen, it denotes either a list told or a list inscribed. Moreover, the duality that inheres in this sense of ἀπόδεξις reinforces the fundamental ambivalence, most famously explicated by Immerwahr, in the notion of ἔργον: at once a deed and a monument of a given achievement – both what happened, and the chronicling of it.[56] In θωμαστά as well we may view hints of that magical conjuring, of the monument's ability to reenact the ἔργον-deed, a power that lists can have as well.[57] So when we arrive at ἀποδεχθέντα later in the passage, again, the sense "enumerative display" obtains. The words ἀποδεχθέντα are those collected in a list, whatever form that may take. Herodotus' ἀπόδεξις, then, is the redisplay, his recataloguing of those collected ἔργα, an elaborate inventory of people, places, events, and their monuments, the word for both the methodology and the product of examining the physical and representing it verbally. On the one hand, this process recalls non-Greek systems of using lists to represent object collections, as we see with the Theban priests. On the other, though, it foreshadows the events, deeds, and physical wealth that Herodotus will collect in words as the work

---

[55] Pelliccia 1992: 74–80. Pollux (*Onom.* 5.150) includes ἐξίτηλος in a list of words describing inscribed texts. While he does not treat the meaning of ἐξίτηλα, Bakker's interpretation of the deictic demonstrative ἥδε at the start of the passage leads him to liken Herodotus' account to an inscription of the type most pointedly described in Svenbro 1993: 30. More recently Dewald 2012: 62 has aligned ἐξίτηλα with Herodotus' desire to "eschew an interest in the themes of traditional myth and legend, in particular, the deeds of gods and superhuman heroes."

[56] Immerwahr 1960, especially 264–266. Along these same lines, Bakker 2002: 31 says of ἀπόδεξις, "the recording of 'great monuments' . . . becomes a great monument itself, an achievement on a par with the *megala erga apodekhthenta*, whose *kleos* it intends to preserve."

[57] For the magical efficacy of lists, see Gordon 1999; for a perspective on words as representative of things in magic, see Weiner 1983: 692.

progresses.[58] The exact objects of this accounting, τὰ γενόμενα, as has been noted, are neither specified nor easily retrievable.[59] But it is ἀπόδεξις that saves them from effacement. While the word may not yet carry a specific oral or written nuance, it is tempting to think of Herodotus' work as a whole as behaving much like a later inscribed inventory: a grand verbal catalogue of all the discrete goings-on of his world, each one an entry to be accounted. Furthermore, if one understands ἀπόδεξις as some sort of list, the λόγιοι, who appear in the following section of the prologue and with whom Herodotus arguably aligns himself, truly act as chroniclers, reckoners, makers of λογίσματα.[60] We might think of them as the logical successors of Pindar's λόγιοι from above, who extol the ἀποδεχθέντα of victors.

Understanding *apodexis* as "an enumerative display in words" not only sheds light on the prologue: the same process describes other sections of the *Histories* in which Herodotus puts his innovative program into practice. It refers, for example, to his own description of the Theban dynasties, which do not require a physical component for his list, or to his extensive catalogues of the Persians' satrapies (Book 3) or armies (Book 7). While other peoples have made displays in material goods, Herodotus makes his using only words; thus only in his work is the transfer to verbal display completely realized. This agenda of innovative redisplay, moreover, may help to account for the discrepancies between Herodotus' own accounts and native ones, a longstanding problem.[61]

In addition to his more grandiose catalogues, Herodotus also engages in a more specific and discrete brand of *apodexis*: the listing of specific objects in specific places, such as the dedications of Croesus, with which this study began. The trajectory of the goods themselves mirrors the shift in the meaning of *apodexis*, beginning as a collection on physical display, possibly accompanied by an inventory at Delphi, but ultimately realized as an autonomous text in Herodotus' reiteration, no longer accompanied by the objects or in need of visual augmentation. Rather, he provides verbal snapshots of the collection, taken at particular moments. It is the list form, I would argue, and the physicality inherent in *apodexis*, that allows for this material quality to emerge,

---

[58] See Immerwahr 1960: 264–266.

[59] Bakker 2002: 18 translates "things made to happen by men"; Dewald 2012: 62 translates "things done by human beings." On objects see also Dewald 1993.

[60] Because this analysis concerns the use of a small genre (the catalogue) more than the reclassification of a large one (history), I do not intend to press this reading much further. For Herodotus' self-identification with the λόγιοι, see Nagy 1987 and 1990, Luraghi 2006 (cf., however, Luraghi 2009: 455–456 and Kurke 2010: 375).

[61] Armayor 1978 addresses the inconsistencies of the Persian catalogues in particular; cf. Laird 1921. See Prakken 1940 for Herodotus' use of Spartan king-lists.

where more standard prose might not. To assist in the facsimile too, it is essential that the list provide as detailed a record as possible – Herodotus notes the precise placements of objects, whether they moved, and their current conditions. This is quite similar to the function that inscriptions will later begin to fulfill in Athens as temple administrators record and publish on stone the contents of treasuries. It is no coincidence, I think, that approximately when *apodeiknumi* comes to denote the verbal display of a collection, the first extant Attic epigraphic inventories appear in the 430s. Of course, displaying a list of Croesus' gifts, and citing Xerxes' inventory of them, reiterates a concept with which these characters are all too familiar: the inescapable perishability of treasure. The vicissitudes of fortune and the threat of plunder encourage – demand, even – that some record of material wealth exist besides autopsy. An inventory initially might complement its contents, but once the physical treasure becomes fragmented, lost, or stolen, the list persists not only as an acceptable substitute, but also as a new original.[62]

Herodotus' facsimile, finally, acts as a virtual collection for an audience who may never lay eyes on everything (or anything) that he has, and so the list also functions as a new original for them. In modern terms, we might think of it as a simulcast, but with no concomitant live performance. Herodotus, meanwhile, becomes an ambassador to an audience preoccupied with, among other things, the seductive luxuriousness of Egypt and the East and the burgeoning prosperity of Athens. It is of vital importance that he provide both an accurate representation of what exists in the non-Greek world and a usable example of how the Greeks should account for and display their own valuable things. And where Croesus' original set of dedications may not be physically accessible, Herodotus furnishes it via *apodexis*.

What, then, is at stake for Greek listmaking on the one hand and Herodotus on the other? First of all, we can observe in the *Histories* a new process and protocol for accounting for possessions. While other peoples have made inventories before, Herodotus introduces the Greek audience to the legitimate way of counting: through naming and illustrative listing, *apodexis*. Though a somewhat similar process occurs in the Homeric

---

[62] Moreover, if the contents were of no import, the list would not be necessary either. Compare this abridged catalogue (8.85):

> ἔχω μέν νυν συχνῶν οὐνόματα τριηράρχων καταλέξαι τῶν νέας Ἑλληνίδας ἑλόντων, χρήσομαι δὲ αὐτοῖσι οὐδὲν πλὴν Θεομήστορός τε τοῦ Ἀνδροδάμαντος καὶ Φυλάκου τοῦ Ἱστιαίου, Σαμίων ἀμφοτέρων.

> I have it at my disposal to list the names of the many captains who captured the Greeks' ships, but I will make use of none except Theomestor the son of Androdamas and Phylacus the son of Histiaeus, both Samians.

poems, the objects there lack the cultural immediacy of those in Herodotus. The poet does not catalogue Priam's ransom or Agamemnon's offering for the audience because they need to be convinced of the lavishness of their contents; rather, he does so out of formulaic protocol and attention to record-keeping and memory practices of the legendary past. Herodotus, by contrast, acts as ambassador to an audience preoccupied with two key phenomena: the luxuriousness of the East, and the burgeoning prosperity of Athens. It is of vital importance that he provide both an accurate representation of what exists in the others' world, and a usable example for the Hellenes of how to count their own things.

Cataloguing the possessions, natural resources, or even practices of the enemy or object of conquest is a mode of taking ownership and control; this, too, is often theorized as the ultimate aim of archivism. While Herodotus' aims may be more modest, he operates on a similar principle, namely that the first step in appropriating the riches of the barbarian is to collect them. Since he cannot amass them in the physical world, he must do so verbally. While this kind of representation is not exclusively or originally Greek, and indeed Herodotus seems to have had plenty of contact with foreign inventories, his own rhetorical practice of catalogue draws on Homeric epic, wisdom literature, and the discourses of medicine, science, and law.[63] By presenting things this way Herodotus succeeds in making two translations: the first of object into word, and the second of foreign into Greek – a rather clever turn. It is an act of cultural transference not unlike the one Croesus articulates when he tells Cyrus that his men are plundering a city that now belongs to him (1.88), yet of course by happy circumstance he might say: the objects he is inventorying for the Greeks are now their own. That the first Athenian records of this kind begin to appear during approximately the same time-frame as Herodotus' composition of the *Histories*, then, should come as no surprise, and forms the subject of the next chapter.

---

[63] Things generally in the domain of the canonical seven sages, themselves the elements of many a list and with a rich history of dedications, as at Delphi:

ἀνέθεσαν τῷ Ἀπόλλωνι εἰς τὸν νεὼν τὸν ἐν Δελφοῖς, γράψαντες ταῦτα ἃ δὴ πάντες ὑμνοῦσιν (Plato, *Protagoras* 343b1–3)

For Herodotus' adoption of medical style (mainly lexical), in addition to the thematic "links" between his and these texts, see Thomas 2000: 73 on gynecological recipes, which provide a good structural comparandum for these lists; Totelin 2009 deals with these texts afresh.

4 | Stone Treasuries

The Apodeictic Inscribed Inventory

In the *Histories*, Herodotus reveals a preoccupation with enacting physical displays of collections in his own text, and an understanding of the
interwoven relationship between displaying objects and making lists of
them. These developments are not made in isolation; as Kosmetatou has
argued, the *Histories* contain stylistic and content-based traces of his
consultation of archival documents from Delphi and Delos.[1] The current
chapter turns to study the epigraphic inventories of the fifth and fourth
centuries, approaching the complex questions of their purpose, uses, and
origins. From the 430s on, the treasurers of Athena maintained and
published stone versions of yearly inventories of the treasures stored in
the buildings on the Acropolis until the practice waned at the end of the
fourth century.[2] A well-preserved example from 420/19 lists items from
the Parthenon[3] (*IG* i[3] 353.49–71):

[τάδε *h*οι ταμίαι τõν *h*ιερõν χρεμάτον τε̃ς Ἀθεναίας Εὐφίλετος Κεφ]ισιε[ὺς καὶ
χσυνάρχοντες, *h*οῖς]

50 [Ἐπιγένες Λυσάνδρο Αἰγιλιεὺς ἐγραμμάτευε, παρέδοσαν τοῖς ταμ]ίασι ⋮ *h*[οῖς
Λυσίδικος ....9....]

[Γαργέττιος ἐγραμμάτευε ⋮ Λύκονι Πρασιεῖ καὶ χσυνάρχοσι, παρ]αδεχσάμ[ενοι
παρὰ τõν προτέρον τα]-

[μιõν, *h*οῖς Νικέας *h*αλιμόσιος ἐγραμμάτευε, ἐν τõι Παρθενõνι] στέφανο[ς χρυσõς
σταθμὸν τούτο ⋮𝌆Δ⋮ ν]

[φιάλα]ι̣ [χ]ρ̣[υσαῖ Γ, σταθμὸν τούτον 𐅈ΗΗΗ𐅇ΔΔΔΗ· χρυσίον ἄσεμον, στ]αθμὸν τ
[ούτο ΗΙΙΙ· καρχέσιον χρυσõν]

---

[1] Kosmetatou 2013.

[2] Davies 1994: 202 alludes to the fact that there was nothing left to account for; D. M. Lewis 1988:
304–305 suggests on the basis of the late inventory texts (where crowns have been erased) that
the system stops following Demetrius' seizure of treasure in 304/303.

[3] Acropolis inventories specify items as being both ἐν τῷ παρθενῶνι or ἐν τῷ ἑκατομπέδῳ; this
implies storage in more than one space. Harris 1995: 4 identifies this "parthenon" with the
western chamber of the Parthenon, leaving slightly open the possibility of its including the
western portico as well.

[τ]ὸμ πυθμένα *h*υπάργ[υρον ἔχον, *h*ιερὸν τõ *h*ερακλέος τõ ἐν Ἐλαεῖ, σ]ταθμ[ὸν τούτο

:ΗΔΔΓΗΗ: ἔλο δύο *h*υ]-

55   παργύρο καταχρύσο, στα[θμὸν τούτοιν :ΗℙΔΔΔΗΗΗ: πρόσοπον *h*υπάργυρον

κατάχρυσον, σταθμὸν τούτ]-

ο :ΗΔΓΗ: φιάλαι ἀργυραῖ :ΗΔΔΔ[ΓΙΙΙ: κέρας ἀργυρõν σταθμὸν τούτον

:ΤΤΧΧΧΗΗΗΓΗ: ἀριθμὸν τάδε· ἀκινάκα]-

ι περίχρυσοι :ΓΙ: λέιον περίχρυ[σον, στάχυες :ΔΙΙ: κανὸ *h*υποχσύλο καταχρύσο

:ΙΙ: θυμιατέριον *h*υπόχσυ]-

λον κατάχρυσον :Ι: κόρε ἐπὶ στέλε[ς κατάχρ]υσ[ος :Ι: κοίτε *h*υπόχσυλος κατάχρυσος

:Ι: γοργόνειον, κάμπ]-

ε ἐπίχρυσα· *h*ίππος : γρύφς, γρυπὸς προτομέ : γρ[ύφς, λέοντος κεφαλέ, *h*όρμος

ἀνθέμον, δράκον, ἐπίχρυσα]

60   ταῦτα· κυν̃ε ἐπίχρυσος : ἀσπίδες ἐπίχρυσοι *h*[υπόχσυλοι :ΔΓ: κλῖναι Χιοργῆς :ΓΙΙ:

κλῖναι Μιλεσιοργῆς :]

Δ: χσιφομάχαιραι :ΓΙΙΙΙ: χσίφε :Γ: θόρακες :ΔΓΙ: ἀσπί[δες ἐπίσεμοι :ΓΙ: ἀσπίδες

ἐπίχαλκοι :ΔΔΔΙ: θρόνοι :ΓΙ:]

δίφροι :ΙΙΙΙ: ὀκλαδίαι :ΓΙΙΙΙ: λύρα κατάχρυσος :Ι: λύραι [ἐλεφάντιναι :ΙΙΙΙ: λύραι :ΙΙΙΙ:

τράπεζα ἐλεφαντομένε]·

κράνε χαλκᾶ :ΙΙΙΙ: κλιν̃ον πόδες ἐπάργυροι :ΔΙΙΙ: πέλτε : φι[άλαι ἀργυραῖ :ΙΙΙΙ: κυλι. .ιο

*h*υπαργύρο ΙΙ: *h*ίππος ἀ]-

ργυρõς : σταθμὸν τούτον :ℙΗΗΗΗ: ἀσπίδε ἐπιχρύσο *h*υπ[οχσύλο :ΙΙ: ἀκινάκες

ἐπίχρυσος, ἄσταθμος· φιάλα]-

65   ι ἀργυραῖ :ΓΙΙΙ: σταθμὸν τούτον :ℙΗΗΗΓΗ: ποτέρια Χαλ[κιδικὰ ἀργυρᾶ :ΙΙΙΙ:

σταθμὸν τούτον :ΗΔΔΗΗΗ: συβ]-

ένε *h*ε παρὰ Μεθυμναίον ἐλεφαντίνε κατάχρυσος : ἀσπ[ὶς ἐγ Λέσβο ἐπίσεμος : κράνος

ἐγ Λέσβο Ἰλλυρι]-

κὸν χαλκõν : φιάλα ἀργυρᾶ :ΙΙ: καρχέσιο ἀργυρὸ :ΙΙ: σταθμὸ[ν τούτον :ℙℙΔΔΔ:

Λέσβιοι κότυλοι ἀργυροῖ ΙΙΙ: στ]-

αθμὸν τούτον :ΗΗΗℙΔΔ: στέφανος χρυσõς, σταθμὸν τούτο :[ΔΓΗΗΙΙΙ: στέφανος

χρυσõς, σταθμὸν τούτο :ΔΔΓ]

ΗΗΗ: Ἀθεναίας Νίκες στέφανος χρυσõς, σταθμὸν τούτο :[ΔΔΓΗΗΗ: στέφανος

χρυσõς, σταθμὸν τούτο :ΔΔ]

70   ΔΗΗ: Ἀθεναίας Νίκες στέφανος χρυσõς, σταθμὸν τούτο :[ΔΔΔΗΗ: τετράδραχμον

χρυσõν, σταθμὸν τούτ]-

ο :ΓΗΗΙϹ: ὄνυχς τὸν δακτύλιον χρυσõν ἔχον, ἄσταθμος *vv*   [*vacat*]

The following things the treasurers of the sacred goods of Athena, Euphiletos of

Kephisia and his colleagues, for whom

50   Epigenes son of Lysander of Aigilia was the secretary, handed down to the treasurers

: for whom Lysidikos . . .

of Gargettos was the secretary : Lykon of Prasiai and his colleagues, having received

them from the previous treasurers,

for whom Nikeas of Halimous was the scribe, in the Parthenon, gold crowns, weight
of these: 60 dr.:
Gold phialai, 5, weight of these :782 dr.: Unmarked gold, weight of this 9 dr.
Goblet, gold,
with the silver plated base, consecrated to Herakles in Elaios, weight of this :138
dr.: Two nails,

55   covered in silver and gold, weight of these: :184 dr.: Mask, covered in silver and
gold, weight of this,
:116 dr.: Silver phialai : 138 : silver horn; weight of these: 2 talents 3307 dr.: The
following things by number. Persian daggers,
gold overlaid :6: Gold wheat, stalks :12: Baskets, wooden, gilded :2: Incense
burner, wooden,
gilded :1: Kore-statue on a pedestal, gilded :1: Bed, wooden, gilded :1: A
gorgoneion, monsters,
gold-plated. A horse : Griffin, bust of a griffin : Griffin, head of a lion, chain of
blossoms, snake, these

60   gold-plated. Helmet, gold-plated : Shields, gold-plated wood : 6 : Couches of
Chian workmanship :7: Couches of Milesian workmanship
:5: sabers : 9 : Swords : 5 : Breast-plates :16: Shields, stamped, 6. Shields,
bronze-plated, 31. Chairs : 6 :
stools :4 : Folding stools : 9 : Lyre, gilded :1: Lyres, ivory :4: Lyres : 4 : table
worked/inlaid in ivory
Helmets, bronze : 4 : feet of couches, silver-plated :13: Light shield. Phialai, silver,
:4: ..... covered in silver :2: horse,
silver, weight of these : 900 dr. : Shields, gold-plated wood : 2 : Persian dagger,
gold-plated, unweighed. Phialai,

65   silver, :8: weight of these : 807 dr. Chalkidian cups :4: weight of these 124 dr.:
aulos-case, the one from Methymna, ivory, gilded : shield, stamped, from Lesbos :
helmet, from Lesbos, Illyrian,
bronze : phialai, silver, : 2 : Goblets, silver : 2 : Weight of these : 580 dr. : Lesbian
cymbals, silver, :3:
Weight of these : 370 dr.: Crown, gold, weight of this :18 dr. 3 ob.: Crown, gold
weight of this :
29 dr. : Crown of Athena Nike, gold, weight of this :29 dr.: Crown, gold, weight of
this : 33 dr.:

70   Crown of Athena Nike, gold, weight of this : 33 dr.: Tetradrachm, gold, weight of
this : 7dr. 2.5 ob.: nail having a gold ring, unweighed.

Already we can observe some features akin to those we have discussed for
literary lists. The text emphasizes formulaics, counting, and value, at
times to distraction. Each numerical measure is offset by three dots on

either side, punctuation that perhaps aids reading but reminds any casual viewer that this is a precise piece of accounting, and that it denotes objects of great importance and worth. Weights of precious metals are given alongside ample reminders of material details, such as gilding, and gold and silver overlay or plating (ἐπίχρυσος, περίχρυσος, and κατάχρυσος, etc.). Moreover, while most singular items go unnumbered, the occasional tendency to count "one" (for the incense-burner, *kore*, and bed in 58, and the gilded lyre in 62) reminds us, like Herodotus' short list of Medes, that marking the act of counting is paramount to the inventory-maker. Finally, the text hints at its own engagement with numeracy, signaling the part of the list that will proceed according to count rather than weight – ἀριθμὸν τάδε, "the following items by number" (56). We will return to this text below, after a discussion of the inventory genre and its central questions.

In addition to the spaces of the Parthenon and Erechtheion, collections of inventories exist from the sanctuary of Artemis Brauronia and the Asklepieion at Athens, the sanctuary at Eleusis and, in the most extensive corpus, from Delos; there is also evidence of regular inventory creation from Boiotia and Didyma.[4] At various points sanctuaries elsewhere in the Greek world also produced isolated occasional inventories of their holdings. Scholars have drawn a distinction between regularly administered yearly records and one-off lists of treasures, terming the latter "offering lists" and not "inventories," and seeing them as generically distinct; here I treat some examples of both.[5] Sanctuary officials across the Greek world likely engaged in some form of temporary record-keeping, but far fewer areas chose to publish and display these documents routinely on imposing stone monuments.[6]

---

[4] Select bibliography relevant to texts discussed in this chapter: Athens: Parthenon and Erechtheion, Kosmetatou 2002, 2003, and 2005, Harris 1995; Asklepieion: Aleshire 1989; Aigina: Prêtre et al. 2002, Polinskaya 2013; Delos: Constantakopoulou 2017, Prêtre 2012, Chankowski 2008 (for an account of the Athenian administration and introduction of inventory practices see 127–146), R. Hamilton 2000; Brauron: Cleland 2005, Linders 1972. See also papers in Knoepfler and Quellet 1988; Scott 2011, and Brøns 2015.

[5] See Dignas 2002 for discussion of "inventories versus offering lists," and her 236 n. for relevant bibliography; cf. Aleshire 1989: 103.

[6] Moreover, those who did publish inventories may have been selective in what they included on *stelai*; for a version of this idea, see Constantakopoulou 2017: 225.

While scholars have often treated inventories primarily as a discrete invention of the fifth-century Athenian administration, here I wish to situate them in the greater context of Greek literary lists. In a culture with a rich tradition of literary catalogue – which, as we have seen, often serves to express and manipulate values – transfers between poetic heritage and documentary behaviors seem almost inevitable. This chapter examines selected texts from Athens, Brauron, Delos, and Samos and their inter-actions with the greater list-poetics of Greek literature. Like Homeric or Herodotean lists, inventories are complex products designed to display, add value to, and eventually replace the commodities in their store. Whether or not they serve as ongoing useful records for officials, they allow both the polis administration and the public to grapple with mul-tiple forms of worth on the one hand, and deterioration on the other. On a large scale, somewhat like catalogic literary creations, Greek inventories and accounts evolve from devices by which to record dedicatory objects and monies, to the very objects of value themselves. This process is related to Davies' model of the shift of public documents from "record to monument."[7] But where Davies' main concern is the transition from a temporary to a permanent text, often the change from record to monument occurs on one and the same stone. Many of the epigraphic lists under discussion here begin their lives as theoretically consultable documents, but end up as symbolic monuments. Objects deteriorate, but even before they do, inventories stand as substitutes for them, with their own dynamics of display, space, and temporality. Yet some have seen the detailed content of the inventories as antithetical to the state project. Davies pointed out that inventories show "a stamp-collector's pleasure in the quiddity of the specimens in their charge [such that] ... we can probably detect a tension between the values of such curatorship (and even connoisseurship) on the one hand and, on the other, the more direct fiscal preoccupations of a Kallias or an Androtion or a Lycurgus."[8] This chapter suggests rather that inventories' meticulous character, their so-called "quiddity," in fact reinforces and validates fiscal interests. While it might seem that inventories should simply record objects with intrinsic worth already, they in fact create value for sacred dedications, and can even become themselves lasting objects of this value, projecting civic wealth by proxy.

[7] Davies 2003.   [8] Davies 1994: 209.

The Purpose of Inventories

Scholars recognize three main types of inventory based on their ancient administrative uses.[9] They correspond to three different official actions: *paradosis* (the most common), the handover of treasure from one set of officials to the next; *exetasmos*, the special, off-schedule inspection of items for some reason or other; and *kathairesis*, the destruction or removal of items from the sanctuary.[10] All three kinds of list thus relate to goods stored in a precinct and often in an explicitly designated architectural space. Diane Harris sketches out a possible portrait of how yearly record-keeping practices for the Parthenon and Erechtheion may have been structured; others have offered interpretations for other major groups of texts.[11]

Inventories and offering lists were just one among many types of serial and enumerative documents produced in Classical Athens and elsewhere in the Greek world. There were lists of people of all kinds: magistrates, navy personnel, archons, war casualties, and ephebes. There were lists of accounts recorded by multiple boards of officials: of moneys lent to groups and to individuals, of moneys expended on buildings and public works, of leases of land. Finally, there were lists of income. In this group, the Athenian Tribute Lists (*IG* i³ 259–290) stand as perhaps the most conspicuous physical example, despite going unmentioned in textual sources.[12] These tallies of place-names and quotas, begun in 454/453 BCE, not only illustrate the continued importance of cataloguing both names and precious items in one cohesive text, but also reveal the degree to which such documents may have been engineered for public consumption: among them the largest inscribed piece of marble ever quarried in Athens. The fact that the tribute lists may have included funds long gone from the polis economy also points to the rising supremacy of text – and monumental text-object – over physical goods. To be sure, all these examples relate intimately to the broader discussion of cataloguing, yet this study concentrates on inventories specifically, precisely because they

---

[9]　Aleshire 1989: 103–107; cf. Constantakopoulou 2017: 183–184.

[10]　For recent interpretation of *paradosis*-inscriptions and inventory practice in Boiotia, see Fröhlich 2011. See Kosmetatou 2003: 43–44 for an account and examples of *kathairesis*; see also her critiques alongside Harris 1992.

[11]　Harris 1995: 22–25. See also, e.g., Tréheux 1959 and R. Hamilton 2000 for Delos; Aleshire 1989 for the Asklepieion; Linders 1972 for the Artemision and (to the extent possible) Brauron.

[12]　The standard references are Meritt, Wade-Gery, and McGregor 1939–1953 and Paarman 2007. For new readings and discussion, see also Tracy 2013.

list objects that often do not have intrinsic monetary value, such as wood and textiles, or that stand to depreciate significantly. These lists of objects, while they may appear trifling in isolation, both account for a significant portion of sacred administrative attention and communication with the public, and impart the disparate material and physical value of the city's finances.

The first extant inscribed inventories are those of the treasurers of Athena and the Other Gods, the earliest of which date from 434/433. In subsequent years, the city administration produced regular records for precious goods stored in or related to the various chambers of the Parthenon, the Erechtheion, and the Asklepieion, as well as in the sanctuaries of Eleusis and Brauron. The inventories of sacred items from Delos span the years 364 to 166 BCE and have often been grouped according to the status of the island at the time as independent or subject to Athens, though Chankowski has argued for more continuity between record-keeping practices at different periods; this body of evidence has caused much speculation on the purpose of the lists it contains, seen as "the crucial issue of the inventories."[13] The main divergence of opinion regards whether the lists were really intended as functional archives to be consulted by those who saw them, or as mere "symbolic" records of some sort. What scholars decide tends to correlate to the particular evidence upon which their attentions focus, from which they reasonably generalize to similar texts. Thus Linders has argued on the basis of the Delian inventories, in which dedications move, disappear, and reappear at random, that all *paradosis*-inventories function as a record of the safe exchange of goods from one set of officials to the next – the act of *paradidomi*, specifically and above all else.[14] More generally, inventories in this view record relationships and transactions of officials rather than serve as financial documents, and accordingly the lists that accompany the prescripts remain largely symbolic.[15] Fröhlich more recently has also argued for a "symbolic" function for *paradosis*-inventories from Boiotia.[16] In studying the inventories of Asclepius, however, Aleshire defended the validity of these and other such archives as usable documentary records.[17] Harris, based on studies of the inventories from the major buildings on the Acropolis, has drawn on

[13] Chankowski 2008; quotation, Harris 1995: 63.
[14] Linders 1988: 37–47 (see last page for generalization to all Greek παραδόσεις).
[15] This, indeed, is the thrust of Linders 1992.
[16] Fröhlich 2011; cf. Knoepfler 2012 for a critique of Fröhlich's periodizations of the Boiotian material.
[17] Aleshire 1989: 103.

Thomas and Linders to argue that these texts hold the polis administration accountable to the citizens and "attest[s] to the power of the public concerning the right to know."[18] These kinds of argument can be aligned with broader-based claims about Athens' commitments to the public dissemination of information, and its importance to the success of the democratic project.[19] While it is tempting to set inventories within a framework of civic cooperation and efficiency, the texts themselves evade easy interpretation along these lines. This chapter thus highlights their incongruities, and the ways in which they manipulate and package data rather than present it wholly objectively.

In this, the chapter supports the idea that inventories may have served different purposes for the public on the one hand and the administrative bodies responsible for their publication on the other. Scholarly focus has shifted away from how magistrates may have employed these records toward their meaning for the individuals who viewed them and whose names were recorded on them. Constantakopoulou has recently argued that the Delian texts display the networks of cult, among other symbolic functions.[20] Scott points out that inventories show "what is not on display," linking sanctuary visitors to city administrations and including them in various facets of polis life, especially the religious and political spheres.[21] Liddel's discussion meanwhile has examined them alongside other epigraphic lists, describing their role as "monuments of fulfilled civic obligations," not unlike honorary decrees.[22] Because of the relative ease of reading lists of names, he argues for their use as *both* practical documents and symbols, "more frequently geared to recording obligations already fulfilled by citizens rather than listing those citizens liable to particular obligations."[23]

Liddel's interest in lists' highlighting of individuals builds conceptually on Dignas' study of the texts from Didyma and other cities in Asia Minor. Dignas recognizes the complexity of the question of the purpose of lists but maintains that "[i]t seems problematic ... to argue that the lists demonstrate the zeal and correctness of the officials and at the same time do not live up to basic requirements of book-keeping."[24] Nonetheless, she concludes that temple offering lists from Asia Minor exhibit a movement

---

[18] Harris 1994: 214.
[19] As developed by, e.g., Ober 2008, though he does not mention these records; see his 156–157 for some other examples.
[20] Constantakopoulou 2017: 225–226.   [21] Scott 2011.
[22] Liddel 2007: 182–183 and 194–195.   [23] Liddel 2007: 184.   [24] Dignas 2002: 241.

toward emphasizing the individuals involved (especially through naming them) and "are apparently not the place to learn about treasures and the wheels of temple administration."[25] But must they always be? The creators of large inscribed monuments likely intended them eventually for some imagined posterity. And yet their value to viewers, even in antiquity itself, is as a testament to the organization and grandeur, and indeed the vast resources, of the body that created them. Through the course of this chapter, then, I follow scholars who believe inventories may be both consultable and symbolic at once; the notion, in Dignas's words, that "the Greeks might have had different ideas both of book-keeping and of what they wanted temple records for."[26] The Greek official inventory tradition takes root in a cultural context already disposed, at least since archaic times, to the use of lists as a means of displaying and codifying wealth, and it in fact may in part stem from it. Furthermore, the diction, physical nature, content, and display of inventory *stelai* suggest that these texts serve an archival purpose on a larger scale than one might expect, documenting the overall grandeur of the treasuries, as well as the exact reality of each of its contents. Yet by approximating an itemized account and showing a version of one (even if inaccurate), the administrators of Greek treasuries succeeded in producing long-lasting analogues of physical collections of precious goods. These in turn, by their conspicuousness and permanence, constituted a calculated and curated display of wealth. Making and displaying an inventory text visually and verbally presents the physical collection of monies and goods to a public that may otherwise not see them. Imposing *stelai* make a show and an account of civic wealth that an ancient viewer can comprehend in a number of ways, many of these not dependent on his level of literate or even numerate skill.[27] Moreover, these *stelai* eventually become objects worthy of viewing and valuable in their own right, long after the items they describe have themselves perished. Inventories create this effect in a number of ways, which the sections below address: their use of deixis and display, their formatting and design choices, their formulaic language, and their attention to fragmentary or damaged objects.

---

[25] Dignas 2002: 243.   [26] Dignas 2002: 241.

[27] On numeracy, see Netz 2002 and Cuomo 2012; on the interface of literacies and numeracy, see Thomas 2009.

The Apodeictic Interface: Showing with Text

The last chapter traced the verb *apodeiknumi* in Herodotus from its initial
physical sense of "display" to the more figurative meanings "show in
words" and "inventory." This semantic broadening corresponded to the
list's inherent ability to make a display. The verb and the Attic noun
apodeixis maintain the technical sense of "inventory" in the fifth and
fourth centuries; in inscriptions, however, the term *apodeixis* is not
explicit. On the one hand, it need not be, for the stone more clearly
makes a visual display than an orally transmitted text, or even one on
a temporary or mobile medium. On the other, this function of inventories
as displays has not always been recognized. As we have seen, trying to
understand the purpose these stone texts serve can "leave[] us with more
questions than answers and does not enable us to assess the quantitative
wealth of the gods."[28] Comparative study can help. By considering the
tradition of lists in Greek literature, however, and their ability there to

Figure 1 Detail of *IG* i³ 353–354.

---

[28] Dignas 2002: 243.

communicate very general impressions of abundance alongside very detailed descriptions of individual items but little in between, we can begin to recognize a similar operation in inscribed inventories. While these texts may seem at first to be an act of financial transparency on the part of the state, they in fact purposely privilege only part of the whole picture.

An attention to the goods' physical presence emerges in the early period of Athenian inventorying in the text quoted earlier, to which we now return. This inventory and the one from the following year (419/418) both appear on a fragment of a large opisthographic *stele*, 0.48 m. high and 0.2 m. wide, now in the Athens Epigraphical Museum (Figure 1). Each year of inventorying begins with a prescript specifying the names of the treasurers in charge of handing over goods from the previous year to the following one (*IG* i³ 354.72–74):

> τάδε οἱ ταμίαι τὸν hιερὸν χρεμάτον τὲς Ἀθεναίας Λύκον Πρασιεὺς καὶ
> χσυνάρχοντες, [οἷς Λυσίδικος Γαργέττιος ἐγραμμάτευε, παρέδοσαν τοῖς
> ταμίασι, οἷς Φορ]|μίον Κυδαθεναιεὺς ἐγραμμάτευε, Χαρίνοι Ἀλεχσιμάχο
> [Π]έλεκι <καὶ χσυνάρχοσι>, παραδεχσάμενοι παρὰ [τὸν προτέρον ταμιὸν,
> οἷς Ἐπιγένες Αἰγιλιεὺς ἐγραμμάτευεν, ἐν τὸι Παρθε]|νὸνι·

> These things the treasurers of the sacred goods of Athena Lykon of Prasiai and colleagues in office, for whom Lysidikos of Gargettos was secretary handed over to the treasurers, for whom Phormion of Kydathenaia was secretary, to Charinos son of Aleximachos of Pelekes and his colleagues in office having received them from the previous treasurers, for whom Epigenes of Aigilia was secretary, in the Parthenon:

The repeated prescripts signal not only the officials' attention to protocol, but their repeated physical handling of the items in their store. The formula also shows considerable consistency throughout the history of the inventory: it gives the names and demotics of the sets of officials responsible for the handover, the officials they gave the treasures to, and those from whom they received them the previous year. Slight variations occur, but one element remains constant: the initial τάδε. Where the beginnings of inventories are extant, they begin with the neuter plural near demonstrative, "these things," which seems doubly deictic, for it makes reference to both the list of objects that follows ("the following things") and the physical collection of treasure that accompanies the official handover ("these things here"). It possibly even refers directly to dedications displayed in the company of the inscription, though this seems a less likely scenario in many cases.[29] The word is always fronted, or pre-posed, and illustrates the general principle that "in isolation, ὅδε signals in ongoing narrative the particular salience of a piece of information being introduced."[30] This comes as no surprise, given the information about to follow the pronoun.

The near demonstrative also has a long history setting up lists of displays, in both oral and written media. We have seen that, in Herodotus, catalogues of objects conceived of as collections employ the demonstrative pronouns as framing devices, beginning with a form of ὅδε and concluding with a form of οὗτος pointing backward; in many instances, Herodotus introduces a series of objects starting with τάδε, and at the end concludes with ταῦτα, referring to the list he just gave.[31] The initial demonstrative signals that a list will follow, and the final one brackets or frames it as a stand-alone piece. The epigraphic inventory employs forward-pointing deixis but generally does not end with a final or capping pronominal statement, at least as far as the extant stones with intact endings suggest. In some ways, it stands to reason that they should not, for inscribed inventories, repeated every year on the same stone, represent a work in progress – a text under regular revision, and one that does not have a formal ending until official procedure ceases. The temple, of course, continues to welcome more gifts. In not putting an end on the list, the inscribed inventory thus allows for its potential to expand indefinitely, outside the frame created by the stone.

Variations in prescript also attest to inventories' capacity for visible display. A well-preserved example from the Amphyctionic period at Delos lists treasures from the Artemision, Temple of the Athenians, and Temple of the Delians (364/363 BCE) (Figure 2). Unlike the previous example, this text contains the additional verb ἀποφαίνω in the prescript, alongside παραδίδωμι (*ID* 104.1–7 = Chankowski 2008 no. 19.1–7):

> ἐπὶ Τιμοκράτους ἄρχοντος Ἀθήνησι, ἐν Δήλωι δὲ Αἰετίωνος.
> τάδε <u>ἀπέφηναν</u> ἐν τῶι Ἀρτεμισίωι καὶ <u>παρέδοσαν</u> σταθμῶι καὶ
> ἀριθμῶι, μετὰ βουλῆς Δηλίων καὶ ἱεροποιῶν Ἀπατουρίου καὶ συν-
> αρχόντων, Ἀμφικτύονες Ἀθηναίων Ἀρίστων Ἀφιδναῖος καὶ συν-

---

[29] Several factors preclude the inscriptions' placement near the actual dedications they depict, such as the fact that only the temple administration could gain access to certain repositories like the west cella of the Parthenon, as noted by Harris 1995: 4–5, 81, or the apparent habit of displaying inventories of objects dedicated elsewhere, as in the case of the records for Artemis Brauronia, for which see Linders 1972: 71–72.

[30] Bakker 2010: 158.

[31] See, e.g., *Histories* 1.50–51. In discussing the functions of the demonstratives in Herodotus, Bakker 2010: 157–158 gives an example from 7.61.1, which begins the catalogue of Xerxes' army: οἱ δὲ στρατευόμενοι <u>οἵδε</u> ἦσαν. Once he has named all the peoples who served, he concludes at 7.81.1: <u>ταῦτα</u> ἦν τὰ κατ' ἤπειρον στρατευόμενά τε ἔθνεα καὶ τεταγμένα ἐς τὸν πέζον.

Figure 2 Inventory of the Delian *hieropoioi*, *ID* 104.

ἄρχοντες, οἷς Πραξιτέλης Πραξιάδου Κεφαλῆθεν ἐγραμμάτευεν,   5
Ἀμφικτύοσιν Ἀθηναίων Θρασωνίδηι Εὐπυρίδηι καὶ συνάρχουσι-
ν, οἷς Μένης Μενεκλέους Πήληξ ἐγραμμάτευεν.

In the archonship of Timokrates at Athens, and in Delos of Aetion. The following things (the undersigned) showed forth and handed over, with their weight and count, along with the council of the Delians and the *hieropoioi* Apatourios and his co-magistrates, the Amphyctions of the Athenians Ariston of Aphidna and his co-magistrates, for whom Praxiteles son of Praxiades of Kephale was secretary, to the Amphyctions of the Athenians Thrasonides of Eupyridai and his co-magistrates, for whom Menes son of Menekles of Pelekes was secretary.

The appearance of the verb ἀποφαίνω, radically "show forth," "display," does not appear in the prescripts of other Delian inventories (aside from its restoration, based on this text, at *ID* 104–12.1). This inscription seems to make explicit mention of the act of inventory-taking itself, not merely the exchange of goods.[32] Like ἀποδείκνυμι and ἀπόδειξις, ἀποφαίνω and ἀπόφασις have

---

[32] Though the prescripts tend to be "to a great extent word for word the same" Linders 1988: 44, slight variation occurs even in records from the same official body. It is reasonable to surmise

initially spatial, physical senses that come to describe virtual displays, and both appear in the specific technical use of "inventory" or "account." Thus here the verb does not mean merely that the officials displayed the items to their colleagues, but that they performed the act of displaying them via the text.

Even in earlier sources ἀποφαίνω bears a relationship to listing and to civic order. Thus Solon describes εὐνομία, lawfulness, as being able to display (ἀποφαίνειν) the right values of the city in an enumerative way (fr. 4.32–38):

> Εὐνομίη δ' εὔκοσμα καὶ ἄρτια πάντ' ἀποφαίνει,
>   καὶ θαμὰ τοῖς ἀδίκοις ἀμφιτίθησι πέδας·
> τραχέα λειαίνει, παύει κόρον, ὕβριν ἀμαυροῖ,
>   αὐαίνει δ' ἄτης ἄνθεα φυόμενα,   35
> εὐθύνει δὲ δίκας σκολιάς, ὑπερήφανά τ' ἔργα
>   πραΰνει· παύει δ' ἔργα διχοστασίης,
> παύει δ' ἀργαλέης ἔριδος χόλον.

> Good law makes clear all that's fit and decorous,
> and swiftly binds the unjust round with chains:
> It smooths the jagged, halts excess, blinds insolence,
> and desiccates the budding bloom of bane.   35
> It straightens crooked justice, actions arrogant
> it mitigates. It stops sedition's work,
> And stops the mean anger of strife.

As the collocation εὔκοσμα καὶ ἄρτια suggests, πάντ' ἀποφαίνει gives a heading of what is to follow: the verb prefigures a list of all the remedial measures εὐνομία effects. We may note too the reiterative property possible in the prefix ἀπό: lawfulness "makes clear again and again" (cf. ἀποδίδωμι in the sense "return, recur").

The word in the Delos inscription, then, signals the role of the inventory text as both a record of showing, and a display in and of itself. ἀποφαίνειν denotes the inscription's ability to make a showing, an inventory, to the later viewer, not just the officials at the moment the document is made. Its inclusion in the prescript formula implies that ἀπόφασις – not just παράδοσις – is an integral part of offical procedure and record, and so the stone itself, as well as

that the inclusion or omission of various pieces of the formula, such as ἀπέφηναν, depends on the whim of the year's administrative staff and perhaps the stonecutter rather than denoting an actual shift in purpose and procedure; thus the action and implications of ἀπέφηναν apply to more texts than just this one. Major reorganizations, such as that which occurred following the Independence period at Delos ca. 200 BCE result in more obvious superficial changes (see, e.g., R. Hamilton 2000: 26 n.92).

Figure 3 Inventory of the Samian Heraion, *IG* xii.6.1.261.

the text recorded on it, performs the display of the treasure for a later audience. Much like the process of reperformance and rededication understood for dedicatory epigrams, the inscribed inventory redisplays the treasure and its count to the audience, as if to another cycle of officials.[33]

The interface between objects and inventories, and visual and verbal display, emerges again in the isolated inventory of the Samian Heraion, a text made in conjunction with Athenian officials in 346/345, following the reestablishment of a cleruchy on the island in 365 (Figure 3).[34] While the text begins with the usual listing of the officials who "received" (παρέλαβον, line 2) the treasures from

---

[33] See Day 2010 for models of reperformance in dedicatory inscriptions.

[34] For discussions of personnel, administration, and prosopography, see Cargill 1995: 116–119, Salomon 1997: 84–85, and further bibliography given by Hallof 2000 (*IG* xii.6) ad loc. For analysis of the placement of the cult statue, see Held 1995: 13–23. Kassel 2000: 132 finds some interesting parallels of diction in this text and in comic fragments. See Dignas 2002: 239–240.

a previous group, a later section (35–41) describes an additional set of objects added to the register (*IG* xii.6.1.121.38–40):[35]

ἐν τῶι μεγάλωι νειῶι· ὅσα ἐν το<ῖ>ς μέρεσιν ἀνεγίγνωσκεν ἐκ τοῦ βιβλίου τοῦ σε-
σημασμένου καὶ ὁ ἱερὸς τῆς θεοῦ Πελύσιος <u>ἀπέφαινεν ὄντα</u> πλὴν τῶν ν ἑτοίμ[ω]-
ν· ἐνέλειπεν σκάφης χαλκῆς, ταύτην ἔφασαν θεσμοθέτας ἔχειν·

In the Great Temple: everything in the parts of the temple (?)[36] which he (?)[37] read about from the sealed book also the priest of the goddess, Pelusios, showed existed, except for the things in hand (i.e., in use?).[38] There was missing a bronze bowl,[39] this they said the *thesmothetai* had.

Here, the verb ἀποφαίνω again denotes the process of making objects manifest from temporary records, as part of the new inventory-taking. While the officials making the text likely gained visual proof from Pelusios of the items he had read about, the inscribed inventory becomes the new *apophasis* of what is in the temple.[40] Furthermore, elements of Pelusios' own "showing" occurs verbally rather than physically. In any event, it is the new stone, and not Pelusios' tour or the temporary or partial record in the "book," that becomes the definitive display of objects. Objects and their inventories, then, participate in a progression of *apophasis*, whereby physical displays give way to the list on stone.

A version of this verbalizing effect can perhaps even be traced in inventory-like murmurings from much earlier in the epigraphic record, such as a bronze dedication of the mid-sixth century, which states (*IG* i³ 510):

ℎοι ταμίαι ⫶ τὰ δὲ χαλκία ⫶ [-----c.12–14---- ἀνέθεσαν]
<u>συνλέχσαντες</u> ⫶ Διὸς κρατερ[όφρονι παιδί. ⫶ ----c.8–10---]
Ἀναχσίον ⫶ καὶ ΕὔδιϞος καὶ Σ[---c.9–10-- καὶ ----c.9–10--]
καὶ Ἀνδοκίδες ⫶ καὶ Λυσίμαχ[ος καὶ --c.8-- καὶ --c.8--].

The treasurers (dedicated) these bronze things . . .

---

[35] The personnel here are somewhat unclear; the previous lines (35–37) describe additions made by one Philostratus, who may also continue as the subject of the verb in line 38.

[36] Hallof 2000, ad loc., "in diversis templi locis," but perhaps this phrase refers to objects organized in "classes" or "categories," as in the philosophical use of ἐν μέρει.

[37] The subject is unclear: Hallof 2000 ad loc. proposes Philostratus, the magistrate from line 35; Dunst proposed another (unnamed) secretary. Could Pelusios be the subject of both verbs?

[38] Hallof 2000 ad loc., "res quas, quamquam in promptu non erant, tamen adesse declaravit Pelysius." This interpretation makes sense in context but is difficult to glean from ἑτοίμων.

[39] Or tub, basin, cradle, or perhaps sundial.

[40] For the technical use of ἀπόφασις for an inventory of (personal) property, see Dem. 42.14 (*Against Phaenippus*), where the noun is used three times in this sense.

collecting them all together, to the stout-hearted [child] of Zeus, . . .
Anaxion and Eudicus and S[. . . and . . .]
and Andocides and Lysimach[us and . . . and . . .].

The verb συλλέχσαντες, describing the action of the ταμίαι, on the surface refers to the collection or acquisition of the bronze objects. Yet, like its cognate καταλέγω, this verb too comes to describe the process of list-making; the most overt example of this sense is provided in Demosthenes' *Against Midias*, in which the orator claims (21.23):

πολλὰ μὲν τοίνυν, ὦ ἄνδρες Ἀθηναῖοι, καὶ περὶ ὧν τοὺς ἄλλους ἠδίκηκεν ἔχω λέγειν, ὥσπερ εἶπον ἐν ἀρχῇ τοῦ λόγου, καὶ <u>συνείλοχ</u>’ ὕβρεις αὐτοῦ καὶ ἀτιμίας τοσαύτας ὅσας ἀκούσεσθ’ αὐτίκα δὴ μάλα. ἦν δ’ ἡ <u>συλλογὴ</u> ῥᾳδία· αὐτοὶ γὰρ οἱ πεπονθότες προσῇσάν μοι.

Many things, Athenians, do I have to say also about ways he wronged others, as I said at the beginning of my speech, and I have catalogued his outrageous deeds and dishonors, all of which you will hear shortly. And the cataloguing was easy: for his victims presented themselves to me.

Here both συλλέγω and the noun συλλογή must describe verbal lists; it is not impossible that συλλέχσαντες in the inscription could have gestured to something similar, with the demonstrative τάδε, again, pointing to the objects as well as the list. Some have even taken the text of the inscription to suggest that the ταμίαι were making inventories earlier on than other evidence would reveal;[41] while this is merely a supposition, it allows us to entertain narratives and timelines of inventory-making that move beyond the immediate contexts of Periclean Athens. The notion that yearly inventories were first produced to prepare for the Peloponnesian War,[42] or because the newly built Parthenon afforded, in the words of Davies, "new and better places to store things,"[43] no longer need be the only explanations.[44] Indeed, as Davies himself pointed out,

[41] E.g. Sickinger 1999: 39–40. Cf. Faraguna 2005, who argues that early examples of financial accounts, such as those from the sanctuary of Nemesis at Rhamnous (I Rhamnous 182 = *IG* i³ 248), show an increasing attention to record-keeping and permanent display starting from early in the fifth century. See also Rhodes 2001.

[42] Lewis 1986: 72.   [43] Davies 1994: 202.

[44] See Harris 1995: 20–21 and 40–41 for another version of these claims. Conclusions about the history and origin of the inventories used to rely in part on the decrees of Kallias (*IG* i³ 52 A and B), which had been taken to mandate the publication and production of these records in 434; in their (different) re-datings of the Kallias inscriptions to later years, however, both Kallet-Marx 1989 and Samons 1996 and 2000 have specified that these texts have nothing to do with the inventories of the buildings on the Acropolis. Kallet-Marx believed the decrees did not institute new procedures but were rather "unfinished business, a one-time 'clean-up' of a backlog" (102). Samons interprets *IG* i³ 383, a hybrid inventory-account of the treasurers of the Other Gods, as

confidence [in these explanations] shrivels somewhat when one contemplates the scale of resources which a few demes were reporting considerably earlier in the fifth century . . . On such evidence it is certain that there had accumulated in Attica major quantities of resource in public or cult hands, in coin or bullion or plate, long before any public accounting of them appears in lapidary form.[45]

While inscribed inventories may seem to be novel and spontaneously generated creations, they in fact interact with and echo the centuries-long tradition of literary inventorying.

The Visual Semiotics of Inscribed Inventories

The idea that inventories can be either "useful" or "symbolic," while interpretively limiting, is an invitation to delve further into *how* an inscribed text might function "symbolically" for a viewer.[46] It is worth therefore considering what it means in the positive for an inscription to operate symbolically, and thus in turn worth examining the visual details of the *stelai* on which texts like this were inscribed. The curious care and assiduousness with which the displayed inventories were created should not be overlooked, especially considering the large audiences that could have seen them on public display: citizens, metics, slaves, visitors, women, and even children.

Most inventories of the Classical Athenian type, are laid out not in columnar, list-looking format, with numbers spaced out from words, but in running block, often stoichedon, text, as if they were continuous prose. This formatting gives inventories the look of more narrative texts such as decrees or treaties than of other financial accounting or catalogic inscriptions, such as many accounts of the Hellenotamiai, Poletai inscriptions, ephebic lists, or the tribute lists (Figure 4). As Thomas notes about Athenian public "list literacy," many such documents seem made to be legible to a public with differing degrees of competence in reading; as she stresses, "people looked at these lists."[47] Cuomo interprets the "interspersed" format as a "default setting" and has associated the tabular format with

the only example of the kind of text the Kallias decrees specify. For recent discussion of this text, and the administration and dates of the terms of the treasurers, see Marcaccini 2015.

[45] Davies 1994: 202–203.

[46] There are many ways in which inventories fail to be "useful": (1) they are difficult to consult as a finding aid, because objects are listed in a haphazard order; (2) they are inaccurate, because objects do not seem to be logged consistently; (3) viewers cannot read them easily or do not have access to the objects in question.

[47] Thomas 2009: 30–36.

Figure 4 Columnar format on the Athenian Tribute Lists, *IG* i³ 280.

accountability practices of the Periclean-era state finances.[48] Yet even the official decision not to present treasure inventories in columnar format when it was still available begs explanation.

While they may not be the very largest *stelai* erected on the Acropolis, the published inventories of the treasurers of Athena and the Other Gods present an imposing stature. The *stele* containing *IG* i³ 353–354 is missing a large portion of its top section, yet it still measures nearly 0.5 m. tall (Figure 5). It may easily have been twice this height, and a new one would have been erected every few years once it became full of text. The heights and arrangement of letters also reveal that the creators of these texts were attentive to visual display. Some inventories show a large and widely spaced Θ Ε Ο Ι as a heading, a reminder to viewers and a pious display of whom both treasure and record

---

[48] Cuomo 2012: 10–12.

Figure 5 Parthenon inventory stele displaying *IG* i³ 353–354.

are intended to honor and even address.[49] The large lettering and liberal use of stone space not only suggest that the inscriptions might reach the gods' eyes but also show that their creators were sufficiently concerned with matters of formatting and visual layout as to leave valuable space blank. Moreover, the earlier years on the *stele* have letters of about 0.01 m. in height – not the largest among Athenian inscriptions, but certainly not tiny, and visible from some distance, especially if they were painted. After the entries for the year 420/419, however, the formatting changes: we see in the entry for 419/418 (*IG* i³ 354) letter heights of 0.006 m. – little more than half the size of those in previous years – and stoichedon rows of 127 letters each versus earlier 78. It is possible the stonecutters feared they would not have space to complete the inventory at the bottom of the *stele*, but should this have been their only motivation, they certainly overcompensated, for there is a sizeable vacat at the bottom of the stone. Aside from this example, Athenian inventory letters from the fifth century tend to stay close to 0.01 m. tall.

---

[49] See also Mack 2018. Note that I am not suggesting the inventories may be intended solely for the gods' eyes, as have others (as, e.g., Harris 1995: 17), but rather acknowledging their attempt to send multiple messages to multiple audiences.

During the fourth century, however, there is a tendency toward smaller lettering, though the *stelai* themselves maintain a similar scale to earlier ones. Thus an intact *stele* listing dedications from the Athenian Asklepieion from 329/328 (*IG* ii² 1532s = Aleshire III) measures 1.265 m. (excluding a tenon, later trimmed), with small, so-called Lycurgan lettering, a scant half of the height of earlier examples (0.004 m.).[50] Again, despite the tiny close stoichedon-style formatting, the letters would have been made more legible from their being painted. In addition to being able to accommodate more information, smaller print on a *stele* of the same size creates an effect of more and closer-knit writing.

The format and scale of many of these texts – oblong slabs or *stelai* slightly shorter than an adult human – convey a sense of both grandeur and accessibility.[51] The entries themselves, generally having the three components of item type, number of items, and an optional description, allow viewers to see the relevant basics and examine more levels of detail if they desire. As we have already seen, after their prescripts, inventories tend to list dedications either singularly or in groups, specifying the material, their weight when possible, and sometimes other distinguishing characteristics. The acrophonic numerals describe the quantities and the weights of the objects; these are often separated with a mark or space in the otherwise continuous text, such as the three-dot interpuncts of *IG* i³ 353–354. These interpuncts offset the individual quantities and weights of the objects, allowing a viewer to zoom in easily on an individual entry or segment, for instance:

> Lesbian cymbals, silver, ⫶3⫶ Weight of these ⫶ 370 dr.⫶ Crown, gold, weight of this ⫶18 dr. 3 ob.⫶

A close reader could proceed through the inscription systematically, line by line, or someone could perhaps just use the punctuation as an anchoring device from which to pick out a few numbers. The format also garners some intrigue in specific items (what is the story behind the Lesbian cymbals, for example?). It also allows for a holistic sense of a large mass of objects. But one would have to do a fair amount of dedicated running arithmetic to gain a sense of the total numerical wealth present in these items, and in turn get a clear idea of overall treasury finances. I do not mean to wholly discount that an educated person might be capable of such calculations. And yet these texts do not easily allow for any visual

---

[50] Aleshire 1989: 127–128.

[51] Meyer 2016 provides a fascinating new account of the predecessors of the documentary *stele* form and its origin, which, she argues, stems from wooden *kurbeis* (posts); instrumental in this progression are the Marathon casualty lists.

estimation of how many pieces or how much metal in weight are stored in a given place.

What they accomplish instead, it seems, is to make the treasures seem individually precious, and generally abundant. One achieves either a very close-up reckoning, which calls to mind mental images of individual items, or a very broad, wide-angle view of a large and overflowing whole collection. It is possible to make out the magnitude of each of the treasure's parts, but not so easy to reckon their actual sum worth. This kind of interaction is "iconic" and "symbolic," yet it depends both on reading individual terms and on viewing the entire *stele*. In combination, these two modes of viewing and counting accomplish something similar to what Homeric ransom formulaics do: one is given a set of specific numbers to examine; upon examination, one determines that the collection is potentially uncountably large.[52]

The effects of seeing this stone, then, are akin to those of the Homeric catalogue on an audience. On the one hand, one can approach the text and become absorbed in each individual item, considering and visualizing it, much as one might Priam's cup at the end of his ransom for Hector. On the other, one can take in the whole portrait of small print and close stoichedon, envisioning an analogue to the treasure-trove itself. And again, this kind of invitation to visualize seems especially important in contexts where objects might not be visible to viewers of the texts because they are stored separately from them. In this sense, the inventories act also as surrogates, ways of materializing goods that are not present to the viewer. The block layout adds to this effect, as do occasional references to the spatial organization of various objects. The inventories thus operate by aligning real, tangible measures and weights with some more, we might say, magical thinking. The combination, as one might imagine, results in a very powerful kind of accountability. The numbers are all there, and they seem to add up to a larger-than-imaginable amount.

These texts thus represent not a transparent act of accountability, as has been suggested before,[53] but an act of some manipulation and conjuring. Davies once described temple inventories as an attempt to "exploit afresh the endless riches and (it seems) unfathomable complexities of democratic Athens."[54] This comment was surely intended to be figurative, yet it aptly reflects the message inventories project: that they themselves contain "unfathomable complexities" and "endless riches." To view the inventories, with or without the objects themselves, is to catch a glimpse of this infinite

---

[52] This is perhaps somewhat like the common crime-movie scenario, in which someone hands over a suitcase of cash and says, "Count it – it's all there." The recipient rarely does this; the visual display coupled with some specific examples are enough to be convincing.

[53] Harris 1994, Scott 2011.   [54] Davies 1994: 202.

potential, and to believe in it. At the same time, the inventories share something with Umberto Eco's theory of "visual lists," a genre he associates with Dutch still life painting. He speaks especially of the piles of fruits, meats, and fish one so depicted: "so clear is the intention to attain the effect of abundance," he muses, "of the ineffability of variety suggested." Yet at the same time, he reminds us, these paintings with their heaped-up piles of delicacies can have just the opposite effect on a viewer: "They stand for all that is perishable, and invite us to think of the transience of worldly goods." Even as they conjure notions of an endless, unlimited supply, inventories also suggest its exhaustion.

Space and Time in Conflict: The Evolution of a Documentary Genre

In addition to finding iconic ways to "show" objects, inventories grapple with the related problem of recording objects across space and time. This turns out to be a complicated project, and we can perhaps attribute the muddled body of evidence that some extant records present to the difficulty of attending to spatial and chronological ordering together. The inventories of the Treasurers of Athena undergo an evolution whereby accounting practices shift between the first extant inventories of 434 and the last ones around 300.[55] As the inventories are consolidated they become further organized into an order better suited to a collation of texts than to an arrangement in a room. Thus, while the earlier fifth-century texts include many years of inventories of one room on the same stone, with the contents arranged in no consistent order but perhaps reflective of spatial organization, later texts group *epeteia*, yearly additions, and arrange the rest of the items by material.

The Delian corpus, meanwhile, comprises inventory texts grouped into three chronological phases based on variations in style, composition, and titling of officials from the Amphyctionic period, the period of Delian independence, and the group produced under Athenian control.[56] Scholars have often associated the independence-era texts with a haphazard, even anarchic brand of record-keeping, for dedicated objects in these inventories shift, apparently at random, from year to year in their

---

[55] See, e.g., R. Hamilton 2000: 274.

[56] See Constantakopoulou 2017: 171–178. Tréheux 1959 grouped independence texts into three phases between 314 and 279, after which they seem to become standardized and follow a regular format.

arrangement, weight, and order of record. The records of the Athenian period, by contrast, give a far greater semblance of order: objects maintain consistent weights throughout, and the *epeteia* – new offerings from the last year – are listed in a separate group rather than mixed in with the old items. The contrast has led to the belief that the independence texts would have been nearly impossible for yearly officials to use for fact-checking.[57] Yet, by the very fact of their inconsistency, these texts can be seen to reflect a more thorough examination on the part of the officials, who, so to speak, re-invent the wheel every time they make them, re-weighing metals and re-composing the list as opposed to merely annotating it. Linders has concluded that the Delian texts are records of the handover from one set of officials to the next rather than usable documents. We might cast the inventory instead as a changing facsimile of the collection, such that the independence texts from Delos could present a shifting portrait, not just a disjointed narrative.

Within their organizational parameters, however, even temporally delineated inventories show second-order attention to spatial placement and markers. Thus we find passages such as this one, from an Athenian inventory of the late fourth century (*IG* ii² 1489.8–16):

φι]-

[άλη ἀργυρᾶ ἐμ πλα]ισίωι : πρ[ὸς]
[τῶι ὑπερτοναίωι] φιάλιον μι[κ]-   10
[ρὸν ἀργυροῦν : π]ρὸς τῆι παρασ-
[τάδι τῆι ἀριστε]ρᾶς εἰσιόντι
[ἕτερον φιάλιον]· πρὸς τῆι παρα-
[στάδι τῆι δεξιᾶ]ς εἰσιόντι vv
[...6... φιάλη ἀ]ργυρᾶ ἐπίχρυσ-   15
[ος, ἣν οἱ διαιτητ]αὶ ἀνέθεσαν.

Silver

phiale, in the box. By
the lintel, a small silver   10
mini-phiale. By the pillar
on the left as you go in,
another little phiale. By the pillar
on the right as you go in
. . . . . . a silver phiale, gilded,   15
which the arbitrators dedicated.

---

[57] This notion is the main impetus behind Linders 1988 and the dissertation of Tréheux (1959); but cf. R. Hamilton 2000: 25–29 and Aleshire 1989: 107 n.3.

The Peloponnesian War–era inventories from Aigina also attend to similar details, as Polinskaya has observed in her study of these texts; as she notes, they seem to be organized first by room and then in "clusters" by material.[58] Sections of the text even imply movement of a viewer with a participle in the dative, similar to that found in Pausanias' or Herodotus' spatial descriptions (*IG* iv² 2.787.26–37):

εἰσιόντι *h*υπὲρ τε͂ς εἰσόδο·
περόναι <ε>ἴκοσι δύο σιδερα[ῖ]·
[ἐ]ν τ͂ο͂ι τε͂ς Αὐζεσίας· λυχ[νε]-
ῖον χαλκὸν *h*έν, θυμιατ[ερί]-
ο χαλκὸ δύο, τοῦτο ΙΟ.. [. . .]   30
ἐστιν τὰ ἄν<ο, θ>ρόνοι δέ[κα]
ξύλινοι, βάθρον θρόνο *h*ε͂[ν],
κανο͂ν χαλκὸν μικρόν, ἄγαλ-
μα Αὐζεσίας *h*έν, ἀγαλμ-
άτιον μικρόν, περόναι   35
σιδεραῖ *h*εκατὸν ὀγδο-
έκοντα

Going in, above the entrance [of Auzesia]:
Pins, twenty-two, iron.
In that of Auzesia: lampstand,
bronze, one. Incense-burners,
bronze, two. [Text   30
damaged]. Thrones, ten,
wooden. Pedestal of a throne, one.
Basket, bronze, small. Image
of Auzesia, one, statuette,
small. Pins, iron,   35
one hundred eighty.

(Trans. Polinskaya)

A reader of the text receives not just an account of what was in the sanctuary but a sense of placement, and even his or her own position in relation to objects.

Many texts also list objects grouped by blocks or rows (*rhumoi*). The aforementioned inventory of the Samian Heraion ends in a dizzying array

---

[58] *IG* iv² 787, *IG* iv² 1037, Polinskaya 2013: 615–624.

of twenty-two rows of phialai, with their weights painstakingly recorded (*IG* xii.6.1.261.63–77):

πρῶτος ῥυμός, φιάλαι : Δ : ἦγε

𐅅ΗΗΗΗΔΓⱵⱵ : δεύτερος ῥυμός, φιάλαι : Δ : ἦγε : 𐅅ΗΗΗΗ𐅄ⱵⱵΙΙΙΙ : τρίτος ῥυμός,

65 ἦγε φιάλαι : Δ : 𐅅ΗΗΗΗ𐅄ΔΔΔΔΓⱵⱵⱵ: τέταρτος ῥυμός, φιάλαι : Δ : ἦγε : 𐅅ΗΗΗΗ

ΓⱵⱵⱵΙΙΙ : πέμπτος ῥυμός, φιάλαι : Δ : ἦγε : 𐅅ΗΗΗΗΔⱵΙΙΙ : ἕκτος ῥυμός, φιάλαι : Δ [:]

ἦγε : 𐅅ΗΗΗΗΔΔΔⱵⱵⱵΙΙΙ : ἕβδομος ῥυμός, φιάλαι : Δ : ἦγε : 𐅅ΗΗΗΗΔΔΓⱵⱵΙ :

ὄγδ[οος]

ῥυμός, φιάλαι : Δ : ἦγε : 𐅅ΗΗΗΗΔΔΔΓⱵⱵΙΙ : ἔνατος ῥυμός, ἦγε φιάλαι : Δ : 𐅅ΗΗΗΗ

𐅄ΔΔΔΔⱵⱵⱵΙΙΙΙ : δέκατος ῥυμός, φιάλαι : Δ : ἦγε : 𐅅ΗΗΗΗΗΓⱵⱵ : ἑνδέκατος

70 ῥυμός, φιάλαι : Δ : ἦγε : 𐅅ΗΗΗΗ𐅄ⱵⱵⱵΙΙ : δωδέκατος ῥυμός, φιάλαι : Δ : ἦγε

𐅅ΗΗΗΗΓΙΙΙ : τρίτος καὶ δέκατος ῥυμός, φιάλαι : Δ : ἦγε : 𐅅ΗΗΗΗΔΔΓⱵⱵⱵ : τέ-

ταρτος καὶ δέκατος ῥυμός, φιάλαι : Δ : ἦγε : 𐅅ΗΗΗΗΗ𐅄Ⱶ : πέμπτος καὶ δέκα-

[τ]ος ῥυμός, φιάλαι : Δ : ἦγε : 𐅅ΗΗΗ𐅄ΔΔΔΔΓΙΙ : ἕκτος καὶ δέκατος ῥυμός, φιάλα[ι]

[: Δ : ἦγε :] 𐅅ΗΗΗΗ𐅄ⱵⱵⱵΙΙΙΙΙ : ἕβδομος καὶ δέκατος ῥυμός, φιάλαι : Δ : ἦγε : 𐅅ΗΗΗ[?]

75 [–c.3–: ὄγδο]ος καὶ δέκατος ῥυμός, φιάλαι : Δ : ἦγε : 𐅅ΗΗΗΗΔΔΔΓⱵΙΙΙ : ἔνατος

[<καὶ δέκατος> ῥυμός, φιάλαι : Δ : ἦ]γε : 𐅅ΗΗΗΗΓⱵⱵⱵ : <εἴκοσ>τὸς ῥυμός, φιάλαι :

Δ : ἦγε : 𐅅ΗΗΗΗΔ *vac.*

[.. : πρῶτος καὶ εἴκοστ]ὸς ῥυμός, φιάλαι : Δ : ἦγε : 𐅅ΗΗΗΗΔΔΔΔΓ :

first row, phialai, 10, weight:

919 dr. Second row, phialai, 10, weight: 952 dr, 4 obols. Third row,

65 weight, 10 phialai: 898 dr. Fourth row, phialai, 10, weight 908 dr., 3 obols. Fifth row, phialai, 10, weight: 911 dr., 3 obols. Sixth row, phialai, 10 weight: 944 dr, 3 obols. Seventh row, phialai, 10, weight: 927dr., 2 obols. Eighth row, phialai, 10, weight: 937 dr., 2 obols. Ninth row, weight of phialai, 10: 994 dr., 4 obols. Tenth row, phialai, 10, weight: 907 dr. Eleventh

70 row, phialai, 10, weight: 953 dr., 2 obols. Twelfth row, phialai, 10, weight: 905 dr., 3 obols. Thirteenth row, phialai, 10, weight: 929 dr. Four-teenth row, phialai, 10, weight: 956 dr. Fifteenth row, phialai, 10, weight: 895 dr., 2 obols. Sixteenth row, phialai, 10, weight: 953 dr., 5 obols. Seventeenth row, phialai, 10, weight: 8 [. .] dr.[59]

75 Eighteenth row, phialai, 10, weight: 936 dr., 3 obols. Nine-teenth row, phialai, 10, weight: 908 dr. Twentieth row, phialai, 10, weight: 91[.] dr. Twenty-first row, phialai, 10, weight: 945 dr.

---

[59] The round number is unique, but the stone does not, according to my autopsy, show any trace of a letter; thus I accept Dunst's reading of a *vacat* following the three etas, as seemingly does Hallof in the apparatus of *IG*, despite printing a [.] with a question mark at the end of line 74.

Yet this text also separates dedications by the time of their recording, and by which ones were missing, and by shelves; it thus reveals competing interests on the parts of the inventory-takers. I would venture that as the interests of organizers of the yearly texts change, they seem to strive to maintain a spatial element, a semblance of spatial iconicity, even though they become increasingly interested in non-spatial modes of organization that specifically privilege the differences between and the relative values of the dedications.

This continued attention to spatiality and placement may reflect a desire for accuracy for purposes of identification, yet it also seems, perhaps ironically, particularly important in a context where viewers of the text cannot see the dedications in question. Such was the case for the inventories of Artemis Brauronia, which show yearly offerings from 355/354–334/333, mainly of women's clothing.[60] Though they contain some objects of precious metal, the bulk of the texts describe fabric garments, along with the names of the women who dedicated them, and include multiple references to their locations within the dedicatory space (*IG* ii² 1514. 38–43):

κατάστικτον διπτέρυγον περὶ τῶι ἔδει [τῶι]
ἀρχαίωι· χλανὶς καρτὴ ἄγραφος παράβολον ἔχο[υσα]·
παιδίου χλανίσκιον λευκὸν καρτόν, ἱερὸν ἐπιγ[έγ]-   40
ραπται Ἀρτέμιδος, παράβολον ἔχει φοινίκιον· χι[τ]-
ωνίσκος κτενωτὸς περιποίκιλος, περὶ τῶι ἀγάλμ[α]-
τι τῶι ὀρθῶι· χιτωνίσκος κτενωτὸς περιήγητος·

A spotted mantle around the old
statue. A smooth wool garment, uninscribed, having border.
A smooth wool white child's cloak, inscribed as sacred   40
to Artemis having a red border. A scallop-edged
cloak, embroidered, around the upright
statue. A scallop-edged cloak with a border around it.

In addition to frequent names of dedicators (elsewhere on the stones) and descriptions of the appearance of the items, here we observe attested two physical details, referring to one dedication's placement by "the old statue" and another's by "the upright statue." An apparent third statue emerges elsewhere and posed problems of identification, given the evidence from

---

[60] *IG* ii² 1514–1531, by additional fragments organized in Linders 1972.

the Acropolis. Further interpretive difficulties arise from references in the inventories to two buildings: the "Parthenon" and the "old temple," neither of which labels seemed apt to describe the Athenian sanctuary of Brauronian Artemis in the southwestern section of the Acropolis, in (or near) which the dedications were thought to have resided.[61] Not until the mid twentieth century, when excavations of Brauron yielded an inscription mentioning these two buildings by the same name, did it become clear that the dedications in the inventories were stored not in Athens but at a sanctuary some 40 km. away.[62] Though there were parallel records at the sanctuary itself, the presence of these copies at Athens speaks to a different kind of representational force from the inventory *stele*: their ability to stand in for items far away but felt as state possessions. Without making the long pilgrimage to Brauron, a visitor to the Acropolis and to the Brauroneion there could at a glance observe an approximation of the bulk of the sanctuary's riches, and, if he or she desired, glean a comprehensive portrait of just what kinds of things were dedicated where, and by whom. He or she might even choose to seek out a specific dedication or detail. Scholars have emphasized the practicality of these inventories' entries for sanctuary officials because of their code-like descriptive words and categories, where the garment titles and adjectives adhere to a finite set of options from which to choose.[63] Yet it is crucial too to understand these texts as designed expressly for an audience who will not see the physical contents.

Formulaics of Description

To examine this notion further, we might return to certain ideas traced out in our discussion of Homer in Chapter 1. In the *Iliad* and *Odyssey*, I argued, catalogues take precious items and display them as a unified collection, but also highlight specific items, using the stock words and phrases upon which formulaic poetry is based. In her study of the Brauron texts, Cleland has argued for formulaics in clothing descriptions, positing that the descriptions include aspects of the objects that "vary meaningfully." In her view,

---

[61] *IG* ii² 1517 lines 217 and 3, respectively. For discussion, see Linders 1972: 70–73.
[62] The inscription in question still awaits publication, but is mentioned by Papademetriou 1956–1961: 24, 1963: 118, Robert and Robert 1963 no.91, Kondis 1967: 169.
[63] Cleland 2005 (especially chapter 2).

the purpose of these descriptions is to "enable the users of the catalogue to discriminate each individual garment within a broadly similar collection."[64] Yet, as I will continue to emphasize, specificity in inventories, as in Homer, operates to materialize objects in the imaginations of those who cannot see them. One lexical example might serve to show how these quite disparate genres work on their audience in similar ways. Of the many curiosities of the Brauron texts we find repeated fourteen times throughout an adjective περιποίκιλος, describing at least four different kinds of garment: eleven χιτωνίσκοι (κιθωνίσκοι), one ἔγκυκλον, one τρύφημα, and one κάνδυς.[65] The word appears nowhere else in Classical literature save once in Xenophon's description of two varieties of hare (one larger and one smaller), in which he says of the creatures (*Cyn.* 5.23):

τὴν δὲ οὐρὰν οἱ μὲν κύκλῳ περιποίκιλον, οἱ δὲ παράσειρον.

The (larger) ones have a tail colored all around in a circle;
the (smaller) ones on one side.

The prefix περι- seems to have its radical spatial connotation related to the arrangement of the coloring, implying that in one hare the color goes all around, whereas the smaller hares have color just on one side of the tail. In fact, the European hare, of which Xenophon likely speaks, along with a relative, has a tail that is colored on top but white beneath, whereas some other varieties have a uniformly colored one. The prefixed adjective περιποίκιλος, then, reflects the meaning given by κύκλῳ and describes the distribution of the color on the material in question. παράσειρον, then, we may take as adverbial, parallel to κύκλῳ rather than περιποίκιλον. The "color" adjective is implicit, but in simplex form, ποίκιλον. In the case of the Brauron garments, I would suggest the word also refers to parts of them colored in a circular way: perhaps a collared band, or, in the case of the ἔγκυκλον, the entire circular garment. The rarity and specificity of the adjective suggest just how precise and technical the Brauron entries are, but also how prone to their own brand of formulaic vocabulary. We might compare the description of the offering Hecuba brings Athena in Book 6 of

---

[64] Cleland 2005: 76.
[65] *IG* ii² 1514.8, 1514.42, 1515.2 (restored), 1516.20, 1517.131, 1517.154–155, 1523.24, 1524.146, 1524.195, 1524.197, 1524.199, 1529.5 (restored), 1530.2–3.

the *Iliad* and repeated in the *Odyssey* as Helen gives a similar item to
Telemachus in the palace of Menelaus (*Il.* 6.289–290):[66]

> ... ἔνθ' ἔσάν οἱ πέπλοι παμποίκιλα ἔργα γυναικῶν
> Σιδονίων.

> ... where were the embroidered woven cloths, works of
> Sidonian women.

The compound παμποίκιλος is slightly more common than περιποίκιλος,
but it appears in only a few attestations between Homer and the fourth
century.[67] While the two words are of course different, they are of similar
formation and have similar distributions of usage. Thus the composers of
object-descriptions in both epic and the Brauronian inventories make use
of the same kinds of relatively rare, technically specific words that they
then employ as formulaic terms, over and over, describing supposedly
unique and different offerings. While I do not claim that the Brauron
officials were drawing specifically on Homer, inventory-making in both
literary and administrative contexts employs a similar brand of formulaic
poetics.[68]

It is thus true that the inventories do not give an individualized
description of each object, and that in some sense "the relationship
between the real and 'written' garment is one of equivalence rather than
identity." And yet, the display of the *stelai* renders the distinction somewhat moot to viewers in Athens.[69] For them, the garments on the stone
are equivalent to what is at Brauron, whether or not there is specific
meaning in the code-like use of fashion terminology. While much study
of yearly inventories imagines their utility as related to tracing a single
object through time, both the monolithic *stele* medium and the textual
layout equally well provide a synchronic facsimile of a physical collected
treasure. Therein, and not in detailed accuracy, lies much of their effect
on a lay viewer.

---

[66] Cf. *Od.* 15.104–105: Ἑλένη δὲ παρίστατο φωριαμοῖσιν, | ἔνθ' ἔσαν οἱ πέπλοι παμποίκιλοι, οὓς
κάμεν αὐτή.

[67] Homeric *Hymn to Aphrodite* 89; Pindar N.10.36, Euripides *Helen* 1359, Herodotus *Histories*
2.116.11.

[68] One could expound further on the resonances between the composer-bard tradition and the
temple official one. Both, for instance, rely on the regular transmission of information and
modes of expression to a changing set of authors, who in turn produce another version of
essentially the same text.

[69] Quotation, Kosmetatou 2006: 2.

Inventory as Archive: Commemoration and Controlled Demolition

The tension Eco identified between the infinite and the perishable, and the attention of the inventory to objects that are far away in space and time, seems directly applicable to the notion of inventories in their capacity as archives. Like Eco's "visual lists," the archive has been theorized as a fundamentally paradoxical and ambivalent kind of product. As Derrida famously noted, "archivization produce[s] as much as it record[s] the event",[70] archives also have an intimate connection to both commemoration and loss. Moreover, as Mbembe observed:[71]

> The relationship between the archive and the state . . . rests on a paradox. On the one hand, there is no state without archives – without its archives. On the other hand, the very existence of the archive constitutes a constant threat to the state. The reason is simple. More than on its ability to recall, the power of the state rests on its ability to consume time, that is, to abolish the archive and anaesthetise the past. The act that creates the state is an act of "chronophagy."
>
> . . .
>
> In contrast, other states have sought to "civilise" the ways in which the archive might be consumed, not by attempting to destroy its material substance but through the bias of commemoration. In this framework, the ultimate objective of commemoration is less to remember than to forget. For a memory to exist, there first has to be the temptation to repeat an original act. Commemoration, in contrast, is part of the ritual of forgetting: one bids farewell to the desire or the willingness to repeat something.

The creators of Athenian inventories, it seems, participated in some combination of these two actions. On the one hand, they controlled the layout, appearance, and display of the texts, formatting them to their purposes. While we do not have direct evidence of the destruction of inventories, Athenian officials did seem to have the power to choose to create a permanent and publicly displayed document or not. Despite the continuation of inventories from the Athenian Asklepieion, the treasurers of Athena and the Other Gods stopped producing inventories at the turn of the third century BCE, for reasons yet unexplained. While this shift may have occurred because officials switched to more temporary records or had

---

[70] Derrida 1996: 17.   [71] Mbembe 2002: 23–24.

nothing left to list,[72] it may also reflect post-Lycurgan attempts to obfuscate public data.[73]

On a larger scale, inventories reflect the control of counting on the part of the polis and ultimately the choice of preservation or demolition. Consequently, they become, in their act of commemoration, "part of the ritual of forgetting." This quality emerges most clearly in *kathairesis* ("removal") inventories, which list objects destined for decommission from a sanctuary, to be melted, and repurposed into new items. The *kathairesis* inscription self-consciously presents items that will not survive far into the future and which it will, by design, outlast. While there are few undisputed examples of *kathairesis* texts,[74] those that survive belie a specific attention to the material nature of the things about to be destroyed. A third-century Athenian decree describes the melting and recasting of old metal dedications for a new propitiatory offering of an oenochoe to the healer Heros Iatros.[75] A list of the old dedications follows the decree concerning the new offering (*IG* ii³ 1.1154.54–88):

[ἐ]ν τ[ῶ]ι τοῦ Ἥρωος τοῦ Ἰατροῦ τὰ καθαιρεθέντα
εἰς τὸ ἀνάθημα· νν ἀργυρᾶ· ν τετράχμον ὃ ἀνέ-   55
θηκεν Καλλίστρατος· ν τύπον ὃν ἀνέθηκε Λα-
μίδιον· ν τύπον ὃν ἀνέθηκεν Ζωῖλος ὑπὲρ τοῦ
παιδίου· ν τύπον ὃν ἀνέθηκεν Καλλίστιον· ν
τύπον ὃν ἀνέθηκεν Λαμίδιον· τύπον ὃν ἀνέθηκεν Ἀσφαλίων· ν τύπον ὃν ἀνέθηκεν Νικοκλῆ[ς]·   60
τύπον ὃν ἀνέθηκεν Καλλίστιον· ν τύπον ὃν ἀνέθηκε Φιλιστίς· ν τύπον καὶ ἀσπίδιον ὃ ἀνέθηκεν Εὔθιον· ν τύπον ὃν ἀνέθηκεν Ζωῖλος· μηροὺ[ς]
δύο οὓς ἀνέθηκεν Ξενοκλῆς· ν τύπον ὃν ἀνέθηκεν Εὔκλεια· ν τύπον ὃν ἀνέθηκεν Ὀλυμπίς· ν   65
τύπον ὃν ἀνέθηκε Καλλίστιον· ν ὀφθαλμοὺς ν
οὓς ἀνέθηκεν Κτήσων· ν τύπον ὃν ἀνέθηκε Καλλί[σ]-
τιον· ν δραχμαὶ ἕξ· ν τετρά[χμον] ἀνεπίγραφον·
τύπον ὃν ἀνέθηκεν Κ[αλλ]ί[σ]τ[ι]ον· μηροὺς οὓς ἀ-
[ν]έθηκεν Σπινθήρ· τύπον ὃν ἀνέθηκε Πατροκλ[. .]·   70
[ὀφθ]αλμοὺς οὓς ἀνέθηκε Λαμίδιον· ν ὀφθαλμοὺς ν
[οὓς] ἀνέθηκε Φιλοστράτη· ἀκροστόλιον ὃ ἀν[έ]-

[72] See Koumanoudes and Miller 1971, Linders 1972: 61–62, Linders 1975 generally, D. M. Lewis 1988, Aleshire 1989: 210.
[73] For the placement of records into closed spaces such as the Metroon in this period, see Sickinger 1999: 122–127.
[74] For a brief discussion of evidence, see Kosmetatou 2003: 43 with nn.56–57.
[75] See recently Lambert 2014.

[θηκ]ε Θεό[δ]οτος· *ν* τύπον ὃν ἀνέθηκε Σόφον· *ν* στῆ-
[θος] ὃ ἀνέθηκε Πύρων· τύπον ὃν ἀνέθηκε Μοσχ[. .]
[ὑπ]ὲρ Καλλιστράτης καὶ Καλλίππου· *ν* τύπον ὃν [ἀ]-   75
νέθηκεν Καλλίστιον· *ν* τύπον ὃν ἀνέθηκεν *ν*
Καλλίστιον· *ν* τύπον ὃν ἀνέθηκεν Καλλίστι[ον]·
τύπον <ὃν> ἀνέθηκε Καλλίστιον· *ν* χεὶρ ἣν ἀνέθη[κε]
Νικοστράτη· *ν* τυπία δύο <ἃ> ἀνέθηκεν Εὐκλῆς.
          vacat 0.022
ἀργυρίου δραχμὰς *ν* ΔΠΗΗΗ *ν* τύπων ὁλκὴ ΗΔΠΗ   80
φιάλη ὁλκὴ *ν* Η *ν* κεφάλαιον *ν* ΗΗΔΔΔΗΗΗ *ν* ἀπὸ τού-
του ἀρεστήριον κατὰ τὸ ψήφισμα *ν* ΔΠ *ν* καὶ συν-
χωνευθέντων τῶν τυπίων καὶ τῆς φιάλης *ν*
ἀπουσία *ν* ΔΗ *ν* καὶ εἰς ἀναγραφὴν τῆς στήλης
ΠΗΗΙΙΙ *ν* ἔργαστρα τῆς οἰνοχόης *ν* ΔΗ *ν* ἡ οἰνοχό-   85
η ἄγει *ν* ΗΡΔΔΔΗΗΙΙΙ *ν* κεφάλαιον *ν* ΗΗΔΔΔΗΗ *ν* λοι-
πὸν *ν* ΗΗ *ν* τοῦτο κατασκευασάμενοι ἀναθήσο-
μεν τύπον.   *vacat*

In the sanctuary of Heros the healer, the things destroyed
to make the dedication. Silver things: a tetradrachm which
Kallistratos dedicated. A statue which La-
midion dedicated. A statue which Zoilos dedicated on behalf
of his child. A statue which Kallistion dedicated.
A statue which Lamidion dedicated. A statue which
Asphalion dedicated. Statue which Nikokles dedicated.   60
Statue which Kallistion dedicated. Statue which Phil-
istis dedicated. Statue and small shield which
Euthion dedicated. Statue which Zoilos dedicated. Two thighs[76]
which Xenokles dedicated. Statue which
Eukleia dedicated. Statue which Olympis dedicated.   65
Statue which Kallistion dedicated. Eyes
which Kteson dedicated. Statue which Kallistion
dedicated. Six drachmas. A tetradrachm, uninscribed.
statue which Kallistion dedicated. Thighs which
Spinther dedicated. Statue which Patrokl [. . .] dedicated.   70
Eyes which Lamidion dedicated. Eyes
which Philostrate dedicated. Stern-ornament which
Theodotos dedicated. Statue which Sophon dedicated. Chest
which Pyron dedicated. Statue which Mosch [. . .] dedicated
on behalf of Kallistrate and Kallipos. Statue which   75
Kallistion dedicated. Statue which

---

[76] On μηρός and dedicatory μῆρα, see Nussbaum 2018.

Kallistion dedicated. Statue which Kallistion dedicated.
Statue which Kallistion dedicated. Hand which
Nikostrate dedicated. Two figurines which Eukles dedicated.
Drachmas of silver, 18. Weight of statues, 116 dr.   80
Phiale, weight, 100 dr. Total: 234 dr. From this
propitiatory offering according to the decree, 15 dr., and
waste from the melted-down figures and phiale,
12 dr., and for the inscription of the *stele*,
8 dr., 3 obols. Fabrication of oinochoe, 7 dr. The oinochoe   85
weighs 183 dr., 3 obols. Total: 232 dr. Left:
2 dr. Having fabricated it we will dedicate
(the resulting) statue.

Even as it might attest to the officials' good faith, the text highlights the new authority of the archival document, which supplants the objects in question in the most literal fashion possible.[77] On the one hand, we can read this kind of source as the very essence of accountability: it clearly states that it is a list of τὰ καθαιρεθέντα εἰς τὸ ἀνάθημα, "the things destroyed to make the dedication," and one has no good reason to doubt the completeness of what follows. By naming the dedicators, it also allows these individuals or their descendants to maintain public recognition and divine favor for their dedications, even as they are erased to make the new statue.[78] Yet on the other hand, this picture of administrative transparency could just as well stand as a mere gesture toward the same, an appeasement of a few important figures. This possibility becomes more likely if we consider the cases in which, as Kosmetatou has noted, "*kathaireseis* can be sometimes deduced when damaged votives disappear from inventories in coming years, and it is possible that assemblages of *ex votos* that were to end up in the furnace some time in the future were created from time to time."[79] This possibility, coupled with the relatively small number of reliably identifiable *kathairesis* texts in the existing corpora, suggests that these records were relatively rare productions under special commemorative circumstances, rather than a display of administrative completeness; more regularly, items might slip silently out of both the treasury and its stone record. Whatever the case,

[77] On this point, see Davies 1994, Harris 1994, Dignas 2002, Liddel 2007: 183.
[78] Dignas 2002 argues that inventory texts dealing with dedications increasingly become lists of names in the late Hellenistic period.
[79] Kosmetatou 2003: 43; she cites here her own study of objects in the Delian inventories of the Chalkotheke and Artemision, which she deduces held damaged items slated for melting.

documents such as this commemorate loss and enact the ritual of forgetting in monumental terms. They display very physical acts of "chronophagy": after the phialai (ritual bowls) and figurines melt into pools of
metal that new visitors to the sanctuary will see only in their new form.
Finally, *kathairesis* texts address the problem of absence by recreating and
immortalizing the dedications in text, lining them up one by one. Thus
they participate in archival control by showcasing officials' power to both
destroy and preserve the items at the same time. In this way these texts
also stand as unlikely counterparts to the Athenian casualty lists,
inscribed monuments that are also created to project specific messages
to the public concerning loss. In both cases, lists are offered up as
satisfying compensation to the public.

The recent reinterpretation of a Lycurgan-era record of melted dedications accords with the idea of the *kathairesis* as a calculated document,
designed to effect both commemoration and forgetting. The so-called
phialai inscriptions are a series of fragments of *stelai* from the last third
of the fourth century, cataloguing collections of silver phialai subsequently melted down to make larger hydriae.[80] The phialai were long
believed to be dedications made by manumitted slaves, and the lists
treated as records of manumission (and hence commonly called the
"manumission inscriptions"). These texts, however, have been convincingly reread by Meyer as unrelated to manumission, and instead as tithe-
dedications from metics who had won compensation money in trials of
dike aprostasiou (a charge of not having a patron or nonpayment of tax).[81]
Furthermore, in Meyer's version of events, the inscriptions record an
inventory of objects dedicated at various years in the past, not within one
short period, and collected out of the place of original dedication; they
also take information directly from the inscriptions on the *phialai*.[82]
A well-preserved excerpt proceeds as follows (*IG* ii² 1559.32–39 =
Meyer 2010: 1559A.144–151):

>   Ὠφελίων ἐν Κολλυ οἰ-
>   κῶ κλινοπ ἀποφυγὼν
>   Εὐπόλεμον Εὐπολέμ-
>   ο Ἀγρυ, φιάλ σταθμὸ :Η·   35
>   – – – – – –

---

[80] *IG* ii² 1553–1578; re-edition with new fragments: Meyer 2010.

[81] Meyer 2010; for reinterpretation, see especially 28–78. The arrangement of fragments in
drawings on pages 84–85 presents an impressive rendering of the reconstructed "great *stele*"; see
also *SEG* 60.181.

[82] Meyer 2010: 65–68.

Μοσχίων ἐμ Πειρ o[ἰκ]-
ῶ ἔμπορο ἀποφυγ[ὼ]ν ν
Λύκιν Βίωνος ['Αχαρν],
φιάλ σταθμὸν [:Η]· *νννν*

Ophelion, a bedmaker in
the house of Kolly., acquitted from (the charge of)
Eupolemos son of Eupolem-
os of Agryle, a phiale, weight : 100   35

– – – – – –

Moschion (a metic) in
the house of Peir., acquitted from (the charge of)
Lykis son of Bion of Acharnae,
a phiale, weight: 100

Viewed as metic and not manumission inscriptions, the phialai texts take on a radically altered symbolic value. Rather than serving as a profound and vitally important proof of a person's changed legal status, these, too, become records of past transactions with selective detail and obfuscation. The names of the dedicators are preserved, but not the circumstances or dates of trials or the dedications, nor the locations of the phialai; as a result, a series of unrelated events and people collapse into a single space and moment. Even the formatting participates in the standardization process: while some entries have differences in wording (in reflection of the original inscriptions on the phialai, according to Meyer), all are fitted into sixteen- or seventeen-letter stoichedon chunks, with abbreviations throughout to maintain consistence. What was likely a more irregular assortment of discrete commemorative objects has become a neat and orderly list that privileges the new collective rather than the individual.

The practice of melting groups of smaller precious-metal objects and reforming them into larger ones has been associated with Lycurgan reform and the consolidation of finances,[83] but it also calls to mind instances of individual erasure in favor of a collective value, such as that which Herodotus describes in his account of the 600-amphora Scythian krater (Hdt. 4.81). This object, produced from melted arrowheads the king demanded from each member of the entire male population, seems

---

[83] By, e.g., Schwenk 1985 and Meyer 2010: 59–60, who discusses Lycurgan style and format features. On a separate note, one can also envision a viewer with limited literacy being able to decipher a name in addition to the other formulaic features.

emblematic of absolute monarchic power over faceless subjects. Perhaps, then, we can read texts like the phiale inscriptions as a calculated effort to project an attention to individual citizens (or metics) on the part of the polis, despite the clear effacements of their contributions. At the same time, they return us to the fundamental fact that the ultimate marker of value and worth is not a collection of small metal objects or even one grand, imposing one: it is the list made from them.

Listing Value in Fragments: From Rags to Riches

kathairesis lists preserve collections that are deliberately destroyed, but whose face value becomes transferred to the text. Moreover, its actual worth, or melt (pure metal) value, is almost completely retained with just minor loss in processing, as carefully outlined, for instance, in the end of the example above for Heros Iatros. There, we read, "the oinochoe weighs 183 dr. 3 obols. Total: 232. Left: 2. Having fabricated this we will dedicate (the resulting) statue." The destruction thus is in the details. But dedicatory objects can also disintegrate or disappear organically, out of age or fragility, with little chance of rehabilitation or repair. Compared with metal dedications, those made of textile, ceramic, and wood not only degrade easily and are prone to damage, they also have little intrinsic material value and certainly no melt value.[84] One would think that this kind of predictable damage would be unremarkable and that worn-out dedications might just deteriorate into oblivion; yet inventories regularly describe dedications in a middling state of preservation. Thus in the Delian texts we find examples of "old couches in the Hieropoion," while the term ῥάκος ("rag") scattered throughout the inventories of Artemis Brauronia seems to refer to threadbare garments.[85] The Samian Heraion inventory specifies chairs that are beat-up (συντετριμμένον) or missing parts (46–47), along with two gilded sparrows whose tail-feathers are missing (34–35). One of the inventories of Asclepius may suggest repair of objects in a fragmentary passage (ἀποκατέστησεν, "he restored"?, *IG* ii^2 1534.17 = Aleshire IV.17). These objects, peppered as they are among other intact and perhaps more impressive specimens, arguably regain lost

---

[84] Textile dedications in particular have received renewed attention; see, e.g., Ekroth 2003, Cleland 2005, Brøns 2015.
[85] See Brulé 1990: 74–76 for adoption of this interpretation of ῥάκος, and not his previous theory of a "rag" showing menstrual blood.

value from juxtaposition to the rest of the items. Things made from non-reusable, non-meltable materials become, in the textual list, placed alongside their precious-metal counterparts. Inclusion in the list becomes itself a source of lasting value.[86] Even texts that separate groups of objects according to material still operate according to the principle of inclusion, and a casual viewer will not easily deduce the relative material worth of the items. On the inscription, at least from the far, "symbolic" viewpoint, all objects become in some respect equalized in value by virtue of being written down at all.

While it is likely ritually and bureaucratically important not to omit damaged things, describing fragments lends them perhaps more prominence in the text than they even had before as complete objects, in a sense adding rather than subtracting value. As we have already noted, inventories are as much an account of the unseen as they are a facsimile of the seen. Several key terms used for fragmentary objects in inventories demonstrate this point: the words κλάσμα and κλασμάτιον ("fragment, broken bit"), ψῆγμα ("scraping, chip"), and ῥάκος ("rag, tatter") each operate in different ways to make what is quantitatively less precious seem qualitatively even more so, somewhat like a modern error coin or rare misprint. κλάσμα (< κλάω, "break") is little known from literature of the Classical period, appearing only in two possible instances, while its diminutive κλασμάτιον appears only in Byzantine literature. Thus it is likely with ingenuity and specific intention that treasury officials frequently employ both words in inventories from Athens and Delos, where they appear dozens of times. A representative passage from an independence-era account of items in the Delian Artemision (279 BCE) shows some of their contexts (*IG* xi.2.161.B.39–42):

ἀριθμὸς ἀμφορέων ·ⴼΓΙΙΙ· στλεγγὶς καὶ στεφάνωγ κλάσματα χρυσᾶ, ὁλκὴν ·ΔΔΗΗΗΙΙΙ· πεντόροβο[ς] | χρυσοῦς, ὁλκὴν ·Ⱶ· στεφάνωγ κλάσματα χρυσᾶ καὶ ἀσπιδίσκαι καὶ στλεγγίδωγ κλάσματα καὶ ἄλλα παντοδαπὰ χρυσία, ὁλκὴ πάντων δρα- | χμαι ·ΗΗΗΔΔΔΔΗΗΗ· μῆλα χρυσᾶ, ἔνια πλήρη γῆς, ἀριθμὸν ·ΔΔΔΙΙΙΙ· καὶ ἀνθεμίου ὑπαργύρου κλάσμα, ὁλκὴ τούτων ·ΔΔΔΔΙΙΙ· περόναι χρυσαῖ καὶ | τούτωγ κλάσματα, ἀριθμὸν ·ΔΔΙΙΙ· ἄστατοι· ὅρμος ὁ Ἐριφύλης χρυσοῦς, ὁλκὴν δραχμαὶ ·ΗⴼΓⱵ·

---

[86] Chankowski 2011 outlines further ways in which cults "generate" value in the Hellenistic period.

Number of amphorae: 58. Scraper and gold fragments of crowns, weight: 14 dr. 3 obols. Golden peony, weight: 1 dr. Gold fragments of crowns, plus disks, plus fragments of scrapers plus various other gold things, weight of all these: 344 dr. Golden apples, some full of earth, number: 34. Plus a fragment of a silver-plated blossom, weight of these: 43 (dr.). Gold pins and fragments of these, number: 23. Unweighed. Golden necklace of Eriphyle, weight, drachmas: 156.

The repeated designation of fragments makes in a sense something out of nothing: a longer entry, and perhaps even a more interesting one, out of what has become diminished. While κλάσμα seems to be part of an official technical vocabulary, the term ῥάκος, for a "rag" of a garment or textile, by contrast gains prestige from its association with Homeric poetry.[87] Like the formulaic terms from the Brauron clothing catalogues discussed above, ῥάκος appears in a mundane context but activates an epic past. A representative passage shows the word in the context of other complete dedications (*IG* ii^2 1514.15–19):

Φείδυλλ[α]   15

ἱμάτιον λευκὸν γυναικεῖον ἐμ πλαισίωι· Μνησὼ β[α]-
τραχίδα· Ναυσὶς ἱμάτιον γυναικεῖον πλατυαλουρ-
γὲς περι[κυ]μάτιον· Κλεὼ ἀμπέχονον· Φίλη περιήγητ-
ον· Τ[ε]ισικράτεια κάνδυν ποικίλον· Μέλιττα ἱμάτιον λευκὸν καὶ χιτωνίσκον, ῥάκος·

Pheidulla,   15

a white woman's *himation* in the box. Mneso, a
frog-green garment. Nausis, a woman's *himation*, broad-purple-
bordered, wave-patterned. Kleo, a shawl. Phile, a bordered
garment. Teisikrateia, a multi-colored Median double. Melitta, a
white *himation* and a *chitoniskos*, a rag.

Although it appears occasionally in Classical prose, ῥάκος is more frequently a poetic word, and one whose most ready association may have been with the *habitus* of Odysseus from iconic moments in epic. In the *Odyssey*, ῥάκος first appears when Odysseus asks Nausikaa to "throw him a rag" to cover himself; later, it becomes a central element of the beggar's costume Athena disguises him in upon his return to Ithaca as the stranger (13.434, 14.342):

---

[87] For discussion of scholarly interpretations of this term in these texts, see Cleland 2005: Glossary s.v. ῥάκος.

ἀμφὶ δέ μιν ῥάκος ἄλλο κακὸν βάλεν ἠδὲ χιτῶνα,

And she cast about him also a dirty rag and a chiton . . .

This ῥάκος will remerge several other times at key moments of Odysseus' disguise and revelation in the second half of the poem. Thus the word used in the Brauronian text recalls one of the most famous clothing rags of Greek legend, and the inventory signals its ῥάκεα not as items to be dismissed or discarded, but as precious relics deeply worthy of record and valuation.

An even more overt example of official preoccupation with the fragmentary comes from an inscription at Miletus. The Milesians' most often-noted contributions to the inventory genre come from the sanctuary at Didyma, where regular accounts were maintained of the copious amounts of new dedications to the temple of Apollo from far and wide, from the end of the fourth century into the 270s. But the following text represents a less-common example of the accounts of a sanctuary within the city. This late second-century offering list from the Heroon shows a series of dedications described in varying states of preservation. A representative sample of the text shows its repeated attention to fragments (*Milet* vi.3.1357.7–11):

> παλαιὸν ἠχρειωμένον, ἁλουργέα παλαιὰ κατακεκομμένα
> ἀχρεῖα ὀκτώ, χλανίδες παλαιαὶ ἀχρεῖαι κατακεκομμέναι τ-
> [ρ]εῖς, ἱμάτια πορφυρᾶ βαπτὰ ἀχρεῖα κατακεκομμένα τρία, κά[ρ-]
> τασος παλαιός, σινδονίτης παλα[ι]ὸς ἀχρεῖος, ὀθόναι λιναῖ π-   10
> [α]λαιαὶ ἀχρεῖαι τρεῖς, ἄλλαι ἡ[μ]ιτριβεῖς κεκομμέναι δύο.

> . . . old, damaged; eight old sea-purple items, threadbare,
> unusable; three old shawls, unusable, threadbare;
> three cloaks dyed purple, unusable, threadbare; an old
> linen item; an old Sidonian garment, unusable; three fine linen   10
> garments, old, unusable; two more half-worn threadbare ones.

As Günther has noted, the entire contents of the list seem to be objects in disuse.[88] The catalogue comprises primarily garments variously described as some combination of old (παλαιά), tattered (κεκομμένα), in disrepair or disuse (ἀχρεῖα), or the like. The adjectives

---

[88] See Günther 1988 and discussion in Herrmann et al. 2006: 214–215. Cf. Brown 2000 for non-Greek damaged sacred objects.

are repeated so often as to seem to have special meanings in a technical language that render the objects, once so described, void in the sacred administrative context. As far as concerns the purpose of the document's publication, both Günther and the editors acknowledge the limitations posed from the broken beginning of the stone, but the latter suggest that it may be a list of disintegrating items meant for removal from the sanctuary. The descriptions of the state of each item, though, in addition to documenting them for removal, also serve to create a snapshot of the collection exactly as it stands at a particular moment in time. Entries such as ἱμάτια πορφυρᾶ βαπτὰ ἀχρεῖα κατακεκομμένα not only point to disuse but give a picture of how the objects might have appeared to a subsequent viewer of the text. Furthermore, the general lack of named dedicators in the inscription testifies to the continued importance of these things themselves, not just of the recognition of individuals. Perhaps some critical event called the inscription into existence and the treasurers felt compelled to compile an inventory; perhaps the gradual accumulation and disintegration of so many items led to their being decommissioned and this record's being created. Or perhaps we can impute to its authors an obsessive attention to record-keeping, the sort that characterizes the figure recounted in versions of the following tale:[89]

> This man was a great taxonomist of the old school – detailed, ordered, meticulous, and industrious to a fault. I was told that two boxes had been found in a desk drawer after his death – one marked "pieces of string for future use," the other marked "pieces of string not worth saving."

Yet as it highlights the diminished state of the original dedications, this inventory, just as others featuring only occasional imperfect objects, immortalizes and restores them in a stone treasury.

Document to Monument

From the inner workings and formatting of the inscribed text, we might finally consider how the *stele* functions as a whole. As we observed at the

---

[89] Purcell and Gould 1992: 44.

start of this chapter, Davies has argued for a multi-stage model whereby ancient documents undergo a process of "monumentalization," shifting from their origins as archives into publicly displayed objects.[90] While his study does not focus on inventories in particular, they too share the qualities he outlines: an inventory, much like a decree, becomes ratified such that people recognize it as an "entity," belonging to a certain category and endowed with certain administrative significance and power. It is not just an isolated text, particularly if it is placed side by side with similar *stelai*.[91] This shift, however, is also analogous to Day's understanding of archaic dedicatory inscriptions, which, he argues, undergo a process of "repetition and reperformance," such that the act of dedication is always re-enacted.[92] If re-engagement with an epigram can stand in for the original dedicatory act, so too can the inventorying and re-inventorying of dedicated objects stand in for their original value.

I have suggested in previous chapters that the list has already long been a recognizable and identifiable genre in the Greek literary world, from the Homeric catalogues to Herodotus' lists in the *Histories*, which stand apart from the narrative flow as delineated, modular items. Thus while these examples fulfill the requirement of Davies that a text must have an established and agreed-upon typology to become a monument, Athenian culture of the mid fifth century was already familiar with the list as a mode of recording and preserving collections of valuable items. The epic and historical traditions had long since established this function, and government inventories may even have been a part of Athenian documentary culture in the sixth century.[93] Thus having taken this first step on the path of record to monument through both their broader literary and their immediate documentary past, the Athenians had a significantly shorter distance to go before producing large inscribed list-*stelai*. The creation of a written record, its preservation, and its placement on public display

---

[90] Davies 2003, especially 324–326 and 335–337 (for outline of steps).   [91] Davies 2003: 324.

[92] Day 2010.

[93] Sickinger 1999: 38–41 suggests that, though we have but scanty epigraphic evidence as such, there was a small and growing practice of taking regular inventories of treasures in Athens in the sixth century. Most of these documents, he suggests, were "rudimentary" and kept on temporary materials, such as wood or bark. He concedes, however, that it was not until much later that the Athenians began committing these records to stone, which development concerns us here.

and subsequent maintenance can then follow. The *stelai,* both grounded in an established and recognizable listing tradition and realized as large, imposing, displayed structures then function as something for a public to seek out and look at as objects in themselves, vested in multiple traditions.

5 | Citizens Who Count

Aristophanes' Documentary Poetics

The previous chapters have examined what we might consider the ancestral roots of Greek inventory poetics. Homer, Hesiod, and Herodotus represent the catalogue at its most traditional and – in proffering war prizes, noble stock, enemy ranks and votives – at its most solemn. The extended catalogues of archaic epic and of Herodotus' *Histories* serve as architectural elements of these works, supporting and bolstering their messages, but informing their overall structure and style too. Through their catalogic and apodeictic rhetoric, these texts come both to define and to express things worth knowing, seeing, and committing to memory. By encompassing important things in lists and then performing them, they create an unending cycle of valuation, whereby objects must have inherent prestige to be included, yet gain further worth by virtue of this very inclusion.

From the mid fifth century on, inscribed lists increasingly formed part of the visual text-world in which Athenians spent much of their daily lives.[1] Even if a citizen was not equipped to read every word of these texts or just did not take the time to do so, they nonetheless played an influential role in the visual landscape. Along with the burgeoning of epigraphic financial documents there arose another genre of publicly disseminated text, one that also put the machinery of Athenian public officials on conspicuous display: comic drama. The list thrived in old comedy, as exemplified by Aristophanes, on whom this chapter focuses, as well as in the work of more fragmentary poets. Amidst the lists that pepper the comic fragments, we can see traces of influence that emerge more fully in the Aristophanic corpus, from the epic tradition on one hand, and the temple inventory tradition on the other. A notable example of the former is Hermippus' dizzying catalogue of all the goods that come to Athens from the global Greek marketplace (fr. 63 K-A.1–9):

---

[1] For an overview of engagement at various levels of literacy with inscribed documentary lists, see Thomas 2009: 30–42.

ἔσπετε νῦν μοι, Μοῦσαι Ὀλύμπια δώματ' ἔχουσαι,
ἐξ οὗ ναυκληρεῖ Διόνυσος ἐπ' οἴνοπα πόντον,
ὅσσ' ἀγάθ' ἀνθρώποις δεῦρ' ἤγαγε νηῒ μελαίνηι.
ἐκ μὲν Κυρήνης καυλὸν καὶ δέρμα βόειον,
ἐκ δ' Ἑλλησπόντου σκόμβρους καὶ πάντα τάριχη,   5
ἐκ δ' αὖ Θετταλίας χόνδρον καὶ πλευρὰ βόεια·
καὶ παρὰ Σιτάλκου ψώραν Λακεδαιμονίοισι,
καὶ παρὰ Περδίκκου ψεύδη ναυσὶν πάνυ πολλαῖς.
αἱ δὲ Συράκουσαι σῦς καὶ τυρὸν παρέχουσαι ...

Tell me now, you muses who hold Olympian homes,
since Dionysus skippered over the wine-dark sea,
how many good things he brought here for mankind on his black ship.
Out of Cyrene, silphium and ox-hide,
out of the Hellespont mackerel and all kinds of saltfish,   5
and then out of Thessaly, wheatmeal and beef flanks.
And from Sitalces, scabies for Spartans,
and from Perdiccas, a whole armada of lies.
And the Syracusans, furnishing pork and cheese ...

The passage, which continues in a similar vein, begins by mimicking the Homeric Catalogue of Ships, quoting the invocation to the muses verbatim and perhaps even emulating its geographic groupings.[2] However, rather than immortalize a series of heroes with *kleos*, Hermippus' catalogue "glorifies the prosperity of Athens, a city on which all routes converge, which attracts commerce and is rich in all the precious products of every land."[3] This distinction is crucial, for it illustrates how the comic list operates – by imbuing a traditional and solemn text-form with the *hic et nunc* sundries of the contemporary polis. These can range from exotic foodstuffs like silphium, apples, and figs (mentioned later in the fragment) to raw materials (ox-hide, ivory), and then incongruous juxtapositions, such as an unpleasant skin condition or an abstract concept like "lies." We will see Aristophanes employ similar tactics. But just as comic lists engage with traditional poetic catalogue, they also appear intimately attuned to the world of documentary inventories. Hermippus' list itself is reminiscent of an account of tribute or dedications, with regularly introduced place-names standing in for the tributaries or dedicators. Yet there were also more overt connections to documentary culture. Evidence points to a whole subgenre of plays in which characters played the part of temple

---

[2] See Olson 2007: 158.   [3] Gilula 2000: 78.

visitors and performed descriptive accounts of sacred treasure.[4] Thus, for instance, Epicharmus in *Thearoi*, much like Herodotus in the *Histories*, or a public official, gives an inventory-like account of what was in the sanctuary at Delphi (fr. 68 K-A.1–2):

> κιθάραι, τρίποδες, ἄρματα, τράπεζαι χάλκιαι,
> χειρόνιβα, λοιβάσια, λέβητες χάλκιοι.

> Lyres, tripods, wagons, bronze tables,
> hand-basins, libation vessels, bronze basins.

These inventories-on-stage suggest a deep cultural engagement and familiarity with forms of documentary record-keeping to the point of reperformance and recasting for entertainment. While it may be difficult to draw conclusions based on incomplete plays, these glimpses of the fragmentary record accord with concerns reflected in the fuller corpus of Aristophanes' plays. In reading Aristophanes, we gain a richer sense of how the public may have interacted with the documentary material displayed all around them, and how these texts in turn influenced comedy's own presentation of Athenian culture. Aristophanes inhabits a social world in which the administrative uses of listing have become increasingly entwined in both civic domestic life and the elite literary arts.

The List in Verse

A more general look at lists in Aristophanes provides a basis for understanding their connections to documentary culture. To the reader interested in less mundane aspects of comedy, an enumeration spoken by an Aristophanic character may seem unremarkable. Nursery-rhymish paratactic strings are inherently funny, and no one doubts that these sequences provoked laughter.[5] Why else, but for the sake of amusement, would the hoopoe in the *Birds* punctuate his sentences with quaint illustrative quartets, whether innocently informing the audience of avian domestic habits (160–161)?[6]

---

[4] See Rusten et al. 2011: 65, who compares Aeschylus' *Temple Visitors* and *In Isthmia*, Eur. *Ion* 185ff., and three mimes.

[5] Gilula 2000: 82 makes a related claim about catalogues in comic fragments.

[6] Texts of Aristophanes are taken from Wilson 2007. Translations are my own except as noted.

νεμόμεσθα δ' ἐν κήποις τὰ λευκὰ σήσαμα
καὶ μύρτα καὶ μήκωνα καὶ σισύμβρια.

We live in gardens, on white sesame,
and myrtle, poppyseeds, and bergamot.

Or expressing unbridled enthusiasm at the prospect of forming a bird-nation (193–194)?

μὰ γῆν, μὰ παγίδας, μὰ νεφέλας, μὰ δίκτυα,
μὴ 'γὼ νόημα κομψότερον ἤκουσά πω·

By earth, by traps, by cloudy skies, by nets!
I never heard as slick a plan as that.

And what of Lysistrata's argument that women can save the city with their adornments, which will charm the men into ending the war (46–48)?

ταῦτ' αὐτὰ γάρ τοι κἄσθ' ἃ σώσειν προσδοκῶ,
τὰ κροκωτίδια καὶ τὰ μύρα χαὶ περιβαρίδες
χἤγχουσα καὶ τὰ διαφανῆ χιτώνια.

These very items, see, will save us all:
our saffron robes, perfumes, and peep-toe flats,
our bronzers and our diaphanous wraps.

Scholars have put forth stylistic explanations for the proliferation of lists in comedy. Willi comments that "long, asyndetic lists, especially of consumption goods, gained in importance" as comedy evolved, and that such examples in Old Comedy likely served as "virtuoso pieces" for lickety-split recitation.[7] Silk convincingly explores the list as a vehicle for the comic poetics of accumulation; in comedy's more general "relish for parallel structures," lists (as well as compounds) can express "exuberance," "satirical gusto," and "plenty."[8] In a more extended study of verbal accumulation, Spyropoulos collates and analyzes the distribution of dramatic effects of series of words in Aristophanes, including their capacity for exaggeration, emphasis, and humor.[9] In contrast to stylistic studies, this chapter

---

[7] Willi 2010: 487. Gilula 2000: 83 identifies this same virtuosity in Hermippus, where "the delivery is important in itself, and there must be a change of style, perhaps a change of pace, and a sharp focus on the performer and his skills, as in the case of the performance of a modern list, that of fifty-seven Russian composers belted out by Danny Kaye in one of his movies" (in fact Kaye recited the list live but not on film).

[8] Silk 2000: 132; for the discussion of accumulation more generally, see 126–135.

[9] Spyropoulos 1974, especially part III.

seeks to address how lists behave within the wider cultural context of comedy, and specifically to examine the motivations and functions of comic catalogue within Greek documentary precedents. Aristophanes' use of the list form weaves together two distinct traditions, one new, present, and mundane, the other archaic, distant, and hallowed: on the one hand, Aristophanes draws on an age-old poetics of epic literary lists; meanwhile, however, comic characters and scenarios display a preoccupation with public and private finances, using lists in precisely the ways the Athenian civic administration does: for counting, valuation, quantifying, and establishing authority. Through listmaking comedy thus enacts a complex integration of the literary and administrative spheres.

Comedy in the fifth and fourth centuries finds itself in the peculiar position of being able to borrow from several areas of literature and culture with impunity – without needing to fulfill any of their requirements of content or even structure. As Carey has put it, comedy "finds amusement at social, legal, and religious derelictions which in life would not amuse."[10] Thus a comic playwright is at liberty to empty the contents of an existing literary form and refill it with whatever lexical content he pleases.[11] Such humor only achieves its effects, of course, before an audience versed in the parodic source. Athenians surely had regular contact with the inscribed lists displayed in public civic spaces and arguably had themselves become caught up in accounting and record-keeping. Observing these same tendencies in Aristophanes' characters, then, argues for their existence in the Athenian social landscape not because we cast Aristophanes as a realist but because of the inherent nature of humor-making. While his use of the list form preserves its functions of naming, displaying, and counting, he exposes these same practices to ridicule, and therein reveals the preoccupations of the Athenian populace.

---

[10] Carey 1994: 79.

[11] This is akin to the parody's functioning "to exploit the humorous potentialities of incongruity by combining high-flown tragic diction and allusions to well-known tragic situations with vulgarity or trivial domestic predicaments," and humor lying in the exaggerated new use of an old literary form (Dover 1972: 73, 76). Silk 2000 perhaps summarizes the situation most elegantly (99): "over and over again [Aristophanes] fills the air with verbal presences evocative of earlier and contemporary literature – evocative of all and any literature, from the old epic to the New Dithyramb, from oratory to oracles, from sophistic quibbles to Aesopian fables – but, above all, evocative of tragedy."

Full of Gold: The Treasure-Record on Stage

Aristophanic characters are almost stereotypically obsessed with quantifying their private wealth, and concomitantly with their own relationships to
other citizens' and the state's economic wellbeing. We can identify these
concerns as early as *Acharnians* (425 BCE), which begins with Dicaeopolis'
lament that he has had no pleasure save "those five talents Cleon coughed
up" (5–6), or *Clouds* (423 BCE), where Strepsiades' motivating force is to
stave off his debt-collectors. Yet they reach their most explicit expression in
the later plays. In *Assemblywomen* (392 BCE) and *Wealth* (388 BCE)
especially, works that probe the ethics of wealth and poverty and present
alternatives to the problems of distribution in early fourth century Athens,
Aristophanes integrates the language and style of public records within the
dramatic dialogue.[12]

This development accompanied an increase in the visibility of public
records and documentary culture in Athens in the late fifth and early fourth
centuries: indeed by the end of the fifth century, the number of documents
had grown so large as to incite the creation of the public archive in the
Metroon.[13] Aristophanes' later use of lists specifically echoes the language
and interests of public records; moreover, these plays demonstrate the
admixture of public and private archival concerns.[14]

The plot of *Wealth*, in which the protagonists plan both to restore the
deified entity of wealth to health and to redefine it as an attribute of the
good and not the corrupt citizen, makes plain the basic issue. More

[12] I make this argument without reference to Aristophanes' own political motivations, which, in
the context of both these plays and the corpus as a whole, remain a source of critical dispute.
Olson 1990 describes the complex ideologies at play in *Wealth*. For some more aspects of the
problem, see Konstan and Dillon 1981, who argue that Aristophanes shifts the central issue
from unequal distribution to that of abundance versus dearth. In a response to the large body of
scholarship that espouses Wilamowitz's "ironic" reading of the play (e.g. Heberlein 1981),
Sommerstein 1996 makes the useful suggestions that the politics of the playwright (a) can shift
over a lifetime, (b) should not be assumed to be reflected accurately in all his works, and (c) need
not interfere with all our interpretations of them; see also McGlew 1997. Zumbrunnen 2006: 319
takes a unifying approach, arguing that Wealth presents a useful economic model that "instills
in [its] audience a complex and challenging sensibility that holds fantasy and irony in tension
with one another." More recently, Sidwell 2009 has seen the parabasis of *Clouds* as indicative of
Aristophanes' support of a radical democracy.
[13] Even if one interprets Athenian record-keeping as having earlier origins (as, e.g., Sickinger
1999: 60–61), the transfer of documents to the Metroon signals an emphatic valuation of the
practice.
[14] According to Davies 2003: 329–333, the "erosion of the public/private boundary" represents a
key phase in the development of archivization; while he culls examples from the third century,
the Aristophanic evidence suggests the admixture begins as early as the fourth.

specifically, though, Chremylus all but defines the concept of wealth in terms of the official polis administration of it. As he announces to bystanders (*Wealth* 1191–1193):

ἱδρυσόμεθ' οὖν αὐτίκα μάλ' – ἀλλὰ περίμενε –
τὸν Πλοῦτον, οὗπερ πρότερον ἦν ἱδρυμένος,
τὸν ὀπισθόδομον ἀεὶ φυλάττων τῆς θεοῦ.

Let's stand him up then right back here – hold on a sec –
Wealth, I mean, right where he stood in place before,
ever guarding the treasury of the goddess.

To position Wealth thus before the Opisthodomos, the rear chamber of the old temple on the Acropolis, is to install him before the city treasury, a repository and display site for precious items and the inventories that account for them. The imagery of a repository, which begins at the civic level, also infiltrates Chremylus' perception of private prosperity. Wealth, as a deified quality, both exists in the forms of movable goods and countable wares and causes mortals to have them. Because of its fundamental physicality and presence in a collection, by extension, images of fullness often accompany discussions of wealth. So just as a full treasury signifies wealth for the polis, a full home signifies wealth for a private citizen. Chremylus' language as he entreats Wealth reflects this notion (*Wealth* 230–233):

σὺ δ', ὦ κράτιστε Πλοῦτε πάντων δαιμόνων,   230
εἴσω μετ' ἐμοῦ δεῦρ' εἴσιθ'· ἡ γὰρ οἰκία
αὕτη 'στὶν ἣν δεῖ χρημάτων σε τήμερον
μεστὴν ποῆσαι καὶ δικαίως κἀδίκως.

And you, Wealth, powerfullest of all deities,   230
come inside, enter here with me. For this is the
house that you have to make full of goods today,
whether you get it done by just or unjust means.

This extreme concretization of wealth, in both anthropomorphic and inanimate material forms, as a physical entity that moves through and takes up space, accords with even more literal concretization of wealth that Athenian stone records enact. The preoccupation with "fullness," and with entering as many items as possible into the record pervades archival culture as well. Not only, as we have seen, did Athenian officials pay meticulous attention to material details:[15] Athenian records show what Finley called a "curious abun-

---

[15] Davies 1994: 209.

dance of precise figures, readily and publicly proclaimed, of the size of individual fortunes or at least of individual financial transactions."[16] Like these records, then, Chremylus' concept of wealth centers around its ability to fill up space, to be collected in a pile, and to be parsed, measured, and weighed.

In fact, the imagery of fullness regarding riches has already emerged earlier in the play, as Cario and Chremylus set out to show Wealth that he is in fact more powerful than Zeus. They begin by citing examples of all the actions Wealth influences, speaking in rhetorical questions to his incredulous replies, but the climactic moment occurs as they conclude that it is of Wealth alone that men can never have a surfeit, listing all manner of items for which this is not the case (188–197):

Χρ.	ὥστ' οὐδὲ <u>μεστός</u> σου γέγον' οὐδεὶς πώποτε.	
	τῶν μὲν γὰρ ἄλλων ἐστὶ πάντων πλησμονή,	
	ἔρωτος, –	190
Κα.	ἄρτων, –	
Χρ.	μουσικῆς, –	
Κα.	τραγημάτων, –	
Χρ. τιμῆς, –		
Κα.	πλακούντων, –	
Χρ.	ἀνδραγαθίας, –	
Κα.	ἰσχάδων, –	
Χρ. φιλοτιμίας, –		
Κα.	μάζης, –	
Χρ.	στρατηγίας, –	
Κα.	φακῆς, –	
Χρ.	σοῦ δ' ἐγένετ' οὐδεὶς <u>μεστὸς</u> οὐδεπώποτε.	
	ἀλλ' ἢν τάλαντά τις λάβῃ τριακαίδεκα,	
	πολὺ μᾶλλον ἐπιθυμεῖ λαβεῖν ἐκκαίδεκα·	195
	κἂν ταῦθ' ἀνύσῃ<ται>, τετταράκοντα βούλεται,	
	ἢ φησιν οὐκ εἶναι βιωτὸν τὸν βίον.	

Chr.	So no one ever gets his fill of you.	
	One can get full of every other thing:	
	Of love,	190
Ca.	of bread,	
Chr.	of music,	
Ca.	of hors d'oeuvres,	
Chr. Of honor,		
Ca.	pancakes,	
Chr.	uprightness,	

---

[16] Finley 1999: 35.

Cᴀ.   dried figs,
Cʜʀ. Ambition!
Cᴀ.   Dough!
Cʜʀ.   Being General!
Cᴀ.   Lentil soup!
Cʜʀ. But of you? Never – no one gets his fill.
          Nope! If he gets his hands on thirteen K,
          then all the more he'll wish he had sixteen.   195
          And if he gets that, forty's what he wants,
          or else life's just not worth living, he says.

The alternation of Chremylus' weighty abstract concepts with the silly food items supplied by Cario, along with the inevitable culmination in the lowly lentil, must have made for entertaining trimeters.[17] It also illustrates the ease and familiarity with which Aristophanes presents and manipulates the list form before an audience who has come to recognize it, using a familiar rubric with surprise items in it. But most importantly, it emphasizes and even upsets the conception of wealth's materiality. On the one hand, the list likens wealth to lesser physical goods: Cario's bread, hors d'oeuvres, pancakes, and figs. On the other, it approximates wealth to Chremylus' abstract pleasures and values, suggesting that having resources is better than – but quantifiably comparable to – love, music, position, and moral virtue. The scene presents a keen understanding of the duality of monetary fortune, which has both practical and symbolic value for person and polis. Furthermore, the conclusion that one can in fact never be "full" of wealth again disturbs the notion of its physicality with a paradox: it seems to behave like other material goods, but ultimately does not, for the more you acquire, the more you lack.

This malleable physical sense of fullness that characterizes prosperity repeatedly accompanies the adjective *mestos* in *Wealth*, but also plays on Athenian financial culture, and in particular inscribed inventories, which explicitly replicate the fullness of sanctuary treasuries. In fact, inventories are the only genre of Greek inscription in which *mestos* appears. We find descriptions of various dedicated objects as full of precious substances, such as, in a fourth-century inventory from the Parthenon, of a krater full of gold (χαλκοῦ μεστός),[18] or "golden apple-shaped vessels full of balm" (μῆλα χρυσᾶ κηρωτῆς μεστά).[19] In *Wealth*, Aristophanes reincorporates this documentary language of fullness and luxury and adapts it to a domestic scale, where the cup that runs over, so to speak, is an entire house. Thus later in the play, Cario

---

[17] For similar tactics cf. *Knights* 1007 and fr. 164 and 404.   [18] *IG* ii² 1638.61.
[19] *IG* ii² 1643.18–19 and *IG* ii² 1644.7.

speaks out a grand inventory of the spaces full of commodities now that Wealth has graced his home (802–815):

ὡς ἡδὺ πράττειν, ὦνδρές, ἐστ᾽ εὐδαιμόνως,
καὶ ταῦτα μηδὲν ἐξενεγκόντ᾽ οἴκοθεν.
ἡμῖν γὰρ ἀγαθῶν σωρὸς εἰς τὴν οἰκίαν
ἐπεισπέπαικεν οὐδὲν ἠδικηκόσιν.   805
ἡ μὲν σιπύη μεστή ᾽στι λευκῶν ἀλφίτων,
οἱ δ᾽ ἀμφορῆς οἴνου μέλανος ἀνθοσμίου.
ἅπαντα δ᾽ ἡμῖν ἀργυρίου καὶ χρυσίου
τὰ σκευάρια πλήρη ᾽στίν, ὥστε θαυμάσαι.
τὸ φρέαρ δ᾽ ἐλαίου μεστόν· αἱ δὲ λήκυθοι   810
μύρου γέμουσι, τὸ δ᾽ ὑπερῷον ἰσχάδων.
ὀξὶς δὲ πᾶσα καὶ λοπάδιον καὶ χύτρα
χαλκῆ γέγονε· τοὺς δὲ πινακίσκους τοὺς σαπροὺς
τοὺς ἰχθυηροὺς ἀργυροῦς πάρεσθ᾽ ὁρᾶν.
ὁ δ᾽ ἰπνὸς γέγον᾽ ἡμῖν ἐξαπίνης ἐλεφάντινος.   815

How sweet it is to be affluent, gentlemen,
and – what's more – have none of it taken from the house.
For a mountain of goods has burst into our home,
although we've not in any way been wrongdoers.   805
The grain silo is full of barley shining bright,
the amphoras, of inky wine with sweet bouquet.
And absolutely all our vessels are full of
silver and gold: you'll wonder at the sight of it.
The well is full of olive oil, our salve-flasks brim   810
with perfume, and the crawl space is stuffed with dried figs.
Every cruet and ramekin and casserole
has turned to bronze; and you can even take a look
at those old rotten planks for fish – they're silver now.
And our kitchen has suddenly become ivory.   815

The passage first imagines the new possessions as an unspecified heap (σωρός), but then details them in the list.[20] And again in individual items, Aristophanes emphasizes the vocabulary of fullness (πλήρη, μεστόν, γέμουσι).[21] Just as the kraters and small vessels of temple inventories, the

---

[20] σωρός is also the term Aristotle applies to an unspecified (as opposed to a specific) quantity at Metaph. 1044a4 and 1084b22.

[21] Cf. also Xenophanes fr. 1.

household vessels are also now full of gold, silver, and perfume. From item to collection, the home has itself become a treasury. The passage further enacts this transformation through its fantastical metamorphosis of everyday materials to precious metals: the cruets, ramekins, and casseroles (ὀξίς, λοπάδιον, χύτρα) have become not household items but their bronze dedicatory counterparts, usually found in sacred treasuries.[22] Thus Cario's inventory list not only recalls and parodies sacred record-keeping, but also performs the duties of sacred treasurers before the audience.

Domestication of the Civic Mind

Characters' enumerations of precious objects likely have multiple motivations. A dramatic explanation could account for these moments: perhaps the playwright is providing visual cues for props that a faraway viewer would be unable to distinguish,[23] or perhaps the staging of the plays varies, sometimes relying more on verbal cues, other times on physical elements.[24] Without dismissing these factors altogether, I contend that the public display of civic financial accounts has also influenced comic fashion. By the last quarter of the fifth century, the gaze of any visitor to the Athenian Acropolis and its sacred monuments would have been overwhelmed by the trinkets and vessels, wreaths and statues accumulated every which way throughout both indoor and outdoor spaces.[25] These objects, moreover, did not stand undocumented but were subject to a rigorous process of registration and cataloguing that annually culminated in the publication of stone inventories, set up for public

[22] Bronze χύτραι are common dedications, appearing frequently in inventories from Athens, Eleusis Delos, and Oropos. ὀξίδες appear in Delian inventories (e.g. *ID* 300.14 and *ID* 313 fr.i.6). λοπάδια do not appear in inventories but are found in a late fourth-century vase inscription of household items, Agora XXI B12.3. Similar household utensils and furniture purportedly appear in an unpublished text from the hestiatorion at Brauron; see *SEG* 37.34 and Themelis 1986: 229. On *thesauroi* (treasuries) as both public and private entities, see Neer 2003.

[23] Deictic pronouns are taken to imply that there were objects on the Aristophanic stage as part of the set even when they were not described (Whitehorne 2002: 33–34).

[24] English 2005: 4 has argued that the earlier plays show more reliance on physical objects on stage, while in the later ones words assume this same dramatic work: "Without a doubt, there is a noticeable decrease in the number of stage properties required for an Aristophanic production near the end of the Peloponnesian War as well as a marked preference for humble, everyday objects rather than the luxury wares coveted during the 420s. Aristophanes also seems to have stopped using objects as the foundation for key dramatic action."

[25] The earliest of the published paradoseis, records of the transfer of goods from one set of treasurers to the next, begin in the mid 430s, but that does not preclude earlier such records on temporary media. For further overviews of the evidence, see Davies 1994. Harris 1995 has made a comprehensive study of the Acropolis texts and their placement.

consumption.[26] Aristophanes' audience and characters, then, inhabit an environment in which the city has mandated a specific formula for dealing with items of value: collect them; put them on display; count them; display the account. By the early fourth century, the symbolic correlation of the inventory document to the concept of wealth sits squarely within the Athenian popular consciousness. As a related phenomenon, characters in the plays voice anxieties about keeping track of their personal resources in the context of an unstable financial climate, using lists in particular to quantify what they own. The household administrative practices of these private individuals mirror the concerns of Athenian public officials, who themselves produce meticulous public financial documents in part to reassure the populace of the state's welfare. The setting and language of a further example from *Wealth* illustrate this point. After the deified Wealth has incubated in the sanctuary of Asclepius to have his blindness cured, Cario again recreates the dedicatory scene in the sacred space and employs the vocabulary of public record-keeping in his account (668–683).[27]

ὡς δὲ τοὺς λύχνους ἀποσβέσας
ἡμῖν παρήγγειλεν καθεύδειν τοῦ θεοῦ
ὁ πρόπολος. εἰπών, ἤν τις αἴσθηται ψόφου,   670
σιγᾶν, ἅπαντες κοσμίως κατεκείμεθα.
κἀγὼ καθεύδειν οὐκ ἐδυνάμην, ἀλλά με
ἀθάρης χύτρα τις ἐξέπληττε κειμένη
ὀλίγον ἄπωθεν τῆς κεφαλῆς του γρᾳδίου,
ἐφ' ἣν ἐπεθύμουν δαιμονίως ἐφερπύσαι.   675
ἔπειτ' ἀναβλέψας ὁρῶ τὸν ἱερέα
τοὺς φθοῖς ὑφαρπάζοντα καὶ τὰς ἰσχάδας
ἀπὸ τῆς τραπέζης τῆς ἱερᾶς· μετὰ τοῦτο δὲ
περιῆλθε τοὺς βωμοὺς ἅπαντας ἐν κύκλῳ,
εἴ που πόπανον εἴη τι καταλελειμμένον·   680
ἔπειτα ταῦθ' ἥγιζεν εἰς σάκταν τινά.
κἀγὼ νομίσας πολλὴν ὁσίαν τοῦ πράγματος
ἐπὶ τὴν χύτραν τὴν τῆς ἀθάρης ἀνίσταμαι.

---

[26] The issue of how these texts functioned has bred much controversy: Linders 1988, followed by Thomas 1989: 82–83, Davies 1994: 202–203, 212, and Harris 1994: 214, has advanced the thesis that inscribed inventories functioned symbolically, while Aleshire 1989 and Sickinger 1999 have maintained that they were practical documents for consultation. Regardless of this issue, it is certain that these stones were intended for public interaction.

[27] Sommerstein 2001 ad loc. (181): "Carion's assumption that the priest is stealing the offerings would be perceived as either disingenuous or, more likely, comically naïve." At the same time, I would not rule out the possibility that Aristophanes may intend a dig at temple administration too. As to the location of the temple, Aleshire 1989 argued that Aristophanes likely means the sanctuary at Zea, and not Athens or Epidaurus.

And when the god's attendant snuffed
the lights announcing it was time to sleep,
and added that, if someone heard a sound   670
he should keep mum, we all lay down to bed.
I couldn't sleep though, 'cause there was this
pot of porridge set by some old lady's head
nearby that just was driving me insane –
the need to sneak up there possessed me so.   675
But then I look up and I see the priest
snatch up the sacred cakes[28] and the dried figs
from off the offering-table. After that,
he went round to the altars one by one
to see if there were any biscuits left,   680
then dedicated them into his sack!
So seeing it would be a holy act,
I went right up to that cauldron of gruel.

This passage employs multiple references to cultic *realia*, and specifically perishable sacred edibles and their treatment. As religious participants, visitors to the sanctuary would have generally suspended disbelief, regarding foods as going to the gods without acknowledging what really became of them behind the ritual scenes.[29] But Cario refuses (or is too ignorant) to play along, instead casting the priest as corrupt, someone who squirrels away dedications and proceeds from altar to altar to steal foods from the gods. His account makes the whole incubation system and the administration of the sanctuary out to be a sham, though in fact priests regularly collected ritual foodstuffs after offering and left them for the needy. To enhance his narration of the events, Cario also uses the vocabulary of ritual administrative texts. His lexicon accords with inventories and *leges sacrae*, where πόπανα, small cakes, ἰσχάδες, dried figs, and φθόεις, either metal bars or bar-shaped cakes, appear alongside descriptions of their placement in the sacred space.[30] Like inventory texts more generally, Cario's account specifies the delineated areas in which the treasure lies and verbally

[28] φθόϊς here could also denote bars of precious metal, as it does in inventory texts.

[29] Aleshire 1989 and 1991 remain standard references for cult practices of Asclepius at Athens; for more recent interpretations of Asklepian ritual, see, e.g., Lamont 2015 and Stafford 2008: 205–221. I have also benefited from the ideas and comments of Donald Mastronarde about these practices and this scene.

[30] φθόϊς (as metal bar): in Hekatompedon inventory *IG* ii² 1443; ἰσχάδες: in Delian inventories, *ID* 401, 406, 440, 442, 445, 452, 464; πόπανα: in *IG* xii.6.1.260.

recreates the dedicatory scene.[31] Yet it also closely parallels a *lex sacra* of the fourth century pertaining to the cult of Asclepius at Zea (Peireios).[32] Face A of the inscription lists prescriptions for the necessary offerings for various gods, followed by (in an apparent later addition) the actions of the priest Euthydemos at Eleusis (*IG* ii² 4962.A.1–18):

θεοί

κατὰ τάδε προθύεσθα-

ι· Μαλεάτηι πόπανα τρ-

ία· Ἀπόλλωνι πόπανα τ-

ρία· Ἑρμῆι πόπανα τρί-   5

α· Ἰασοῖ πόπανα τρία· Ἀ-

κεσοῖ πόπανα τρία· Πα-

νακείαι πόπανα τρία·

κυσὶν πόπανα τρία· κυ-

νηγέταις πόπανα τρί(α).   10

  vac. 0.13

Εὐθύδημος

Ἐλευσίνιος

ἱερεὺς Ἀσκληπιῶ

τὰς στήλας ἀνέθηκ[ε]   15

τὰς πρὸς τοῖς βωμοῖς

ἐν αἷς τὰ πόπανα πρῶτος

ἐξηικάσατο, ἃ χρὴ πρ[ο]-

θύεσθ[αι – –

Gods.

These things are to be consecrated as follows: to Maleates, three biscuits. To Apollo three biscuits. To Hermes three biscuits. To Iaso three biscuits. To Akeso three biscuits. To Panakeia three biscuits. To the dogs three biscuits. To the hunter thr(ee) biscuits.

Euthedemos of Eleusis priest of Asclepius set up the *stelai* by the altars on which he first made likenesses of the biscuits which it was fitting to offer to . . .

---

[31] Inventories of the Hekatompedon (e.g. *IG* ii² 1443) and the inventory from the Samian Heraion (*IG* xii 6.1.261) in particular attend to the spatial arrangements of objects, describing them as situated on numbered rows (ῥυμοί, originally "poles" or "logs" but, in the inventory context, apparently sets of shelves).

[32] Lamont 2015 argues for this connection as well; this argument, composed before Lamont's article appeared, reaches a similar conclusion. For further discussion of this inscription and its implications for the Asklepian cult, see von Eickstedt 2001, Stafford 2008, Pirenne-Delforge 2011: 123–130.

This text lists items identical to the ones Cario mentioned; it also provides an idea about what priests are meant to do with consecrated πόπανα based on the example of Euthydemos. The inscription is so specific as to state that in addition to setting up *stelai* to account for the offerings, the priest had visual likenesses of them produced (ἐξηικάσατο).[33] Thus in describing the sanctuary in minute detail, Cario enacts this same enumeration of offerings and establishment of sacred custom as the *lex sacra*. The humor of the scene depends as much on Cario's archetypal buffoonery as it does on the audience's familiarity with public record-keeping and cult practice.

Assemblywomen shows similar administrative poetics at work. The heroine Praxagora's plans for a reformed economic system in which all citizens share resources, with women as overseers, exhibit the influence of Athenian accounting culture. The connection is apparent from the moment she announces her proposition (210–212):

> ταῖς γὰρ γυναιξὶ φημὶ χρῆναι τὴν πόλιν
> ἡμᾶς παραδοῦναι. καὶ γὰρ ἐν ταῖς οἰκίαις
> ταύταις ἐπιτρόποις καὶ ταμίαισι χρώμεθα.

> I say, we ought to put the city in
> The women's hands! For in our homes
> We employ them as guards and treasurers.

Here Praxagora re-appropriates the title of the polis treasurer and inventory-maker, the ταμίας, suggesting by syllogism that because they are domestic ταμίαι women should also be civic ones.[34] Coupled with ἐπιτρόποις, the ambiguous form ταμίαισι may well come from the masculine agentive ταμίας rather than feminine ταμία; if this is the case, she also makes a grammatical effort to neutralize the gender of the noun and subsume both domestic and civic affairs under one (female) body, in distinction to the usual gendered division of domestic and public. Moreover, it only adds to this fusion of male and female that these lines

[33] For a summary of previous interpretations, see Lamont 2015: 48 n.44, who contends that this verb means only that Euthydemos had the ritual practices inscribed; I rather follow those who read the verb more literally (cf. e.g. *Knights* 230, where the verb refers to a portrait mask).

[34] This is not to say that the term originates in the polis context; that use likely developed from the domestic context. It appears in Homer of stewards who distribute food (*Il.* 19.44), and Pindar refers to peace as τάμι' ἀνδράσι πλούτου (O.13.7). Herodotus applies it to the Athenian treasurers (8.51). That Xenophon uses the term in *Oeconomicus* (9.10.2, 9.11.1, etc.) suggests that it had been transferred to denote a member of the household by the date of that text (perhaps 362, nearly thirty years after the production of *Assemblywomen*), or perhaps had remained in use in private contexts.

are delivered from beneath an elaborate layering of gendered guises, in
which a man (Chremes) quotes the lines of a woman (Praxagora) disguised
as a man (and played by a male actor). And Praxagora's appropriation of
the role of public treasurer pervades more than just her diction: she herself
performs the role of official record-keeper in her speech. As quoted by
Chremes, she (dressed as a man) argues that women are better and more
discreet financiers than men, and more trustworthy in an exchange economy (446–450):[35]

> ἔπειτα συμβάλλειν πρὸς ἀλλήλας ἔφη
> ἱμάτια, χρυσί', ἀργύριον, ἐκπώματα,
> μόνας μόναις, οὐ μαρτύρων ἐναντίον,
> καὶ ταῦτ' ἀποφέρειν πάντα κοὐκ ἀποστερεῖν,
> ἡμῶν δὲ τοὺς πολλοὺς ἔφασκε τοῦτο δρᾶν.   450

> Then he said that women lend to one another
> their dresses, their gold jewelry, silver, drinking cups,
> among themselves, private, and without witnesses,
> and that they return everything and never steal,
> whereas most of us men, he claimed, we do just that.   450

At first glance, this list of exchanged goods might appear to be a simple
extended example, a means of sounding more convincing than just a mere
statement of purported truth. But in enumerating the very objects of worth
women exchange – ἱμάτια, χρυσί', ἀργύριον, ἐκπώματα – Praxagora produces a list of the sort that an actual record of such an exchange might
entail in the public – rather than the private – sphere. From Chremes'
mouth comes not an argument, but a virtual inventory, which he has
presumably repeated from Praxagora's statements in the assembly, much
as someone might in reading a copy of an official document. Women, as
domestic ταμίαι, make listed accounts of goods much like actual city
officials.[36] And the specific items she mentions are no accident: just as in
the case of Cario's description, the extended entry in Praxagora's home-
catalogue recalls the lexicon of inventories, and the types of items often
presented as dedications or exchanged by women among themselves. Small
gold objects and pieces of silver appear regularly across the corpus of
inventories, while ἐκπώματα specifically appear as dedications in a number

---

[35] For a similar idea, cf. *Thesm.* 819–823.

[36] Bowie 1993: 256 observes a similar infiltration of the public lexicon: "Praxagora calls the store-
rooms 'stoas' and the word is significant, because 'stoa' is not found of the store-rooms of
houses, but always of the large public ones[.]"

of Attic and Delian texts of the late fifth and fourth centuries.[37] Moreover, the stark asyndeton of her line 442 is reminiscent of administrative style, such as this fourth-century example from the Delian inventories, *ID* 104.86–87 (364/3 BCE):

> ἐν τούτοις τάδε ἐστάθη· λεβήτια ΙΙ· ἀλάβαστοι · λέοντος κεφαλή·
> [οἰ]νοχόαι ΙΙΙ· ἔκπωμα· κέρας· καρχήσιον Ι· κυλιχνὶς Ι.

> Among these the following were weighed: Brazierettes, 2. Alabastra, 5. Lion head. Oinochoes, 3. Beaker. Drinking-horn. Drinking cup, 1. Cup, 1.

Finally, Praxagora's list recalls not just inventories of dedicatory objects generally, but the special cataloging of women's dedications in particular, in which *himatia* (her first item) figure prominently. Most relevant in this context is the set of fourth-century treasure-records for Brauronian Artemis, displayed on the Athenian Acropolis but recording dedications from Brauron. As we have seen, these inventories specifically and almost exclusively give the names of female dedicators,[38] allowing us to imagine a women's economy similar to the exchanges Praxagora discusses, as at *IG* ii² 1514.17–22:

> Ναυσὶς ἱμάτιον γυναικεῖον πλατυαλουρ-
> γὲς περι[κυ]μάτιον· Κλεὼ ἀμπέχονον· Φίλη περιήγητ-
> ον· Τ[ε]ισικράτεια κάνδυν ποικίλον· Μέλιττα ἱμάτι-
> ον λευκὸν καὶ χιτωνίσκον, ῥάκος· Γλυκέρα Ξανθίππ-   20
> ου γυνὴ χιτωνίσκον περιήγητον ἐκπλύτωι ἀλουρ[γ]-
> εῖ καὶ [τ]ριβώνια δύο· Νικολέα χιτῶνα ἀμόργινον.

> Nausis, a woman's *himation*, broad-purple-bordered, wave-patterned (?). Kleo, a shawl. Phile, a bordered garment. Teisikrateia, a multicolored Median double. Melitta, a white *himation* and a *chitoniskos*, a rag. Glykera wife of   20
> Xanthippus, a bordered frock of faded sea-green and two threadbare cloaks. Nikolea, a flax tunic.

Thus Aristophanes presents Praxagora to an audience not only in general political terms, but using pointed bureaucratic diction and, most importantly, the list format. The audience's perception of this moment requires a

---

[37] ἐκπώματα: *IG* i³ 342.14, *IG* ii² 1382.13, *ID* 104.87, etc.
[38] Linders 1972 is the most comprehensive study. While the relevant evidence from the excavations at Brauron still remains to be published, Y. Kalliontzis reveals in a recent conference paper that a new Brauronian text from Oropos mentions a male dedicator.

familiarity with how official accounting functioned, and by the time of *Assemblywomen*'s production, between 392 and 388, annual inventories would have been published for the Acropolis for the better part of the last half-century.[39] It is with close attention to this official tincture that we should examine Praxagora's more extended description of her plan as she outlines it to her skeptical husband Blepyrus and neighbor (596–607):

Πρ.   μὰ Δί', ἀλλ' ἔφθης μ' ὑποκρούσας.
τοῦτο γὰρ ἤμελλον ἐγὼ λέξειν· τὴν γῆν πρώτιστα ποιήσω
κοινὴν πάντων καὶ τἀργύριον καὶ τἄλλ', ὁπόσ' ἐστὶν ἑκάστῳ.
εἶτ' ἀπὸ τούτων κοινῶν ὄντων ἡμεῖς βοσκήσομεν ὑμᾶς
ταμιευόμεναι καὶ φειδόμεναι καὶ τὴν γνώμην προσέχουσαι.   600
Γε.   πῶς οὖν ὅστις μὴ κέκτηται γῆν ἡμῶν, ἀργύριον δὲ
καὶ Δαρεικούς, ἀφανῆ πλοῦτον;
Πρ.   τοῦτ' εἰς τὸ μέσον καταθήσει.
Βλ.   κεἰ μὴ καταθεὶς ψευδορκήσει; κἀκτήσατο γὰρ διὰ τοῦτο.
Πρ.   ἀλλ' οὐδέν τοι χρήσιμον ἔσται πάντως αὐτῷ.
Βλ.   κατὰ δὴ τί;
Πρ.   οὐδεὶς οὐδὲν πενίᾳ δράσει· πάντα γὰρ ἕξουσιν ἅπαντες,   605
ἄρτους, τεμάχη, μάζας, χλαίνας, οἶνον, στεφάνους, ἐρεβίνθους.
ὥστε τί κέρδος μὴ καταθεῖναι; σὺ γὰρ ἐξευρὼν ἀπόδειξον.

Pr.   By Zeus, you're preempting me with your interruptions!
For I was about to say that I first will make the land the common property
                of everyone,
and the money and everything else each person has in his possession.
Then from these things, being now common property,
we will feed, acting as treasurers, sparing and attentive to you.   600
Ne.   What about those of us who don't have land, but silver
and gold coins, invisible wealth?
Pr.   They'll put that in the kitty too.
Bl.   And what if they swear falsely and don't put it in? For that's how they
                acquired it in the first place.
Pr.   But there will be no point in their doing that.
Bl.   How come?
Pr.   No one will do anything out of poverty, for everyone will have
everything: bread, sliced fish, barleycakes, shawls, wine, garlands,
                chickpeas.   605

---

[39] The *terminus post quem* for the play comes from internal evidence, 392 being the first time during the Corinthian War in which the Athenians might have had reason to express any optimism, such as occurs at lines 202–203. The *terminus ante quem* is the date of the production of *Wealth*.

So what would he gain by not putting his money in the pot? Think about it
– show me.

The Greek literary tradition and the fifth-century Athenian polis administration dealt with precious objects with a similar process: amass them into a
contained collection, put them on display, count them in an inventory, and
then display the account. Praxagora aims to effect precisely this scheme for
the resources, once private and soon to be communal, of the whole
population. In the first phase of her plan, participants bring all precious
objects together in one place. This collection, composed of both money and
goods (καὶ τἀργύριον καὶ τἄλλ᾽, 598) will reside "in the middle" (εἰς τὸ
μέσον, 602), that is, in a literal central space for a figurative shared benefit.[40]
The μέσον, then, functions as would a city treasury, a physical repository.
And like the collections of funds on the Acropolis, Praxagora's too require
officials to keep watch over them, which roles the women will serve, acting
as treasurers and being frugal (ταμιευόμεναι καὶ φειδόμεναι). A neighbor
naturally thus wonders what will become of moveable wealth (πλοῦτος
ἀφανής), the usual contents of city treasuries and private hoards – will
people not hoard them for the sake of personal gain (κέρδος)?[41] Praxagora
insists that no one will hoard because no one will be wanting, but her
system also devalues gold and silver insofar as they have no worth for
exchange. They thus have no place in her communal system, in which all
resources are shared and there is no such thing as a currency.[42] To prove
her point, she again turns to the tactics of bureaucratic administrative
practice.[43] Explaining to Blepyrus what *will* have value in the new system,
she produces that crucial tool of official financial management: an

---

[40] Ussher 1973: 159.

[41] Fear of hoarders is no new phenomenon. We can observe a reversal of roles here, I think, that
from the model proposed for the archaic period, in which the reactionary elite seeks to maintain
a traditional economic order that privileges material wealth above coined money, for which see
Kurke 1999: 32–40 and 2002: 93–94. ἀφανὴς οὐσία is the normal designation for coined money,
as opposed to φανερά, the latter for visible possessions such as land. For further discussion of
these terms, see Gabrielson 1986 and Ferrucci 2005, and O'Connell 2016: 50–52.

[42] Exchangeability is one of three defining features that post-Keynesian writers have used to define
types of money, the other two being (a) inherent prestige and, in its absence, (b) value imparted
by communal agreement. Galbraith 1975: 72 sees all three as different versions of the "fact of
scarcity," common to all, and which would not figure into Praxagora's new order.

[43] A more obvious instance of this kind of diction that has not escaped the notice of commentators
is Blepyrus' question τί δῆτ᾽ ἔδοξεν (455), inverting the formulaic words of inscribed resolutions
of the dēmos and boulē.

inventory. Her charming list of ἄρτους, τεμάχη, μάζας, χλαίνας, οἶνον, στεφάνους, ἐρεβίνθους takes account not just of all that each citizen might require (as she envisions it), but also of the physical material in the collection – in other words, the very contents of τὸ μέσον.[44] The enumeration does not simply exemplify the oft-invoked assumption that "there is, of course, in comedy, much emphasis on food."[45] Instead, it signals the complete integration of the poetic and the documentary list, including the same admixture of comestibles and clothing that often populate a sanctuary, but which are here transferred to the domestic sphere. I would venture, finally, that Praxagora invokes Athenian documentary culture in her last challenge to Blepyrus, saying that, if he can think of anything that a would-be hoarder would gain, he should "make it clear" (ἀπόδειξον). While the verb is generally taken here to mean "prove it," it again recalls accounting language as well, where an *apodeixis* is an authoritative inventory of goods and a verbal showing on the part of an official body.[46] Thus Praxagora asks Blepyrus here literally to make a list, following upon her own, of any other valuable items one might gain from hoarding silver and gold. Her triumph lies in his empty set.

Count Your Blessings

Earlier Aristophanic plays, while they do not so directly mimic Athenian financial documents, nonetheless show a similar attention to the enumeration of personal resources. In these contexts, Aristophanes' lists seem to resonate with fifth-century civic concerns in content, yet in other ways draw on the enumerative stylistics of archaic poetry. Often lists appear at the outset to illustrate a qualitative or descriptive point, but in fact end up doing so quantitatively. Furthermore, the list does not just illustrate an arbitrary group of items under a heading (or implied heading), but rather purports to tell *all* of them. For example, when in *Acharnians* Dicaeopolis asks the Theban peddler what goods he's brought, he responds (*Acharnians* 873–876):

---

[44] That this list may fail to comprise quite all that one might require does not pose an interpretive roadblock. Poetic license here and the time constraints of dramatic performance call for a shorter list, but the list form always has the ability to invoke the infinite.
[45] Ussher 1973: 160.
[46] For this use of the term in Herodotus, see Casson 1921 and A. Kirk 2014.

ὅσ’ ἐστὶν ἀγαθὰ Βοιωτοῖς ἁπλῶς,
ὀρίγανον, γλαχώ, ψιάθως, θρυαλλίδας,
νάσσας, κολοιώς, ἀτταγᾶς, φαλαρίδας,
τροχίλως, κολύμβως.

Just all the good things Boiotia has:
oregano, mint, rushes, candlewicks,
ducks, jackdaws, francolins, baldheaded coots,
plovers and pigeons.

The introductions to this enumeration contain quantitative markers, such as a form of the demonstrative ὅσος or the adjective πᾶς – a correlative whose interrogative equivalent would not be "what kind," but rather "how many." The Theban's response, beginning with ὅσα, thus reformulates the list to answer an implicit question that would be posed by πόσα: "*How many* good things does Boiotia have?" A similar example occurs after Bdelycleon's promise to accommodate his father, culminating in a lewd joke (*Wasps* 736–740):

καὶ μὴν θρέψω γ’ αὐτὸν παρέχων
ὅσα πρεσβύτῃ ξύμφορα, χόνδρον
λείχειν, χλαῖναν μαλακήν, σισύραν,
πόρνην, ἥτις τὸ πέος τρίψει
καὶ τὴν ὀσφῦν.   740

And I will care for him, providing him
everything healthful for an old man: gruel
to lick, a soft mantle, a goat-hair cloak,
a prostitute who'll wear his penis down,
his tailbone too.   740

Variations of the same scheme, with (ἁ)πάντα in place of the demonstrative pronoun, occur late in *Acharnians* with a list of dinner preparations, and in the Stronger Argument's list of all one misses out on by being decent (σωφρονεῖν) in *Clouds*.[47] In each instance, the list responds to the quantifying word and answers the same implicit "how many?" However, should we abstract the implicit question "How many things are helpful for an old man?," the most natural answer would be a number ("5"). The list, in providing the answer instead, acts as a count, and fills in for a number.[48]

---

[47] *Acharnians* 1089–1094; *Clouds* 1071–1074.

[48] This is not unlike Barney's assessment of lists in Chaucer, which treats them as "adjectival," stating that "the ingredients of a list are more specific and concrete than the general and abstract principle on which the list depends." For this reason, he points out, Chaucer uses the word "undo"(in the sense of "tease out") to describe what a list does for a more abstract rubric (Barney 1981: 191). Thus, for Aristophanes, Gruel, Mantle, Cloak, and Whore "undo" the general idea of Old Men's Needs.

Quantifiers like ὅσα sometimes do not have such precise numeric semantics (they can appear in contexts almost interchangeably with the relative), and certain lists do not include quantifying language.[49] Nevertheless, Aristophanes reminds the audience of their radical force by correlating them to actual numbers as well. So Dicaeopolis' lament starts *Acharnians* (1–6):

> ὅσα δὴ δέδεγμαι τὴν ἐμαυτοῦ καρδίαν,
> ἥσθην δὲ βαιά, πάνυ δὲ βαιά, τέτταρα·
> ἃ δ' ὠδυνήθην, ψαμμακοσιογάργαρα.
> φέρ' ἴδω, τί δ' ἥσθην ἄξιον χαιρηδόνος;
> ἐγᾦδ' ἐφ' ᾧ γε τὸ κέαρ ηὐφράνθην ἰδών·   5
> τοῖς πέντε ταλάντοις οἷς Κλέων ἐξήμεσεν.

> How many times I'm bitten in my heart,
> and had paltry pleasures, most paltry: four.
> But pains I've suffered? Sandgrainjillions.
> Let's see – what pleasure I've had worth a smile?
> I know, when I saw this my heart rejoiced: 5
> Those five talents, the ones Kleon coughed up.

---

[49] Notable exceptions include Strepsiades' account of his upwardly mobile marriage at *Clouds* 49–52, where he "climbed into the bed / smelling like young wine, dried figs, fleece, surplus, / and she, like perfume, saffron, French kissing, / feasts, decadence, Kolias, Genetyllis"; and Trygaios' vision of what the former, peaceful life entailed at *Peace* 571–581:

> ἀλλ' ἀναμνησθέντες, ὦνδρες,
> τῆς διαίτης τῆς παλαιᾶς,
> ἣν παρεῖχ' αὕτη ποθ' ἡμῖν,
> τῶν τε παλασίων ἐκείνων,
> τῶν τε σύκων, τῶν τε μύρτων,   575
> τῆς τρυγός τε τῆς γλυκείας,
> τῆς ἰωνιᾶς τε τῆς πρὸς
> τῷ φρέατι τῶν τ' ἐλαῶν
> ὧν ποθοῦμεν,
> ἀντὶ τούτων τήνδε νυνὶ   580
> τὴν θεὸν προσείπατε.

> But, remember, gentlemen, please
> the life we knew in the old days,
> which this goddess then gave to us:
> the life of those little fruitcakes,
> life of figs, and life of cherries,   575
> and of unfermented sweet wine,
> and the bed of violets over
> by the well, and of the olive
> trees we long for,
> in exchange for all these things, now,   580
> to this goddess give your thanks.

The humor arises here initially because the first line smacks of the tragic, and because ὅσα causes the audience to anticipate a vague exclamation that might end without a real quantification, after βαιά.[50] The punchline, though, lies in the unexpected and overly specifying τέτταρα, which interrupts the maudlin flow with a specific count and renders absurd the question implicit in ὅσα and continued in the next line.[51] τέτταρα also sets up an aftershock punchline in the next line, where the listener, now wise to the game, anticipates another cardinal number but gets a tongue-twisting neologism instead: ψαμμακοσιογάργαρα. This form entertains at the outset for its structural parody of heavily compounded Greek arithmetical jargon words, such as ἑπτακαιεικοσαπλάσιος, "twenty-seven fold." But its comic thrust extends further, for its three components ("grains of sand," *-illion*, and a word like "gaggle") recall the frequent literary use of sand to denote the infinite, or at least uncountable, as expressed, e.g. in Pindar (*Ol*.2.98–100 and *Ol*.13.43–46):[52]

> ἐπεὶ ψάμμος ἀριθμὸν περιπέφευγεν,
> καὶ κεῖνος ὅσα χάρματ' ἄλλοις ἔθηκεν,
> τίς ἂν φράσαι δύναιτο;   100

> Since sand has fled numeration,
> and how many joys that man has made for others,
> who would be able to speak?   100

> ὅσσα τ' ἐν Δελφοῖσιν ἀριστεύσατε,
> ἠδὲ χόρτοις ἐν λέοντος, δηρίομαι πολέσιν
> περὶ πλήθει καλῶν· ὡς μὰν σαφές   45
> οὐκ ἂν εἰδείην λέγειν ποντιᾶν ψάφων ἀριθμόν.

> And as to how many times you emerged the best in Delphi,
> and among the grasslands of the lion, I contend with many
> concerning the count of your wins, since I would not know   45
> to tell clearly the number of the pebbles in the sea.

50 Olson 2002: 64 points to Euripides fr. 696.8 as the tragic source; Starkie 1909 had thought it might parody the lost beginning of *Telephus*.

51 This number poses a problem for commentators, because Dicaeopolis then goes on to name only two pleasures. Suggestions that τέτταρα means "some, a few," or is somehow otherwise idiomatic (Dover 1987: 227) seem unnecessary. Rennie 1909: 86 seems closer to an explanation in pointing to its contrast with ψαμμακοσιογάργαρα, while Olson 2002: 66 recognizes the word as a punchline, but ventures no further.

52 Olson 2002: 66 supplies this and other relevant citations, to which I would add, along with O.13., Plato *Th*. 173d. The sentiment, in any case, has paratragic overtones generally, and specifically of uncountable troubles, as the chorus at Sophocles *OT* 168–169: ὦ πόποι, ἀνάριθμα γὰρ φέρω | πήματα.

In these instances, the poet invokes sand to avoid disclosing an actual sum or even engaging in further discussion, though he has already made some approximation of the victor's acts of generosity and successes known over the course of the ode. In similar fashion, upon pronouncing them countless, Dicaeopolis proceeds to list those very troubles in alternation with his joys in the lines that follow. With his numeric *praeteritio*, he thus also engages in a similar scheme the *recusatio* of the Homeric narrator of the Catalogue of Ships (*Il.* 2.488–489):

> πληθὺν δ' οὐκ ἂν ἐγὼ μυθήσομαι οὐδ' ὀνομήνω,
> οὐδ' εἴ μοι δέκα μὲν γλῶσσαι, δέκα δὲ στόματ' εἶεν

> And I could not speak nor name the multitude,
> not even if I should have ten tongues and ten mouths

As in *Acharnians* an accounting of the "multitude" in catalogue form follows the speaker's very refusal to state one. Here too, then, counting and cataloguing become inseparable activities. Moreover, Dicaeopolis' opening lines foreshadow a desire to quantify that preoccupy the characters on the comic stage before an audience embedded in a city with the same concerns.

A similar tendency emerges in *Wasps* between Bdelycleon and his father, Philocleon, a character "being treated as a fool by a group of political swindlers, who claim to be his protectors but are in fact manipulating the city's affairs for their own benefit and who accordingly laugh at him behind his back."[53] Attempting to open Philocleon's eyes, his son bids him take stock and count the ways the city's powers-that-be actually take all the goods for themselves. This account is realized as a list and thus Bdelycleon is able to help his father come up with a sum at the end (*Wasps* 655–663):

> ἀκρόασαί νυν, ὦ παππίδιον, χαλάσας ὀλίγον τὸ μέτωπον·   655
> καὶ πρῶτον μὲν λόγισαι φαύλως, μὴ ψήφοις ἀλλ' ἀπὸ χειρός,
> τὸν φόρον ἡμῖν ἀπὸ τῶν πόλεων συλλήβδην τὸν προσιόντα·
> κἄξω τούτου τὰ τέλη χωρὶς καὶ τὰς πολλὰς ἑκατοστάς,
> πρυτανεῖα, μέταλλ', ἀγοράς, λιμένας, μισθώσεις, δημιόπρατα·
> τούτων πλήρωμα τάλαντ' ἐγγὺς δισχίλια γίγνεται ἡμῖν.   660
> ἀπὸ τούτου νυν κατάθες μισθὸν τοῖσι δικασταῖς ἐνιαυτοῦ
> ἓξ χιλιάσιν – κοὔπω πλείους ἐν τῇ χώρᾳ κατένασθεν –,
> γίγνεται ἡμῖν ἑκατὸν δήπου καὶ πεντήκοντα τάλαντα.

---

[53] Olson 1996: 135. The statement would of course apply to Strepsiades with Socrates and his followers in place of the politicians, and the Thinkery in place of the city.

> Then listen, Pops, and relax your frown a bit. First of all, calculate roughly, not with counters but on your fingers, how much tribute we receive altogether from the allied cities. Then make a separate count of the taxes and the many one percents, court dues, mines, markets, harbors, rents, proceeds from confiscations. Our total income from all this is nearly 2,000 talents. Now set aside the annual payment to the jurors, all 6,000 of them, "for never yet have more dwelt in this land." We get, I reckon, a sum of 150 talents.

When he reiterates his point just a few lines later and explains everything corrupt city leaders are given, Bdelycleon provides another list for his father to emphasize the unfair treatment of average Athenian citizens, who receive no such gifts (675–677):

> τούτοισι δὲ δωροφοροῦσιν
> ὕρχας, οἶνον, δάπιδας, τυρόν, μέλι, σήσαμα, προσκεφάλαια,
> φιάλας, χλανίδας, στεφάνους, ὅρμους, ἐκπώματα, πλουθυγίειαν·

> These men they present with bribes:
> pickle jars, wine, tapestries, cheese, honey, sesame, headrests,
> saucers, mantles, garlands, necklaces, drinking-cups, health and wealth.

These enumerations are general markers of abundance, replete with "goods which represent the high-life generally and a very luxurious banquet and symposium in particular."[54] But the collections of items here, in form and content, also precisely echo the kind of inventory that the very officials in question might cause to be made of state treasure on display.

Here, we observe a private citizen's difficulties in accounting for his own resources; ultimately he is brought to understand the inequitable distribution of goods at the state level. For Philocleon, domestic and public life become increasingly indistinguishable as he struggles to maintain a sense of authority as citizen and *head of* household, if we may apply the term, culminating in his replication of the law-courts in his home.

An Aristophanic *Teichoskopia*

Aristophanes' use of the structures and diction of civic public records in the service of humor sets his works apart from numerous other poets that employ the catalogue form. Yet he combines with this official idiom a

---

[54] Olson 1996: 135.

completely separate tradition of listmaking, from the literary, rather than the epigraphic, record. And unlike his use of other textual forms that align comedy with tragedy, Aristophanes' use of lists draws primarily on non-dramatic literary predecessors and above all epic.[55] When the Athenian comic audience encountered lists in performed plays, the Homeric poems would have stood as a familiar exemplar.[56] The mere presence of a catalogue on its own, though, does not necessarily and obviously dictate an epic precedent, and the influence of the archaic version of the list form does not emerge so obviously as does, say, Aristophanes' use of the hexameter; these moments require a rather more nuanced analysis.[57]

Tereus' introduction of the chorus in *Birds* to Euelpides and Pisthetaerus, despite its surface tragic allusions and wordplay, shares the formal characteristics of a Homeric passage. The two men have arrived in what will become Cloudcuckooland, and Tereus summons the birds before them describing each one in succession – some as they parade out, others once they have assembled on stage (lines 268–310).[58] The scene as a whole might call to an audience's mind one of the similes that precedes the Iliadic Catalogue of Ships, which compares the marshalled forces to so many collected birds (*Il.* 2.459–468):

> τῶν δ' ὥς τ' ὀρνίθων πετεηνῶν ἔθνεα πολλά
> χηνῶν ἢ γεράνων ἢ κύκνων δουλιχοδείρων   460
> Ἀσίω ἐν λειμῶνι Καϋστρίου ἀμφὶ ῥέεθρα
> ἔνθα καὶ ἔνθα ποτῶνται ἀγαλλόμενα πτερύγεσσι
> κλαγγηδὸν προκαθιζόντων, σμαραγεῖ δέ τε λειμών,
> ὣς τῶν ἔθνεα πολλὰ νεῶν ἄπο καὶ κλισιάων
> ἐς πεδίον προχέοντο Σκαμάνδριον· αὐτὰρ ὑπὸ χθών   465
> σμερδαλέον κονάβιζε ποδῶν αὐτῶν τε καὶ ἵππων.

---

[55] That is not to say that catalogue falls wholly outside the tragic repertoire: notable examples include the catalogue of Persian dead in Aeschylus' *Persians* (302–330); the Chalkidean women's catalogue of the Greek fleet at *Iph. Aul.* 231–303; Antigone's description of the army at *Phoen.* 110–117. E. Hall 1996: 108–109 discusses the *Persians* passage in relation to epic; Ebbott 2000 to Athenian casualty lists; Scodel 1997 compares the Euripidean passages to their Homeric precedents. See also Allen 1901.

[56] Platter 2007: 109 attributes the lack of epicism in Aristophanic comedy to the considerable attention and imitation that genre already received from the literary tradition itself (109). Harriott 1986: 63–64 seems to recognize some epic flavor in *Knights*; Willi 2010: 496 essentially dismisses engagement with epic outside of hexameter oracles and metrical puzzle pieces. Parodies of Homeric catalogue itself, such as Hermippus fr. 63 (Gilula 2000), have received less attention. Moulton 1996 argues for mythical innovation in *Birds*.

[57] For a study based on five hexameter scenes, see Platter 2007: 111, who claims that "in each case a speaker attempts to assert rhetorical control of a situation by appeal to epic-oracular authority."

[58] Gelzer 1996: 206–207 gives a colorful and useful account of the expectations that Aristophanes sets up and dashes for the audience throughout the parodos and introduction to it.

ἔσταν δ' ἐν λειμῶνι Σκαμανδρίῳ ἀνθεμόεντι
μυρίοι, ὅσσά τε φύλλα καὶ ἄνθεα γίγνεται ὥρῃ.

And just as the many types of winged birds,
the wild geese, or the cranes, or the swans with long-necks,   460
in the Asian meadow by Caüstrius' streams,
fly this way and that way exalting in their wings,
perch with shrill chirping, and the whole meadow resounds,
so too out of the ships and huts their many tribes
poured out onto the Scamandrian plain; the earth   465
beneath echoed with sounds of their horses and feet.
And in the ever-blooming Scamandrian plain
they stood, countless, just as the leaves and buds in spring.

This focus on the birds' song and dance on the plain is equally at home in the Athenian theatrical setting; there are, however, even more specific resonances to be found. Throughout the first part of the Aristophanic characters' conversation, a pattern emerges; triggered by the sight of a bird, one of the visitors asks (often with a deictic reference) which bird presents itself before him, and Tereus answers with a short description and name, as at 269–273:

ΕΥ.   νὴ Δί' ὄρνις δῆτα. τίς ποτ' ἐστίν; οὐ δήπου ταῶς;
ΠΕ.   οὗτος αὐτὸς νῷν φράσει· τίς ἐστιν οὔρνις οὑτοσί;   270
ΤΕ.   οὗτος οὐ τῶν ἠθάδων τῶνδ' ὧν ὁρᾶθ' ὑμεῖς ἀεί,
          ἀλλὰ λιμναῖος.
ΕΥ.   βαβαί, καλός γε καὶ φοινικιοῦς.
ΤΕ.   εἰκότως <γε>· καὶ γὰρ ὄνομ' αὐτῷ 'στὶ φοινικόπτερος.

ΕΥ.   Well, that sure is a bird. What is it? Not a peacock, right?
ΡΙ.   This guy here will tell us. What bird is this over here?   270
ΤΕ.   That one isn't one of those ones that you see every day;
          It's a marsh bird.
ΕΥ.   Oh wow, look, he's so pretty and purple!
ΤΕ.   He sure is! And that's how come he's called the purple-wing.

The exchange continues as the birds emerge first in dribs and drabs, then as a body on stage, and Pisthetaerus and Euelpides come to know through inquiry the number and names of the residents they plan to colonize. The ambassador and ornithological expert, Tereus, identifies the birds individually, giving some salient attributes for each. By the end, we have heard a full catalogue of the twenty-four-member chorus. Commentators offer little guidance as to why the chorus comprises these species to the exclusion of others.[59] For the most part, they note the scene's use of tragic diction and quotation and then turn their attention to the names, studying each in detail.[60] But in content and structure, and in some sense effect, the scene bears a close resemblance to a distinct poetic predecessor: the *teichoskopia*, Helen's account to Priam of the Greek commanders as seen from the walls of Troy (*Il.* 3.162–242). That scene follows the same pattern, repeating multiple times the series of sighting trigger, question, and identifying answer. Summoning Helen to his side, Priam asks her in succession who each warrior is, an exchange marked unusually by the narrator with ordinal numbers. Thus in the case of Odysseus, the second figure Helen identifies and discusses, the exchange proceeds as follows (*Il.* 3.191–202):

> Δεύτερον αὖτ' Ὀδυσῆα ἰδὼν ἐρέειν' ὁ γεραιός·
> εἴπ' ἄγε μοι καὶ τόνδε φίλον τέκος ὅς τις ὅδ' ἐστί·
> μείων μὲν κεφαλῇ Ἀγαμέμνονος Ἀτρεΐδαο,
> εὐρύτερος δ' ὤμοισιν ἰδὲ στέρνοισιν ἰδέσθαι.
> τεύχεα μέν οἱ κεῖται ἐπὶ χθονὶ πουλυβοτείρῃ,   195
> αὐτὸς δὲ κτίλος ὣς ἐπιπωλεῖται στίχας ἀνδρῶν·
> ἀρνειῷ μιν ἔγωγε ἐΐσκω πηγεσιμάλλῳ,
> ὅς τ' οἰῶν μέγα πῶϋ διέρχεται ἀργεννάων.
> Τὸν δ' ἠμείβετ' ἔπειθ' Ἑλένη Διὸς ἐκγεγαυῖα·
> οὗτος δ' αὖ Λαερτιάδης πολύμητις Ὀδυσσεύς,   200
> ὃς τράφη ἐν δήμῳ Ἰθάκης κραναῆς περ ἐούσης
> εἰδὼς παντοίους τε δόλους καὶ μήδεα πυκνά.

> Second the old man asked, seeing Odysseus,
> "Tell me, dear child, this one, who is this man right here?
> He's shorter, true, than Agamemnon Atreus' son,
> but broader, looks like, in his shoulders and his chest.
> His armor all lies on the much-nourishing earth,   195
> but he sweeps like a ram through rank and file of men.
> Really, he looks like a thick-fleecy ram to me,
> cleaving through the great flock of shining-white sheep."
> Then Helen, born from Zeus's line, replied to him:
> "That is wily Odysseus, Laertes' son,   200

---

[59] "[t]he evidence suggests that, although the majority would be familiar to Athenians by sight and/or sound, Ar. was moved to include at least three ... by his experience of poetry rather than of birds; but ... colour-effects were also in his mind" (Dunbar 1995: 244).

[60] E.g. line 275 adapts Sophocles' *Tyro* fr. 65, and in 276 Pisthetaerus asks which bird is the μουσομάντις, an Aeschylean compound.

raised in the land of Ithaca, rough though it be,
who knows of cunning tricks and clever-plotted plans."

The Aristophanic and Iliadic scenes share parallel characters: both show-case an expert and a novice, a compatriot sharing his or her familiarity with a foreigner requesting information. Helen and Tereus occupy the same role in identifying for Priam on the one hand, and Euelpides and Pisthetaerus on the other, the members of the opposing force from an insider's position. And both sets of descriptions, which include names and a few attributes, once they are complete, form a small catalogue. On a narrative level, both scenes also allow the audience to view the main characters as they self-consciously view a third display: not quite a play-within-a-play, but some-thing further into the depth of the scene, which we might term endotheater.[61] The act of observation, as marked by the verb ὁράω, is common and essential to each, though it must be narrated in the epic poem (Ὀδυσῆα ἰδὼν ἐρέειν᾽ ὁ γεραιός), while it can be spoken directly in the play, e.g. 263–268:

ΠΕ. ὁρᾷς τιν᾽ ὄρνιν;
ΕΥ.   μὰ τὸν Ἀπόλλω 'γὼ μὲν οὔ·
καίτοι κέχηνά γ᾽ εἰς τὸν οὐρανὸν βλέπων.
ΠΕ. ἄλλως ἄρ᾽ οὖπωψ, ὡς ἔοικ᾽, εἰς τὴν λόχμην   265
ἐμβὰς ἐπόπωζε χαραδριὸν μιμούμενος.
ΤΕ. τοροτὶξ τοροτίξ.
ΠΕ. ὦγάθ᾽, ἀλλ᾽ <εἷς> οὑτοσὶ καὶ δή τις ὄρνις ἔρχεται.

ΡΙ. You see a bird yet?
ΕΥ.   By Apollo, no, not me.
Though I've been looking open-mouthed up at the sky.   265
ΡΙ. I guess then the Hoopoe mimicked the mountain stream
going into the woods and crying epopoi!
ΤΕ. Torotix, torotix!
ΡΙ. I'm sure he did, pal, but look here, here comes one now!

Just as in the Homeric example, a verb of seeing introduces the subject to be named and then catalogued by the interlocutor. After several iterations of the process, we end up in both passages with a catalogue of names and

---

[61] Narratology prefers the terms metadiegetic or hypodiegetic. For a treatment of the similar phenomenon of the play-within-a-play, see Redfield 1990: 316–317. In this example, though, both epos and drama behave in the same way, since Tereus acts as diegetic narrator, as does Helen. The displays that they narrate, however, function both within and outside the narrative, since they are cataloguing for both a diegetic interlocutor and for an extradiegetic audience.

attributes that correspond to actual physical entities within the world of the literary work. Priam and Helen's catalogue-dialogue closes after three lengthy entries, and the Aristophanic bird-catalogue begins in like manner, with four protracted examples, until the Athenian visitors notice the full chorus of birds collected at the stage entrance (294–296):

> Πε. ὦ Πόσειδον, οὐχ ὁρᾷς ὅσον συνείλεκται κακὸν
> ὀρνέων;
>
> Ευ.   ὦναξ Ἄπολλον, τοῦ <u>νέφους</u>. ἰοὺ ἰού,   295
> οὐδ' ἰδεῖν ἔτ' ἔσθ' ὑπ' αὐτῶν πετομένων τὴν εἴσοδον.

> Pɪ. Poseidon! Don't you see that there are birds collecting?
> Eυ.   Lord Apollo, what a cloud! Gol-ly!   295
> You can't see the entrance now with them flying!

The exclamation of νέφος subtly lends the scene more Homeric flavor: we first see the figurative use of a cloud for a collection of animate beings at *Il.* 4.274 (ἅμα δὲ νέφος εἵπετο πεζῶν, "and a cloud of footmen followed at the same time") and then again at 17.755, where the Achaean forces descending on Aeneas and Hector are compared to ψαρῶν νέφος . . . ἠὲ κολοιῶν, a cloud of starlings or jackdaws.[62] After hundreds of years in the poetic tradition the cloud might seem a somewhat defused metaphor, but the decision to name the city ἐκ τῶν νεφελῶν καὶ τῶν μετεώρων χωρίων, "based on the clouds and the lofty places" (and so Cloudcuckooland), argues that the idea retains some charge. Though the new state must indeed be replete with literal clouds, the "clouds" also refer metonymically to the citizens within them. Moreover, figurative clouds reappear later in the play in the language of divination and fable: the oracle read at 977–978 states that anyone who follows its orders "will become an eagle among the clouds" (αἰετὸς ἐν νεφέλῃσι), while the one who does not will become not even a turtledove, a thrush, or a woodpecker (οὐ τρυγών, οὐ λάϊος, οὐ δρυκολάπτης). A subsequent injunction asks that the law enforcement smite all phony participants at the sacrifice and "cut no slack, not even for an eagle among the clouds" (φείδου μηδὲν μηδ' αἰετοῦ ἐν νεφέλῃσιν) (987). The *Birds* scene diverges from its Homeric model, however, as it progresses and accelerates. Whereas the *teichoskopia* retains throughout an almost reverent tone in its studied descriptions capped with elaborate naming

---

[62] Dunbar 1995 notes the parallel. The application to an army occurs again with the repetition of εἵπετο νέφος πεζῶν at *Il.* 23.133 (of the Myrmidons at Patroclus' funeral), while there is a dark cloud of Trojans at *Il.* 16.66.

formulae, the capping entries to the bird catalogue begin as jokes, then devolve an accelerated list of mere names. Thus when Euelpides notices an owl has entered, Pisthetaerus responds (301):

τί φής; τίς γλαῦκ' Ἀθηναζ' ἤγαγεν;

Say what? Who brought an owl to Athens?

The echo of the proverbial "owls to Athens" seems included exclusively for the audience's amusement and receives no response from the next speaker, who immediately bursts into a rapid-fire list of bird names as the scene reaches its dramatic peak (302–304):[63]

κίττα, τρυγών, κορυδός, ἐλεᾶς, ὑποθυμίς, περιστερά,
νέρτος, ἱέραξ, φάττα, κόκκυξ, ἐρυθρόπους, κεβληπυρις,
πορφυρίς, κερχνῇς, κολυμβίς, ἀμπελίς, φήνη, δρύοψ.

Jay. Turtledove. Lark. Reed Warbler. Thyme Finch. Rock Dove. Vulture. Hawk. Ring Dove. Cuckoo. Redshank. Red-head Shrike. Porphyrion. Kestrel. Dabchick. Bunting. Lammergeier. Woodpecker.

(Trans. Henderson)

As Gordon has observed, "a list that occurs in the context of continuous discourse … by that very token draws attention to its refusal of the connecting power of language … and thereby alerts us to its own expectations of rhetorical gain."[64] Here, instead of the extended and amplified entries earlier in the scene, Aristophanes alters and condenses the catalogue, reducing both form and content to an onslaught of items impossible to ignore and achieving the utmost in absurdity and parodic excess.

This condensed version also comes with none of the optional bells and whistles of catalogue, but only the essential elements: names. At the most basic semiotic level, names are the minimal part of the catalogue that the "experts" supply, and what the asking observers require.[65] For this reason, Priam asks specifically that Helen come near him to speak out their names in succession, beginning with Agamemnon, whom he sees first: ὥς μοι καὶ τόνδ' ἄνδρα πελώριον ἐξονομήνῃς (*Il.* 3.166); "tell me the name also of this huge man." The singular act of naming leads to successive listing, and, as we have already seen in the case of Homeric ὀνομαίνω, verbs of naming

---

[63] It is unclear who speaks these lines: Dunbar 1995 gives them to Tereus, Henderson 2000 to Euelpides; Sommerstein 2001 prints the text as alternating between the two Athenians, based on the comparandum of Chremylos and Karion's alternating list of things that men can have their fill of at *Wealth* 190–192. It is perhaps not impossible to imagine some mix of all three voices involved here.

[64] Gordon 1999: 246.   [65] Gordon 1999: 252 calls these simplest versions "natural lists."

introduce lists. A similar evolution of naming into listing begins at *Birds* 287–288:

> Εγ. ὦ Πόσειδον, ἕτερος αὖ τις βαπτὸς ὄρνις οὑτοσί.
>   τίς <u>ὀνομάζεταί</u> ποθ᾽ οὗτος;
> Επ.   οὑτοσὶ κατωφαγᾶς.

> Eu. Poseidon! there's some other bright-dyed bird now, that one there.
>   Whatever could that one be named?
> Te.   That there's a vultureglut.

The catalogue that builds from Euelpides' series of questions attends to naming each bird, an act that culminates in counting them. The eighteen birds that form the final paratactic sequence top up the total of the chorus, while this list also prefigures a similar one that will appear later in the play, as Pisthetaerus calls out to the new avian deities that replace the Olympian gods (864–888). While this latter catalogue clearly imitates the poetics of a sacrificial invocation,[66] it also recalls for the audience – and parodies – the deep connections between religious practice and lists.[67] In its own twenty-four members, it exactly doubles the twelve anthropomorphic Olympians, reminding us again of the counting function of lists, as well as suggesting by extension the sheer quantity of offerings these gods will need. The enumeration soon goes too far, threatening to add more birds than the sacrifice can accommodate. As Pisthetaerus cries out to put an end to it, "παῦσαι καλῶν. ἰοὺ ἰού,/ἐπὶ ποῖον, ὦ κακόδαιμον, ἱερεῖον καλεῖς/ ἁλιαιέτους καὶ γῦπας; ("Quit calling them! Whoa, whoa! What kind of victim are you calling the eagles and vultures to, you nut?!"). At this point, the list's inherent extendable nature – its recursive ability to continue on adding entries *ad infinitum* – comes into direct tension with the priest's desire for it to define an exclusive set.

Birds presents the comic list at its most flamboyant and perhaps most ekphrastic as well: the audience conceives not only of a number of items, but also physical and aesthetic details of the collection. Meanwhile, Blepyrus' insistence and Praxagora's response bring to light a peculiar feature of lists in Aristophanes: that despite their echoes of documentary texts, they persist in occupying an intermediate space between traditional modes of reckoning wealth and innovative record-keeping practices, a binary that in the scheme

---

[66] Payne 2010: 94 makes this point and notes that the list of birds, as long as it is, remains a mere sample of the extant species; it thus, for him, highlights the Athenians' wonder at the abundance of the natural world.

[67] Gordon 1999 outlines the functions of lists in magic, but many of his conclusions may equally refer to these examples.

of our evidence maps onto a balance between archaic poetic tradition on the one hand and Athenian public records on the other. Aristophanes' lists are the pivot, in a sense, between an old financial model and the new, rooted in old cultural practice yet essential to any economic system, real or, as so often in comedy, imagined. Aristophanes exploits both these associations, sometimes in the selfsame catalogue, to comedic advantage.

Characters like to enumerate things to a greater extent in comedy than in other genres, arguing their points and punctuating their claims with them. This tendency is aligned both with archaic expressions about infinity, Homeric catalogue, and a preoccupation with making accurate counts of real, non-infinite goods. We find a progression from a more impressionistic and personal approach to reckoning, such as Dicaeopolis and Philocleon show and attempt to remedy, to the full domestication of polis administrative practice that emerges in *Assemblywomen* and *Wealth*. The implications of Aristophanes' use of the list form in all these spheres are manifold. Including mock inventories reinforces the legitimacy of comedy as "a sophisticated dramatic form utilizing public-spirited themes and offering timely political advice."[68] At the same time, these lists and characters' interactions with them reflect a population seriously concerned about their livelihoods in the possible economic downturn of the early fourth century, but, quite independent of fiscal realities, enthralled by government practice in dealing with resources. In *Wealth*, the notion emerges that each man's house is a treasury, a place to collect and display his goods. Consequently, like city officials, the characters of private citizens exhibit Davies' "tension between the values of such curatorship (and even connoisseurship) on the one hand and, on the other, the more direct fiscal preoccupations of a Kallias or an Androtion or a Lycurgus – a tension perhaps further complicated by considerations of cultic or human propriety."[69] Scenes such as Cario's description of the newly filled house do not simply reflect a backward-looking picture, "conjur[ing] up the spontaneous abundance of the golden age."[70] Rather, these moments evoke a mindset rooted in poetic forms of the legendary past, but ultimately blossoming in very local Athenian soil.

---

[68] A. T. Edwards 1991: 157.   [69] Davies 1994: 209.
[70] Quotation from Konstan and Dillon 1981: 380.

6 | Unified Infinities, Catalogic Chronotopes

Disordering Lists in Early Hellenistic Poetry

This book has focused on the archaic and Classical traditions of Greek listmaking, but the story of literary catalogue continues well beyond these periods. Greek poets engage directly and explicitly with earlier catalogic texts, and with epic in particular. Thus Aristophanes' mock-*teichoskopia* in *Birds*, with which Chapter 5 concluded, likely represents an example of a larger practice of epic parody.[1] For poets of the early Hellenistic period, archaic poetic catalogue inspired a robust tradition of erudite reception and self-conscious innovation.[2] These literary antiquarian interests have often been connected with the resources and development of the library and *mouseion* at Alexandria, though the history of that institution remains opaque.[3] Regardless of the precise details of how and where poets accessed texts, researched catalogic works such as Callimachus' *Aetia* or Aratus' *Phaenomena* became popular, and poetic catalogue gained status as "not simply an expected epic conceit but a highly esteemed and desirable art form *per se*."[4] Scholars have increasingly shown the ways in which the Hesiodic *Catalogue of Women* held particular sway on poets of this period.[5]

In addition to discrete poetic catalogues, intellectual interest in anthologizing and compilation resulted in catalogic groupings that treated shorter texts such as epigrams as objects to be inventoried, in potentially

---

[1] For an overview of this tradition, see Olson and Sens 1999: 5–12.

[2] On Hellenistic catalogue poetry generally, see Asquith 2006, Lightfoot 2008, Lightfoot 2009b: 220–224, 2009a: 149, Harder 2012: 312–314, and Overduin 2014: 29–31. On reception of the Hesiodic *Catalogue* specifically, see below, n.5.

[3] See Harder 2013 on the influence of the library on Callimachus and Apollonius with other papers in König et al. 2013, particularly that of Jacob. For critique of the usual narrative of the library, see Hendrickson 2014 and Johnstone 2014, who downdate the creation of the library as a political institution to the second century BCE, and decentralize its development, moving it away from one prototype or place. Bagnall 2002 provides earlier critique.

[4] Clauss 1993: 26–27.

[5] Cameron 1995: 380–385, Asquith 2005, Hunter 2005; cf. Sistakou 2009, who rethinks the question of Hesiod's influence on Callimachus, highlighting differences. On Aratus, see Fakas 2001: 77–84.

encyclopedic fashion.[6] These learned literary catalogues also bear implicit connections to the collecting of books, as both sources of information and objects of value themselves.[7] Here we might place such anthologies as the *soros*, "heap," of epigrams, or Posidippus' collection of ekphrastic gemstone epigrams, the *Lithika*, which exploits the connections between precious object and precious text. This text has been productively explored as a fictive temple inventory on papyrus. As Kuttner imagines it: "For a reader, the tidy columns of pseudo-inscriptions (ἐπιγράμματα) on the papyrus could easily seem a humorous miniature of stone temple walls where engraved columns of a text listed the god's treasures and their donors."[8] Outside the realm of poetry, lists such as Callimachus' *Pinakes*, described in the Suda as the "Tables of Men Distinguished in Every Branch of Learning, and Their Works, in 120 Books," allude to an abiding interest in exhaustive cataloguing.[9] These kinds of lists are closely linked to ideas about object display and connoisseurship in this period, topics that have received a good deal of scholarly attention.[10]

Within this variegated context, poetic catalogue held the potential for multifaceted use and usurpation; the catalogic texts of this period can hardly be subsumed under a single model of reception or influence. Accordingly, I offer here two specific groups of poetic catalogues from the third century BCE, both of which subvert expectations, using the list form largely to deconstruct and disorder, rather than to order, knowledge. In the first, we can trace an interest in the specifically numeric and "uncountable" nuances of Homeric catalogue presented in Chapter 1, through selected interactions with the Homeric *recusatio* formula and the proem to the Catalogue of Ships, and the key verb καταλέγω. Here, however, instead of presenting lists that are potentially unending, poets cause us to imagine paradoxical singular lists, containing just one element. The second set of examples focuses on Callimachus and Hermesianax in particular, who exploit the catalogue form as a mode of manipulating objects in space and time. Rather than deploying the mimetic powers of catalogue, which earlier poetry did so well, these poets create verbal

---

[6] See Krevans 2007 on epigram collections; Hatzimichali 2013 on encyclopedism. On collecting, see Higbie 2017.

[7] On the history of book-collecting and the "objectification" of the book, see Johnstone 2014: 368–373; for book-collecting in the fourth century BCE, see Pinto 2013, and Hanink 2018 on tragedy.

[8] Kuttner 2005: 146. Cf. Jones 2015.

[9] On the *Pinakes* and Callimachus' other bibliographic works, see Blum 1991: 124–184, Fantuzzi and Hunter 2004: 43; Call. frr. 429–53 Pfeiffer. While many scholars assume the *Pinakes* have a relationship to a physical book collection of the Alexandrian library, this is unclear; see Krevans 2011: 123, Johnstone 2014: 370.

[10] These concepts are usefully explored by Shaya 2005 and Platt 2010, more recently by Jones 2015 and Higbie 2017.

collections that challenge the orders and limits of chronology and geography. While certain earlier genres introduced this possibility (the Homeric infinite, or sanctuary inventories that might include objects that were no longer there, for instance), we find in Callimachus' and Hermesianax's works a progressive interest in pressing the boundaries of lists. They enact what we might call chronotopic fantasies, allowing chronologically and spatially distant objects to coexist. From geographic catalogues to the space of the human body, Callimachus and Hermesianax construct reorganized fictive time–spaces through serial collections of words.

From Many, One: The Listed Singularity

The so-called *recusatio* formula of Homeric poetry we explored earlier, οὐκ ἂν ἐγὼ μυθήσομαι οὐδ' ὀνομήνω, was a well-known beginning that enjoyed an afterlife well into late antiquity.[11] Fourth- and third-century iterations of this formula can be understood as deconstructing the notion of the potentially infinite catalogue with which it is associated in Homer.[12] Epic parodist Matro of Pitane deploys the Homeric *recusatio* in an amusing effort to subvert the numerical potentialities of the catalogue form (Olson-Sens fr. 3):

> σόγκους δ' οὐκ ἂν ἐγὼ μυθήσομαι οὐδ' ὀνομήνω
> μυελόεν βλάστημα, καρηκομόωντας ἀκάνθαις,
> βολβίνας θ', αἳ Ζῆνος Ὀλυμπίου εἰσὶν ἀοιδοί
> ἃς ἐν χέρσῳ θρέψε Διὸς παῖς ἄσπετος ὄμβρος,
> λευκοτέρας χιόνος, ἰδέειν ἀμύλοισιν ὁμοίας·   5
> τάων φυομένων ἠράσσατο πότνια γαστήρ.

> And I could not speak or name the sowthistle,
> a shoot full of marrow, long-haired with its thistles,
> and the starflowers, who are Olympian Zeus's singers,
> whom the boundless rain, child of Zeus, nourished on land,
> whiter than snow, with a look like mealcakes.   5
> My mistress belly fell in love with these as they grew.

---

[11] E.g.: in the epitome of Cassius Dio's *Roman History* (77.6.1), it is stated of the number of "fine men killed without justification" by the Emperor Caracalla, a catalogue of whose names followed; in the fifth century CE, it becomes a much-repeated segment in the Homeric centos of the Empress Aelia Eudocia. For a full list of ancient citations and references, see West 2006: 66. On Eudocia, see Sowers (forthcoming).

[12] See e.g. Lightfoot 2008: 12, Hunter 2004 and 2005.

At a basic level, the poem trades on the typical comic substitution of hairy foodplants for lofty Homeric nouns; thus σόγκους, sowthistles of the dandelion tribe, and later βολβίνας, an unidentified bulbous plant, together replace the Iliadic *plethun*, or the Odyssean form of *pas*.[13] But at the same time, Matro eliminates the possibility of a countable catalogue, naming the "unnameable" things even as he refuses to do so: his new objects cannot be further individuated. In this he also plays on the semantics of *onomaino*, which here means "to call by name," but in the Homeric formula means "to enumerate," "to name successively in a list." Finally, the end of the fragment implies that rather than provide more examples, the poet has gotten lost in this singular one, and this can be a catalogue of only one item.

The idea of the one-member catalogue enters into Apollonius of Rhodes' *Argonautica*, where we find further engagement with the numeracy of the Iliadic Catalogue of Ships, in the proem to the catalogue of Argonauts (1.18–25):

νῆα μὲν οὖν οἱ πρόσθεν ἔτι κλείουσιν ἀοιδοὶ
Ἄργον Ἀθηναίης καμέειν ὑποθημοσύνῃσιν.
νῦν δ' ἂν ἐγὼ γενεήν τε καὶ οὔνομα μυθησαίμην   20
ἡρώων, δολιχῆς τε πόρους ἁλός, ὅσσα τ' ἔρεξαν
πλαζόμενοι· Μοῦσαι δ' ὑποφήτορες εἶεν ἀοιδῆς.
πρῶτά νυν Ὀρφῆος μνησώμεθα...

The ship, at any rate, the bards of old still tell
that Argos wrought it by Athena's guidelines.
But as it is I shall speak the stock and names   20
of the heroes and their paths on the lengthy sea, and all they did while
wandering. May the muses illuminate my song.
Now first let us mention Orpheus...

While scholars have sometimes characterized this passage as an homage to its Homeric predecessor, it overturns the catalogic model through its figure of one singular, named ship, not many.[14] Moreover, his description of the catalogue he does give is qualitative rather than quantitative. By reworking the *recusatio* formula with the single verb μυθέομαι (γενεήν τε καὶ οὔνομα μυθησαίμην, versus μυθήσομαι οὐδ' ὀνομήνω), he pointedly privileges the narrative, storytelling act of the catalogue, rather than the enumerative listing implicit in *onomaino*. And where the Iliadic poet gave names and

[13] For botanical discussion, see Olson and Sens 1999: 145–146. See Telò 2017 for a sensory reading.
[14] Many scholars have read this catalogue as a more straightforward emulation of the Homeric one, with some technological improvements. For versions of this idea, see Clauss 1993: 26–27 and Vian 1974–1981: 5.

numbers, Apollonius shies away from numerical data, promising instead everything the heroes *did* on their travels (ὅσσα τ' ἔρεξαν πλαζόμενοι). Finally the muses' role shifts from those who remind to ὑποφήτορες, "suggesters," or perhaps more tangentially, "interpreters" of the song.[15] The shift further marks this as a text less interested in numbers than its predecessor.

Theocritus also adapts Homeric-style catalogic plurality into a poetics of oneness. *Idyll* 17, the encomium to Ptolemy II, opens with a priamel that starts by mentioning Zeus but quickly gives way to markedly enumerative praise of Ptolemy.[16] ἀνδρῶν δ' αὖ Πτολεμαῖος ἐνὶ πρώτοισι λεγέσθω καὶ πύματος καὶ μέσσος, "but of men, let Ptolemy be stated among the first, and last and middle." In an imaginary catalogue of high-status figures such as those of archaic epic, where an audience might expect to hear of countless heroes, the single Ptolemy will be counted three times; moreover, he appears repeatedly in this context in which it would be an honor to be included just once.[17] Thus the poem replaces listed multiplicity with singularity, and the variegated collection with the repeated individual.

Theocritus continues this playful engagement with traditional list poetics at the end of the proem, again highlighting the singularity of one listed item rather than all (11–12):

> τί πρῶτον καταλέξω; ἐπεὶ πάρα μυρία εἰπεῖν
> οἷσι θεοὶ τὸν ἄριστον ἐτίμησαν βασιλήων

> What should I list first? As I could state thousands of ways
> in which the gods honored the best of kings.

---

[15] This is not, *pace* Clauss 1993: 27, a "parallel request" to that in the Homeric catalogue, but a total change in the muses' role. ὑποφήτορες has long presented an interpretive problem. Hesychius (Υ 789) glossed it as ὑποτεταγμένοι, "subordinates," an understanding followed in the extreme by Gercke 1889: 135–137, who suggested that the later invocations in the poem constitute a palinode to this hubristic exposition. Many scholars follow LSJ and take the word to be equivalent in sense to ὑποφῆτες, "interpreters," as it seems to be in its attestation at *A.P.* 14.1; Mooney 1912 followed Seaton 1888: 84 in seeing it as "suggesters." Vian 1974–1981: 239 claims the muses are the poet's "inspirers" and not his "docile interpreters," but gives little explanation. Acosta-Hughes 2010: 47 has proposed that the word signifies "subsequent voices" and points forward to the muses that will emerge in the proems to books 3 and 4; thus the poet will begin the poem with the catalogue, and the muses will take over the narrative later.

[16] For discussion of the Hellenistic tradition of "beginning with Zeus," see Hunter 2003b: 98–99.

[17] The poem arguably bears out this desire; as Hunter observes, "Ptolemy is in fact named in the third and third-to-last verses, and the story of his birth occupies the central section of the poem."

Hunter notes that "alleged embarrassment before the richness of potential material is a familiar hymnic and rhetorical trope," and we can contextualize this question specifically within the Homeric potentially infinite catalogue.[18] It similarly evokes the Homeric "boundless recompense" (*apereisia apoina*) formula, which we have observed often signals the presence of an enumeration;[19] here too the poet undoes his own hesitation, later counting out all of Ptolemy's holdings by name and number (77–94).[20] But the *Idyll* makes an important distinction, focusing us on the singular element rather than the abundant plurality of catalogue. These lines, as is well known, echo Odysseus' question to the Phaeacians at the start of his own story (*Od.* 9.14–15):

> τί πρῶτόν τοι ἔπειτα, τί δ᾽ ὑστάτιον καταλέξω;
> κήδε᾽ ἐπεί μοι πολλὰ δόσαν θεοὶ Οὐρανίωνες.

> What first, what last should I catalogue?
> Since the Ouranos-born gods gave me many troubles.

By excluding Odysseus' second member τί δ᾽ ὑστάτιον ("what last") from the question, Theocritus highlights a single item in the catalogue, here the first element, rather than two or more.[21] What is important will be this one, rather than the last, or the potential myriad in between. Here he invokes the repetitive and serial connotations of καταλέγω only to undermine them with a singular object. Moreover, his addition of the second verb παρειπεῖν to describe the potential speaking of a long list further emphasizes the contrast.

Geo-Catalogic Fantasy in Callimachus

These permutations of traditional catalogue poetics suggest that we should not treat fourth- and third-century lists as merely fulfilling or amplifying traditional functions, nor as texts easily reconcilable with the worlds they purport to mirror. While they may seem to represent human realities, and while they often employ human rather than supernatural narrators, they in fact resist

---

[18] Hunter 2003b: 106.

[19] Hunter points out (2003b: 155) that Theocritus' use of rare ἄπειρος, "dry land" later at line 77 etymologically evokes ἄπειρος, "boundless"; if so, Theocritus may be thinking of the formula despite not quoting it.

[20] For analysis of these numbers and the epic styling of the counts, see Hunter 2003b: 155.

[21] Hunter 2003b: 106 surmises, "T. suggests again that there can be no end to the praise of Ptolemy." In this vein he also contrasts πολλά in the Homeric passage with Theocritus' μυρία.

real-world possibility. This is true in the world of numbers, which are not always what they seem. It is also true of space and time, on which this section focuses. In the chronological sphere, catalogues collapse time so that new collected items can coexist at once. As such they resonate with Susan Stewart's observations about the collection, which "seeks a form of self-enclosure which is possible because of its ahistoricism." For her, "[t]he collection replaces history with classification, with an order beyond the realm of temporality."[22] These catalogues also destabilize their contents in geographical terms. Earlier Greek geographical catalogues, such as those of Hecataeus of Miletus and the later traditions of *periplous* and *periodos* concern themselves with the verbal organization of physical space.[23] Yet the lists in this chapter defy expectations, deconstructing the known world and creating new imaginary landscapes.[24]

Perhaps the most explicit example of this kind of temporal and geographical destabilization occurs at the start of Callimachus' *Hymn to Zeus*, where the poet describes the primeval Arcadian landscape with a catalogue of not-yet-extant rivers (18–27):

> Λάδων ἀλλ' οὔπω μέγας ἔρρεεν οὐδ' Ἐρύμανθος,
> λευκότατος ποταμῶν, ἔτι δ' ἄβροχος ἦεν ἅπασα
> Ἀζηνίς· μέλλεν δὲ μάλ' εὔυδρος καλέεσθαι
> αὖτις· ἐπεὶ τημόσδε, Ῥέη ὅτ' ἐλύσατο μίτρην,
> ἦ πολλὰς ἐφύπερθε σαρωνίδας ὑγρὸς Ἰάων
> ἤειρεν, πολλὰς δὲ Μέλας ὤκχησεν ἀμάξας,
> πολλὰ δὲ Καρνίωνος ἄνω διεροῦ περ ἐόντος
> ἰλυοὺς ἐβάλοντο κινώπετα, νίσσετο δ' ἀνὴρ
> πεζὸς ὑπὲρ Κρᾶθίν τε πολύστιόν τε Μετώπην
> διψαλέος· τὸ δὲ πολλὸν ὕδωρ ὑπὸ ποσσὶν ἔκειτο.

> But Ladon did not yet flow, nor Erymanthus,
> glitteriest of rivers; still unsoaked was all
> Azenis. But it would be called well-watered
> soon. Since then, when Rhea loosened her sash,
> watery Iaon lifted many oak trees on high,
> and Melas sustained many wagons,
> and many earth-movers cast their lairs above
> the Carnion (though wet), and a man could go
> on foot over the Krathis and the pebbly Metope,
> in thirst. All the water lay underfoot.

---

[22] Stewart 1993: 151.

[23] For illuminating discussion, see Ceccarelli 2016: 66–74 on Hecataeus' use of catalogue.

[24] Hunter 2004: 225. Hunter 2003a [Dionysius] reviews aspects of the progression of catalogic stylistics from Homer through earlier Hellenistic poetry to Dionysius' *Periegesis*.

The passage aims to paint a portrait of the rainless and lifeless Arcadian world before Zeus, to be understood as the etymology of Ἀ-ζην-ίς. The catalogue describes a region whose rivers could in reality dry up in hot weather; hence it can be envisioned parched. Yet the passage forces the reader to imagine Arcadia at once dry and not: it invokes the white or sparkling quality of the Erymanthus, the wateriness of the Iaon even as it provides ground to trees, and the explicitly contradictory Carnion, which snakes inhabit despite its wetness. While commentators tend to render διεροῦ περ ἐόντος as "although now wet," no adverb actually distinguishes this temporality. Rather, the passage creates a time–space of simultaneous irrigation and dryness. Moreover, while the water is explicitly underfoot – latent and, like Zeus, yet to spring up – each description invokes only the motion on top, through the rhetoric of lifting and raising. Despite not yet existing above, these dry riverways are still viable for transport, like their watery counterparts. The final image of the thirsty man walking perhaps epitomizes this unstable eco-chronology, incongruously inserting a contemporary human figure into a supposedly lifeless landscape. On a broader level, the passage usurps the geographic-catalogue for a subversive purpose: whereas this is a form traditionally employed to impose cognitive order on an unfamiliar place (e.g. Herodotus' Scythia, or Homer's Troy), Callimachus' list instead defamiliarizes a well-known landscape.

Callimachus' catalogue of Sicilian cities in the *Aetia* behaves in similar ways. Despite its fragmentary nature, its opaque selection principles and order can be understood to construct a geography untethered to time and space (fr. 43.42–57 Harder):

φήσω καὶ Καμάριναν ἵν' Ἵππαρ⌋ ι̣ι̣ς⌋ ἀγκύλος ἕρ⌊πει
    ⌋λειν
    ⌋γύλο̣ν̣η̣[
        ⌋ ν
οἶδα Γέλ⌊α⌋ ποταμο⌊ῦ⌋ κεφαλ⌊ῇ ἔπι κεί⌋ μ̣ε̣ν̣ι̣ ον ἄστυ
Λίνδοθεν ἀρχαίη [σ]κ̣ιμπτ[όμενο]ν̣ γενε[ῇ,
Μινῴη[ν] καὶ Κρῆσ[σ]αν, ἵ[να ζείο]ν̣τα λοετ[ρὰ
χεῦαν ἐ[π'] Εὐρώπης υἱέϊ Κ̣[ωκαλί]δες·
οἶδα Λεοντίνους [ ]δεδρα[.........] .....[
καὶ Μεγαρεῖς ἕτερ[οι] τ̣ο̣ὺ̣ς ἀ[πέ]ν̣ασσα̣ν̣ ἐκεῖ

Νισαῖοι Μεγαρῆες, ἔχω δ' Εὔβοιαν ἐνισπε[ῖν
φίλατο κα[ὶ] κεστ[ο]ῦ [δ]εσπότις ἣν Ἔρυκα·
τάων οὐδεμιῇ γὰ[ρ ὅτ]ις πο[τὲ] τεῖχος ἔδειμε

νωνυμνὶ νομίμην ἔρχ[ε]τ᾽ ἐπ᾽ εἰλαπίνην.
ὣς ἐφάμην· Κλειὼ δὲ τὸ [δ]εύτερον ἤρχ[ετο μ]ύθ[ου
χεῖρ᾽ ἐπ᾽ ἀδελφειῆς ὦμον ἐρεισαμένη·

"I will say also Kamarina, where, where the bendy Hipparis creeps
I know the town that lies at the mouth of the river Gela
boasting its ancient roots from Lindos,
and Minoa and Crete, where the Cocalids poured
boiling bathwater upon Europa's son;

I know of Leontini. . .
and of the Megarians, whom the other Megarians from Nisa
sent over there, and I can tell of Euboia,
and the one she, the mistress of the charmed girdle, loved: Eryx.
for in no one of these cities does the man who once built its wall
come unnamed to the traditional sacred feast."
Thus I spoke. And Clio began her story again,
setting a hand on her sister's shoulder.

Discussion of this passage has often focused on the poetic voice and the relationship of the poet to the muses, which seems to represents a departure from archaic epic invocation models, and in particular from the Homeric proem discussed above.[25] But the contents of the catalogue inspire equal intrigue. Commentators have noted that the cities as listed have no discernable organizing principle; Harder provides a possible reconstruction of the complete series as: Syracuse, Catane, Selinus, Naxus, Thapsus?, Aetna?, Kamarina, Gela, (Heraclea) Minoa, Leontini, Hadranum?, Megara, Euboia, Eryx.[26] The sequence corresponds to no predictable order, whether chronological (by date of foundation), spatial (by geographical location or size, or arrangement relative to a fixed center), or otherwise, such as according to an older tradition, to the cities' relative fame, or even to the alphabet.[27] Moreover, this collection represents no single historical

---

[25] On the relationship of the poet and the muses, see Krevans 1984: 234, Harder 1988, Hunter 1993: 125, and Harder 2012: 302–303.

[26] Harder 2012: 312.

[27] The comparable catalogue in Thuc. 6.3–5 is in chronological order by foundation. Alphabetization was seemingly used in the *Pinakes*; see Blum 1991: 153 and the alphabetical example cited by Athenaeus, *Deipnosophistae* 14.51 = Call. fr. 435 Pfeiffer:

οἶδα δὲ καὶ Καλλίμαχον ἐν τῷ τῶν παντοδαπῶν συγγραμμάτων Πίνακι ἀναγράψαντα πλακουντοποιικὰ συγγράμματα Αἰγιμίου καὶ Ἡγησίππου καὶ Μητροβίου, ἔτι δὲ Φαίτου.
I know that Callimachus in the "Pinax of all kinds of writings" records the writings related to cake-baking of Aigimios and Hegesippus and Metrobios, and then Phaitos (Trans.Olson).

moment: these cities did not all coexist at one time.[28] While Harder has connected these inconsistencies with Callimachus' general wish to project learnedness or make a programmatic gesture echoing the universalizing timespan of the *Aetia*,[29] they more immediately signal a deconstructive manipulation of the catalogue form. Instead of an archaic epic grouping of simultaneous figures or objects, instead of a catalogue of one empire's holdings, Callimachus creates a new diachronic super-Sicily that encompasses present and past. Moreover, the geographical scrambling of cities across the island, despite the one close cluster of Gela and Kamarina, stands in stark opposition to the organization of locations in a traditional precedent such as the Homeric Catalogue of Ships, a text Hunter has memorably called (in relation to Dionysius Periegetes) "the authorising model for later *Periegeseis*."[30] The Homeric Catalogue, Clay has argued, is organized geospatially according to natural geography, with clusters of poleis; these clusters are further reflected in syntactic groupings.[31] Callimachus' list would seem to purposefully reject this model of place-listing, instead zigzagging back and forth across the Sicilian land mass and retracing steps. While it is tempting to want to align this passage with Callimachus' erudite self-image of, as Hunter puts it, "the writer as a gatherer of vast amounts of information, but a gatherer who may remain stationary in one spot,"[32] the passage seems to confuse as much information as it provides.

At the same time, this indiscernible order also presents the notion that Callimachus may be more interested in names than locations. While scholars tend to refer to this as a list of "towns," Callimachus suggests that it is more basically a list of multivalent names, signifiers applied not only to Sicilian cities, but also to founding peoples and adjacent land formations. The theme and concept of naming frames the episode, which seems to list cities with named founders as counterexamples leading to the aetion of Zancle, a city with an anonymous founder-cult.[33] Subsequently the passage presents onomastic ambiguities. Following the more straightforward relationship of Kamarina and the Hipparis, line 46 (οἶδα Γέλᾳ ...) leads us through a circular geographical path from the river Gela to the town with whose name the line began; really what the poet seems to be claiming to know is the name Gela and its multiplicity. Similar ambiguity is set up in the

---

[28] On destruction dates, see Harder 2012: 314; see also 326.   [29] Harder 2012: 313–314.
[30] Hunter 2004: 225; see also Lightfoot 2008: 12 for further elaboration.
[31] Clay 2011: 117–118; for a visualization, see Clay's *Mapping the Catalogue of Ships*, https://ships.lib.virginia.edu/ Cf. Danek 2004.
[32] Hunter 1996: 288, cf. 2004: 81–83, where he develops the figure of the poet as armchair geographer rather than *periegetes*.
[33] Harder 2012: 312, 333.

sequence of οἶδα Λεοντίνους ("I know [the town] Leontini") followed by καὶ Μεγαρεῖς – either "and [the town] Megara," as Pfeiffer thought, or "and the Megarians."[34] The multivalence again is clarified in the next line, with the distinction of ἕτεροι ... Νισαῖοι Μεγαρῆες, the "other ... Nisaean Megarians." The disyllabic epic ending seems to mark a difference, but we again understand "same name, different people." Next, the laconic sequence ἔχω δ᾽ Εὔβοιαν ἐνισπεῖν, "I am able to tell of Euboia," promises an epic tale but delivers only a name unexplained, either of the colonial town or its founders' home island.[35] The list culminates in Eryx, the name with the most signifieds – not only the northwestern city, but a nearby mountain and an eponymous founder. Though the feminine relative rules out the founder, this final entry seems to prove the poet's underlying message: names, the stuff of lists, can refer to multiple physical spaces in multiple times. Finally, the closing idea that none of the cities' founders "goes unnamed to the traditional feast" (νωνυμνὶ νομίμην ἔρχ[ε]τ᾽ ἐπ᾽ εἰλαπίνην) provides an ironic summation, for the list seems to have named few if any of them (with the possible exception of Theocles, founder of Naxos, restored in line 36).

The list as a mechanism of geographical reorganization and semantic ambivalence finds parallel, and fuller exposition, in Callimachus' *Hymn to Delos*, a poem that foregrounds imagined geographical displacement in the overall narrative. At its start, various lands flee from the pregnant Leto, while later the island Asteria herself wanders the sea before taking root as Delos. Within this framework, the list becomes a vehicle for delivering a sense of unimaginable movements. The opening praise of Delos places her at the head of an island chorus (*Hymn* 4.19–22 Pfeiffer):

ἡ δ᾽ ὄπιθεν Φοίνισσα μετ᾽ ἴχνια Κύρνος ὀπηδεῖ
οὐκ ὀνοτὴ καὶ Μάκρις Ἀβαντιὰς Ἑλλοπιήων
Σαρδώ θ᾽ ἱμερόεσσα καὶ ἣν ἐπενήξατο Κύπρις
ἐξ ὕδατος τὰ πρῶτα, σαοῖ δέ μιν ἀντ᾽ ἐπιβάθρων.

Phoenician Corsica follows behind in her footsteps
Not to be scorned, and Abantian Macris [Euboia] of the Ellopians
And Sardinia, lovely, and onto whom Cypris first
swam out of the water; and she safeguards her in return for the landing.

Like the cities of Sicily, the selection of Corsica, Euboia, Sardinia, and Cyprus does not follow an obvious logic. Stephens, in contrast to

[34] Pfeiffer ad loc. interprets this as the town name of Megara Hyblaea; Harder follows Hunt and Massimilla to read this as "Megarians."
[35] On this word and Callimachus' usurpation of the muses' role, see Harder 1988.

flummoxed earlier commentators, has argued that "the choice is comprehensible, since the four [islands] act as a geographical bracket encompassing the whole Greek world."[36] This solution, while attractive, is not altogether satisfactory. The choice of Euboia as the northeastern bracket leaves out a good deal of the Aegean (why not Lesbos?). Moreover, it does not account for the list's order, which the poet seems to emphasize (ὄπιθεν, ὀπηδεῖ). The route among these islands zigzags in a geographical synchysis, akin to that of the Sicilian cities – on what map could Corsica be said to "follow" Delos? Rather, the list suggests an interest in emphasizing choral motions and reorganizations, movements possible and relevant specifically in the verbal imaginary of this poem.[37] Although the opening of the poem purports that Delos is "fixed in the sea," Callimachus' reordering of islands in the list and presentation of them as a moving chorus prefigures the more explicit migrations of lands we will hear of later in the hymn. In this way it also collapses the distinction between the island's wandering past (as Asteria) and fixed present (as Delos).

Klooster has read the poem as surrealistic, arguing that in difficult-to-visualize passages "it would seem that Callimachus is really defying his reader's ability to imagine what he is describing, all the while tantalizingly inviting him nevertheless to try."[38] Her reading helps account for characterizations of the poem as "chaotic" or "frenzied,"[39] a reaction inspired by the catalogic description of locations that are said to "flee" from the pregnant Leto (70–78):

> φεῦγε μὲν Ἀρκαδίη, φεῦγεν δ' ὄρος ἱερὸν Αὔγης
> Παρθένιον, φεῦγεν δ' ὁ γέρων μετόπισθε Φενειός,
> φεῦγε δ' ὅλη Πελοπηῒς ὅση παρακέκλιται Ἰσθμῷ,
> ἔμπλην Αἰγιαλοῦ γε καὶ Ἄργεος· οὐ γὰρ ἐκείνας
> ἀτραπιτοὺς ἐπάτησεν, ἐπεὶ λάχεν Ἴναχον Ἥρη.
> φεῦγε καὶ Ἀονίη τὸν ἕνα δρόμον, αἱ δ' ἐφέποντο   75
> Δίρκη τε Στροφίη τε μελαμψήφιδος ἔχουσαι
> Ἰσμηνοῦ χέρα πατρός, ὁ δ' εἵπετο πολλὸν ὄπισθεν
> Ἀσωπὸς βαρύγουνος, ἐπεὶ πεπάλακτο κεραυνῷ.

---

[36] Stephens 2015: 183. For a summary of previous views, mainly regarding the absence of Crete, Lesbos, and Sicily, see Mineur 1984: 67–68, who himself thinks "the choice of names is arbitrary." Cf. Giuseppetti 2013.

[37] For a compelling and original recent account of the interface between catalogue and choruses in archaic poetry and visual imagery, see Steiner 2017.

[38] Klooster 2012: §11; cf. Williams 1993.

[39] Bing 1988: 113 and 127, and Bulloch 1984: 218, respectively; see also Stephens 2003: 114–121 for the idea of cosmogenic chaos.

And Arcadia fled, and the holy mountain Parthenion of Auge
fled, and old Pheneios fled behind,
and the whole part of the Peloponnese that abuts the Isthmus fled,
except Aigialos and Argos. For those pathways she did not
tread, since Hera was allotted Inachus.
Aonia also fled by the same route, and there followed   75
the Dirce and the Strophia, holding the
hand of their dark-pebbled father Ismenos, and followed
far behind Asopus, his knees heavy, since he had been thwarted by a
thunderbolt.

The mainland geographical characters here, though generally clustered around Arcadia, the Argolid, and Boiotia, are haphazardly arranged; moreover, the repeatedly emphasized idea that they "flee" (φεῦγε ... φεῦγε ...) is not easily understandable without treating it as completely metaphoric.[40] But I agree with Klooster that this is no simple metaphor, and it may well be that Callimachus, as she concludes, is "trying to show up the contradictions inherent in earlier poetic representations of animated landscapes."[41] Moreover, we can place this passage within a larger program of catalogic manipulation, in which Callimachus bends the list into a medium of fantastical realization, a formal space in which new versions of previously fixed ideas can be expressed. This imaginary potential is available to lists in particular, and perhaps uniquely, because of their rich tradition as a mode of expressing value and translating the material into the verbal. Instead of simply upholding these characteristics, Callimachus rather tries to "show up" earlier catalogue as comparatively unimaginative, and overly tethered to a physical reality.

A Catalogic Joke

Callimachus thus deploys catalogue to scramble expected orders and distort, rather than faithfully represent, perceived spatial realities and connections. These playful meditations on the possibilities of catalogue and of geographical space pave the way for a learned pun later in the *Hymn to Delos*, and one that also proves deconstructive to the catalogue. At the close of the story of Apollo's birth, Asteria gives a speech exalting both the island and the god over other divine sacred places, after which the poet addresses her directly (268–274):

[40] As did e.g. Mineur 1984.   [41] Klooster 2012: §13.

"ἀλλ᾽ ἀπ᾽ἐμεῖο
Δήλιος Ἀπόλλων κεκλήσεται, οὐδέ τις ἄλλη
γαιάων τοσσόνδε θεῷ πεφιλήσεται ἄλλῳ,   270
οὐ Κερχνὶς κρείοντι Ποσειδάωνι Λεχαίῳ,
οὐ πάγος Ἑρμείῃ Κυλλήνιος, οὐ Διὶ Κρήτη,
ὡς ἐγὼ Ἀπόλλωνι· καὶ ἔσσομαι οὐκέτι πλαγκτή."
ὧδε σὺ μὲν κατέλεξας· ὁ δὲ γλυκὺν ἔσπασε μαζόν.

"But from me
Apollo will be called Delian, and no other
land will be as much loved by any other god,   270
not Cerchnis by Poseidon who rules Lechaeum,
not the crag of Cyllene by Hermes, not Crete by Zeus,
as I by Apollo. And I will no longer be a wanderer."
Thus you recounted; and he sucked your sweet breast.

Mineur, following Wilamowitz, saw the final line (ὧδε σὺ μὲν κατέλεξας· ὁ δὲ γλυκὺν ἔσπασε μαζόν) as a moment of "brilliant brevity," where the poet moves quickly from Asteria's grand pronouncement of alliance to her wet-nursing. For him, "the impact of Asteria's lofty speech is humorously undone by the picture of the babe Apollo feasting upon the nymph's milk, a reference to Delos' function as Apollo's τιθήνη."[42] This abrupt shift in register seems to be achieved by the epic-rhetorical loftiness of καταλέγω (274) followed by the intimate domestic scene. The catalogic undertones of κατέλεξας seem apparent, for the verb refers to not just Asteria's speech generally, but more precisely the short enumeration of places with which she ended it.

Yet a closer look reveals a more complex humor at play, in the form of a pun for the hyper-learned reader. Like Theocritus above, Callimachus also seems to allude here to a specific Homeric line.[43] Line 274 is notable for its placement of καταλέγω in the first hemistich, a relatively uncommon position for this verb in Homer.[44] The line most closely echoes *Od.* 19.44, where καταλέγω also appears early in the line, again with μέν … δέ and a second person subject. There Odysseus speaks to Telemachus before they part for the night (44–45):

ἀλλὰ σὺ μὲν κατάλεξαι, ἐγὼ δ᾽ ὑπολείψομαι αὐτοῦ
ὄφρα κ᾽ ἔτι δμῳὰς καὶ μητέρα σὴν ἐρεθίζω

But you go to bed, and I will stay right here
So I can go on to press the slave-women and your mother.

---

[42] Mineur 1984: 221; Stephens 2015: 223 cites further examples of islands nursing.

[43] Giuseppetti 2013: 166–183 discusses the hymn's rich use of the Homeric lexicon, with many examples.

[44] Only at *Od.* 4.327, 17.44, 19.44, 19.497, 23.321 – five out of sixty-three instances in both epics.

	1. "recount," aor. active	2. "go to bed," aor. middle	3. "put to bed," aor. active
Homer:	κατέλεξας (6x, line-final only)	κατάλεξαι (1x)	ἔλεξα, λέξον (2x)
Callimachus:	κατέλεξας	---	κατέλεξας

Figure 6 Aorist καταλεξ- in Homer and Callimachus.

Clearly the verb in the Homeric passage means something different. κατάλεξαι here is not καταλέγω, "recount" but a homonymic aorist from κατα + λέχεται, "lie down" (cf. λέχος, "bed") – an infrequent epic word.[45] Here the contexts and the contrast in voice (active κατέλεξας in Callimachus, middle κατάλεξαι in Homer) might seem to contradistinguish the verbs, since with the prefix κατα-, the "bed" verb in Homer appears only in the middle, with the reflexive sense "put oneself to bed, lie down." However, in Homer the simplex aorist active λεξ- "put [someone] to bed, lay down" appears twice (λέξον, *Il.* 24.635, ἔλεξα, *Il.* 14.252). Figure 6 summarizes this.

In Homer, κατέλεξας, "you recounted" invariably appears in line-final position. By placing this form instead in the same early-*sedes* position as κατάλεξαι, "go to bed," Callimachus playfully suggests an alternate derivation, from a compound stem of active -λεξ- "put to bed" (column 3 above). Read this way, the poet's grand summation of Asteria's speech ὧδε σὺ μὲν κατέλεξας· ὁ δὲ γλυκὺν ἔσπασε μαζόν becomes: "so you put him to bed, and he sucked your sweet breast." The preceding list goes wholly unacknowledged, and it is perhaps the catalogue form itself that "is humorously undone," or at least characterized as suitable for the feminine, domestic context.

The pun also points to a nuanced reception of both the identity of the cataloguer and the role of Odysseus, who, as this book has argued, is presented in Homer as a figure with specialized catalogic knowledge, who repeated Agamemnon's reparations list and who proved his identity by listing trees. On this reading, the line entwines Asteria's and Odysseus' status as parents with their roles as performers of listed information. It also comments on the gender of catalogue – a traditionally male-focused textual genre. While Asteria first seems exceptional in her ability to perform the list, the double entendre re-situates her in a more traditional parental role. Meanwhile, it defies the audience's expectations for allusion, pointing to a non-list passage of Homer in which Odysseus, the would-be cataloguer, is instead performing an act of intimate, even mundane, parenting.

---

[45] For a list of Homeric *hapax* and *dis legomena* in the Callimachus hymn, see Giuseppetti 2013: 169–171.

Bodies in Time–Space

A combination of geographical revision and playful reception also pervades the catalogic work of Hermesianax of Colophon, Callimachus' approximate contemporary of the early third century.[46] The *Leontion*, three books of elegies dedicated to the poet's beloved of the same name, contained in Book 3 a "catalogue of love affairs" (κατάλογον ἐρωτικῶν), as described and quoted at length by Athenaeus. Many of the "affairs" are humorous fictions: Homer loved Penelope, Alcaeus loved Sappho, Socrates loved Aspasia; as Caspers has argued, these revisionist biographies turn epicists and others into "crypto-love poets," and Hermesianax's catalogue provides new backgrounds for familiar works.[47]

Within the list, authors are ordered in a recognizable genre-based sequence that is internally chronological, but in the overall series they are reorganized.[48] While the ordering of genres places some "older" forms before "newer" ones (e.g. epic before tragedy), the sequence intermingles figures of earliest legend, Hellenistic contemporaries, and everyone in between. Poets of different periods often appear together, as in the case of elegists Mimnermus and Antimachus, and time meanders in nonlinear fashion. In addition to this temporal reordering, Hermesianax's catalogue reimagines the geographical movements of living poets and embodies them within the landscapes of new places.[49]

Peregrination is a crucial element of most characters' narratives in the fragment.[50] One can detect a theme of spatial disorientation from the very start of the text. In the entry for Orpheus and "Agriope" (Eurydice), the location of the story is momentarily confused (fr. 3 Lightfoot, 1–4):[51]

> οἵην μὲν φίλος υἱὸς ἀνήγαγεν Οἰάγροιο
> Ἀγριόπην Θρῆσσαν στειλάμενος κιθάρην
> Ἀιδόθεν· ἔπλευσεν δὲ κακὸν καὶ ἀπειθέα χῶρον,
> ἔνθα Χάρων κοινὴν ἕλκεται εἰς ἄκατον ψυχὰς οἰχομένων.

---

[46] For dating, see Lightfoot 2009a: 148.

[47] Caspers 2006: 25. Asquith 2005: 286 also argues for aetiological influence of the Hesiodic *Catalogue* here.

[48] For the order of entries in the fragment, by genre and chronologically, see, e.g., headings in the text in Sider 2016. For the traditional ordering of the first four poets, Orpheus, Museaus, Hesiod, Homer, cf. Plato *Apology* 41a, with Nagy 2008: 3.99–101.

[49] On the poem see Giangrande 1977–1978a, b, Bing 1993, Kobiliri 1998, Asquith 2005, Caspers 2005 and 2006, Hunter 2005, Gärtner 2012, and Sider 2016 no. 27.

[50] This has been emphasized before, e.g. by Hanink 2008: 115.

[51] Passages of this unsatisfactory text are quoted from Lightfoot's 2009 edition, with exceptions as noted.

Such a woman as the dear son of Oiagros led back,
Agriope the Thracian, taking up his lyre,
from Hades. He sailed to pernicious, uninviting country,
where Charon drags the souls of the departed into his light boat.

Sider calls line 3 "a quick chronological reversal in the narrative, from Hades . . . to Hades,"[52] but it also turns us around geographically. Before arriving at Charon's name in line 4, the reader does not know where Orpheus is meant to have sailed. A natural assumption in context might be back to Thrace – a region potentially imaginable to some ancient readers as κακός and ἀπειθής.[53] Whatever the case, we are primed to attend to the unexpected movements of figures between both real and imagined places.

In perhaps the best-known entry of the poem, the poet gives an alternate account of Hesiod's arrival in Ascra[54] (fr. 3.21–26):

φημὶ δὲ καὶ Βοιωτὸν ἀποπρολιπόντα μέλαθρα
Ἡσίοδον, πάσης ἤρανον ἱστορίης,
Ἀσκραίων ἐσικέσθαι ἐρῶνθ' Ἑλικωνίδα κώμην·
ἔνθεν ὅ γ' Ἠοίην μνώμενος Ἀσκραϊκὴν
πόλλ' ἔπαθεν, πάσας δὲ λόγων ἀνεγράψατο βίβλους   25
ὕμνων, ἐκ πρώτης παιδὸς ἀνερχόμενος.

And I say that leaving his house did also Boiotian
Hesiod, keeper of all knowledge,
come to Ascra, Heliconian village, in love.
Where wooing Eoie the Ascraean
He suffered much and titled whole scrolls of words   25
in hymnic praise, proceeding from the girl first.

As has long been recognized, the invented name "Eoie" puns on the phrase *ehoie* ("or such a woman as . . . "), the formulaic beginning to the entries in the Hesiodic *Catalogue of Women* and the name by which (in the plural) the poem came to be known.[55] The creative merging of catchphrase and woman also leads to a slippage between poem and place in the phrase ἐκ

[52] Sider 2016: 327.
[53] The Thracian reputation for wildness might also lurk behind the name Agriope, found only here. Might Hermesianax intend this Thracian "wild-voiced" wife of Orpheus as a dark analogue of Kalliope, his mother and muse of poetry? See e.g. Kobiliri 1998 ad loc. for a defense of the MS reading (versus Zoega's suggestion Ἀργιόπην).
[54] The poet in the *Works and Days* claims that his father (not he) went to Ascra – Caspers argues that Hermesianax is revising this account (2006: 22). For issues in the text, see Sider 2016: 329 and Kolibiri ad loc.: the preposition ἐκ presents problems with the verb; thus others read ἐναρχόμενος or ἀπερχόμενος.
[55] See, e.g., Asquith 2005: 275–276 especially, Hunter 2005, Caspers 2006: 22–23.

πρώτης παιδὸς ἀνερχόμενος, which has puzzled commentators. It could mean that Hesiod began each section of the poem "from the girl" (i.e., with the words ἢ οἵη), or that he first "went up" to Ascra (on Mt. Helicon) because of love for her – a reading that makes better sense of the manuscript reading ἀνέρχομαι and explains Hesiod's new migration story. Thus Hermesianax aligns the lover's physical movement with the physical writing of poetry and conflates the writing-space of the poem with geographical space.

The entry for Homer similarly revises the poet's geographical history as it mingles poetic composition with spatial movement, and poetic content with land mass. As the poet explains (29–32):

> λεπτὴν ἧς Ἰθάκην ἐνετείνατο θεῖος Ὅμηρος
> ᾠδῇσιν πινυτῆς εἵνεκα Πηνελόπης·
> ἣν διὰ πολλὰ παθὼν ὀλίγην ἐσενάσσατο νῆσον,
> πολλὸν ἀπ' εὐρείης λειπόμενος πατρίδος·

> Godlike Homer stretched out slender Ithaca,
> In songs on account of discreet Penelope.
> Suffering much for her he settled on a small island,
> Leaving off far from his broad homeland.

Here Hermesianax not only displaces Homer to Ithaca; he also puns on the poet's epic aggrandizement of the narrow island, which Homer "stretched out" by setting it to verse – the metaphoric sense of ἐντείνω usually understood here.[56] The catalogue thus imagines the composition of poetry as a literal expansion of geographic space, through both Homer's fictive far travel and his elongation of Ithaca.

While Homer travels far, Anacreon travels often and across time, imagined to compete with Alcaeus for Sappho's affections (51–56):

> καὶ γὰρ τὴν ὁ μελιχρὸς ἐφημίλλητ' Ἀνακρείων
> στελλομένην πολλαῖς ἄμμιγα Λεσβιάσιν·
> φοίτα δ' ἄλλοτε μὲν λείπων Σάμον, ἄλλοτε δ' αὐτὴν
> οἰνηρῇ δείρῃ κεκλιμένην πατρίδα,
> Λέσβον ἐς εὔοινον· τὸ δὲ Μύσιον εἴσιδε Λεκτόν[57]   55
> πολλάκις Αἰολικοῦ κύματος ἀντιπέρας.

> For honey-sweet Anacreon vied for her
> as she withdrew, mingled with all the Lesbian women.

---

[56] Cf. Giangrande 1977–1978a: 106, who analyzes the verb as "make reference to."
[57] Lightfoot: Λέκτον.

> Sometimes he departed Samos, other times his
> own homeland that lies on the viny ridge,
> for Lesbos, good for wine. And he often looked on Mysian　　55
> Lektos across the Aeolian waves.

While it is possible to read a predictable joke about Sappho's uninterest in men at line 52, the rest of the entry focuses on surmounting spatial and temporal distance. The life of Anacreon (perhaps born in the late 570s, fl. 536/5 according to Eusebius) probably barely overlapped with that of Sappho (born in the second half of the seventh century), but Hermesianax compresses them into contemporaries; meanwhile, the diction emphasizes the frequency of Anacreon's visits to Samos (φοίτα, ἄλλοτε, ἄλλοτε), an unlikely arrangement, as if he commuted regularly from Polycrates' Samian court or Teos. The final reference to his looking out at Lektos (the cape at the western tip of the Troad, modern Babakale), visible only from the north coast of Lesbos, urges us to visualize Anacreon on the island within the greater geographical landscape, mindful of his position and displacement from home.

　　The entries that place Mimnermus next to Antimachus effect a similar but more subtle cross-temporal union, aligning two elegists who composed poems named for women (*Nanno* and *Lyde*).[58] The entry for Antimachus delves further into the geography of poetry. As if to signal the inseparability of place, the beloved, and the poem itself, Hermesianax calls Antimachus "struck by love for Lydian Lyde" (Λυδῆς δ' Ἀντίμαχος Λυδηίδος ἐκ μὲν ἔρωτος πληγείς), a heavy-handed etymological figure (41–42).[59] In the corrupt lines that follow, Lyde dies and Antimachus laments; he then composes his poem after more travel (44–46):

> . . . †αἶζαον δ' ἦλθεν ἀποπρολιπὼν
> ἄκρην ἐς κολοφῶνα,[60] γόων δ' ἐνεπλήσατο βίβλους
> ἱράς, ἐκ παντὸς παυσάμενος καμάτου.

> And leaving forth from. . .?
> he came to high summit, and he filled sacred
> books with laments, ceasing from all his toil.

---

[58] Both are also from Colophon, though the poem does not emphasize this connection. See Caspers 2006: 28. For the tradition of naming elegiacs for a beloved woman, see Lightfoot 2009a: xi.

[59] Could there also be a play on an instrument struck in the Lydian mode here? Cf. Orpheus earlier in the fragment (13), described in the MS reading as λυδιάζων, "Lydianizing," a *hapax* that could refer to speech, dramatic acting, or musical performance.

[60] Lightfoot: Κολοφῶνα.

While many capitalize Κολοφῶνα, reading Antimachus' home city, the word can also be understood as a spatial metaphor, "the highest level in poetry."[61] If this is so, the undertone of the place-name likely can still be heard, and Hermesianax thus again interweaves geographical and literary progress through double entendre; subsequently the final phrase idea of ceasing from all his toil ambiguously refers either to his successful summiting of the ridgeline or to his completion of the poem.

Hellenistic poets often revise myth and history; yet Hermesianax's permutations of literary lives across geographies and generations reveals the catalogue to be a particularly fertile form for reinvention and reorientation. In his catalogue, poets sail effortlessly back and forth through spaces and times, performing migrations that fix them in wholly new lands. This is a move perhaps akin to the well-documented tradition of fictionalized poets' tombs, which materialize the body of the poet in a particular location;[62] it also allows Hermesianax to create unexpected poetic and amorous alliances, reordering the canon and adding new names to it – as he purportedly did with the Graces, among whom Pausanias reports he included Peitho, against tradition.[63]

Space of the Body

A final example, by way of conclusion, reveals the catalogue's capacity for reimagining the spaces not only of the world, but of the body itself. The "Tattoo Elegy," a fragmentary curse poem of uncertain authorship but sometimes attributed to Hermesianax, imagines elaborate mythological scenes etched onto the recipient, with repetitions of the verb στίξω, "I will tattoo."[64] On the back, the centaur Eurytion does battle with Heracles; on the head presses the rock of Tantalus; on the forehead, the Calydonian boar. While lists are common in magic-related genres, including that of *arae* (curse poems) with which the poem has been identified, this text uniquely re-envisions the body as a dynamic and extendable canvas for

---

[61] Kobiliri 1998 ad loc. The archaeological site of Colophon, despite sitting among hills, is not particularly steep between the valley and the Acropolis; see Bruns-Özgan et al. 2011. κολοφών in the modern sense of a statement at the end of a written text seems to be later.

[62] For recent discussions of this rich form of reception, see essays in Goldschmidt and Graziosi 2018, and particularly Platt's, on the materiality of the poet's body and its interface with the text.

[63] Fr. 12 Lightfoot = Pausanias 9.35.5: Ἑρμησιάνακτι δὲ τῷ τὰ ἐλεγεῖα γράψαντι τοσόνδε οὐ κατὰ τὴν τῶν πρότερον δόξαν ἐστὶν αὐτῷ πεποιημένον, ὡς ἡ Πειθὼ Χαρίτων εἴη καὶ αὐτὴ μία.

[64] For a summary of theories about dating and authorship, see Rawles 2016: 42–43.

elaborate pictorial narrative.[65] In this it also differs from more common instances of punitive tattooing with isolated words or marks, while it elaborates on the traditional curse practice of listing body parts for punishment.[66] The poem, like the *Leontion* and the geographical catalogues of Callimachus, stretches and alters the possibilities of physical surfaces – here, not of earth but of skin. The first column of the poem foregrounds the size and complexity of the images (P. Brux. Inv. E. 8934 + P. Sorb. Inv. = Lightfoot Hermesianax ("dubiously attributed") 13 col. i.1–24):

```
                         ].[                                          1
                ].[......].. .[.].. .[
         ].π.[..].μνήσονται ἀοιδαὶ
         ]..[.].[.]. ὥς τε πυρὶ φλέγομαι
         ]νῶτον στίξω μέγαν Εὐρυτι[ω]να             5
       Ν]εφέλης υἱὸν ἀτρεστοβίην
Ἀμφιτρυωνι]άδαο δαϊζόμενον ὑπὸ χερσίν
         ]κ..τος τε μνηστεύετο κούρην
      ἀνθ]ρώπων ἀζόμενος νμεσιν
         ]ας δεινὸν χόλον, ὅς τ᾽ ἐπὶ δειλ[.].        10
         ].ον δριμὺν [ἀεὶ] τίθεται
         ]τίσις τω.σ..ο.οι· ἦ γὰρ ὅ γ᾽ οὐδὲν
         ]π[.] .....κακῆς ὕβριος
         ]...ε [τ]ρίποδα μμέγαν......
         ]. φο ..[.] ις κρατὸς ὕπε[ρ] λασίου           15
         ].ει μέσσον δ᾽ εἰς στῆθ[ο]ς ἔρεισεν
         ]ν ἀνέρος οὐδεμίαν
         ]εθηκε βέλος Τριτωνὶς Ἀθήνη
         ]του φειδομένη μεγάλως
      ἑτ]έρηι μὲν ὑπ᾽ ἀσφάραγον λάβε χειρί,              20
τῇ δ᾽ ἑτέρηι ῥ]όπαλον σκληρὸν ἀνασχόμενος
         ] κρόταφον σύν [τ᾽ ὀ]στέα πάντα ἄραξεν
         ]νων ἔκπεσεν [ἐγ]κέφαλος
         ]πλήγην ψυχὴ [δ᾽] ἀνὰ ἠέρα δῦνε
```

...songs will remind
...how I burn with fire
...I will tattoo a great Eurytion on your back   5
... son of Nephele, of unwavering strength

---

[65] On *arae*, see Watson 1991.

[66] On punitive tattooing, see Jones 1987: 147–150; cf. 145–146 for discussion of representations of Thracian women with occasional figural tattoos. See also Phanocles fr. 1.23–28 Powell, who gives a story of punitive tattooing of the Thracian women.

Being torn up by son of Amphytrion's hands
...he was pursuing a girl
...(no) fear of people's indignation
... (or) terrifying (divine) wrath which on a wretch...   10
...always makes an acrid
...revenge ... because nothing ...
...of evil arrogance
...a large tripod
...over his hairy head   15
...and plunged into the middle of his chest
...of a man ... no ...
...Tritonian Athena placed a spear
...greatly sparing
... he grabbed his throat with one hand,   20
and with the other raising his hard cudgel,
...he blasted the side of his head
...and his brains dropped out
...and on impact his soul was engulfed in air.

In his typology of ancient tattoos, Jones placed this example under "metaphorical stigmata," yet the speaker in the poem takes pains to describe the images vividly, as if we are to imagine the spatial mechanics of their actual presence on the body.[67] As Bernsdorff has argued, it is difficult to pinpoint precisely where the visualization is intended to cede to verbal elaboration. For him, the poem presses the bounds of ekphrasis and catalogue, and the compounded descriptions prolong the dread and pain of the tattooing; the scenes thus work to extend and elongate both the time and bodily space of the punishment.[68]

But these features also align with a greater third-century program of manipulating physical spaces through catalogue. Eurytion and the tripod are both described as "large" ($\mu\acute{\epsilon}\gamma\alpha\varsigma$), as are later listed items to be tattooed; indeed, the word appears six times in the fragment. While this adjective and its repetition may seem otiose, it forces the poet's audience to continually imagine bodily space as larger than life as it negotiates between image size and life-size. Is a "large" Eurytion just one bigger than other depictions (e.g. on a vase or sculpture), or is it one larger-than-life-size? In either case we encounter something beyond the scope of a human back, especially if we add in the rest of the scene. As well as expanding one bodily canvas, the fragment also inserts violence (Heracles' cleaving of Eurytion and

---

[67] Jones 1987: 150–151.   [68] Bernsdorff 2008.

shattering of his skull) that superimposes still further bodily surfaces onto the tattooed person's back, which itself remains whole, if not unscathed.

The second, better-preserved column of the poem extends the rhetoric of size to body parts beyond (and smaller than) the back (col. ii.1–24):

μείδησεν [δ]ὲ Δίκη παρθένος ἀθάνα[τος],   1
ἥτε ἀναπεπ|ταμένοις ἀτενὲς βλέπε[ι
    ὀφθαλμοῖσιν],
ἐν δὲ Διὸς Κρ[ο]νίδεω στήθεσιν ἑδριά[ει].
στίξω δ' ἐν κ|ορυφῆι σε μέγαν καὶ ἀναιδέα λᾶαν,
ὅς τε καὶ εἰν Ἄϊδ|εω κρατὸς ὑπερκρέμαται   5
Ταντάλωι ἀ|ξυνέτου γλώσσης χάριν· ἦ μέγ'
    ἐκείνωι
πῆμα καὶ εἰν | Ἄϊδεω δώμασιν ἐστρέφετο.
ἦ μὲν δὴ καὶ | θεοῖσιν ὁμέστιος ἀθανάτοισιν,
ἦεν καὶ Ζην|ὸς παῖς νεφεληγερέος,
καὶ πλούτωι | καὶ παισὶ μέγας καὶ τίμιος αὔτως.   10
ἀλλ' οὐδ' ὡς γλ|ώσσηι δοὺς χάριν ἀξυνέτωι
ποινὴν ἐξή|λυξε· σὺ δ' ἔλπεαι ἐκφεύξεσθαι;
μήπω τοῦτο [θ]εοῖς ἀνδάνοι ἀθανάτοι[ς].
αὐτὰρ ὑπέρθ' ὀ|φρύων στίξω σῦν ἀργιόδοντα,
ὅς ποτ' ἀν' Αἰτ[ω]λῶν ἐρχόμενος καμάτ[ους]   15
Ἀρτέμιδος βο|υλῆισι – τὸ γὰρ φίλον ἔπλετ[ο]
    κούρηι –
σίνετο μὲν [σῖτ]ον, σίνετο δὲ σταφυλάς,
πολλοὺς δὲ σκ[ύλ]ακας θηρήτορας ἐξενά[ρι]ξεν,
πρίν γ' ὅτε οἱ μ|ελίην πῆξεν ὑπὸ λλαπά[ρ]ην
Οἰνεΐδης | Μελέαγρος· ὁ γὰρ θηρέστατος ἦεν   20
πολλῶν ἡρώ|ων σὺν τότ' ἀθροισαμένων.
ἦλυθε μὲν Θη|σεὺς Πιτθηΐδος, ἦλυθε δ' Αἴθων,
ἦλυθε δ' Ἀγκ|αῖος σὺμ μεγάλωι πελέκει,
ἦλθον δὲ Λή|δης κοῦροι καὶ Ζηνὸς ἄνακτος

Deathless maiden justice smiled,   1
she who stares with eyes wide open,
and seats herself in Cronian Zeus's chest.
And I will tattoo a large and brazen stone on your head,
the one that also in Hades hangs over the head   5
of Tantalus because of his witless tongue; really
a great burden circled round him, even in Hades.
Yes he, messmate of the deathless gods,
and yes, cloud-gathering Zeus's child,
with large funds and large family, and well-respected.   10

> But he indulged his stupid tongue
> and couldn't outrun vengeance; so you think you'll escape?
> May that never please the deathless gods.
> And I will tattoo a white-tusked boar above the brow,
> which once came upon the Aetolian's works   15
> ordered by Artemis (it was what she wanted)
> and wrecked the grain, wrecked the grapes,
> and killed many hunting pups,
> until he pierced his ash beneath his flanks,
> he, Oeneus's son Meleager. For he was the best hunter   20
> of the many heroes then together for the chase.
> Theseus of Pittheus came, and Aithon came,
> and Ankaios came with a large axe,
> and Leda and lord Zeus's boys came.

The visuals of Zeus and Dike hint at these engineerings of bodily surface: if the restoration of line 3 is correct (στήθεσιν ἑδριά[ει]), then we can imagine a Dike somehow sitting on Zeus's chest – not just "lodged inside it," like Metis.[69] Meanwhile the thematization of μέγας continues, and the poet suggests yet more unrealistically sized objects on comparatively small body parts, in the form of Tantalus' great stone on the victim's head, and the boar on the forehead. While Rawles suggests that the relative clauses associated with these objects mitigate the ekphrasis, telling stories about the pictured objects rather than describing their tattooed appearance, I contend with Bernsdorff that we cannot be so precise. We instead become lost in the description and the body's seemingly infinite spatial possibility.

As they enact an extension of skin space, these stories also conflate mythical and present time. The poet seems to collapse the accursed person's head with both the rock with which it will be adorned and Tantalus' own head, in a kind of time–space mashup. The relative clause referring to the stone suggests not so much that we are going into a narrative separate from the ekphrasis, but that the stone to be tattooed is one and the same as the one that hung above Tantalus. Moreover, the tenses of the verbs that follow further confuse past and present, mythical object and tattooed image. The abrupt shift from a present "hangs over" (ὑπερκρέμαται, of the rock) to the similar but imperfect ἐστρέφετο in the next sentence (his punishment continually "turned about him," or perhaps "tortured him") dislocates the temporality of the myth: is Tantalus still in Hades? Is this rock that rock? Lines 11–12 at first seem to separate Tantalus and the victim chronologically, yet they leave the question open ("Yet, giving licence to his

---

[69] *pace* Huys 1991: 59.

foolish tongue, even so / He could not sidestep punishment; and you hope to flee?"). Again, catalogue affords wormholes through which mythical past and physical present, legendary objects and future depictions, can meet in the flesh.

The final phase of punishment connects the victim with the Calydonian boar in part of an elaborate interplay that equates human and animal bodies, a general feature of the poem noted by Huys.[70] Meleager's "sticking" (πῆξεν) of the boar with his spear evokes the στίξω of the tattooer, and the animal's pierced flesh adorns the accursed person's own. The poem here makes its most extreme expansion of the human body, imagining what might be the most elaborate scene of the poem on what might be the smallest space of skin – the forehead. But here the poet also introduces a geo-spatial component: he sets the scene in Aetolia, reminding us of the boar's ravaging of the land itself. The tattooed body becomes coterminous with this landscape in the careful choice of the location of the scene ὑπέρθ' ὀ̣|φρ̣ύ̣ων – above the eyebrows, but also traditionally the "brow" of a hill or cliff.[71] Even as the victim's skin becomes animal hide, it also recalls the extended space of an entire geographical formation. Catalogue thus enables not only effective and extensive punishment but material, temporal, and spatial transfers of bodies and objects.

---

[70]   See his note, e.g., on ἐξεναρίξεν, 1991: 68. On Homeric resonances in this passage see Rawles 2006: 490–493.

[71]   At, e.g., *Il.* 20.151, Pi.*Ol.*13.106, etc.

7 | Conclusion and Epilogue

The Materialization of Lists

The previous chapters of this book have attempted to draw a trajectory through the genre and poetics of catalogues and inventories from the earliest and least-fixed texts of the oral tradition to those quite literally set into stone. This tradition culminated in the multifaceted Hellenistic reception of the Greek catalogic past, and the creation of catalogues interested in representing and dissolving the boundaries of time and space. Meanwhile, this book has traced the monumentalization of documents that inventory objects, becoming not only impressive substitutes for contents invisible to viewers, but in some cases something to see in and of themselves. The Greek inventory should be treated not as a mere text-format but rather recognized as the enduring medium in which the Greeks express cultural value. Across oral poetry, written document, and the many genres in between, the list creates, embodies, and ultimately even replaces the objects it purports to represent. Furthermore, its cultural weight and its generative capacities only increase in influence with time.

To gesture to the impact centuries of cataloguing and inventorying had on Greek modes of preservation and valuation, this chapter briefly addresses two final Hellenistic examples of inscribed documents, each of which presses the catalogic habit to an unprecedented extreme by creating a monumental list of essentially manufactured records. These texts recall the poetic catalogue's ability to represent and misrepresent time and space, as we saw in the last chapter, but do so as they create new monuments that both fabricate and conflate past and present. Meanwhile, they interact with the catalogue tradition in the *longue durée*, with connections to earlier inscribed inventories, to the aims of historiographical catalogue, and to the aspirational nostalgia of epic. I discuss both only briefly here, as products of a deep and enduring cultural technique and as provocations to further engagement with catalogue as a genre.

The Parian Marble (ca. 264/3 BCE) purports in both physical form and style to be a historical document, yet it focuses on events of the remote legendary past, listing them by date as if they had occurred within the realm of recorded history, and focusing viewers on the amounts of time from the present to each past event. The Lindian Chronicle (99 BCE), an officially produced *stele* from Rhodes, lists objects from the sanctuary of Athena Lindia, many of which had long since perished at the time of its publication, or that were so legendary and evanescent to have perhaps existed only in the treasury of the mind. Ultimately, it is precisely through the list's long-established history of documenting, authenticating, and displaying power that it becomes a tool for embellishment, fabrication, and posturing. These two objects exemplify the inventory-list as a precious object to see in and of itself, the inventory-monument as a virtual collection to stand in for items that never existed at all, and the inventory monument as a material record of bygone times.

Materialized Time in the Parian Marble

The Parian Marble, a partially lost inscription discovered in two separate fragments from Paros, dated to 264/3 BCE, gives a compendium of important historical, political, and cultural events beginning over a millennium before its own time (1581/0 BCE).[1] While this text has traditionally been thought to align with texts of the so-called "Chronographic" genre, such as king-lists, Olympic victor lists, and historical Chronicles, it also draws on inventory texts of the Classical period for its formatting and reckoning of time. The lacunose prescript of the text sets out its aims but is lacking key phrases (A1, prescript):[2]

> [– – –]ΟΥ[– – –]ν παν[τοί]ων [– – –]νων ἀνέγραψα τοὺς ἀν[– – –] | ₂ [– – –]
> ἀρξάμ[εν]ος ἀπὸ Κέκροπος τοῦ πρώτου βασιλεύσαντος Ἀθηνῶν εἴως
> ἄρχοντος ἐμ Πάρωι [– – –] | ₃ [– – –]υάνακτος, Ἀθήνησιν δὲ Διογνήτου.
> (*vac.* ca. 5)

> . . . of all sorts . . . I recorded the. . ., starting from Cecrops, the first king of Athens, until . . . uanax was archon in Paros, and Diognetus in Athens.

Part of the missing text contained the object of the first person ἀνέγραψα, "I wrote up." Jacoby's suggestion of τοὺς ἀν[ωθεν χρόνους], "I wrote up the times of old," has long stood as a placeholder, though Rotstein reasonably removes this and others from among Jacoby's copious restorations. If

---

[1] For details about historical and epigraphic concerns, see Sickinger 2016 and Rotstein 2016; see also standard treatments in *CIG* 2.2374, pp. 293–343, *IG* xii.5.444, pp. 100–111; and Jacoby 1904: v–xviii.
[2] Texts and translations of the Parian Marble taken from Rotstein 2016. Numbers in subscript refer to lines in the inscription.

Jacoby was on the right track, however, this text would present itself not so much as an inventory of events but as one of times, literal counts of years. While we cannot base conclusions on restored text, the extant entries on the fragments lend credence to the notion of counting time. Here is a representative sample of entries from the beginning of the Ashmolean fragment (A2. 30–31):

ἀφ' οὗ Φ[εί]δων ὁ Ἀργεῖος ἐδήμευσ[ε τὰ] μέτ[ρα καὶ | στ]αθμὰ κατεσκεύασε καὶ νόμισμα ἀργυροῦν ἐν Αἰγίνηι ἐποίησεν, ἐνδέκατος ὢν ἀφ' Ἡρακλέους, ἔτη ΓΗΔΔΔΙ, βασιλεύοντος Ἀθηνῶν | [Φερεκλ]είους.

ἀφ' οὗ Ἀρχίας Εὐαγήτου δέκατος ὢν ἀπὸ Τημένου ἐκ Κορίνθου ἤγαγε τὴν ἀποικίαν [καὶ ἔκτισε] Συρακού[σσας, ἔτη – – – | β]α[σι]λεύ[ο]ντος Ἀθηνῶν Αἰσχύλου ἔτους εἰκοστοῦ καὶ ἑνός.

From the time the Argive Ph[ei]don mad[e] [the] meas[ures] public [and] determined [we]ights and produced silver coins in Aigina, being eleventh from Heracles, 631 years (= 895/3 BCE), when [Pherecl]es was king of Athens.

From the time Archias, son of Euagetes, being tenth from Temenus, led the settlement from Corinth [and founded] Syracu[se, ... years], when Aeschylus w[a]s [k]ing of Athens, in his twenty-first year.

The entries are formulaic and invariably begin with the temporal phrase ἀφ' οὗ (ever since, from the time when). They give a synopsis of an event or series of events in the past and state, with a number, how many years it has been since; they then include an alternative form of dating reference, by king or archon. Immediately the entries seem to undermine the notable events they describe by focusing on the idea of an amount of time ("since the time when") and also by focusing on the present, which, rather than the past, becomes the benchmark for the text's own internal dating system.

The repeated opening sequence importantly marks this text as participating in the catalogue genre in this context where it may not be so self-evident. A key generic precursor to the Chronicle in this regard is found in the Hesiodic *Catalogue of Women*, whose successive entries all famously begin with the connective element ἢ οἵη, "or such a woman as...." There, as we have seen, the formulaic phrasing is a key marker of both the poetic-catalogue genre and of the unit being counted (women); in the Parian Marble, the repetition of ἀφ' οὗ reminds us that we are in a list concerned, always, with tallying amounts of time. The phrase does not so much connect one set of events to the next as continuously relate each one to the present.

And although the entire series is in chronological order, there is little emphasis on the distance between events. Moreover, as has been observed previously, the spacing of events in the text is uneven: some get clustered, and there are gaps of several hundred years at a time. The text is famous for hitting many highlights one would hope to see in the period it covers, like the Trojan War and Persian Invasion and Panhellenic Games, but also for omitting such major events as the Peloponnesian War or Olympic Games. Yet all these disparate occurrences, from cosmic events and natural disasters to battles, inventions, sacred history, and the lives of poets, are all flattened into a single rubric. This is a monument for a present public, composed for the present moment.

Many inscriptions reckon time in some way or other. But the Parian Marble, in addition to signposting so forcefully its focus on a number of years, has another curious feature: it gives all the counts for years in the acrophonic numeral system. This seems incongruous for a few reasons. First, Greek acrophonic numerals are commonly understood to have been replaced by the third century BCE with the standardized system of alphabetic notation. It is only in Attica that the 'legacy' acrophonic system continued to be used, down to sparse examples in the first century BCE.[3] Second, even in their Athenian democratic heyday, the acrophonic numerals were most commonly used for quantities such as weights and monetary sums, not for dates, nor often, as Threatte noted, for inscriptions of "connected prose" such as decrees.[4] There is also no evidence that they were used directly for counting.[5] Even Attic texts that employ acrophonic numerals do not use them for all numerical data: an Athenian account, now lost, of Delian temples from the 430s, for instance, gives amounts of funds in acrophonic numerals but spells out the numbers of years in letters.[6] Thus in its use of the acrophonic system, the Parian Marble gestures to Classical inventories, the genre of texts with which the system was most closely associated. Yet it also hypergestures by using them to denote time, presenting its parcels of years as if they were monies or treasure.

The Parian Marble also counts years distinctly from examples closer to its own genre. Rotstein has called this kind of text "the count-down chronicle," a sub-genre of chronographic text to which she adduces the

---

[3] For examples, see Threatte 1980: 113.   [4] Threatte 1980: 112.

[5] See Cuomo 2012: 11ff on the difference between what she terms "tabular" and "interspersed" formats, which she relates to the Athenian democracy and accountability.

[6] *IG* i³ 402; see, e.g., lines 20–21, which include acrophonic numerals for amount of principal followed by δέκα ἔτη ("ten years"). For discussion of practices in this and other texts, see Faraguna 2008.

closest parallels as two Imperial texts, the two Chronicles that are included in the texts of the *Tabulae Iliacae*. While those objects seem contextually different from the Parian Marble, the surface similarities of the texts are striking. They both begin with the ἀφ' οὗ formula and both include many events similar in kind to those of the Parian Marble. Yet they do not use acrophonic numerals either. There is a clear distinction even here between acrophonic numerals as a quantity-counting device and written-out numbers as referring to a number of years. The use of them in the Parian Marble, then, seems calculated and unique. The Marble even gives years of age in acrophonic numerals – an unusual practice without obvious parallel (B 15):

> ἀφ' οὗ Σωσιφά|νης ποιητὴς τελευτᾶι, ἔτη ΔΔΔΔΠΙΙΙΙ, ἄρχοντος Ἀθήνησιν Θεοφράστου, βι[οὺ]ς ἔτη ΔΔΔΔΠ.

> From the time Sosiphanes the poet dies, 49 years (= 313/12 BCE), when Theophrastus was archon in Athens, being 45 years of [age].

One could just call this an archaizing feature, intended to give the text some feel of the earlier eras it may have purported to describe, if inaccurately so. But I make a more specific claim: the Parian Marble is treating the time it counts as a tangible entity, almost as a physical, material commodity to be valued and quantified. Beginning in the hundreds and thousands, the years seem like so many drachmas of silver, gold, or bronze. Thus the presentation of time here models itself on object-inventory texts rather than merely following the conventions of chronographic texts, inviting viewers to marvel at the years and at the richness of *now*. In this sense, its closest comparanda may be the treasury records we examined earlier. At the same time, this physicalization of years gone by into an almost tangible format, and direct reckoning from the inscription's present, recalls the collapses of mythical and present time we have seen in Callimachus and Hermesianax. In the context of the third century BCE, the text positions itself as a wormhole that conducts us directly to events of the legendary pasts.

The Visible Manifestation of Time

Like accounts and inventory-lists, the Parian Marble also focuses on the illusion of the visible manifestation of what it is counting. That is to say, it attempts to "materialize" events, and in doing so often collapses disparate kinds of temporalities into one mode. In four entries of the text, the author uses the key verb φαίνω to describe certain events of note – recall that compounds of this verb characterized inventory texts as well. The first describes a divine apparition, or perhaps the spontaneous appearance of a statue or relic (A 10):

[ἀφ᾽ οὗ Ἐριχ]|₁₈θόνιος Παναθηναίοις τοῖς πρώτοις γενομένοις ἅρμα ἔζευξε καὶ τὸν ἀγῶνα ἐδείκνυε καὶ Ἀθηναίους [- - - ΟΝ - - -], κ]αὶ [ἄγαλμα | θ]εῶν μητρὸς ἐφάνη ἐγ Κυβέλοις, καὶ Ὕαγνις ὁ Φρὺξ αὐλοὺς πρῶτος ηὗρεν ἐγ Κ[- - -] τοὺς Φρύγας…

[From the time Erich]thonius yoked a chariot in the first Panathenaea that took place, and showed forth the contest and . . . the Athenians, [a]nd [an image] of the Mother of the [g]ods appeared on the ridge of Cybele, and the Phrygian Hyagnis first invented the auloi in C . . . the Phrygian ones

The second, giving credence to the idea that the first is an epiphanic moment, describes the appearance of a comet (B 25):

ἀφ᾽ οὗ [κομήτης ἀσ]τὴρ ἐφ[ά]ν[η], καὶ Λυσίμαχ[ο]ς [εἰς τὴν Ἀσίαν διέβη (?), ἔτη ΔΔΔΠΙΙΙΙ, ἄρχοντος Ἀθήνησι] Λ[εωστ]ρ[άτου].

From the time [a comet] ap[p]eare[d], and Lysimach[u]s [crossed over to Asia (?), 39 years (= 303/2 BCE), when] L[eost]r[atus was archon in Athens].

In both these instances, ἐφάνη describes a literal apparition of some kind: brief, unexpected, and somewhat supernatural. These are special and momentary occurrences that rely on visual perception for their importance. And yet the verb φαίνω appears twice more to describe the times of two of the most famous cultural presences in the Marble, Homer and Hesiod. In a pair of entries, both poets are said to have "appeared" a certain number of years ago. While the text mentions many other poets, none are described in this way. The statement may not seem so remarkable because it is readily translatable, yet it has puzzled commentators on the text with no real consensus – are we speaking of a birth or a *floruit*? Taking into account the idea of ἐφάνη as describing an apparition, however, we can see its application to Homer and Hesiod as an attempt to engage with the visual component of moments in time and, more pointedly, to collapse what are surely not momentary events into one epiphanic and miraculous occurrence. Like a temple treasury record, the Parian Marble considers its events as if they were valuable objects. Just as those things must be listed, measured, weighed, and kept track of, so too must the events of the past be "measured," labeled, and recorded according to their worth in years. The combination of temporal focalizing words, acrophonic numeration, and epiphanic language makes these often-legendary events, and the evanescent concept of time itself, into visible, quantifiable, and almost physical entities. Moreover, the stone itself becomes a singular manifestation of what is in truth a multifaceted, irregular collection of disparate events and times. Its material and unifying presence *here*, along with the consistent reckoning by the standard of the *now*, consolidate, solidify, even, the ephemeral happenings of before into a unified whole.

The Lindian Chronicle as Fabricated Inventory

This kind of transfer – from evanescent to permanent, and from document to monument – is one we find writ in the largest terms on the Lindian Chronicle. This monumental inscription composed in 99 BCE catalogues the dedications made at the sanctuary of Athena Lindia at Rhodes throughout its history, as well as four recorded epiphanies of the goddess. Many of the dedications themselves are no longer extant by the time of the inscription's composition (the temple burned in a fire of 392/1 BCE), and the authors are thus exhorted to reconstruct "whatever details are fitting (*harmozonta*) about the offerings and the epiphanic appearance of the goddess" from the available sources. The *stele* has already provided fertile ground for examining the relationship of text and object, both in its individual entries and as a singular, composite monument. It has been interpreted, and rightly so, as a "relic of relics," a record of the temple as "community museum," and a document of a "lost and partially imagined world."[7] Perhaps most pertinent here, Platt has called it a "rematerialization" of the lost items it lists, an analysis that calls to mind the functions of earlier temple inventories.[8] In this sense, the Lindian Chronicle presents us with a permutation of the quintessential inventory, one that signals a new level of abstraction in Greek collecting and listmaking. In 1922, less than a decade after Blinkenberg's *editio altera*, Elizabeth Douglas Van Buren published what is possibly the first brief treatment in English of the inscription. Due perhaps to some combination of its opaque title, anthropological approach, and journal of publication, her article, "Museums and Raree Shows in Antiquity," receives little

---

[7] "Relic of relics": Koch Piettre 2005: 98; "Community museum": Shaya 2005; "lost ... world": Higbie 2003: 15. See also Shaya 2014 on cultures of collecting and the Chronicle.
[8] Platt 2011: 165; see also Kirk 2018.

attention from present students of the Lindian Chronicle. Yet Van Buren makes an astute observation in her claim that the Lindian temple of Athena functioned much as the modern museum, where objects "by degrees accumulated a hoary crust of traditions, never allowed to lack picturesqueness by the custodians who discoursed to an admiring crowd of sight-seers about the treasures which enriched the sanctuary." This portrait, couched as it is in baroque prose, does not differ so greatly from Higbie's dramatization of an ancient trip to Rhodes: "a visitor might have gleaned information . . . from conversations with a local priest or from reading the inscriptions on display. He might have come across the most important survivor of these inscriptions, the stone now known as the Chronicle of Lindos, and he could have learned from it something about those early centuries of the sanctuary."[9] Undoubtedly the two works do not share scholarly objectives, yet both insist on the significance of the tourist – the viewer – at this sanctuary and especially in the face of this text. This is an important intersection, and less self-evident than it seems, if we are to consider the Lindian Chronicle alongside the inventories of the fifth-century Attic tradition. Whereas these texts seem to exist, at least in theory, to provide an account of extant items, the inscription from Lindos states its purpose as precisely the opposite (lines 2–10):[10]

> . . . ἐπεὶ τὸ ἱερὸ]ν τᾶς Ἀθάνας τᾶς Λινδίας ἀρχαιότατόν τε καὶ ἐντιμό[τα]|τον ὑπάρχον πολλοῖς κ[αὶ καλοῖς ἀναθέμασι ἐκ παλαιοτ]άτων χρόνων κεκόσμηται διὰ τὰν τᾶς θεοῦ ἐπιφάνειαν,| συμβαίνει δὲ τῶν ἀνα[θεμάτων τὰ ἀρχαιότατα μετὰ τᾶν ἐ][11]πιγραφᾶν διὰ τὸν χρόνον ἐφθάρθαι, τύχαι ἀγαθᾶι δεδόχθαι [μ]αστροῖς καὶ Λινδίοις κυρ[ωθέντος τοῦδε τοῦ ψαφίσματος ἐλέ]σθαι ἄνδρας δύο, τοὶ δὲ αἱρεθέντες κατασκευαξάντω στάλαν|[λ]ίθου Λαρτίου καθ᾽ ἅ κα ὁ ἀρχ[ιτέκτων γράψηι καὶ ἀναγραψάντ]ω εἰς αὐτὰν τόδε τὸ ψάφισμα, ἀναγραψάντω δὲ ἔκ τε τᾶν | [ἐπ]ιστολᾶν καὶ τῶν χρηματ[ισμῶν καὶ ἐκ τῶν ἄλλων μαρτυρί]ων ἅ κα ἦι

---

[9] Higbie 2003: 5.

[10] Text of the Lindian Chronicle is taken from Blinkenberg 1941, which Higbie 2003 follows closely except where noted.

[11] The proposals for the effaced middle of this line – essentially all suggestions of the accusative subject for ἐφθάρθαι that is partitive to τῶν ἀνα[θεμάτων] – generally fall into two groups: those that highlight the age of the destroyed dedications, and those that emphasize their quantity. Thus alongside Blinkenberg's ἀρχαιότατα we see ἀρχαιότερα (Wilhelm 1930), while Higbie, following Blinkenberg's 1915 text (= Holleaux 1913) for reasons somewhat obscure, gives τὰ πλειστά. In his review of Higbie, Bresson most recently has provided a convincing rationale for his own restoration τούτων τὰ πολλά, which he presents as a "more neutral" text, since it does not make a direct claim as to the relative age of the destroyed objects or imply that none of the old dedications survived the years or the fire of 330 (Bresson 2006: 538–539). Though his proposal is bolstered by a precise and calculated rejection of previous versions on both epigraphic and thematic grounds, one cannot see it as a definitive restoration *per se*.

ἁρμόζοντα περὶ τῶν ἀναθεμάτων καὶ τᾶς ἐπιφανείας | [τ]ᾶς θε<ο>ῦ
ποιούμενοι τὰν ἀ[ναγραφὰν παρεόντος καὶ τοῦ γρ]αμματέως τῶν
μαστρῶν τοῦ νῦν ἐν ἀρχᾶι ἐόντος, τοὶ δὲ ἱεροτα-|μίαι τελεσάντω τοῖς
αἱρεθεῖσι [τέλεσμα εἰς τὰν κατασκευὰν τᾶ]ς στάλας καὶ τὰν ἀναγραφὰν μὴ
πλεῖον οὗ ἀποφαίνεται Πυργο|τέλης ὁ ἀρχιτέκτων δραχμᾶν διακοσιᾶν·

Since the hieron of Athena the Lindian, both the most archaic and the most venerable in existence, has been adorned with many beautiful offerings from the earliest times on account of the visible presence of the goddess, and since it happens that the oldest of the offerings together with their inscriptions have been destroyed on account of time, it has been resolved with the presumption of good fortune by the *mastroi* and the Lindians, with the authorization of this decree, that two men be selected. Let these men, once selected, set up a *stele* of stone from Lartos according to what the architect writes and let them inscribe on it this decree. Let them inscribe from the letters and from the public records and from the other evidence whatever may be fitting about the offerings and the visible presence of the goddess, making the copy of the *stele* with the secretary of the mastroi, the [secretary] now in office. (Trans. Higbie, modified.)

Even if we momentarily disregard the disputed restoration of the fourth line, it is clear from what remains that we must understand some accusative as complement to τῶν ἀνα[θεμάτων] and, more importantly, subject for ἐφθάρθαι. Thus as opposed to a usual inventory, whose prescripts state at the outset that a given set of officials handed over (*paredosan*) the following things (*tade*), the Lindian Chronicle takes as its responsibility everything that is no longer in the temple. To what end? Higbie has advanced the thesis that the Chronicle served to resurrect the sanctuary's now-faded glory; Bresson disagrees. The Chronicle, he believes, "n'était donc nullement destinée à ressusciter le passé du sanctuaire. Un seul et même principe de rédaction avait été établi: celui de dresser la liste de toutes les dédicaces importantes qui n'étaient plus visibles ou identifiables en 99 a.C."[12] But this is not all: the Chronicle represents the ultimate extension of the inventorying genre, to the point that no real amount of money or prestige objects is at stake any more. It is the act of listing that matters to the listmakers, and to visitors to the sanctuary, who come to see a list rather than a collection of actual goods, even if some remain. The collection, once physical, now has been replaced by the text.[13]

---

[12] Bresson 2006: 547.

[13] On the relationship between text and object Swann 2001, especially chapter 3, has presented several studies of textual collecting in early modern England, and the temple administrative body at Lindos seems to operate on principles similar to those she identifies in English individuals of the seventeenth century.

We can perhaps trace roots of textual collecting in any inventory that alludes to the placement of physical objects and subsequently removes them from view. As we have seen in several examples already, inventories often refer to things that were not visible for a variety of reasons. Perhaps, as in the case of some of the Acropolis buildings, they were put away into an inaccessible part of the sanctuary. Perhaps, as at Brauron or Delos, they were in a different region altogether from their place of record. Perhaps they had been removed or melted for another purpose; perhaps, as in the case of the Samian Heraion, they were temporarily in use. Indeed, the inventory in earlier times had begun to assume an autonomous existence and a power unto itself, yet in the case of the Lindian Chronicle, the relationship of object to text becomes further complicated because almost all of the dedications in question were themselves inscribed at some point, arguably before publication of inventories (or perhaps even inventorying itself) was prevalent in the Greek world. Each entry in the Chronicle systematically lists the dedicators along with known physical details of the offerings, but then expends the most chiseling on the citation of the inscriptions and their sources. Entry VIII(=B48-53) provides a typical example:

[Τήλ]εφος φιάλαν χρυσόμφαλον, ἐφ᾽ ᾶς ἐπεγέ-
[γρ]απτο· Τήλεφος Ἀθάναι ἱλατή[ρι]ον, ὡς ὁ Λύκιος
Ἀπόλλων εἶπε. περὶ τούτων ἱστ[ορ]εῖ Ξεναγόρας   50
ἐν τᾶι α τᾶς χρονικᾶς συντάξιος, Γόργων
ἐν τᾶι α τᾶν περὶ Ρόδου, Γοργοσθένης ἐν τᾶι ἐ-
πιστολᾶι, Ἱερόβουλος ἐν τᾶι ἐπ[ιστολᾶι].

Telephus, a phiale with a golden boss. On which had been inscribed: "Telephus to Athena a supplicatory gift, as Lycian Apollo said." About these things Xenagoras reports in his investigations in the first book of his Annalistic Account, Gorgon in this first book of his work About Rhodes, Gorgosthenes in his letter, Hieroboulus in his. (Trans. Higbie)

Thus from the time of the dedication – sometime in the distant or legendary past – to the time of the Chronicle, the original text has been cut off from its context but reattached to another one. The steps in making this one *stele* represent on a small scale the historical progression of the dedicatory text's relation to the dedicatory object in Greece: beginning as part of it and ending up as completely divorced from it. Figure 7 elucidates these stages.

At the first stage, characteristic of our earliest alphabetic Greek texts and possibly many of the archaic votives in the Lindian Chronicle, the

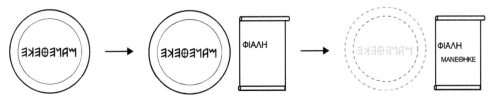

Figure 7 Diagram of the process from dedication to inventory. Image by Gareth Long

dedicatory text exists only as a physical part of the object. In the middle stage, an inscribed *stele* describing the dedications stands alongside the object (inscribed or uninscribed), as is characteristic of standard inventories throughout the Greek world.[14] The third stage signals the disappearance of the votive, and the subsequent grafting of its dedicatory text onto the accompanying *stele*, which then becomes the only item on display. In a series, multiple dedicatory objects become replaced by one conglomerate text. Thus it becomes immediately apparent that the authors of the Chronicle and of the decree – regardless of the realities of the lacuna – have concerned themselves with the complex relationship of dedicated object and text. They have published a list that shares several distinguishing features of a Greek inventorying tradition almost three centuries old, yet that exhibits an elevation of the archive to the status not only of monument but also artifact.[15] If we subsequently return to the notion of the sanctuary as museum (seemingly so rational) it emerges somewhat distorted: imagine visiting a modern museum to observe a list of pieces it had once owned but were now missing, stolen, or repatriated. For the Lindians, though, textual collection, or connoisseurship through listing, is possible and acceptable. The dedicatory object, once something of prestige, becomes a perishable vehicle through which a dedicatory inscription moves from temporary surface to its final and permanent medium of the list on stone. We need not be limited, then, to seeing a grandiose nostalgic rationale for making such a list, for in many senses it is as natural as any other inventory. If Attic inventories in the fourth century can be displaced from what they describe, and if the second-century Milesians can commission and display a list of disintegrated dresses, the Lindians merely continue an archival tradition already bordering on the absurd, or at least far more concerned with

[14] They frequently identify objects as ἀνεπίγραφος, a designation I would adduce as further evidence for the inventory's superseding the object, for the specification implies that the text must reflect exactly what is or is not physically manifest on it.

[15] Davies 2003 explores the monumentalization of the archive and alludes to its origin in dedicatory formats 335–337, such as public gravestones and manumission documents of the fifth and fourth centuries; his account applies equally well to inventory texts.

cataloguing than object-based wealth. For them, though, the cycle is complete: in the total loss of the original offerings, the new monolithic list, complete with dedicatory inscriptions stands in their stead. It is only in a rich context of cultural association, of deep connections among catalogues, inventories, and concepts of value and worth, that such transitions can occur. The Parian Marble and Lindian Chronicle represent two more remarkable specimens, perhaps the products of authors remarkably attuned to the past, yet the tradition of replacing physical wealth with a textual list-object was far older, and far larger, than they.

These two inscriptions stand merely as two examples of the richness of the catalogue tradition in Greek, and its profound capacity for self-referentiality and diachronic engagement, in both content and form. In a world that we so often consider to be divorced from many of modernity's abstractions of representation and virtual media, lists stand as perhaps the closest precursors to technologies of encoding, digitality, and information processing. These are topics to be explored at greater length elsewhere, along with meta-questions about catalogue. Throughout the Greek past, however, we can remain certain that the list, like stone, and like time itself, went on and on and on.

Bibliography

Acosta-Hughes, B. (2010) *Arion's Lyre: Archaic Lyric into Hellenistic Poetry.* Princeton.

Alden, M. J. (2000) *Homer beside Himself: Para-Narratives in the Iliad.* Oxford.

Aleshire, S. B. (1989) *The Athenian Asklepieion: The People, Their Dedications, and the Inventories.* Amsterdam.

   (1991) *Asklepios at Athens: Epigraphic and Prosopographic Essays on the Athenian Healing Cults.* Amsterdam.

Allen, T. W. (1901) "The Euripidean Catalogue of Ships," *The Classical Review* 15: 346–350.

   (1910) "The Homeric Catalogue," *Journal of Hellenic Studies* 30: 292–322.

   (1921) *The Homeric Catalogue of Ships.* Oxford.

Andersen, Ø. and D. T. T. Haug, eds. (2012) *Relative Chronology in Early Greek Epic Poetry.* Cambridge and New York.

Anscombe, G. E. M. (1957) *Intention.* Cambridge, Mass.

Armayor, O. K. (1978) "Herodotus' Catalogues of the Persian Empire in the Light of the Monuments and the Greek Literary Tradition," *Transactions of the American Philological Association* 108: 1–9.

Arrington, N. T. (2011) "Inscribing Defeat: The Commemorative Dynamics of the Athenian Casualty Lists," *Classical Antiquity* 30: 179–212.

   (2012) "The Form(s) and Date(s) of a Classical War Monument: Re-Evaluating IG I³ 1163 and the Case for Delion," *Zeitschrift für Papyrologie und Epigraphik* 181: 61–75.

   (2015) *Ashes, Images, and Memories: The Presence of the War Dead in Fifth-Century Athens.* Oxford.

Asheri, D. (2007) *A Commentary on Herodotus Books I–IV.* Oxford.

Asheri, D., A. B. Lloyd, A. Corcella, O. Murray, and A. Moreno. (2007) *A Commentary on Herodotus Books I–IV,* ed. O. Murray and A. Moreno. Oxford.

Asquith, H. (2005) "From Genealogy to 'Catalogue': The Hellenistic Adaptation of the Hesiodic Catalogue Form," in *The Hesiodic Catalogue of Women: Constructions and Reconstructions,* ed. R. L. Hunter. Cambridge and New York: 266–286.

   (2006) "Listed Narratives in Greek Poetry from Hesiod to Callimachus: The Development of a Genre." Doctoral dissertation.

Austin, J. L. (1975) *How to Do Things with Words*. 2nd ed. Ed. J. O. Urmson and M. Sbisà. Cambridge, Mass.

Austin, J. N. (1965) "Catalogues and the Catalogue of Ships in the Iliad." Doctoral dissertation.

Bagnall, R. S. (2002) "Alexandria: Library of Dreams," *Proceedings of the American Philosophical Society* 146: 348–362.

Bakewell, G. (2007) "Written Lists of Military Personnel," in *Politics of Orality*, ed. C. Cooper. Leiden: 89–101.

Bakker, E. J. (2002) "The Making of History: Herodotus' Histories Apodexis," in *Brill's Companion to Herodotus*, ed. E. J. Bakker, H. van Wees, and I. J. F. de Jong. Leiden: 3–32.

  (1997) *Poetry in Speech: Orality and Homeric Discourse*. Ithaca, N.Y.

  (2010) "Pragmatics: Speech and Text," in *A Companion to the Ancient Greek Language*, ed. E. Bakker. Chichester, UK: 151–168.

Bakker, E. J., H. van Wees, and I. J. F. de Jong, eds. (2002) *Brill's Companion to Herodotus*. Leiden.

Ball, R. (1976) "Herodotos' List of the Spartans Who Died at Thermopylai," *Museum Africum* 5: 1–8.

Barney, S. (1982) "Chaucer's Lists," in *The Wisdom of Poetry*, ed. S. Wenzel and L. D. Benson. Kalamazoo, Mich.: 189–223.

Beck, I. (1971) *Die Ringkomposition bei Herodot und ihre Bedeutung für die Beweistechnik*. Hildesheim.

Beecroft, A. (2010) *Authorship and Cultural Identity in Early Greece and China: Patterns of Literary Circulation*. Cambridge.

Beekes, R. (2010) *Etymological Dictionary of Greek*. Leiden.

Belknap, R. E. (2004) *The List: The Uses and Pleasures of Cataloguing*. New Haven.

Bellos, A. (2010) *Here's Looking at Euclid*. New York.

Berkel, T. A. van. (2017) "Voiced Mathematics: Orality and Numeracy," in *Voice and Voices in Antiquity*, ed. N. Slater. Leiden: 321–350.

Bernsdorff, H. (2008) "Mythen, die unter die Haut gehen: Zur literarischen Form der Tätowierelegie (P. Brux. inv. E 8934 und P. Sorb. inv. 2254)," *Mnemosyne* 61: 45–65.

Bertelli, L. (2001) "Hecataeus: From Genealogy to Historiography," in *The Historian's Craft in the Age of Herodotus*, ed. N. Luraghi. Oxford: 67–94.

Beye, C. R. (1964) "Homeric Battle Narrative and Catalogues," *Harvard Studies in Classical Philology* 68: 345–373.

Bichler, R. (2004) "Herodotus' Ethnography. Examples and Principles," in *The World of Herodotus. Proceedings of an International Conference. Nicosia, September 18–21, 2003, Nicosia 2004, 91–112*, ed. V. Karageorghis and I. Taifacos. Nicosia: 143–160.

Bing, P. (1988) *The Well-Read Muse: Present and Past in Callimachus and the Hellenistic Poets*. Göttingen.

(1993) "The Bios-Tradition and Poets' Lives in Hellenistic Poetry," in *Nomodeiktes*, ed. R. Rosen and J. Farrell. Ann Arbor: 619–631.

Blinkenberg, C. (1941) *Lindos: Fouilles de l'Acropole 1902–1914*, vol. II: *Inscriptions*. Berlin.

Boegehold, A. L., ed. (1984) *Studies Presented to Sterling Dow on His Eightieth Birthday*. Durham, N.C.

Bounia, A. (2004) *The Nature of Classical Collecting: Collectors and Collections, 100 BCE–100 CE*. Aldershot and Burlington, Vt.

Bowie, A. M. (1993) *Aristophanes: Myth, Ritual, and Comedy*. Cambridge.

Bowie, A. M., ed. (2007) *Herodotus Histories Book VIII*. Cambridge.

Bowra, C. M. (1952) *Heroic Poetry*. London.

Bradeen, D. W. (1969) "The Athenian Casualty Lists," *Classical Quarterly* 19: 145–159.

Bresson, A. (2006) "Relire la *Chronique de temple lindien*" [review of Higbie 2003], *Topoi: Orient-Occident* 14.2: 527–551.

Brøns, C. (2015) "Textiles and Temple Inventories: Detecting an Invisible Votive Tradition in Greek Sanctuaries in the Second Half of the First Millennium BC," *Acta Hyperborea: Danish Studies in Classical Archaeology* 14: 43–83.

Brosius, M., ed. (2003) *Ancient Archives and Archival Traditions: Concepts of Record-Keeping in the Ancient World*. Oxford.

Brown, L. A. (2000) "From Discard to Divination: Demarcating the Sacred through the Collection and Curation of Discarded Objects," *Latin American Antiquity* 11: 319–333.

Brulé, P. (1990) "Retour à Brauron: Repentirs, avancées, mises au point," *Dialogues d'histoire ancienne* 16: 61–90.

Bruns-Özgan, C., V. Gassner, and U. Muss. (2011) "Kolophon: Neue Untersuchungen zur Topographie der Stadt," *Anatolia Antiqua* 19: 199–239.

Bulloch, A. (1984) "The Future of a Hellenistic illusion: Some Observations on Callimachus and Religion," *Museum Helveticum* 41: 209–230.

Burr, V. (1944) *Neōn Katálogos: Untersuchungen zum homerischen Schiffskatalog*. Leipzig.

Cameron, A. (1995) *Callimachus and His Critics*. Princeton, N. J.

Camus, A. (1946). *The Stranger*, trans. S. Gilbert. New York.

Carey, C. (1994) "Comic Ridicule and Democracy," in *Ritual, Finance, Politics: Athenian Democratic Accounts Presented to David Lewis*, ed. R. Osborne and S. Hornblower. Oxford: 69–83.

Cargill, J. (1995) *Athenian Settlements of the Fourth Century B.C.* Leiden.

Caspers, C. L. (2005) "Hermesianax fr. 7.75–8 Powell: Philitas, Bittis … and a Parrot?" *Mnemosyne* 58: 575–581.

(2006)" The Loves of the Poets: Allusions in Hermesianax fr. 7 Powell," in *Beyond the Canon*, ed. M. A. Harder, R. F. Regtuit, and G. C. Wakker. Leuven and Dudley, Mass.: 21–42.

Casson, S. (1914) "The Persian Expedition to Delphi," *The Classical Review* 28: 145–151.

(1921) "ΑΠΟΔΕΙΞΙΣ, 'Inventory,' in Herodotus and Thucydides," *The Classical Review* 35: 144–145.

Ceccarelli, P. (2016) "Map, Catalogue, Drama, Narrative: Representations of the Aegean Space," in *New Worlds from Old Texts: Revisiting Ancient Space and Place*, ed. E. Barker, S. Bouzarovski, C. Pelling, and L. Isaksen. Oxford: 61–80.

Chankowski, V. (2008) *Athènes et Délos à l'époque Classique: Recherches sur l'administration du sanctuaire d'Apollon délien*. Athens.

(2011) "Divine Financiers: Cults as Consumers and Generators of Value," in *The Economies of Hellenistic Societies, Third to First Centuries BC*, ed. Z. Archibald, J. K. Davies, and V. Gabrielsen. Oxford: 142–165.

Christ, M. R. (1994) "Herodotean Kings and Historical Inquiry," *Classical Antiquity* 13: 167–202.

Christensen, J. P. (2010) "First-Person Futures in Homer," *American Journal of Philology* 131: 543–571.

Cingano, E. (2005) "A Catalogue within a Catalogue: Helen's Suitors in the Hesiodic *Catalogue of Women* (frr. 196–204)," in *The Hesiodic Catalogue of Women: Constructions and Reconstructions*, ed. R. Hunter. Cambridge: 118–152.

Clauss, J. J. (1993) *The Best of the Argonauts: The Redefinition of the Epic Hero in Book 1 of Apollonius's Argonautica*. Berkeley.

Clay, J. S. (1984) "The Hecate of the Theogony," *Greek, Roman, and Byzantine Studies* 25: 27–38.

(2011) *Homer's Trojan Theater*. Cambridge.

Cleland, L. (2005) *The Brauron Clothing Catalogues: Text, Analysis, Glossary and Translation*. Oxford.

Clifford, J. and G. Marshall, eds. (1986) *Writing Culture: The Poetics and Politics of Ethnography*. Berkeley.

Collins, A. and W. Ferguson (1993) "Epistemic Forms and Epistemic Games: Structures and Strategies to Guide Inquiry," *Educational Psychologist* 28: 25–42.

Collins, D. (2008) *Magic in the Ancient Greek World*. Malden, Mass.

Constantakopoulou, C. (2017) *Aegean Interactions: Delos and Its Networks in the Third Century*. Oxford.

Couloubaritsis, Lambros. (2006) "Fécondité des pratiques catalogiques," *Kernos* 19: 249–266.

Crielaard, J. P., ed. (1995) *Homeric Questions: Essays in Philology, Ancient History and Archaeology, Including the Papers of a Conference Organized by the Netherlands Institute at Athens, 15 May, 1993*. Amsterdam.

Crossett, J. (1969) "The Art of Homer's Catalogue of Ships," *Classical Journal* 64: 241–245.

Cuomo, S. (2012) "Exploring Ancient Greek and Roman Numeracy," *BSHM Bulletin* 27: 1–12.

D'Alessio, A. (2005) "Ordered from the Catalogue: Pindar, Bacchylides, and Hesiodic Genealogical Poetry," in *The Hesiodic Catalogue of Women: Constructions and Reconstructions*, ed. R. Hunter. Cambridge: 217–238.

Danek, Georg. (2004) "Der Schiffskatalog der « Ilias »: Form und Funktion," in *Ad fontes!: Festschrift für Gerhard Dobesch zum 65. Geburtstag*, ed. H. Heftner and K. Tomaschitz. Vienna: 59–72.

Davies, J. K. (1994) "Accounts and Accountability in Classical Athens," in *Ritual, Finance, Politics: Athenian Democratic Accounts Presented to David Lewis*, ed. R. Osborne and S. Hornblower. Oxford: 201–212.

    (2003) "Greek Archives: From Record to Monument," in *Ancient Archives and Archival Traditions: Concepts of Record-Keeping in the Ancient World*, ed. M. Brosius. Oxford: 323–343.

Day, J. W. (2010) *Archaic Greek Epigram and Dedication: Representation and Reperformance*. Cambridge.

Deger-Jalkotzy, S., S. Hiller, and O. Panagl, eds. (1999) *Floreant studia Mycenaea: Akten des X. internationalen Mykenologischen Colloquiums in Salzburg vom 1.–5. Mai 1995*. Vienna.

de Jong, I. J. F. (2001) *A Narratological Commentary on the Odyssey*. Cambridge.

DeMarrais, E., C. Gosden, and C. Renfrew, eds. (2004) *Rethinking Materiality: The Engagement of Mind with the Material World*. Cambridge.

Dench, E. (2007) "Ethnography and History," in *A Companion to Greek and Roman Historiography*, ed. J. Marincola. Oxford and Malden, Mass.: 493–503.

Derrida, J. (1996) *Archive Fever*. Chicago.

Dewald, C. (1993) "Reading the World: The Interpretation of Objects in Herodotus' Histories," in *Nomodeiktes: Greek Studies in Honor of Martin Ostwald*, ed. R. M. Rosen and J. Farrell. Ann Arbor: 55–70.

    (2002) "I Didn't Give My Own Genealogy: Herodotus and the Authorial Persona," in *Brill's Companion to Herodotus*, ed. E. J. Bakker, I. J. F. de Jong, and H. Van Wees. Leiden and Boston: 267–289.

    (2012) "Myth and Legend in Herodotus' First Book," in *Myth, Truth, and Narrative in Herodotus*, ed. E. Baragwanath, E. and and M. de Bakker. Oxford: 59–86.

Dewald, C. and J. Marincola, eds. (2006) *The Cambridge Companion to Herodotus*. Cambridge.

Dignas, B. (2002) "'Inventories' or 'Offering Lists'? Assessing the Wealth of Apollo Didymaeus," *Zeitschrift für Papyrologie und Epigraphik* 138: 235–244.

Dillery, J. (2005) "Chresmologues and Manteis: Independent Diviners and the Problem of Authority," in *Mantikê: Studies in Ancient Divination*, ed. S. I. Johnston, and P. T. Struck. Leiden and Boston: 167–231.

Dobrov, G. W., ed. (1995) *Beyond Aristophanes: Transition and Diversity in Greek Comedy*. Atlanta.

    (2010) *Brill's Companion to the Study of Greek Comedy*. Leiden.

Donlan, W. (1982) "Reciprocities in Homer," *Classical World* 75: 135–174.

(1989) "The Unequal Exchange between Glaucus and Diomedes in Light of the Homeric Gift-Economy," *Phoenix* 43: 1–15.

(1993) "Duelling with Gifts in the *Iliad*: As the Audience Saw It," *Colby Quarterly* 29: 155–172.

Dorati, M. (2011) "Travel Writing, Ethnographical Writing, and the Representations of the Edges of the World in Herodotus," in *Herodot und das persische Weltreich = Herodotus and the Persian Empire: Akten des 3. internationalen Kolloquiums zum Thema «Vorderasien im Spannungsfeld klassischer und altorientalischer Überlieferungen» Innsbruck, 24.–28. November 2008*, ed. R. Rollinger, B. Truschnegg, and R. Bichler. Wiesbaden: 273–312.

Dore, J. (1975) "Holophrases, Speech Acts and Language Universals," *Journal of Child Language* 2: 21–40.

Dougherty, C. (2001) *The Raft of Odysseus: The Ethnographic Imagination of Homer's Odyssey*. Oxford and New York.

Dougherty, C. and L. Kurke, eds. (1998) *Cultural Poetics in Archaic Greece: Cult, Performance, Politics*. New York and Oxford.

(2003) *The Cultures within Ancient Greek Culture*. Cambridge.

Dover, K. J. (1972) *Aristophanic Comedy*. Berkeley.

(1987) *Greek and the Greeks: Collected Papers*. Vol. I. Oxford and New York.

DuBois, P. (1978) "Sappho and Helen," *Arethusa* 11: 89–99.

Dunbar, N., ed. (1995) *Aristophanes: Birds*. Oxford.

Ebbott, M. (2000) "The List of the War Dead in Aeschylus' 'Persians,'" *Harvard Studies in Classical Philology* 100: 83–96.

Eco, U. (2009) *The Infinity of Lists: An Illustrated Essay*. New York.

Edwards, A. T. (1991) "Aristophanes' Comic Poetics: τρύξ, Scatology, σκῶμμα," *Transactions of the American Philological Association* 121: 157–179.

Edwards, M. W. (1980) "The Structure of Homeric Catalogues," *Transactions of the American Philological Association* 110: 81–105.

(1991) *The Iliad: A Commentary*. Vol. V: *Books 17–20*. Cambridge.

(1997) "Homeric Style and Oral Poetics," in *A New Companion to Homer*, ed. I. Morris and B. Powell. Leiden: 261–283.

Eickstedt, K.-V. von. (2001) *Das Asklepieion im Piräus*. Athens.

Ekroth, G. (2003) "Inventing Iphigeneia? On Euripides and the Cultic Construction of Brauron," *Kernos* 16: 59–118.

Elsner, J. and R. Cardinal, eds. (1994) *The Cultures of Collecting*. London.

English, M. (2005) "The Evolution of Aristophanic Stagecraft," *Leeds International Classical Studies* 4: 1–16.

Ernst, W. (2003) "Telling Versus Counting? A Media-Archaeological Point of View," *Intermédialités* 2: 31–44.

Fakas, C. (2001) *Der hellenistische Hesiod: Arats Phainomena und die Tradition der antiken Lehrepik*. Wiesbaden.

Fantuzzi, M. and R. L. Hunter. (2004) *Tradition and Innovation in Hellenistic Poetry*. Cambridge.

Faraguna, M. (2005) "Scrittura e amministrazione nelle città greche: Gli archivi pubblici," *Quaderni urbinati di cultura classica* 80: 61–86.

Faraone, C. A. (2013) "The Poetics of the Catalogue in the Hesiodic 'Theogony'," *Transactions of the American Philological Association* 143: 293–323.

Fayer, V. V. (2013) "The Art of Memory and Composition of 'The Catalogue of the Ships'," in *Indo-European Linguistics and Classical Philology 17: Proceedings of the 17th Conference in Memory of Professor Joseph M. Tronsky: June 24–26, 2013*, ed. N. N. Kazansky. Saint Petersburg: 895–906.

Fehling, D. (1989) *Herodotus and His Sources*. Liverpool.

Ferrucci, S. (2005) "La ricchezza nascosta: Osservazioni su ἀφανής e φανερά οὐσία," *MedAnt* 8: 145–69.

Filbey, E. J. (1917) *The Supplementary Participle in Herodotus*. Urbana, Ill.

Finkelberg, Margalit. (1998) *The Birth of Literary Fiction in Ancient Greece*. Oxford.

Finley, M. I. (1999) *The Ancient Economy*. Berkeley.

Ford, Andrew L. (1992) *Homer: The Poetry of the Past*. Ithaca, N.Y.

Fowler, R. L., ed. (2004) *The Cambridge Companion to Homer*. Cambridge.

Fröhlich, P. (2011) "La «Paradosis» entre magistrats dans les cités grecques: Le dossier béotien," in *Philologos Dionysios: Mélanges offerts au professeur Denis Knoepfler*, ed. N. Badoud. Neuchâtel: 183–229.

Frost, F. J. (1971) "Themistocles and Mnesiphilus," *Historia* 20: 20–25.

Gaertner, J. (2001) "The Homeric Catalogues and Their Function in Epic Narrative," *Hermes* 129: 298–305.

Gärtner, T. (2012) "Der Erotikerkatalog in der Elegie «Leontion» des Hermesianax von Kolophon: Überlegungen zu Aufbau und Überlieferung," *Zeitschrift für Papyrologie und Epigraphik* 180: 77–103.

Galbraith, J. K. (1975) *Money, Whence It Came, Where It Went*. Boston.

Galjanić, A. (2007) "Three and Then Some: A Typology of Poetic Enumeration in Greek and Related Indo-European Traditions." Dissertation: Harvard University.

Gelzer, T. (1996) "Some Aspects of Aristophanes' Dramatic Art in the *Birds*," in *Oxford Readings in Aristophanes*, ed. E. Segal. Oxford and New York: 194–215.

Gercke, A. (1889) "Alexandrinische Studien (Fortsetzung)," *Rheinisches Museum für Philologie* 44: 127–150.

Giangrande, G. (1977–1978a) "Textual and Interpretative Problems in Hermesianax," Ἐπιστημονικὴ Ἐπετηρὶς τῆς Φιλοσοφικῆς Σχολῆς τοῦ Πανεπιστημίου Ἀθηνῶν 26: 98–121.

(1977–1978b) "Textual problems in Hermesianax," *Bollettino dell'Istituto di Filologia Greca dell'Università di Padova* 4: 188–191.

Gilhuly, K. (2014) "Corinth, Courtesans, and the Politics of Place," in *Space, Place, and Landscape in Ancient Greek Literature and Culture*, ed. K. Gilhuly and N. Worman. Cambridge: 171–199.

Gilula, D. (2000) "Hermippus and His Catalogue of Goods," in *The Rivals of Aristophanes: Studies in Athenian Old Comedy*, ed. F. D. Harvey, J. Wilkins, and K. J. Dover. London: 75–90.

Giovannini, A. (1969) *Étude historique sur les origines du catalogue des vaisseaux*. Bern.

Giuseppetti, M. (2013) *L'Isola esile: Studi sull'«Inno a Delo» di Callimaco*. Rome.

Goldschmidt, N. and B. Graziosi. (2018) *Tombs of the Ancient Poets: Between Literary Reception and Material Culture*. Oxford.

González, J. M. (2010) "The 'Catalogue of Women' and the End of the Heroic Age, (Hesiod fr. 204.94–103 M-W)," *Transactions of the American Philological Association* 140: 375–422.

   (2013) *The Epic Rhapsode and His Craft: Homeric Performance in a Diachronic Perspective*. Washington, D.C.

Goody, J. (1977) *The Domestication of the Savage Mind*. Cambridge.

Gordon, R. (1999) "'What's in a List?' Listing in Greek and Graeco-Roman Malign Magical Texts," in *The World of Ancient Magic: Papers from the First International Samson Eitrem Seminar at the Norwegian Institute at Athens, 4–8 May 1997*, ed. D. R. Jordan, H. Montgomery, and E. Thomassen. Bergen: 239–277.

Greetham, D. (1999) "'Who's in, Who's out': The Cultural Poetics of Archival Exclusion," *Studies in the Literary Imagination* 32: 1–28.

Griffin, J. (1995) *Iliad. Book Nine*. Oxford.

Grimes, R. L. (2006) *Rite out of Place: Ritual, Media, and the Arts*. Oxford.

Günther, W. (1988) "«Vieux et inutilisable» dans un inventaire inédit de Milet," in *Comptes et inventaires dans la cité grecque: Actes du colloque international d'épigraphie tenu à Neuchâtel du 23 au 26 septembre 1986 en l'honneur de Jacques Tréheux*, ed. D. Knoepfler and N. Quellet. Neuchâtel: 215–237.

Haas, C. (1996) *Writing Technology: Studies on the Materiality of Literacy*. Mahwah, N.J.

Hackstein, O. (2010) "The Greek of Epic," in *A Companion to the Ancient Greek Language*, ed. E. Bakker. Chichester: 401–423.

Hainsworth, B. (1993) *The Iliad: A Commentary. Books 9–12*. Cambridge.

Hall, A. E. W. (2013) "Dating the Homeric Hymn to Selene: Evidence and Implications," *Greek, Roman, and Byzantine Studies* 53: 15–30.

Hall, E., ed. (1996) *Persians*. Warminster.

Hallof, K., ed. (2000) *Inscriptiones Graecae, XII, 6. Inscriptiones Chii et Sami cum Corassiis Icariaque. Pars I. Inscriptiones Sami Insulae. Decreta. Epistulae, sententiae, edicta imperatoria. Leges. Catalogi. Tituli Atheniensium. Tituli honorarii. Tituli operum publicorum. Inscriptiones ararum, nos. 1–536*. Berlin.

Hamilton, C., et al., eds. (2002) *Refiguring the Archive*. Dordrecht.

Hamilton, R. (2000) *Treasure Map: A Guide to the Delian Inventories.* Ann Arbor.

Hanink, J. (2008) "Literary Politics and the Euripidean Vita," *The Cambridge Classical Journal* 54: 115–135.

(2018) "Scholars and Scholarship on Tragedy," in *Greek Tragedy after the Fifth Century: A Survey from ca. 400 BC to ca. AD 400,* ed. V. Liapis and A. Petrides. Cambridge: 324–349.

Harder, A. (1988) "Callimachus and the Muses: Some Aspects of Narrative Technique in *Aetia* 1–2," *Prometheus* 14: 1–14.

(2012) *Callimachus – Aetia.* Oxford.

(2013) "From Text to Text: The Impact of the Alexandrian Library on the Work of Hellenistic Poets," in *Ancient Libraries,* ed. J. König, K. Oikonomopoulou, and G. Woolf. Cambridge and New York: 96–108.

Harder, M. A., R. F. Regtuit, and G. C. Wakker, eds. (2006) *Beyond the Canon.* Leuven.

Harriott, R. M. (1986) *Aristophanes: Poet & Dramatist.* Baltimore.

Harris, D. (1992) "Bronze Statues on the Athenian Acropolis: The Evidence of a Lycurgan Inventory," *AJA* 96: 637–652.

(1994) "Freedom of Information and Accountability: The Inventory Lists of the Parthenon," in *Ritual, Finance, Politics,* ed. R. Osborne and S. Hornblower. Oxford: 213–225.

(1995) *The Treasures of the Parthenon and Erechtheion.* Oxford.

Harvey, F. D., J. Wilkins, and K. J. Dover, eds. (2000) *The Rivals of Aristophanes: Studies in Athenian Old Comedy.* London.

Hatzimichali, M. (2013) "Encyclopaedism in the Alexandrian Library," in *Encyclopaedism from Antiquity to the Renaissance,* ed. J. König and G. Woolf. Cambridge: 64–83.

Haubold, J. (2007) "Xerxes' Homer," in *Cultural Responses to the Persian Wars: Antiquity to the Third Millennium,* ed. E. Bridges, E. Hall, and P. J. Rhodes. Oxford and New York: 47–63.

Heberlein, F. (1981) "Zur Ironie im Plutos des Aristophanes," *Würzburger Jahrbücher für die Altertumswissenschaft* 7: 27–49.

Heftner, H. and K. Tomaschitz, eds. (2004) *Festschrift für Gerhard Dobesch zum fünfundsechzigsten Geburtstag am 15. September 2004: Dargebracht von Kollegen, Schülern und Freunden.* Vienna.

Heiden, B. (2008) "Common People and Leaders in *Iliad* Book 2: The Invocation of the Muses and the Catalogue of Ships," *Transactions of the American Philological Association* 138: 127–154.

Held, W. (1995) "Wo stand die Hera von Samos?," *Istanbuler Mitteilungen / Deutsches Archäologisches Institut, Abteilung Istanbul* 45: 13–23.

Henderson, J. (1997) "The Name of the Tree: Recounting *Odyssey* XXIV 340–2," *JHS* 117: 87–116.

(1998–2000) *Aristophanes:* Vols. I–IV. Cambridge, Mass.

Hendrickson, T. (2014) "The Invention of the Greek Library," *Transactions of the American Philological Association* 144: 412–413.

Herodotus. (1996) *The Histories*, trans. A. de Sélincourt, ed. with an introduction and notes by J. M. Marincola. London.

Herrmann, P., W. Günther, N. Ehrhardt, D. Feissel, and P. Weiss. (2006) *Milet. 6, Inschriften von Milet. 3, Inschriften n. 1020–1580*. Berlin.

Heubeck, A., J. Russo, and M. Fernández-Galiano. (1992) *A Commentary on Homer's Odyssey: Books XVII–XXIV*. Oxford.

Higbie, C. (2003) *The Lindian Chronicle and the Greek Creation of Their Past.* Oxford.

    (2017) *Collectors, Scholars, and Forgers in the Ancient World: Object Lessons.* Oxford.

Hirschberger, M. (2004) *Gynaikôn Katalogos und Megalai Ehoiai: Ein Kommentar zu den Fragmenten zweier hesiodeischer Epen*. Munich and Leipzig.

Holleaux, M. (1913) "Notes sur la 'Chronique de Lindos'," *Revue des études grecques* 26: 40–46.

Hömke, N. and M. Baumbach, eds. (2006) *Fremde Wirklichkeiten: Literarische Phantastik und antike Literatur*. Heidelberg.

Hunter, R. (1993) *The Argonautica of Apollonius: Literary Studies*. Cambridge.

    (1996) "Callimachus Swings (frr. 178 and 43 Pf.)," *Ramus* 25: 17–26.

    (2003a) "Aspects of Technique and Style in the «Periegesis» of Dionysius," in *Des Géants à Dionysos: Mélanges de mythologie et de poésie grecques offerts à Francis Vian*, ed. D. Accorinti and P. Chuvin. Alexandria: 343–356.

    (2003b) *Theocritus: Encomium of Ptolemy Philadelphus*. Berkeley.

    (2004) "The «Periegesis» of Dionysius and the Traditions of Hellenistic Poetry," *Revue des Études Anciennes* 106: 217–231.

    (2005) "The Hesiodic Catalogue and Hellenistic Poetry," in *The Hesiodic Catalogue of Women: Constructions and Reconstructions*, ed. R. L. Hunter. Cambridge: 239–265.

Huxley, George L. (1966) "Numbers in the Homeric Catalogue of Ships," *Greek, Roman and Byzantine Studies* 7: 313–318.

Huys, M., ed. (1991) *Le Poème élégiaque hellénistique P. Brux. inv. E. 8934 et P. Sorb. inv. 2254*. Brussels.

Immerwahr, H. R. (1960) "Ergon: History as a Monument in Herodotus and Thucydides," *AJP* 81.3: 261–290.

    (1966) *Form and Thought in Herodotus*. Cleveland.

Irwin, E. (2005) "Gods among Men? The Social and Political Dynamics of the Hesiodic *Catalogue of Women*," in *The Hesiodic Catalogue of Women: Constructions and Reconstructions*, ed. R. L. Hunter. Cambridge: 35–84.

Jachmann, G. (1958) *Der homerische Schiffskatalog und die Ilias*. Cologne.

Jacob, C. (2013) "Fragments of a History of Ancient Libraries," in *Ancient Libraries*, ed. J. König, K. Oikonomopoulou, and G. Woolf. Cambridge and New York: 57–81.

Jacoby, F. (1904) *Das Marmor Parium*. Berlin.

Janko, R. (1992) *The Iliad: A Commentary*. Vol. IV: *Books 13–16*. Cambridge.

Jeffery, L. H. (1990) *The Local Scripts of Archaic Greece: A Study of the Origin of the Greek Alphabet and Its Development from the Eighth to the Fifth Centuries B. C.* Oxford.

Johnson, W. A. and H. N. Parker (2009) *Ancient Literacies: The Culture of Reading in Greece and Rome*. Oxford.

Johnstone, S. (2014) "A New History of Libraries and Books in the Hellenistic Period," *Classical Antiquity* 33: 347–393.

Jones, C. P. (1987) "Stigma: Tattooing and Branding in Graeco-Roman Antiquity," *Journal of Roman Studies* 77: 139–155.

Jordan, D. R., H. Montgomery, and E. Thomassen, eds. (1999) *The World of Ancient Magic: Papers from the First International Samson Eitrem Seminar at the Norwegian Institute at Athens, 4–8 May 1997*. Bergen.

Kallet-Marx, L. (1989) "The Kallias Decree, Thucydides, and the Outbreak of the Peloponnesian War," *Classical Quarterly* 39: 94–113.

Kassel, R. (2000) "IG XII 6, 1," *Zeitschrift für Papyrologie und Epigraphik* 132: 132.

Kirk, A. (2014) "The Semantics of Showcase in Herodotus's *Histories*," *Transactions of the American Philological Association* 144: 19–40.

(2018) "Σήματα νίκης: Inscribed Objects in the Lindian Chronicle," *Mètis* N.S. 16: 107–124.

Kirk, G. S., ed. (1985) *The Iliad: A Commentary. Books 1–4*. Cambridge.

Kittler, F. (1996) "Museums on the Digital Frontier," in *The End(s) of the Museum*, ed. T. Keenan. Barcelona: 67–80.

Klooster, J. (2012) "Visualizing the Impossible: The Wandering Landscape in the Delos Hymn of Callimachus," *Aitia* 2: n.p.

Knoepfler, D. (2012) "Bulletin Épigraphique no. 183," *Revue des Études Grecques* 125: 572.

Knoepfler, D. and N. Quellet, eds. (1988) *Comptes et inventaires dans la cité grecque: Actes du colloque international d'épigraphie tenu à Neuchâtel du 23 au 26 septembre 1986 en l'honneur de Jacques Tréheux*. Neuchâtel.

Kobiliri, P. (1998) *A Stylistic Commentary on Hermesianax*. Amsterdam.

Koch Piettre, R. (2005) "La Chronique de Lindos, ou comment accommoder les restes pour écrire l'histoire," in *Les Objets de la mémoire*, ed. P. Borgeaud and Y. Volokhine. Bern and Berlin: 95–121.

Kondis, J. (1967) "Ἄρτεμις Βραυρωνία," *ArchDelt* 22: 156–206, 221–226.

König, J. and T. Whitmarsh, eds. (2007) *Ordering Knowledge in the Roman Empire*. Cambridge.

König, J., K. Oikonomopoulou, and G. Woolf. (2013) *Ancient Libraries*. Cambridge.

Koning, H. (2017) "Helen, Herakles, and the End of the Heroes," in *Poetry in Fragments: Studies on the Hesiodic Corpus and Its Afterlife*, ed. C. Tsagalis. Berlin and Boston: 99–114.

Konstan, D. and M. Dillon (1981) "The Ideology of Aristophanes' Wealth," *AJP* 102: 371–394.

Kosmetatou, E. (2002) "The Athenian Inventory Lists: A Review Article," *L'Antiquité classique* 71: 185–197.

(2003) "Reassessing *IG* II² 1498–1501A: Kathairesis or Eksetasmos?," *Tyche* 18: 33–46.

(2005) "Περιτραχήλιον/περιτραχηλίδιον in the Athenian Inventory Lists," *Epigraphica: Periodico internazionale di epigrafia*, 67: 17–22.

(2006) "The Brauron Clothing Catalogues: Text, Analysis, Glossary and Translation," (Review) *AJA* 110.4, n.p.

(2013) "Herodotus and Temple Inventories," in *Inscriptions and Their Uses in Greek and Latin Literature*, ed. P. Liddel and P. Low. Oxford Studies in Ancient Documents. Oxford: 65–77.

Koumanoudes, S. N. and S. G. Miller (1971) "*IG* ii² 1477 and 3046 Rediscovered," *Hesperia* 40: 448–458.

Krevans, N. (1984) *The Poet as Editor: Callimachus, Virgil, Horace, Propertius and the development of the poetic book*. Princeton.

(2007) "The Arrangement of Hellenistic Epigram Collections," in *The Brill Companion to Hellenistic Epigram*, ed. P. Bing and J. S. Bruss: 131–146.

(2011) "Callimachus' philology," in *Brill's Companion to Callimachus*, ed. B. Acosta-Hughes, L. Lehnus, and S. Stephens. Leiden: 118–133.

Krischer, Tilman. (1965) "Die Entschuldigung des Sängers (Ilias B 484–493)," *Rheinisches Museum für Philologie* 108: 1–11.

(1971) *Formale Konventionen der homerischen Epik*. Munich.

Kühlmann, W. (1973) *Katalog und Erzählung: Studien zu Konstanz und Wandel einer literarischen Form in der antiken Epik*. Freiburg.

Kullmann, W. (2009) "Poesie, Mythos und Realität im Schiffskatalog der «Ilias»," *Hermes* 137: 1–20.

(2012) "The Relative Chronology of the Homeric Catalogue of Ships and of the Lists of Heroes and Cities within the Catalogue," in *Relative Chronology in Early Greek Epic Poetry*, ed. Ø. Andersen and D. T. Haug. Cambridge and New York: 210–223.

Kurke, L. (1991) *The Traffic in Praise: Pindar and the Poetics of Social Economy*. Ithaca, N.Y.

(1999) *Coins, Bodies, Games, and Gold: The Politics of Meaning in Archaic Greece*. Princeton.

(2002) "Money and Mythic History: The Contestation of Transactional Orders in the Fifth Century BC," in *The Ancient Economy*, ed. W. Scheidel, and S. von Reden. Edinburgh: 87–113.

(2010) *Aesopic Conversations: Popular Tradition, Cultural Dialogue, and the Invention of Greek Prose*. Princeton.

Kyriakidis, Stratis. (2007) *Catalogues of Proper Names in Latin Epic Poetry: Lucretius, Virgil, Ovid*. Newcastle.

Kyriakou, I. (2017) "Female Ancestors in the Hesiodic *Catalogue of Women*," in *Poetry in Fragments: Studies on the Hesiodic Corpus and Its Afterlife*, ed. C. Tsagalis. Berlin and Boston: 135–162.

Laird, A. G. (1921) "The Persian Army and Tribute Lists in Herodotus," *Classical Philology* 16: 305–326.

Lamont, J. (2015) "Asklepios in the Piraeus and the Mechanisms of Cult Appropriation," in *Autopsy in Athens: Recent Archaeological Research on Athens and Attica*, ed. M. M. Miles. Oxford: 37–50.

Latacz, J., M. L. West, and A. Bierl, eds. (2000) *Homers Ilias: Gesamtkommentar*. Munich.

Lateiner, D. (1989) *The Historical Method of Herodotus*. Toronto.

(1990) "Deceptions and Delusions in Herodotus," *Classical Antiquity* 9: 230–246.

(2004) "The *Iliad*: An Unpredictable Classic," in *The Cambridge Companion to Homer*, ed. R. Fowler. Cambridge: 11–30.

Latour, B. (1993) *We Have Never Been Modern*. Cambridge, Mass.

Lattimore, R. (1939) "The Wise Adviser in Herodotus," *Classical Philology* 24–35.

Lazenby, J. F. and R. Hope Simpson (1970) *The Catalogue of the Ships in Homer's Iliad*. Oxford.

Leaf, W. (1922) "The Homeric Catalogue of Ships," *The Classical Review* 36: 52–57.

Lewis, D. M. (1986) "Temple Inventories in Ancient Greece," in *Pots and Pans: A Colloquium on Precious Metals and Ceramics in the Muslim, Chinese, and Greco-Roman Worlds*, ed. M. Vickers. Oxford: 71–81.

(1988) "The Last Inventories of the Treasurers of Athena," in *Comptes et inventaires dans la cité grecque: Actes du colloque international d'épigraphie tenu à Neuchâtel du 23 au 26 septembre 1986 en l'honneur de Jacques Tréheux*, ed. D. Knoepfler and N. Quellet. Neuchâtel: 297–308.

Lewis, R. C. (2015) *Voyage of the Sable Venus and Other Poems*. New York.

Liapis, V. and A. Petrides, eds. (2018) *Greek Tragedy after the Fifth Century: A Survey from ca. 400 BC to ca. AD 400*. Cambridge.

Liddel, P. (2007) *Civic Obligation and Individual Liberty in Ancient Athens*. Oxford.

Liddel, P. and P. Low (2013) *Inscriptions and Their Uses in Greek and Latin Literature*. Oxford.

Lightfoot, J. L. (2008) "Catalogue Technique in Dionysius Periegetes," *Ramus* 37: 11–31.

(2009a) *Hellenistic Collection: Philitas, Alexander of Aetolia, Hermesianax, Euphorion, Parthenius*. Cambridge, Mass and London.

(2009b) "Ovid and Hellenistic Poetry," in *A Companion to Ovid*, ed. P. E. Knox. Oxford: 219–235.

Linders, T. (1972) *Studies in the Treasure Records of Artemis Brauronia Found in Athens*. Skrifter utgivna av Svenska Institutet i Athen 19. Lund.

(1975) *The Treasurers of the Other Gods in Athens and Their Functions*. Beiträge zur klassischen Philologie 62. Meisenheim am Glan.

(1988) "The Purpose of Inventories: A Close Reading of Delian Inventories of the Independence," in *Comptes et inventaires dans la cité grecque: Actes du colloque international d'épigraphie tenu à Neuchâtel du 23 au 26 septembre 1986 en l'honneur de Jacques Tréheux*, ed. D. Knoepfler and N. Quellet. Neuchâtel: 37–47.

(1992) "Inscriptions and Orality," *Symbolae Osloenses* 67: 27–40.

Liverani, M. (2000) "The Libyan Caravan in Herodotus IV.181–185," *Journal of the Economic and Social History of the Orient* 43: 496–520.

Lloyd, A. B. (2002) "Egypt," in *Brill's Companion to Herodotus*, ed. E. J. Bakker, I. J. F. de Jong, and H. van Wees. Leiden: 415–456.

Lloyd-Jones, H. (1975) *Females of the Species: Semonides on Women*. London.

Loraux, N. (1993) *The Children of Athena: Athenian Ideas about Citizenship and the Division between the Sexes*. Princeton.

Low, P. (2010) "Commemoration of the War Dead in Classical Athens: Remembering Defeat and Victory," in *War, Democracy and Culture in Classical Athens*, ed. D. M. Pritchard. Cambridge and New York: 341–358.

Luraghi, N., ed. (2001) *The Historian's Craft in the Age of Herodotus*. Oxford.

(2006) "Meta-historiē: Method and Genre in the *Histories*," in *The Cambridge Companion to Herodotus*, ed. C. Dewald and J. Marincola. Cambridge: 76–91.

(2009) "The Importance of Being λόγιος," *Classical World* 102: 439–456.

(2013) "One-Man Government: The Greeks and Monarchy," in *A Companion to Ancient Greek Government*, ed. H. Beck. Blackwell Companions to the Ancient World. Chichester: 131–145.

Lyons, D. (2003) "Dangerous Gifts: Ideologies of Marriage and Exchange in Ancient Greece," *Classical Antiquity* 22: 93–134.

Mack, W. (2018) "Vox populi, Vox deorum? Athenian Document Reliefs and the Theologies of Public Inscription," *Annual of the British School at Athens*, 113: 365–398.

Macleod, C. (1982) *Homer, Iliad Book XXIV*. Cambridge.

Marcaccini, C. (2015) "The Treasurers of Athena in the Late 5th Century BC: When Did They Take Office?" *Hesperia* 84: 515–532.

Marincola, J. (1997) *Authority and Tradition in Ancient Historiography*. Cambridge.

(2005) Review of Higbie 2003, *Bryn Mawr Classical Review* 4: 59.

(2007) "Odysseus and the Historians," *Syllecta Classica* 18: 1–79.

Marks, J. (2012) "Ἀρχοὺς αὖ νεῶν ἐρέω: A Programmatic Function of the Iliadic Catalogue of Ships," in *Homeric Contexts: Neoanalysis and the Interpretation of Oral Poetry*, ed. F. Montanari, A. Rengakos, and C. Tsagalis. Berlin and Boston: 101–122.

Martin, R. P. (1989) *The Language of Heroes: Speech and Performance in the Iliad*. Ithaca.

(2008) "Words Alone Are Certain Good(s): Philology and Greek Material Culture," *Transactions of the American Philological Association* 138: 313–349.

Martínez, J. (2011) "Onomacritus the Forger, Hipparchus' Scapegoat?," in *Fakes and Forgers of Classical Literature = Falsificaciones y falsarios de la literatura clásica*, ed. J. Martínez. Madrid: 217–226.

Maslov, Boris. (2016) "The Genealogy of the Muses: An Internal Reconstruction of Archaic Greek Metapoetics," *American Journal of Philology* 137: 411–444.

Mbembe, A. (2002) "The Power of the Archive and Its Limits," in *Refiguring the Archive*, ed. C. Hamilton et al. Dordrecht: 19–27.

McGlew, J. (1997) "After Irony: Aristophanes' Wealth and Its Modern Interpreters," *AJP* 118: 35–53.

Meritt, B. D., H. T. Wade-Gery, and M. F. McGregor. (1939–53) *The Athenian Tribute Lists*. Cambridge, Mass. and Princeton.

Meyer, E. A. (2010) *Metics and the Athenian Phialai-Inscriptions: A Study in Athenian Epigraphy and Law*. Stuttgart.

(2016) "Posts, Kurbeis, Metopes: The Origins of the Athenian 'Documentary' Stele," *Hesperia* 85: 323–383.

Michailidou, A., P. Kalogerakou, and K. Voutsa, eds. (2001) *Manufacture and Measurement: Counting, Measuring and Recording Craft Items in Early Aegean Societies*. Athens.

Minchin, E. (1996) "The Performance of Lists and Catalogues in the Homeric Epics," in *Voice into Text: Orality and Literacy in Ancient Greece*, ed. I. Worthington. Leiden: 3–20.

Mineur, W. H., ed. (1984) *Hymn to Delos*. Leiden.

Minton, W. W. (1962) "Invocation and Catalogue in Hesiod and Homer," *Transactions of the American Philological Association* 93: 188–212.

Mitchell, L. G. and L. Rubinstein, eds. (2009) *Greek History and Epigraphy: Essays in Honour of P. J. Rhodes*. Swansea.

Montanari, F., A. Rengakos, and C. Tsagalis, eds. (2009) *Brill's Companion to Hesiod*. Leiden.

(2012) *Homeric Contexts, Neoanalysis and the Interpretation of Oral Poetry*. Berlin.

Morris, I. and B. Powell, eds. (1997) *A New Companion to Homer*. Leiden.

Most, G. W. (2007) *Hesiod: The Shield, Catalogue of Women, Other Fragments*. Cambridge, Mass.

Moulton, C. (1996) "Comic Myth-Making and Aristophanes' Originality," in *Oxford Readings in Aristophanes*, ed. E. Segal. Oxford: 216–228.

Moyer, I. S. (2002) "Herodotus and an Egyptian Mirage: The Genealogies of the Theban Priests," *JHS* 122: 70–90.

Muellner, L. (1996) *The Anger of Achilles*. Ithaca.

Muensterberger, W. (1994) *Collecting: An Unruly Passion: Psychological Perspectives*. Princeton.

Murnaghan, S. (2006) "Farming, Authority, and Truth-Telling in the Greek Tradition," in *City, Countryside, and the Spatial Organization of Value in Classical Antiquity*, ed. R. M. Rosen and I. Sluiter. Leiden and Boston: 93–118.

Murray, O. (2007a) "Herodotus and Oral History," in *The Historian's Craft in the Age of Herodotus*, ed. N. Luraghi. Oxford: 16–44.

(2007b) "Herodotus and Oral History Reconsidered," in *The Historian's Craft in the Age of Herodotus*, ed. N. Luraghi. Oxford: 314–325.

Nagy, G. (1987) "Herodotus the λόγιος," *Arethusa* XX: 175–184.

(1990) *Pindar's Homer: The Lyric Possession of an Epic Past*. Baltimore.

(2008) *Homer the Classic*. Hellenic Studies Series 36. Washington, D.C.

(2009) "Hesiod and the Ancient Biographical Traditions," in *Brill's Companion to Hesiod*, ed. F. Montanari, A. Rengakos, and Ch. Tsagalis. Leiden: 271–311.

Nasta, M. (2006) "La Typologie des catalogues d'Éhées: Un réseau généalogique thématisé," *Kernos* 19: 59–78.

Neer, R. (2003) "Framing the Gift: The Siphnian Treasury at Delphi and the Politics of Architectural Sculpture," in *The Cultures within Ancient Greek Culture*, ed. C. Dougherty and L. Kurke. Cambridge: 129–152.

Netz, R. (2002) "Counter Culture: Towards a History of Greek Numeracy," *History of Science* 40: 321–351.

Newmyer, S. T. (2006) *Animals, Rights, and Reason in Plutarch and Modern Ethics*. New York.

Nieling, J. and E. Rehm, eds. (2010) *The Achaemenid Impact in the Black Sea: Communication of Powers*. Aarhus.

Niese, B. (1873) *Der homerische Schiffskatalog als historische Quelle*. Kiel.

Noegel, S. (2010) "Greek Religion and the Ancient Near East," in *The Blackwell Companion to Greek Religion*, ed. D. Ogden. London: 21–37.

Nünlist, R. (2013) "Homers Schiffskatalog," in *Geographische Kenntnisse und ihre konkreten Ausformungen*, ed. D. Boschung, T. Greub, and J. Hammerstaedt. Paderborn: 50–73.

Nussbaum, A. J. (2018) "A Dedicatory Thigh: Greek μηρός and μῆρα Once Again," in *Farnah: Indo-Iranian and Indo-European Studies in Honor of Sasha Lubotsky*, ed. L. Beek et al. Ann Arbor and New York: 232–247.

Ober, J. (2008) *Democracy and Knowledge: Innovation and Learning in Classical Athens*. Princeton.

O'Brien, T. (1990) *The Things They Carried: A Work of Fiction*. Boston.

O'Connell, P. A. (2016) "The Rhetoric of Visibility and Invisibility in Antiphon 5, *On the Murder of Herodes*," *CQ* 66: 46–58.

Ogden, D. (2010) *A Companion to Greek Religion*. Chichester.

Olsen, S. (2017) "The Fantastic Phaeacians: Dance and Disruption in the *Odyssey*," *Classical Antiquity* 36: 1–32.

Olson, S. D. (1990) "Economics and Ideology in Aristophanes' *Wealth*," *Harvard Studies in Classical Philology* 93: 223–242.

(1996) "Politics and Poetry in Aristophanes' *Wasps*," *Transactions of the American Philological Association* 126: 129–150.

(2002) *Aristophanes: Acharnians*. Oxford.

(2007) *Broken Laughter: Select Fragments of Greek Comedy*. Oxford.

Olson, S. D. and A. Sens (1999) *Matro of Pitane and the Tradition of Epic Parody in the Fourth Century BCE: Text, Translation, and Commentary*. Oxford.

Ormand, K. (2004) "Marriage, Identity, and the Tale of Mestra in the Hesiodic *Catalogue of Women*," *AJP* 125.3: 303–338.

(2014) *The Hesiodic Catalogue of Women and Archaic Greece*. New York and Cambridge.

Osborne, R. (2005) "Ordering Women in Hesiod's Catalogue," in *The Hesiodic Catalogue of Women: Constructions and Reconstructions*, ed. R. Hunter. Cambridge: 5–19.

Osborne, R. and S. Hornblower, eds. (1994) *Ritual, Finance, Politics: Athenian Democratic Accounts Presented to David Lewis*. Oxford.

Overduin, F. (2014) *Nicander of Colophon's Theriaca: A Literary Commentary*. Leiden.

Paarman, B. (2007) "Aparchai and Phoroi: A New Commented Edition of the Athenian Tribute Quota Lists and Assessment Decrees." Dissertation: Fribourg.

Page, D. L. (1959) *History and the Homeric Iliad*. Berkeley.

Palaima, T. G. (2003) "'Archives' and 'Scribes' and Information Hierarchy in Mycenaean Greek Linear B Records," in *Ancient Archives and Archival Traditions: Concepts of Record-Keeping in the Ancient World*, ed. M. Brosius. Oxford: 153–194.

Parry, A., ed. (1987) *The Making of Homeric Verse: The Collected Papers of Milman Parry*. Oxford.

Payne, M. (2010) *The Animal Part: Human and Other Animals in the Poetic Imagination*. Chicago.

Peacock, M. (2013) *Introducing Money*. London.

Pearce, S. M. (1994) *Interpreting Objects and Collections*. London.

(1995) *On Collecting: An Investigation into Collecting in the European Tradition*. London and New York.

Pearce, S. M., A. Bounia, K. Arnold, and P. Martin, eds. (2000) *The Collector's Voice: Critical Readings in the Practice of Collecting*. London.

Pelliccia, H. (1992) "Sappho 16, Gorgias' Helen, and the Preface to Herodotus' Histories," *Yale Classical Studies* 29: 63–84.

Perceau, S. (2002) *La Parole vive: Communiquer en catalogue dans l'épopée homérique*. Louvain and Paris.

(2015) "Visualisation, oralisation, dramatisation: La poétique des listes de noms dans l'épopée homérique," *Gaia* 18: 117–132.

Peters, J. D. (2015) *The Marvelous Clouds: Toward a Philosophy of Elemental Media*. Chicago.

Peterson, A. (2017) *Too Fat, Too Slutty, Too Loud: The Rise and Reign of the Unruly Woman*. New York.

Pinto, P. M. (2013) "Men and Books in Fourth-Century BC Athens," in *Ancient Libraries*, ed. J. König, K. Oikonomopoulou, and G. Woolf. Cambridge and New York: 85–95.

Pirenne-Delforge, V. (2011) *"Les Codes de l'adresse rituelle en Grèce: Le cas des libations sans vin," in "Nourrir les dieu: Sacrifice et représentation du divin: Actes de la VIe rencontre du Groupe de recherche européen «FIGURA. Représentation du divin dans les sociétés grecque et romaine» (Université de Liège, 23–24 octobre 2009)*. Ed. V. Pirenne-Delforge and F. Prescendi. Liège: 117–148.

Platt, V. (2011) *Facing the Gods: Epiphany and Representation in Graeco-Roman Art, Literature, and Religion*. Cambridge.

   (2018) "Silent Bones and Singing Stones: Materializing the Poetic Corpus in Hellenistic Greece," in *Tombs of the Ancient Poets: Between Literary Reception and Material Culture*, ed. N. Goldschmidt and B. Graziosi. Oxford: 21–50.

Platter, C. (2007) *Aristophanes and the Carnival of Genres*. Baltimore.

Polinskaya, I. (2013) *A Local History of Greek Polytheism: Gods, People and the Land of Aigina, 800–400 BCE*. Leiden.

Powell, J. E. (1938) *A Lexicon to Herodotus*. Cambridge.

Prakken, D. W. (1940) "Herodotus and the Spartan King Lists," *Transactions of the American Philological Association* 71: 460–472.

Prêtre, C. (2012) *Kosmos et Kosmema: Les offrandes de parure dans les inscriptions de Délos*. Liège.

Prêtre, C. et al. (2002) *Nouveau choix d'inscriptions de Délos. Lois, comptes et inventaires*. Paris.

Pritchard, D., ed. (2010) *War, Democracy and Culture in Classical Athens*. Cambridge.

Pritchett, W. K. (1993) *The Liar School of Herodotus*. Amsterdam.

Pucci, P. (1996) "Between Narrative and Catalogue: The Life and Death of the Poem," *Mètis* 11: 5–24.

Purcell, R. W. and S. J. Gould (1992) *Finders, Keepers: Eight Collectors*. New York.

Purves, A. (2006) "The Plot Unravels: Darius's Numbered Days in Scythia (Herodotus 4.98)," *Helios* 33: 1–26.

Rabel, R. J. (1997) *Plot and Point of View in the Iliad*. Ann Arbor.

Race, William H. (1982) *The Classical Priamel from Homer to Boethius*. Leiden.

Rajewsky, I. (2005) "Intermediality, Intertextuality, and Remediation: A Literary Perspective on Intermediality," *Intermédialités: Histoire et théorie des arts, des lettres et des techniques* 43–64.

Rawles, R. (2006) "Homeric Beginnings in the 'Tattoo Elegy'," *Classical Quarterly*, N.S. 56: 486–495.

   (2016) "The Tattoo Elegy," in *Hellenistic Poetry: A Selection*, ed. D. Sider. Ann Arbor: 40–55.

Redfield, J. M. (1985) "Herodotus the Tourist," *Classical Philology* 80: 97–118.

(1990) "Drama and Community: Aristophanes and Some of His Rivals," in *Nothing to do with Dionysos?: Athenian Drama in Its Social Context*, ed. J. J. Winkler and F. I. Zeitlin. Princeton: 314–335.

(1995) *Nature and Culture in the Iliad: The Tragedy of Hector* (expanded edition) Durham, N.C.

Reger, G., F. X. Ryan, and T. F. Winters, eds. (2010) *Studies in Greek Epigraphy and History in Honor of Stephen V. Tracy*. Pessac.

Renfrew, C. (2004) "Towards a Theory of Material Engagement," in *Rethinking Materiality: The Engagement of Mind with the Material World*, ed. E. DeMarrais, C. Gosden, and C. Renfrew. Cambridge: 23–31.

Rennie, W. (1909) *The Acharnians of Aristophanes: With Introduction, Critical Notes and Commentary*. London.

Rhodes, P. J. (2001) "Public Documents in the Greek States: Archives and Inscriptions, Part I," *Greece & Rome* 48: 33–44.

Riggsby, A. M. (2019) *Mosaics of Knowledge: Representing Information in the Roman World*. Oxford.

Robert, J. and L. Robert. (1963) "Bulletin épigraphique," *RÉG* 76: 121–192.

Rollinger, R., B. Truschnegg, and R. Bichler, eds. (2011) *Herodot und das persische Weltreich = Herodotus and the Persian Empire: Akten des 3. internationalen Kolloquiums zum Thema «Vorderasien im Spannungsfeld klassischer und altorientalischer Überlieferungen» Innsbrück, 24.–28. November 2008*. Wiesbaden.

Rosen, R. M. and J. Farrell, eds. (1993) *Nomodeiktes: Greek Studies in Honor of Martin Ostwald*. Ann Arbor.

Rotstein, A. (2016) *Literary History in the Parian Marble*. Washington, D.C.

Rowe, K. (1995) *The Unruly Woman: Gender and the Genres of Laughter*. Austin, Tex.

Rubin, G. (1975) "The Traffic in Women: Notes on the 'Political Economy' of Sex," in *Toward an Anthropology of Women*, ed. R. R. Reiter. New York and London: 157–210.

Rusten, J. S., J. Henderson, D. Konstan, and R. Rosen. (2011) *The Birth of Comedy: Texts, Documents, and Art from Athenian Comic Competitions, 486-280*. Baltimore, Md.

Rutherford, I. (2000) "Formulas, Voice, and Death in *Ehoie*-Poetry, the Hesiodic *Gunaikon Katalogos*, and the Odysseian *Nekuia*," in *Matrices of Genre*, ed. M. Depew and D. Obbink. Cambridge, Mass: 81–96.

Sale, W. M. (1993) "Homer and Roland: The Shared Formular Technique, Part I," *Oral Tradition* 8: 87–142.

(1994) "The Government of Troy: Politics in the Iliad," *Greek, Roman and Byzantine Studies* 35: 5–102.

Salomon, N. (1997) *Le Cleruchie di Atene: Caratteri e funzione*. Pisa.

Sammons, B. (2010) *The Art and Rhetoric of the Homeric Catalogue*. Oxford.

(2017) "The Hesiodic *Catalogue of Women*: A Competition of Forms," in *Poetry in Fragments: Studies on the Hesiodic Corpus and Its Afterlife*, ed. C. Tsagalis. Berlin and Boston: 163–190.

Samons, L. J. (1996) "The 'Kallias Decrees' (*IG* i³ 52) and the Inventories of Athena's Treasure in the Parthenon," *CQ* 46: 91–102.

(2000) *Empire of the Owl: Athenian Imperial Finance*. Stuttgart.

Schaps, D. M. (2004) *The Invention of Coinage and the Monetization of Ancient Greece*. Ann Arbor.

Scheidel, W. and S. von Reden, eds. (2002) *The Ancient Economy*. New York.

Schmidt, M. (2006) "Die Welt des Eumaios," in *Geschichte und Fiktion in der homerischen Odyssee*, ed. A. Luther. Munich: 117–138.

Schwenk, C. J. (1985) *Athens in the Age of Alexander: The Dated Laws and Decrees of "The Lykourgan Era" 338–322 B.C.* Chicago.

Schwink, F. W. (1999) "The Efficacy of Linear B as a Writing System," in *Floreant studia mycenaea: Akten des X. internationalen Mykenologischen Colloquiums in Salzburg vom 1.–5. Mai 1995*, ed. S. Deger-Jalkotzy, S. Hiller, and O. Panagl. Vienna: 549–554.

Scodel, R. (1997) "Teichoscopia, Catalogue, and the Female Spectator in Euripides," *Colby Quarterly* 33: 76–93.

(2008) *Epic Facework: Self-Presentation and Social Interaction in Homer*. Swansea.

Scott, M. C. (2011) "Displaying Lists of What Is (Not) on Display: The Uses of Inventories in Greek Sanctuaries," in *Current Approaches to Religion in Ancient Greece: Papers Presented at a Symposium at the Swedish Institute at Athens, 17–19 April 2008*, ed. M. Haysom and J. E. Wallensten. Stockholm: 239–252.

Seaton, R. C. (1888) "Notes on Ap. Rhod." *The Classical Review* 2: 83–84.

Segal, E., ed. (1996) *Oxford Readings in Aristophanes*. Oxford.

Sergueenkova, V. V. (2016) "Counting the Past in Herodotus' Histories," *The Journal of Hellenic Studies* 136: 121–131.

Shapiro, H. A. (2007) *The Cambridge Companion to Archaic Greece*. Cambridge.

Shaya, J. (2005) "The Greek Temple as Museum: The Case of the Legendary Treasure of Athena from Lindos," *American Journal of Archaeology* 109: 423–442.

(2014) "Greek Temple Treasures and the Invention of Collecting," in *Museum Archetypes and Collecting in the Ancient World*, ed. M. Wellington Gahtan and D. Pegazzano. Leiden: 24–32.

Sickinger, J. P. (1999) *Public Records and Archives in Classical Athens*. Chapel Hill.

(2016) "Marmor Parium," in *Brill's New Jacoby*, No. 239: https://referenceworks .brillonline.com/entries/brill-s-new-jacoby/marmor-parium-239-a239

Sider, D., ed. (2016) *Hellenistic Poetry: A Selection*. Ann Arbor.

Sidwell, K. (2009) *Aristophanes the Democrat: The Politics of Satirical Comedy during the Peloponnesian War*. Cambridge.

Silk, M. S. (1996) "The People of Aristophanes," in *Oxford Readings in Aristophanes*, ed. E. Segal. Oxford: 229–251.

(2000) *Aristophanes and the Definition of Comedy*. Oxford.

Sistakou, E. (2009) "Callimachus Hesiodicus Revisited," in *Brill's Companion to Hesiod*, ed. F. Montanari, A. Rengakos, and C. Tsagalis. Leiden: 219–252.

Skinner, J. (2012) *The Invention of Greek Ethnography: Ethnography and History from Homer to Herodotus*. Oxford and New York.

Sokolowski, F. (1969) *Lois sacrées des cités grecques*. Paris.

Sommerstein, A. H. (1996) "Aristophanes and the Demon Poverty," in *Oxford Readings in Aristophanes*, ed. E. Segal. Oxford: 252–281.

Sommerstein, A. H., ed. (2001) *The Comedies of Aristophanes*, vol. II: *Wealth*. Warminster.

Spyropoulos, E. S. (1974) *L'Accumulation verbale chez Aristophane: Recherches sur le style d'Aristophane*. Thessaloniki.

Stafford, E. (2008) "Cocks to Asklepios: Sacrificial Practice and Healing Cult," in *Le Sacrifice antique: Vestiges, procédures et strategies*, ed. P. Brulé and V. Mehl. Rennes: 205–221.

Starkie, W. J. M. (1909) *The Acharnians of Aristophanes*. London.

Steiner, D. (2017) "Choruses and Catalogues: The Performative and Generic Context of the Asopids in the Hesiodic *Catalogue of Women*," in *Poetry in Fragments: Studies on the Hesiodic Corpus and Its Afterlife*, ed. C. Tsagalis. 47–82.

Steinrück M. (1994) *Regards sur la femme: Analyse rythmique et interprétation de Sémonide fr. 7 Pellizer-Tedeschi*. Rome.

Stephens, S. A., ed. (2003) *Seeing Double: Intercultural Poetics in Ptolemaic Alexandria*. Berkeley, Calif.

(2015) *Callimachus: The Hymns*. Oxford.

Stewart, S. (1993) *On Longing: Narratives of the Miniature, the Gigantic, the Souvenir, the Collection*. Durham, N.C.

Strauss, B. (2005) *The Battle of Salamis: The Battle That Saved Greece – and Western Civilization*. New York.

Strauss Clay, J. (2011) *Homer's Trojan Theater*. Cambridge and New York.

Svenbro, J. (1993) *Phrasikleia: The Anthropology of Reading in Ancient Greece*, trans. J. Lloyd. Ithaca.

Swann, M. (2001) *Curiosities and Texts: The Culture of Collecting in Early Modern England*. Philadelphia.

Tanselle, G. T. (1998) "A Rationale of Collecting," *Studies in Bibliography* 51: 1–25.

Telò, M. (2017) "Tastes of Homer: Matro's Gastroaesthetic Tour through Epic," in *Taste and the Ancient Senses*, ed. K. C. Rudolph. Abingdon and New York: 72–89.

Themelis, P. (1986) "Brauron, la stoà delle arktoi," *Magna Graecia* 21: 6–10.

Thomas, R. (1989) *Oral Tradition and Written Record in Classical Athens*. Cambridge.

(1992) *Literacy and Orality in Ancient Greece*. Cambridge.

(2000) *Herodotus in Context*. Cambridge.

(2009) "Writing, Reading, Public and Private 'Literacies': Functional Literacy and Democratic Literacy in Greece," in *Ancient Literacies*, ed. W. A. Johnson and H. N. Parker. Oxford: 13–45.

Threatte, L. L. (1980). *The Grammar of Attic Inscriptions. I: Phonology*. Berlin and New York.

Totelin, L. M. V. (2009) *Hippocratic Recipes: Oral and Written Transmission of Pharmacological Knowledge in Fifth- and Fourth-Century Greece*. Leiden.

Tracy, S. V. (2013) "*IG* i^3 259–272: The 'Lapis Primus': Corrigenda Selecta," *Zeitschrift für Papyrologie und Epigraphik* 187: 191–198.

Tréheux, J. (1959) "Études critiques sur les inventaires de l'independance délienne." Thesis. Paris.

(1965) *Études sur les inventaires attiques*. Études d'Archéologie Classique 3. Nancy.

(1988) "Une Nouvelle Lecture des inventaires d'Apollon à Délos," in *Comptes et inventaires dans la cité grecque: Actes du colloque international d'épigraphie tenu à Neuchâtel du 23 au 26 septembre 1986 en l'honneur de Jacques Tréheux*, ed. D. Knoepfler and N. Quellet. Neuchâtel.

Trüb, H. (1952) "Kataloge in der griechischen Dichtung." Dissertation. Zurich.

Tsagalis, Christos C., ed. (2009) "Poetry and Poetics in the Hesiodic Corpus," in *Brill's Companion to Hesiod*, ed. F. Montanari, A. Rengakos, and C. Tsagalis. Leiden: 131–179.

(2010) "The Dynamic Hypertext: Lists and Catalogues in the Homeric Epics," *Trends in Classics* 2: 323–347.

(2017) *Poetry in Fragments: Studies on the Hesiodic Corpus and Its Afterlife*. Berlin.

Tuplin, C. J. (2010) "Dareios' Scythian Expedition Revisited," in *The Achaemenid Impact in the Black Sea: Communication of Powers*, ed. J. Nieling and E. Rehm. Aarhus: 281–312.

Ussher, R. G., ed. (1973) *Aristophanes: Ecclesiazusae*. Oxford.

van Buren, E. D. (1922) "Museums and Raree Shows in Antiquity," *Folklore* 33: 337–353.

van Thiel, H., ed. (1991) *Homeri Odyssea*. Hildesheim.

(2010) *Homeri Ilias*. Hildesheim and Zurich.

Vannicelli, P. (2001) "Herodotus' Egypt and the Foundations of Universal History," in *The Historian's Craft in the Age of Herodotus*, ed. N. Luraghi. Oxford: 211–240.

Vian, F. (1974–1981) *Apollonios de Rhodes: Argonautiques*. Paris.

Vickers, M. J., ed. (1986) *Pots and Pans: A Colloquium on Precious Metals and Ceramics in the Muslim, Chinese and Graeco-Roman Worlds, Oxford, 1985*. Oxford.

Visser, E. (1997) *Homers Katalog der Schiffe*. Stuttgart.

Watkins, C. (1995) *How to Kill a Dragon: Aspects of Indo-European Poetics.* New York.

Watson, L. C. (1991) *Arae: The Curse Poetry of Antiquity.* Leeds.

Weiner, A. B. (1983) "From Words to Objects to Magic: Hard Words and the Boundaries of Social Interaction," *Man* 18: 690–709.

Wenzel, S. and L. D. Benson, eds. (1982) *The Wisdom of Poetry: Essays in Early English Literature in Honor of Morton W. Bloomfield.* Kalamazoo, Mich.

West, M. L. (1985) *The Hesiodic Catalogue of Women: Its Nature, Structure, and Origins.* Oxford.

(2014) *The Making of the Odyssey.* Oxford.

West, S. (1985) "Herodotus' Epigraphical Interests," *The Classical Quarterly* 35: 278–305.

(1991) "Herodotus' Portrait of Hecataeus," *The Journal of Hellenic Studies* 111: 144–160.

Whitehorne, J. (2002) "Aristophanes' Representations of 'Intellectuals'," *Hermes* 130: 28–35.

Willi, A. (2010) "The Language of Old Comedy," in *Brill's Companion to the Study of Greek Comedy*, ed. G. Dobrov. Leiden: 471–510.

Williams, F. (1993) "Callimachus and the Supranormal," in *Callimachus*, ed. M. A. Harder, R. Regtuit, and G. C. Wakker. Groningen: 217–225.

Wilson, D. (2002) *Ransom, Revenge, and Heroic Identity in the Iliad.* Cambridge.

Wilson, N. G. (2007) *Aristophanis Fabulae.* Oxford.

Winkler, J. J. and F. I. Zeitlin, eds. (1992) *Nothing to Do with Dionysos? Athenian Drama in Its Social Context.* Princeton.

Worthington, I., ed. (1996) *Voice into Text: Orality and Literacy in Ancient Greece.* Leiden.

Yeroulanou, M. and M. Stamatopoulou, eds. (2005) *Architecture and Archaeology in the Cyclades: Papers in Honour of J. J. Coulton.* Oxford.

Zumbrunnen, J. (2006) "Fantasy, Irony, and Economic Justice in Aristophanes' Assemblywomen and Wealth," *The American Political Science Review* 100: 319–333.

Index Locorum

General Index

accountability, 15, 86, 127, 131, 143, 214
Achilles, 26, 30, 35, 41–42, 48–50, 70, 127
  catalogue of reparations for, 27–31
Aeschylus, 2, 51, 74, 76, 155, 178, 213
Agamemnon, 18–20, 22–24, 28–31, 33–35,
    37–38, 40, 41, 47–50, 56, 70, 82, 96, 109,
    180, 183, 200
Aigina, 97, 113, 134, 213
Ajax, 49–50
Alcaeus, 201, 203
Alcmene, 56
Alexandria, 186
Amasis, 80, 83–84, 95
Amazons, 89
Anacreon, 203–204
animals
  in Semonides' catalogue of women, 57–60
Anscombe, Elizabeth, 7–8
Antimachus, 201, 204–205
apodeiknumi/apodeixis, 91–108, 123
Apollonius of Rhodes, 186, 189–190
  catalogue of Argonauts, 189–190
apophaino/apophasis, 125
Aristophanes
  Acharnians, 172–177
  Assemblywomen, 167–172
  Birds, 177–184
  Clouds, 158, 173–174
  Homeric influences, 179–184
  use of lists, 156–157
  Wealth, 158–167
Artemis, 46, 121, 136–137, 146, 169
Artemisia, 81
Asclepius, 116, 164
Asia Minor, 117
Athena, 46, 70–71, 84, 96, 116, 120, 128, 132,
    138, 140, 207, 212, 217–220
  sanctuary of Athena Lindia. *See* Lindian
    Chronicle
Athenian Tribute Lists, 115, 127
Athens, 15, 73–74, 76, 108–109, 113, 115–116,
    120–122, 126, 131, 137, 139, 151–152,
    158, 163–168, 183, 212–213, 215–216

authority, 31–36
  of inscriptions, 104
  of lists, 14, 19–20, 31, 79–81, 157

boundless ransom, 38–43
Brauron, 113–116, 137–139, 148, 163, 169, 220
Briseis, 40, 48, 50

Callimachus
  Aetia
    Catalogue of Sicilian cities, 193–196
    Homeric influences, 199–200
    Hymn to Delos, 196–200
    Hymn to Zeus, 192–193
Cambyses, 80
Cario, 160–161, 163–168, 185
casualty lists, 73–77
catalogue (as opposed to list), 7
Catalogue of Ships, 20–31, 41–53, 154, 176,
    178, 187–189, 195
Chremylus, 158–161
chronology, listed, 20, 25, 74, 188, 193
chronophagy, 140, 144
collecting, 6, 13, 19, 108, 182, 187, 217, 219–220
commodities, listed, 51
counting, 18–20, 25–31, 109
Croesus, 44, 78–109
cultural technique, 17, 211

dedications, 3, 46, 79, 108, 116, 151
  in the Lindian Chronicle, 222
  of Amasis, 84
  to Asclepius, 163–167
Delos, 80, 110, 113, 115, 121–123, 133, 147, 163,
    196–199, 199, 220
  Temple of Apollo, 116
  Temple of the Athenians, 121
Delphi, 44, 80, 83, 89, 91–93, 107, 110, 155, 175
Demodike, 69–70
demosion sema, 74
Dicaeopolis, 12, 158, 172, 174–176, 185
Didyma
  Temple of Apollo, 149

For EU product safety concerns, contact us at Calle de José Abascal, 56–1°,
28003 Madrid, Spain or eugpsr@cambridge.org.

www.ingramcontent.com/pod-product-compliance
Ingram Content Group UK Ltd.
Pitfield, Milton Keynes, MK11 3LW, UK
UKHW030904150625
459647UK00022B/2822